HAROLD RAEBURN

THE STEPS OF A GIANT

PETER J BIGGAR

First published in 2024 by Scottish Mountaineering Press.

Copyright © Peter J Biggar and individual authors 2024.

All photos © as credited.

The author and contributors have asserted their rights under the Copyright, Design and Patents Act 1988 to be identified as the authors of this work.

A catalogue record of this book is available from the British Library.

ISBN: 978-1-907233-50-0

All rights reserved. No part of this publication may be reproduced, stored in or introduced into a retrieval system, or transmitted in any form or by any means (electronic, mechanical, photocopying, recording or otherwise), without the prior written permission of the publisher.

Every effort has been made to obtain the necessary permissions with reference to copyright material. We apologise for any omission in this respect and will be pleased to make the appropriate acknowledgements in any future edition.

Edited by Deziree Wilson.
Designed by Gino Di Meo Studio.

Printed & bound in Europe by Latitude Press.

In memory of Michael Robson, teacher and historian of St Kilda.

SCOTLAND PART 1

Chapter 1   28
1888–1896: Early Days, Hillwalking to Climbing

Chapter 2   44
1896–1897: Salisbury Crags, Joining SMC, Yacht Meet

Chapter 3   56
1897–1898: Glencoe, Tarmachan, Skye Controversy

Chapter 4   68
1898: Castle on Nevis, Raeburn's Gully Lochnagar

Chapter 5   78
1899–1901: Liathach, Black Shoot, Gardyloo, Observatory Buttress

Chapter 6   86
1901: Observatory Ridge, Douglas-Gibson Attempt

Chapter 7   94
1902: Arran, Sgòran Dubh Gleann Eanaich

Chapter 8   100
1902: Observatory Buttress, Raeburn's Arête Lochnagar

Chapter 9   110
1902–1903: Beinn an Lochain, Skye, Glencoe

Chapter 10   118
1903–1904: Creag Meagaidh, Garbheinn, Nevis

Chapter 11   128
1904–1905: Sgòrr Ruadh, Aonach Beag

Chapter 12   138
1897–1919: Lakeland Forays by Mike Jacob

SCOTLAND PART 2

Chapter 13   162
1905: 'Scottish Snow'

Chapter 14   174
1905–1906: Cobbler, Cuillin Easter Meet

Chapter 15   184
1906: The Chasm and Green Gully

Chapter 16   196
1906: Creag Meagaidh in June

Chapter 17   200
1907: Quinag, Stob Coire nan Lochan

Chapter 18   210
1907–1908: Shelter Stone, Ben Nevis, Lochnagar, Càrn Dearg

Chapter 19   222
1909–1910: Some Triumphs and an Accident

Chapter 20   230
1910–1918: Pre- and During-War Period

Foreword   6

Preface   8

Introduction   12

Origins, Pre-Climbing and Ornithology   16

THE ALPS AND NORWAY

Chapter 21   244
1901–1903: Early Alps, Norway, Slogen

Chapter 22   256
1904–1906: The Meije, Grande Casse, Aiguille Noire de Peuterey, Petit Dru

Chapter 23   270
1907–1908: Meije II, Dôme de la Sache–Pourri Traverse, Mont Blanc, Dent Blanche, Dru Traverse

Chapter 24   286
1909: Grépon, Aiguille Verte, Monte Rosa, Gabelhorn

Chapter 25   298
1910: North Face of Disgrazia, Crast, Agüzza, Scerscen

THE CAUCASUS

Chapter 26   314
1913: The Caucasus Expedition—Chanchakhi

Chapter 27   330
1913: Nuamkuam, Ushba

Chapter 28   354
1914: The Caucasus Expedition—Karagom, Laboda

Chapter 29   366
1914: The Journey Home

LAST CLIMBS IN THE ALPS AND SCOTLAND

Chapter 30   378
1919: Solo Traverse of the Meije

Chapter 31   382
1920: First Ascent of Observatory Ridge in Winter

Chapter 32   390
Mountaineering Art: A Brief Study

Chapter 33   396
1920: The Himalaya

Chapter 34   406
1921: Everest Reconnaissance Expedition—Part 1

Chapter 35   416
1921: Everest Reconnaissance Expedition—Part 2

Chapter 36   428
1921: Everest Reconnaissance Expedition—Part 3

Chapter 37   434
1922–26: Illness and Decline

Epilogue   444

Acknowledgements   450

Bibliography   452

Index   460

FOREWORD

When I was 18 years old, I spent two days hitchhiking from the South of England to Fort William. The following day I climbed Green Gully on Ben Nevis with my university friend Steve Anderson. It was my first ever Scottish climb, and I was captivated by the Scottish winter climbing experience. By modern standards our equipment was basic—a Curver ice-axe, an ice hammer and Salewa bendy crampons—but our tools were light years ahead of those used by Harold Raeburn and Eberhard Phildius on the first ascent over 70 years earlier. Raeburn climbed Green Gully by cutting a ladder of steps up near-vertical ice with a single 116cm-long ice-axe. It was almost certainly the hardest ice climb in the world at the time and was not superseded in difficulty in Scotland for nearly 30 years.

The Victorians were exceptional mountaineers and they pretty much invented the sport of climbing mountains. By the end of the 19th century, they had made first ascents of many of the major alpine peaks, and following the opening of Scotland's railways, they turned their attention to the Highlands. From a modern perspective, the technical standard of the early Scottish mountaineers was breathtaking. Raeburn's first ascent of Green Gully is nowadays rated IV,4, but his ascents of Right-Angled Gully (IV,5) on The Cobbler in 1896 and Arrow Chimney (IV) on Meall nan Tarmachan in 1898 were just as inspired. These routes were years ahead of their time and only received their contemporary grades nearly a century after they were first climbed. Without doubt, Edinburgh-born Harold Raeburn was the finest climber of his generation. A wiry man with an athletic build, he was a powerful and forceful rock climber who honed his craft on his home city's Salisbury Crags. However, Raeburn is best known as a winter climber, and he made over two dozen new winter climbs across the Highlands, leaving his mark from Ladhar Bheinn in the west to Lochnagar in the east. Raeburn's Route (IV,4) on Stob Coire nan Lochan and Crowberry Gully (IV,4) on Buachaille Etive Mòr remain two of the most sought-after winter lines in Scotland. Climbing alone, he also made the first ascents of two of the great structural features on Ben Nevis: Observatory Ridge and Observatory Buttress. Unlike Green Gully, which has been tamed by modern equipment, Observatory Ridge, climbed in 1920, retains its reputation as one of the longest and most serious winter mountaineering routes on the Ben.

Yet Raeburn's mountaineering prowess extended far beyond Scotland. In the Alps he made the first British guideless ascent of the Zmutt Ridge on the Matterhorn, added new routes to the Aiguille d'Argentière and Monte Disgrazia and made the first solo traverse of the Meije. Further afield he pioneered climbs in Norway and the Caucasus, joined an expedition to Kangchenjunga and was climbing leader on the 1921 British Mount Everest reconnaissance expedition. He was also a keen sailor and ornithologist.

Despite Raeburn's outstanding mountaineering record, little has been written about the man himself. He was naturally modest, his diaries are sometimes brief, and he was notoriously poor at recording his climbs. Whilst his Scottish ascents are now well recognised, his overseas contributions are less widely appreciated. Peter Biggar is ideally placed to write this book. As well as being an accomplished exploratory climber, Peter is a past editor of the *Scottish Mountaineering Club Journal* (SMCJ). This puts him in a unique position to place Raeburn's achievements in perspective and reveal more about the man behind the famous climbs. Extensive use has been made of William Ling's and other climbing partners' diaries, and Peter has been able to dig beneath Raeburn's determined efforts to exclude his personality from public view. The result is a portrait of a talented and self-effacing man who was also fiercely proud. Everest would prove to be Raeburn's undoing, and Peter writes with great sensitivity about the 1921 Expedition and its aftermath.

Harold Raeburn stands alongside Jimmy Marshall, Tom Patey and Andy Nisbet as one of Scotland's greatest ever mountaineers. A biography is long overdue, and Peter Biggar has done an outstanding job of bringing together this fascinating, insightful and detailed story of a remarkable man.

Simon Richardson, 7 September 2023

PREFACE

Harold Raeburn, a giant in Scottish and British mountaineering, is a fascinating and intriguing figure. My first winter climb was Raeburn's Gully on Lochnagar in 1970 in a snowstorm. Two years later, in rather similar conditions, my friend Mike Jacob and I escaped from the windswept upper pitches of Eastern Corner on Creag Meagaidh by descending another Raeburn's Gully to the relative calm of Corrie Ardair. With our shortish wooden axes we cut many steps up the Corner, but we had twelve-point Salewa crampons, 120 feet of kernmantle rope and even a few slings, nuts, pegs and a deadman belaying device with which to protect ourselves. Raeburn, by contrast, had 80 feet of hemp rope and a long ice-axe, excellent as a walking aid, but excessively tiring as an ice-cutting tool. He had boots shod with a pattern of nails but no other technical equipment.

Mike became fascinated by Raeburn and started to research his history. In May of the same year as our Meagaidh climb, Robin Campbell published his famous article 'The First Scottish Ice Climbers', which did so much to rescue Raeburn and his fellow Victorians from obscurity. Of this, more later. I, too, became fascinated by Raeburn. This biography grew partly out of the researches of Jacob and Campbell and I am happy to acknowledge a large debt to them. For one reason or another neither of them completed a book on Raeburn, but it seemed to me that such a seminal figure in British mountaineering needed a biography. I was fortunate, as Editor of the *SMCJ* from 2014 to 2020, to have a full set of *SMCJ*, a vital primary source for the study of Raeburn.

Robin Campbell helped and encouraged in many ways, but most particularly by sending me an electronic copy of another crucial primary source:

the incomparable diary of William Ling, Harold's most frequent companion on the hill. Without it any narrative of Raeburn's mountaineering would be poor indeed. Needless to say, the published writings of Jacob and Campbell have had a huge influence on my view of Raeburn, and this is frequently documented in the text.

I have also been fortunate with the publication, in 2015 and 2017, of Ken Crocket's two-part history of *Mountaineering in Scotland*. As well as having valuable insights into Raeburn's career, Crocket also helpfully sets that career in the context of Scottish climbing at the time. (I also had frequent recourse to his excellent index, which, among many other things, helped me out with the Christian names, seldom mentioned in those days, of many of Raeburn's companions.)

When describing climbing action it is useful, though by no means necessary, to have some personal knowledge of the scene. Alas, I have never climbed in Norway, the Caucasu or in the Himalaya, and my knowledge of the Western Alps is limited to the Mattertal. In Scotland, too, I have my blind spots, the Island of Arran being the most obvious. However, I decided that it would be pure folly for me to attempt to describe Raeburn's many trips to the Lake District as I know very little about it, and Mike Jacob, who knows it well, kindly agreed to contribute a full chapter describing the action there.

Many other people have helped where my knowledge failed, notably a large contingent of my fellow Scottish Mountaineering Club (SMC) members, and this will be acknowledged in the text and in the Acknowledgments at the end.

A rather unexpected advantage I have in writing about Raeburn is that my adoptive parents in Edinburgh were old enough to be my grandparents. My father was a soldier in the First World War—he probably wasn't one of the soldiers to whom the girls escorted back from France by Raeburn wished to throw sweets from the train, but he could have been. I also had quite a flock of elderly aunts who, having grown up at the end of Victoria's reign, were cheerfully Victorian or Edwardian in their outlook, so despite the fact that, as John Betjeman says, 'No motor coach can take me back to that Edwardian erstwhile', I feel oddly at home in that world. I find myself saying, 'Cleanliness is next to Godliness', 'Manners maketh man', and going for 'brisk walks for the sake of my health', even when the rain is pouring down. Similar maxims and habits were probably part of Harold Raeburn's makeup.

My father also departed from these shores for a career in India just after the War in 1920 and, although not a mountaineer himself, he took a great interest in the early Everest expeditions. Who knows, he may even have rubbed shoulders with Raeburn, either in Calcutta or even Darjeeling. (This is not as speculative as it sounds. My father took a great interest in the Everest Expeditions; there is even a photograph of Edward Shebbeare from 1924 in our family album.) He also had many tales to tell of both places, and a photograph of Kangchenjunga taken from the Mall in Darjeeling adorned his bedroom wall in Edinburgh.

Thus, although unlike Robin Campbell I have never chosen to wear Edwardian costume at SMC Dinners, I do have a strange affinity with the period.

INTRODUCTION

Harold Andrew Raeburn (1865–1926) was the leading Scottish climber of his day and certainly one of the best in Britain. He accomplished new routes all over Scotland, in the Lake District, the Alps and Norway, climbed virgin summits in the Caucasus (on occasion by very demanding routes), made two separate reconnaissance trips to Kangchenjunga and was appointed Climbing Leader of the 1921 British Reconnaissance Expedition to Mount Everest. On that expedition he became seriously ill and had to spend many weeks recuperating away from the scene of activity. He made a hazardous and exhausting trek to rejoin the expedition, but by then his place as Climbing Leader had been taken over by George Mallory. After returning to Britain, he suffered a devastating mental collapse and spent the last years of his life in a mental asylum in his native Edinburgh.

Anyone who climbs in Scotland will know that Raeburn made new routes on most of our best-known mountains. There are routes which bear his name on Ben Nevis, Lochnagar, Creag Meagaidh, the Shelter Stone in the Cairngorms and on Skye, to name but five places. Raeburn accomplished what he did with different companions and the most rudimentary equipment. The golden rule was that the leader should not fall. They did not take what we would regard as proper belays, but merely 'hitched' the rope behind convenient projections. It was usual, for rather obvious reasons, for the best climber to do all the leading. On almost every climb Harold was involved in, he was the leader. Although he was once pulled off by falling seconds, he never fell himself, and no member of any party he climbed with anywhere in the UK or abroad suffered serious injury. He was extremely safe. By the time he became Climbing Leader of the Everest Expedition, he had written a book on mountaineering—*Mountaineering Art* (1920)—he had published numerous articles on his various climbs, and was regarded as an authority on the subject.

Through Harold's writings and those of his contemporaries, we know a lot about his mountaineering life, but no man is just a mountaineer. Every man has a personal life, but Raeburn's is partly shrouded in mystery. We know who his antecedents were; we know a little about his family life—his 10 siblings. We know what he did for a living and, through his writings and theirs, we become acquainted with some of his climbing friends and companions. We know what he did in the Great War, but we don't know who he loved or why he never married. We know he was patriotic, but we don't know much about his political opinions or whether he was a religious believer. We must piece together his tastes in literature, art and music from echoes and references in his writings. In other words, many of the usual elements of a biography are lacking. Though presenting difficulties for the biographer, it makes the subject all the more intriguing.

We know remarkably little about Harold's life away from the mountains because very few of his diaries and letters have survived, and these, with some exceptions, are rather unilluminating. There may have been a considerable store of Raeburn memorabilia inherited by his surviving sisters after his death, but when Ruth, the last of them, died in 1962, it seems that whatever relics she still held were dispersed and can no longer be traced, even if they still exist.

Obvious sources of knowledge about a person are the opinions of relations, friends and acquaintances, but, alas, nobody thought to interview Ruth Raeburn, or any other member of his family, about their famous brother. We have to rely on such clues as can be disinterred from Harold's own writing and the writings of those who knew him, and what we mainly rely on are chance remarks in climbing articles and books, and the obituaries written by friends after his death, which are naturally somewhat partial.

Modern literature about mountaineering personalities often contains a wealth of information about the subject, but the late Victorians and Edwardians tended to be extremely unforthcoming about personal matters. In many climbing articles of the period we learn little more about the protagonists than their names—their surnames at that. It was the custom of the times to be reticent. In some of his own notes in the *SMCJ*, Harold himself carries this habit of reticence to extremes by not even acknowledging that he himself was a member of the party climbing the route being discussed! Self-effacement ruled. Fortunately, in certain moods he was more forthcoming.

[Fig 1] One can look at the stiff, buttoned-up studio portrait of Harold Raeburn and think, 'This man must have been made of pure cardboard.' But he was a human being like the rest of us, with the same desires and passions, the same capacity for happiness and unhappiness.

This book is called *The Steps of a Giant* because it is from mountaineering literature of one sort or another that most of our information about Raeburn comes. Any good biography is evidence-based assertion, but when this is conspicuously lacking, a certain amount of speculation or theorising is inevitable. It is important, however, to be aware of the difference between evidence-based assertion and speculation.

This author's modest hope is that this volume documents all we know about Harold Raeburn's mountaineering achievements at home and abroad, paints a convincing portrait of the man and tells the fascinating story of his many-sided life.

A note on Gaelic spellings: where these are contained in quotations, the original spelling will be retained even if it is the crudest anglicisation, e.g. 'Lurven' for Ladhar Bheinn, 'Corrie Labain' for Coire Lagan etc. At other times the received version of Gaelic will be used.

Fig 1

Harold Raeburn, studio portrait: notice the fingers clenched tightly around the ice-axe. He was almost always an awkward, and sometimes unwilling, subject for the camera. Photo: SMC Image Archive

ORIGINS, PRE-CLIMBING AND ORNITHOLOGY[1]

Harold Raeburn's grandparents were William Raeburn and Elizabeth Mary Meakin. William was a wine and spirit merchant in Edinburgh with premises at Castlehill between the Castle Esplanade and the Lawnmarket. William and Elizabeth had two sons, William and John, who followed their father's trade at Castlehill. Grandfather died in 1846 and was interred in Warriston Cemetery.

Grandfather's sons William and John went into brewing and around 1860 bought the J&T Usher brewery at 12 Merchant Street. This was a good investment: it prospered and the Raeburn family moved up the social scale, relocating several times to more prestigious districts of Edinburgh, ending up in 49 Manor Place for many years. William, Harold's father, had married Margaret (Jessie) Ramsay in October 1849. On Friday, 21 July 1865, just one week after Edward Whymper climbed the Matterhorn, Harold, their fourth son and eighth child was born at 12 Grange Loan. The family was large: Harold had ten siblings, all of whom reached adulthood.

Little is known about Harold's early life. He attended Merchiston Castle School, which in those days was situated in the actual old Merchiston Castle on the Borough Muir, only moving to its present site in Colinton in 1924. JJ Rogerson was the Headmaster of the School for 35 years; a formidable figure, the boys called him 'the Chief'.

Life at Merchiston seems to have been exhausting and rigorous. The day began with prayers at 7.30 am, followed by breakfast, lessons, games,

---

1   Most of the material in this chapter is taken from the researches, published and unpublished, of Mike Jacob. Unless noted otherwise, it can be assumed that a quotation comes from his unpublished manuscript on Harold Raeburn.

late dinner, lessons, tea and preparation ending at 9 pm, then bed. As was usual in those days, discipline was strict, at times enforced by the use of the tawse. It is not clear whether Harold was a day-boy or a boarder, but if the former he would have had an even earlier start in the morning. Apparently, he played rugby and was fast and skilful enough to be a three-quarter. He had a good sense of balance, and later in life he sailed, skated, skied and was reputedly a proficient ballroom dancer. One suspects that his sporting accomplishments made school life a little easier.

It is true that the gentler emotions were repressed in public schools and that pupils tended to acquire a tough outer shell, and this may be something of a clue as to Harold's rather taciturn character. However, one should remember that George Mallory, who probably had the same sort of experience at his public school in England, was quite different: exuberant and endlessly expressive of his thoughts and feelings.

Whatever the emotional effects of life at Merchiston, the school seems to have given Harold a very good grounding in science and literature, and he developed a lucid and at times imaginative prose style. Echoes of Shakespeare, the Romantic poets (particularly Coleridge) and Oscar Wilde are evident in his writings, which were frequently published in mountaineering club journals, notably those of the SMC and later the Alpine Club. His academic career flourished at Heriot-Watt College, as the Watt College became. In May 1889 he is listed as being successful at Science, Art and Technological Subjects in the City and Guild of London examinations. He obtained a first advanced pass in Organic Chemistry (Practical) and second advanced passes in Inorganic Chemistry (Practical and Theory) and in Organic Chemistry (Theory). All of this appears to have been achieved while he was undergoing something of an apprenticeship in the family brewing business, indicating an ability to manage his time proficiently and a capacity for hard work which stayed with him until his final years, when he succumbed to illness.

By the time Harold left Merchiston he had already had his first experience of the death of a family member, for his older brother, William, drowned in April 1880 in a yachting accident off Granton Harbour. A report in *The Scotsman* said that young William 'was a most promising young man and his death a source of great grief not only to his relatives but also to a wide circle of friends'.

Among his large family Harold seems to have been particularly close to two of his sisters, Ethel and Ruth. Ethel Maud Raeburn was an artist who painted in oils and watercolours, often Venetian views. She exhibited between 1892 and 1940 in Glasgow, Liverpool, the Royal Institution (London) and in the Royal Scottish Academy. A signed watercolour called *Dappled Sunlight at the Outdoor Café* was sold by Christie's in 2008 for £813. She shared a house with her sisters, Edith and Ruth, at 14 Abercromby Place, and sometimes went hillwalking with Harold.

Ruth Mabel Raeburn was the 39th pupil at St George's Hall classes for girls, which became St George's High School for Girls in 1888. The founders of the school followed the German philosopher Froebel, who believed that every child should be valued for doing their best, not for competing, and that equality for women could only come through education. Ruth left in 1890 to go to a foreign boarding (perhaps 'finishing') school, whose whereabouts are unknown. She contributed a brief chapter on mountain clothing for women to Raeburn's book, *Mountaineering Art* (1920). Harold, doubtless inspired by the women with whom he had climbed, said that when bouldering, a girl should:

> *Select those boulder climbs where activity and balance are of greater value than muscle strength and arm-pulls. She will, there, often be able to show a more experienced and much more powerful man how a short piece of difficult rock can be climbed with ease and grace ...* (ibid.)

Ruth often accompanied Harold and his friend Willie Ling on climbing trips in the UK and the Alps and was herself a founder member, and later President, of the Ladies' Scottish Climbing Club (LSCC). She was also an expert photographer and eventually became an Honorary President of the Edinburgh Photographic Society. Plainly, Ruth Raeburn did her very best.

The question naturally arises: how did young Harold, city-born and bred, come to take an interest in mountaineering? Ken Crocket (1988) wrote a splendid little story about Raeburn going bird-nesting in Edinburgh as a young teenager and finding exhilaration in the activity of climbing to the nest. The kernel of truth in this fiction is Harold's lifelong interest in birdlife.

Most people know that Harold Raeburn was a mountaineer and some have a hazy notion that he also took an interest in ornithology. Few know just how organised and systematic his researches in this area were. In fact, his extensive egg collection and the nineteen diaries in which he described and catalogued the collection are in the Ornithological section of Edinburgh's Royal Museum. The main collection and the diaries were donated by Ethel and Ruth, his executors, three years after his death in 1929. The museum also has a grey partridge from Hoperig in East Lothian and a ptarmigan from Ben Cruachan, donated by Harold in 1888 and 1896, respectively. At this time he was not averse to shooting wild birds, but soon gave it up for photography.

Commenting on the collection and the diaries, Bob McGowan, Senior Curator (Ornithology), said:

> *His interest was clearly a serious one, as the eggs were neatly side blown with a single hole, in the 'professional' manner and inscribed with locality and date of collection ... [the] collection of full clutches, personally collected [not purchased from dealers] complemented with collection data ... were indicative of more methodical and determined individuals. Raeburn's collection is a good example of this type of 'scientific collection' ... Not only did Raeburn inscribe his eggs, but he recorded much useful information in a series of notebooks.* [Fig 1]

One notebook actually records a series of fresh weights of eggs during the period 1885–1895. He collected in Edinburgh, Fife, Peeblesshire, Shetland and Orkney, East Lothian, the Forth Islands and in Essex. His first egg was taken from the nest of a sandwich tern on the Farne Islands when he was nine, but his serious interest developed much later.

Harold's approach to the study of birds' eggs was that of an objective analyst, basing his work on accurate observation and record keeping. The results of his researches were later published in learned periodicals of the time. So notable was his ornithological work that on 18 March 1885, before he was twenty, he was elected to the prestigious Royal Physical Society of Edinburgh, becoming one of the youngest, perhaps even the youngest ever, to have been granted this honour.

Raeburn developed an interest in seabirds and made several visits to the Shetland Islands to study them. In order to reach the nests a considerable amount of rock scrambling and climbing was required and it seems that, partly by accident, Raeburn discovered that he enjoyed and was good at this.

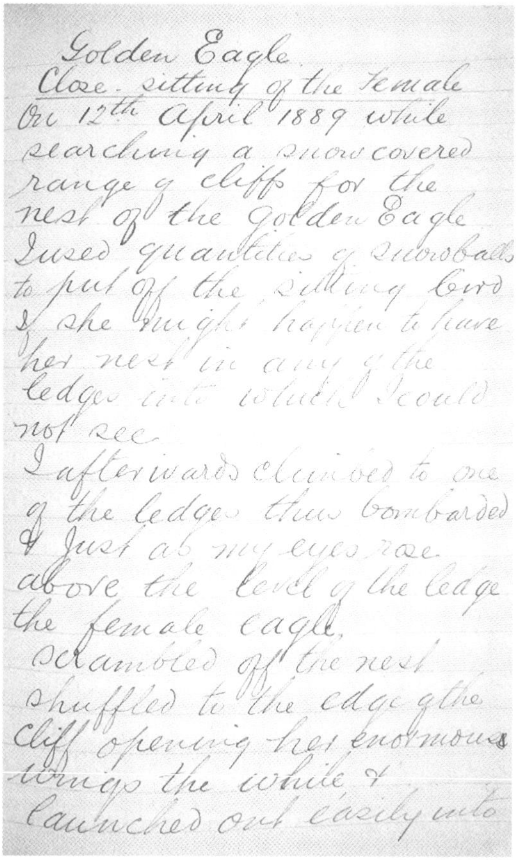

> Golden Eagle.
> Close sitting of the female
> On 12th April 1889 while
> searching a snow covered
> range of cliff for the
> nest of the Golden Eagle
> I used quantities of snowballs
> to put off the sitting bird
> if she might happen to have
> her nest in any of the
> ledges into which I could
> not see.
> I afterwards climbed to one
> of the ledges thus bombarded
> & just as my eyes rose
> above the level of the ledge
> the female eagle
> scrambled off the nest
> shuffled to the edge of the
> cliff opening her enormous
> wings the while &
> launched out easily into

Fig 1

Raeburn's ornithology diary: neat writing, well organised, pages numbered. Photo: Noel Williams

One day in particular stands out and is described at length in his diary:

> In the old times the men of Papa [Papa Stour] had a reputation as climbers little inferior to those of Unst or Foula ... but ... I was informed that only two men on the island are now able to make the ascent of the Lyra Skerry. [One of these] rejoices in the name of 'Long Peter' ... standing some 6 ft 3 ins in his 'rivlins' (raw cowhide shoes worn by the Shetlanders). I had a good illustration, during the course of the day, of the great advantage his enormous reach gives him in cliff climbing.

Raeburn and his frequent host, Mr Scott of Melby, set off to cross the Sound to Papa and made arrangements for a visit to the stacks of Fogla and Lyra. Harold wanted to find the burrows of the manx shearwater (known locally as lyries). He quickly established that there were no burrows on Fogla and they moved on to the so-called Lyra Skerry, which Raeburn noted:

> [I]s really a huge 'Stack' of porphyritic rock, 180 ft high and about a quarter of a mile in circumference ... Lyra is perpendicular, or overhanging, on all sides except one small portion at the S.E. corner, just to the right of the magnificent sea-floored cavern that passes through the island. This was pointed out to me as 'the road up'. Peter now took a coil of codline in his hand and, watching his opportunity as the light boat rose on the swell, jumped clear of the water on to a dry ledge. Though I did not relish the look of the said 'road up', there was no other way of getting to the top; so I followed him. Peter now explained to me that there were only two 'bad bits'—one about halfway up, and the other just at the very top. The first of these is where the rock projects so far as to overhang the sea below, and from where—the men were careful to inform me—a climber had fallen some years before but, striking the water, was picked up by his comrades in the boat, escaping with a broken arm and a severe shock from a fall of 90 ft. They added, perhaps unnecessarily, that he did not again attempt the ascent ...
>
> The ascent for the first 90 ft is comparatively easy for the rock, although almost perpendicular, is firm. At this place occurs the first 'bad bit', as it is necessary to round a point which projects clear over the water, and the ledges have a nasty outward slope. However, the finger

grip is good and, watching where my guide put his feet, we were soon both past this.

By this point Raeburn had taken off his 'India rubber shoes' and was climbing in stockings, like Peter, because 'they afford more freedom for the toes'. Harold continues:

Above this part the climbing is comparatively easy till the top is neared. Here, within fifteen feet of the summit, we brought up against what appeared to me a totally unscaleable place. We were clinging in a sort of shallow niche of the cliff, which above our heads narrowed to a crack about eight inches wide. If it had been a foot wider the ascent would have been comparatively easy by bracing the body against the sides, but its narrowness precluded this. I now watched Long Peter's movements with interest, and here was the point where his great height and long arms stood him in good stead for, stretching himself up the left-hand edge of the crack, he seized a small ledge nearly eight feet above the niche we stood in, and slowly and carefully he drew himself up, finding a crevice for his toes, and, getting another grip higher up, he was at the summit in a few seconds. He then passed the doubled codline down to me, which I fastened under my arms and, Peter putting a 56 lb[2] strain on it, I swarmed up the edge of the crack, and stood beside him on the top.

Raeburn was much impressed by the diversity of the birdlife he discovered on the stack, but after a careful search of all the likely burrows, he could find no evidence of manx shearwater occupation.[3] He concludes his climbing description by saying:

My enjoyment of the scene upon the summit had been somewhat dashed by thoughts of the descent; but, with the aid of Peter's codline for the top piece, it was soon accomplished, and I was exceedingly glad to again jump aboard our boat.

2   How did Raeburn know this? Or does he just mean that Peter kept the line tight?
3   Raeburn must have known that manx shearwaters spend the daylight hours at sea and only return to their burrows after dark, apparently to avoid predators.

Part of what is fascinating about Raeburn's account is his ability, at this stage in his career, to describe, just as a climber would, how the route was achieved. It also demonstrates how clearly he writes. After all, he is not writing for publication, only as a record in his diary,[4] and the only things that he might, on reflection, have changed are the repeated phrase 'comparatively easy' and the split infinitive near the end ('to again jump'). It is also true that he exhibits very strong nerves, for Peter and he have been solo-climbing steep rock in a very exposed situation. Naturally, Raeburn was nervous, as his remarks about the descent make clear, but he remains in perfect control of himself at all times, even having the coolness to change his footwear when necessary. Lyra Skerry was recorded as a rock climb in May 1992 (SMC, 2004), probably by Andy Nisbet, Mick Fowler, C Jones and J Lincoln, and graded Severe.

We also find Harold accidentally beginning his career in winter climbing while he was pursuing ornithology: on 12 April 1889, just as he was nearing the end of his time at Heriot-Watt College, he climbed a snowy crag to collect two eggs from the eyrie of a golden eagle. Again, his diary records the incident:

I used quantities of snowballs to put off the sitting bird as she might happen to have her nest in any of the ledges into which I could not see. I afterwards climbed to one of the ledges thus bombarded and just as my eyes rose above the level of the ledge the female eagle scrambled off the nest and shuffled to the edge of the cliff opening her enormous wings the while and launched out easily into the air.

The eagle vanished in the mist and snow and Harold collected two eggs. He saw no more of the female or her mate. The eggs are item 131 in his collection. Harold gives few details of this escapade, partly one suspects, to protect the eagles (ironically enough). But eagles nest in inaccessible places and, particularly in winter, this ascent cannot have been without climbing hazards.[5]

[Fig 2]

---

4   Raeburn's account was eventually published, unchanged, in *The Zoologist* (1891).
5   It must be remembered that Victorian/Edwardian attitudes towards shooting wild birds and collecting eggs were not the same as our own. Nowadays enlightened opinion frowns upon such activities, but then they were accepted as normal. In any case, Raeburn soon gave up egg-collecting and shooting.

Fig 2

Raeburn's golden eagle eggs carefully blown and labelled. Photo: Noel Williams

As well as being a keen ornithologist, Harold was also a splendid yachtsman. He and his brother John bought between them the nine-ton cutter, *The Teal,* in 1903, and in 1904 won the Corinthian Match Challenge Cup organised by the Royal Forth Yacht Club, of which they were members. Harold and John won this cup again in 1906 and 1907. As three-time winners they were presented with the cup in perpetuity but returned it to the Club, and to this day it is still competed for under the name 'The Raeburn Cup'. Harold's career as a yachtsman was only gradually superseded by mountaineering, and for several years they overlapped. On one memorable occasion he sailed on the Forth until very late in the day and completed a new route on Ben Nevis the following day with only a few hours' sleep in between.

Raeburn was also a competent member of the oldest skating club in Britain, which held its Meets on Duddingston Loch in Edinburgh; by the end of the 19th century its membership comprised the professional and merchant classes. To join, prospective members had 'to skate a perfect circle on each foot consecutively, to form a figure-of-eight on the ice and then jump over one top hat, then two, and finally three piled one on top of the other. There was then a ballot among the council members and, if successful, the candidate had to pay for a silver medallion' (Jacob, 2018) with the club emblem on one side and the names of the member and the club on the other. Henry Raeburn's famous portrait of the Rev Robert Walker skating on Duddingston Loch about a hundred years earlier probably gives a good idea of the gracefulness of the style of skating. There is, incidentally, no known family connection between the artist and the mountaineer.

Raeburn also skied when conditions allowed, which, according to him, was not often. A picture begins to develop of a young man full of energy and enthusiasm for outdoor pursuits, with a secure family background and rewarding employment. It was not long before his attention turned to the mountains and, first of all, to those in his native land.

SCOTLAND PART 1

1. EARLY DAYS, HILLWALKING TO CLIMBING   1888–1896

So far as we know, Harold Raeburn climbed his first large Scottish mountain in September 1888 at the age of 23. That hill was Ben Vorlich in Perthshire. The scanty information we have about young Harold's early excursions in the hills comes from his application form (SMC Archive) for the SMC, which he would eventually join in 1896. This form asks candidates to supply the dates of their ascents, the names of any companions, and comments on the weather and conditions. In his early entries, Raeburn discloses nothing but the month of ascent; his first seven ascents took place in autumn and summer. By the time he was 27 he had climbed Ben Lawers, Stùc a' Chroin and, for variety, 'Chaoruinn', probably the hill now called A' Bhuidheanaich Bheag, really a high point on the rolling plateau east of Drumochter, and as unlike Stùc a' Chroin and Lawers as can be imagined.

He did not confine his hillwalking to Scotland, for he also lists all the principal summits of Yorkshire, Helvellyn in the Lake District and Snowdon in Wales. The Yorkshire summits are not named or even dated. So far, Raeburn's progress as a mountaineer is taking a very usual course, starting with hillwalking and going on from there.

The first comment on weather and conditions comes after Raeburn climbed High Street in the Lake District in 'deep snow and heavy snow-storms'. This ascent, unlike the ones listed above, took place in March, and Raeburn, possibly struck by the difference between summer and winter conditions, saw fit to comment. Winter conditions were to play a large part in his future career; perhaps this early experience was special enough to warrant a few words on the form.

After he climbed III Bell at Froswick in June 1894, things became progressively more serious: in August and September he climbed Great End, the Pikes, Scafell Pinnacle and Scafell 'by Chimney'. The Pinnacle and Chimney routes are the first indication of Raeburn applying his climbing talents in the mountains. The Chimney referred to is probably Slingsby's Chimney, currently graded Very Difficult, and the ascent of the Pinnacle by the easiest route is Moderate.[1]

There followed ascents of Pillar Fell and Great Gable in the Lakes, the Snowdon Horseshoe, Tryfan and the Glyders in Wales. By now, Harold was really getting into his stride. In April 1895, he climbed Ben Lomond and the Central Peak of The Cobbler (or Ben Arthur), an ascent which attracts the brief comment: 'Snow last 200 feet.' In September of that year, now 30, he climbed Ben Nevis for the first time, making the acquaintance of a mountain which was to play an important role in his life. The other mountain in this list which holds some special significance for him is Stùc a' Chroin in Perthshire, where he later suffered a serious accident (see Chapter 19).

The list of routes Raeburn presented to the SMC committee continued with an energetic trip to Arran, also in September 1895, on which he climbed 'Chir Mhor, A' Chir / Casteil Abhail, Goatfell and N. Goatfell'.[2]

We don't know how Raeburn came to be acquainted with William Douglas, the second Editor of the *SMCJ*, but Douglas's voluminous correspondence has survived and in it are letters from Raeburn which show a common interest in Salisbury Crags, in Edinburgh. In one of these letters (1895) Raeburn reports a new ascent to the Editor, and the tone of this letter makes it clear that they have established a friendly relationship. Raeburn ends by hoping that Douglas's cold is better, and he recommends *Tartarin Sur Les Alpes* by Daudet as a book Douglas might enjoy. Whether Raeburn met Douglas on Salisbury Crags or wrote to him first as Editor to record routes we don't know, but their friendly relationship was important in introducing Harold to the SMC and thus providing him with many possible climbing partners and a wealth of information and advice from other members.

[Fig 1]

At the end of December 1895 Harold was invited, probably by Douglas, to be a guest at the SMC's New Year Meet at Tyndrum. Normally a guest at

---

1   Raeburn's Lakeland outings are dealt with in detail in Chapter 12.
2   Direct quotation usually retains the author's spelling.

one of these august occasions would be a little shy and perhaps stay in the background, but Harold seems to have had no lack of social confidence, distinguishing himself in the smoking room at 'Pike's Peak', an American board game which Willie Naismith had brought along. Apparently 'Raeburn and [James] Parker qualified themselves to act as guides' (SMCJ, 1896).

The serious action began on New Year's Day when Raeburn, Douglas and Gilbert Thomson climbed the Central Couloir of Ben Lui. Thomson's brief notes in the Meet Report indicate a fairly straightforward day: two pitches were 'troublesome on account of the slight adhesion of the snow to the rock', but otherwise 'the ascent was rather tame'. They descended by the Fox's Couloir.

The following day, after heavy rain overnight, most of the meet made for Ben Lui again. It was cold, and the snow was in better condition. Raeburn, Douglas, Thomson and Naismith climbed the North Rib. It took four hours of 'continuous scrambling', the holds throughout being 'poor and scarce'. Thomson notes that the size of the party made them rather slow. They saw that John Bell and James Maclay, who were descending the Central Couloir, were laboriously having to cut steps, so they elected again to descend by the Fox's Couloir. These two climbs formed a steady uneventful introduction of Raeburn to the SMC. One isn't sure if his efforts at 'Pike's Peak' were appreciated or tolerated, but crucially, he had completed a couple of respectable climbs in good company and must have shown competence.

These routes were added to his application form, as were Earth Ledge Route and Red Ridge Route at Salisbury Crags, and Raeburn was invited to the Easter Meet at Fort William in April 1896. The September issue of the SMCJ carries a long and entertaining report by Willie Douglas (SMCJ, 1896) of the first ascent of the Direct Route on what has come to be known as the Douglas Boulder, which forms the base of The Tower Ridge.

Raeburn and Douglas were accompanied by William Brown and Lionel Hinxman, both noted members of the club. Douglas was very modest about his own ability as a climber (unnecessarily so) and refers to himself as 'the baggage'. He obviously had great respect for his three companions:

> [T]he insatiable appetite of three of these mountain maniacs ... not only felt equal to the Tower Ridge but insisted on demolishing as well what they irreverently christened 'Douglas's Boulder'.

Fig 1

Raeburn as a young man soloing nonchalantly on Salisbury Crags Crags, Edinburgh. Unobserved, he seems quite relaxed. Photo: SMC Archive

Fig 2

The crags of Coire Ardair on Creag Meagaidh. Raeburn's Gully is at the base of the prominent Pinnacle Buttress beyond which Easy Gully slants up to the plateau. The three famous Post routes are clearly visible on the main face. Photo: Henning Wackerhage

Douglas pointed out that all the holds sloped the wrong way, but the die was cast, and the pinnacle was 'tackled at its lowest point'.

They climbed on 160 ft of rope, it was too steep and difficult to wear gloves, and there were long delays as the seconds waited for the leaders, initially Brown, later, either he or Raeburn. At one point, Douglas and Hinxman had to untie to give the leader more rope. Eventually, Douglas was left unroped standing alone on a long thin ledge: 'Half an hour passed, and no rope.' There were 'showers of hail and keen blasts of cutting wind'. Just as Douglas was wondering if he could climb down the way they came up—and it's probably as well he didn't—'Raeburn's cherubic visage' appeared over the top of an overhanging rock and he dropped the rope to Douglas (the attempt to throw it down having left it stuck on a ledge). The party gained the top of the Boulder 'and enjoyed a halt there, and a new and original drink, of which Raeburn is the patentee'. Needless to say, there was no time to continue up Tower Ridge. They avoided the gap descent 'by descending towards the west, and traversing backwards along a snowy ledge into the snowy gully on the west'. (It's possible that they descended most of the south-west ridge of the Boulder, but Douglas doesn't say how far west they went, so one can't be sure.)

Raeburn's first appearance in a fully-fledged article in the SMCJ comes in William Tough's article, 'Corrie Arder' (1896). Tough begins with a description of the corrie. It doesn't, he says rather surprisingly, have 'grandeur' but has a beauty and character all its own, and, he adds, 'a character which, as yet, little attempt has been made to understand'. Thus Douglas, Raeburn and he were really exploring, 'intent on making an investigation into the nature of the precipices and "Posts"'. As it turned out, they knew a great deal more about Creag Meagaidh after their exploration. [Fig 2]

Their first mistake, instead of taking 'the excellent path' from Aberarder Farm, was to go up the left side of the glen, where they became entangled in thick birchwoods. However, they realised what they had done and gained the path, got to the lochan and examined 'the precipices and gullies ... with the interest always excited by the prospect of a new ascent'. They wanted to climb one of the 'Posts' or discover a route up one of the great buttresses, neither of which, they thought, 'would prove very easy of accomplishment'. How right they were. Tough notes that 'The rocks everywhere ... seemed unfavourable for climbing purposes ... their uniformly downward dip indicated insecurity of hold.' What was worse was that 'the cliffs were crowned by a considerable depth of snow rising nearly perpendicularly from the rock', and in places these slopes were 'overhanging in some of the finest cornices we had ever seen in Scotland'.

Although none of them seems to have realised it at the time, worse still was that 'the air was warm and muggy, and in the lower regions the thaw was proceeding apace'. It would have been wise simply to be content with having seen the Posts, but they attempted what we now know as Centre Post, the long, steep central gully which splits the face. It was full of soft snow, and soon they were sinking to the knees at every step, hoping it would firm up as they got higher. It was not as if Tough and his party were innocent of avalanche risk. They noticed that there were 'traces of avalanche action ... on every side', but they persisted until the point where the Post 'assumed the character of a real chimney', which they could not climb because it was too steep and their axe-heads slipped through the snow 'as if it had been so much sawdust'. Providentially, they were forced to retreat.

They had not gone far 'when a loud crash above our heads announced that something like a real avalanche had fallen and it came past us on both sides'. A large block of snow struck Raeburn 'fairly on the head, while the smaller fragments which followed covered his head and shoulders as he lay prone upon the steep slope'. (One wonders if he had his trademark hat on?) By good fortune, which they hardly deserved, 'the snow was quite soft, so that no harm was done'.

The state of the snow meant they couldn't descend fast, but they reached a sheltering island of rock when they were struck again. This time Tough was hit 'three heavy blows on the head, back and ribs'. Again, because the snow was recently fallen, no real damage was done, and they were let off with a warning.

Nothing deterred, Tough, Raeburn and Douglas returned to Coire Ardair the following day, only to find that 'matters were very much worse. The older snow was ... coming down mixed with earth, stone, and all kinds of detritus'. They watched as 'one large mass of cornice, carrying with it great blocks of rock, swept directly over our track ... Had we been there ... the most appropriate name for that particular Post would have been, as one of the party remarked with grim jocularity, Post Mortem.' Raeburn or Douglas? Both were capable of making this remark; perhaps Raeburn is the slight favourite.

Tough does not state where they were at this point but it seems likely that they were on the lower slopes of the buttress separating Centre Post from South Post, because he says: 'Traversing to the right (looking down)[3] over alternate patches of rock and snow, we scrambled down into the great gully (i.e. Easy Gully) which separates the Pinnacle Ridge[4] from the central face of the corrie'. They went up the gully, crossed it and only then realised that climbing the face of the Pinnacle Ridge was beyond them.

They travelled back to Dalwhinnie, making a visit to Creag nan Adhaircean on the way, partly to view the remarkable gorges and partly, as Tough kindly puts it, because 'the ornithologist wanted to interview a Peregrine' which was known to nest there. Raeburn's love of birds is like a leitmotif which follows him throughout his career. At the end of Tough's article, he provides a list of 28 species which he had spotted during their time out. In Easy Gully he noticed a pair of snow buntings on both days and notes that they were probably settling down to breed.

Although by modern standards this attempt to climb on the Post Face of Creag Meagaidh must seem most ill-advised—one of the first lessons in winter climbing is 'don't attempt gullies in thawing conditions'—it must be remembered that winter climbing in Scotland was in its infancy and the effects of temperature on snow were not well understood. Indeed, many Scottish climbers got their knowledge of snow and ice from trips to the Alps, where conditions were very different. Also, at the time, there was not the modern distinction between winter and summer climbing in Scotland: there was just climbing; one climbed 'the rocks' in whatever condition one found them. Despite these factors, Raeburn appears to have learned from his experience in Coire Ardair. In a long career in Scotland, he does not appear to get into trouble with avalanches again.

William Tough was plainly impressed by Raeburn because he climbed with him again in October 1896, on The Cobbler (*SMCJ*, 1897). Raeburn describes their day in an 'Excursions'[5] piece, beginning with a description of the view permitted by the unusual absence of mist:

3   Writers of this period often give descriptions of crags looking down: they call these directions 'True right' and 'True left'; this can be a source of confusion, especially as they are not always consistent. I have tried to highlight this difficulty where appropriate.
4   Now called Pinnacle Buttress.
5   The 'Excursions' section of the *SMCJ* was meant for writers who did not want to write a full-blown article to give the bare details of their climbs.

[S]nowy peaks, glittering lochs, and dark green valleys, and when the sun began to sink behind the mountains of Jura, the whole sky, with the piled masses of cumulus clouds, was flooded with the most glorious colouring. Especially fine was the backward view through the pass between Arthur and Narnain, the inky-black pinnacles of The Cobbler standing up sharp and jagged against the green and gold sky, and the peak of Ben Ime filling up the background, its snows shining rosy pink in the afterglow.[6]

Raeburn is not only sensitive to birds and animals but has an artist's and geographer's appreciation of landscape.

Their attempt to climb began at the foot of North Peak. A short way up a grassy gully it branched and the left branch ended in a cave 'fantastically ornamented with huge icicles'. They explored 'two stories of this' (shades of tall Edinburgh houses) but couldn't make progress because the roof overhung badly and did not possess 'a skylight'. They tried the right branch, but after some 80 ft it diminished to a crack 'which Tough and I, not being mountaineering illustrations,[7] declined to attempt'. They tried a grassy ledge which traversed the face to the left, but it came 'to an abrupt end on the face of the cliff on the right-hand wall of the very straight gully or chimney ... running up the peak immediately to the right of the northmost beak'. It seems possible, Raeburn notes, 'to gain this gully by ascending the rock face, but we allowed it to stop us, and retraced our steps to the bottom'.

[Fig 3]

Following Raeburn's progress on The Cobbler is not straightforward. Tom Prentice comments that it is:

[H]ard to know exactly where Raeburn went at the start of this description ... However, Recess Route does start with a short bit of grassy gully at the foot of the South Face of North Peak. The general feeling is that Raeburn tried the lower pitches of Recess Route (the left-hand line, see photograph) and Fold Direct (the right-hand line),

---

6   Raeburn goes far beyond the limits of the 'Excursions' piece here. This is not an isolated example. We learn much about him from these pieces.

7   Probably, as Tom Prentice has suggested, the sorts of wildly exaggerated pictures of climbers that accompanied Edward Whymper's *Scrambles Amongst the Alps* (1871).

Fig 3

The Cobbler, South Face of North Peak. Right-Angled Gully starts in the obvious gully on the upper crag: the line traverses to the right halfway up. The Direct Finish, which defeated Raeburn, continues straight up. Ramshead Gully is the dark slit in the centre of the picture with Halfway Terrace to the right of its base. The Fold starts from the right end of this terrace. Recess Route takes the prominent gully in the centre of the lowest crag.
Photo: Tom Prentice

reaching the grassy ledge (now known as the Halfway Terrace) before retreating. From the Halfway Terrace both routes join to continue up the only viable line at the grade, the steep chimney/groove of The Fold which is at the right end of the terrace. (2022)

Ken Crocket (2015) has a slightly different version:

On the North Peak they [Raeburn and Tough] had attempted what would eventually become Ramshead Gully ... failing due to ice. A right traverse on Halfway Terrace took them to The Fold, the crux pitch of Recess Route. Declining to attempt this they retreated.

At least there seems to be no doubt that in 1896 they did reach Halfway Terrace. Eight years later, Raeburn would return to this part of The Cobbler.

After this reversal they proceeded to make the second ascent of Right-Angled Gully.[8] Indeed, they attempted the direct finish, but the last 15 ft proved too much for them because the 40 ft chimney had 'a snow cornice several feet thick overhanging its outlet'. Instead, they escaped to the right 'by a most convenient grass ledge' and gained the summit by the steep 15 ft rock wall. The conditions must have been wintry for they found axes useful on the 'grassy southern peak'. (The Direct Finish to Right-Angled Gully was not climbed until 1930 and is now graded Severe).

By this time Raeburn would have submitted his application to the SMC, and his hill activities continued apace. On 7 November, he joined forces with William Brown and George Duncan on a trip to Ben Nevis (SMCJ, 1897), where Brown thought he had discovered a direct way of climbing Staircase Gully on Càrn Dearg Buttress.

A useful discovery made by the party was finding a better way of reaching the north face from Glen Nevis. On this occasion they approached by the Pony Track to just below the halfway house, crossed the hill above the height of Lochan Meall an t-Suidhe and only had to descend a couple of hundred feet to reach the foot of Castle Ridge. This was much less tiring than grinding up the grassy slopes of Meall an t-Suidhe. (It is fascinating

---

8   The first ascent of Right-Angled Gully was made by Naismith and M'Gregor on 27 September 1896.

how things change: this 'new way' of getting to the cliffs is, nowadays, occasionally used for variety, but the main traffic pounds up and down the Allt a' Mhuilinn glen.)

Alas for their ambitions so early in what would be to us the Winter Season, but to Raeburn and his companions was just another autumn day, the rocks were covered in verglas. They had no chance of doing what they wanted to do and were reduced to 'the tame alternative of cutting [their] way out of Coire na Ciste up one of the snow gullies'. Even in 1897 merely ascending Number Three Gully is seen by Raeburn as tame. He disdains to lead and stays at the tail end of the rope from where he enjoys 'fine views of the precipices from the towering battlements of the Castle—round which were circling a pair of golden eagles—to the steep giant profile of the N.E. Buttress'. In passing they saw that what we now know as Waterfall Gully was 'a mass of huge ribs and stalactites of ice twisted into all kinds of curious forms, but not stable enough to allow of steps being cut in them'.

While Brown cut the steps, Raeburn had plenty of time to admire the scenery which, circumscribed as it was, presented 'scenes of fairy-like loveliness'. With the possible exception of WH Murray, it is difficult to think of any other writer who would use such words to describe a scene on Ben Nevis, but Raeburn fully justifies their use: [Fig 4]

The towering rockwalls ... black in their natural nakedness, were now draped all over in a lace mantle sewn with millions of jewels—fog crystals in fact—overlapping each other plate upon plate and feather upon feather, so that not a trace of stone was visible.

Raeburn the creative writer responds to the beauty, and Raeburn the scientist seeks an explanation:

The size of these masses of opaque ice was astonishing. On the ridges of the rocks several pieces I broke off measured almost a foot from the point of attachment to the rock to the latest born of the outermost feathery crystals. They all pointed in the same direction—downwards at the same angle as the gully.

Why? Because:

> [T]he N. and N.E. winds gathering the mists in Coire na Ciste, and
> pouring them in a constant stream over the edges of the cliffs and up ...
> the gullies, while rising as they did from warmer regions lower down to
> strike the surface of the rocks chilled to 20°F ... deposited their moisture
> in the form of these exquisite fog crystals.

Accurate or not this is a careful, well-thought-out explanation, clearly demonstrating Raeburn's analytical ability: the other side of his artistic insight.

These late Victorian expeditions abounded in energy and high spirits. After enjoying 'a hospitable cup of hot coffee' in the Observatory, someone suggested that they might descend Observatory Gully on the way back. This forms a comic interlude. They took a good double-axe belay and dangled Brown over the cornice 'of that rather gruesome spot'. The precautions were 'not unnecessary', says Raeburn with a smile, 'for otherwise the stern commands of the law of gravity, in conjunction with a slope of 80° or so on icy snow, acting on a man of so law-abiding disposition as Brown, would probably have induced him to leave us *en route* for the bottom of the gully in record time.' Dry as the east wind, there is no doubt about the existence of Raeburn's sense of humour ... Brown was hauled up again.

This incident appears to have been at the top of what we now call Tower Gully. Raeburn mentions that the left-hand branch of the gully is still unclimbed and 'appears hopeless from above'. Gardyloo Gully is indeed much more formidable than Tower Gully, but climbs, we now know, tend to look much more difficult from above. In fact, Raeburn and Harry Lawson were to make the second ascent of Gardyloo in 1901.

On their way down the snow slopes of Càrn Dearg, Raeburn observed that:

> [T]he sun, which had been hidden all day, suddenly appeared in a
> narrow clear strip between the dense masses of the black clouds and
> the horizon, staining the western hills and seas with a blood-red colour,
> while far away to the N. and N.E. the sky assumed a most ghastly, livid
> corpse-like hue, below which the icy mountains shone with a startling
> whiteness. It was in truth a strange and eerie effect, which, despite
> the sharp wind we lingered to gaze upon as it slowly faded before the
> creeping shadows of the dark closing in from the eastwards.

The imagery of this passage, particularly 'corpse-like hue', implies that Raeburn is keenly alive to the unearthly suggestion of the atmosphere. As well as responding sensitively to natural beauty, something in him—a kind of feyness—is brought out by these darker suggestions. By this time, of course, his own life had been touched by tragedy in the death by drowning of one of his brothers. We do not know if Harold, who was only 15 at the time, had a close relationship with William, but it is certainly true that they had a mutual interest in sailing. William's tragic death may be much more significant for Raeburn's later mental state than we know.

Fig 4

'Fairy-like loveliness'? The Ben in early winter condition. Coire na Ciste centre. Photo: Noel Williams

2. SALISBURY CRAGS, JOINING SMC, YACHT MEET   1896–1897

Raeburn's application to join the SMC was, by the standards of the day, quite a strong one, but much better than this, he had now been climbing with SMC members of repute for the past 12 months. His correspondence with *SMCJ* Editor, Willie Douglas, is just the sort of thing which might form the content of emails between climbing partners nowadays: 'Can I borrow your rope? Where can I purchase a helmet?'[1] (He means a balaclava—one of the few forms of headgear Raeburn was ever photographed in apart from his trademark hat.)[2] There was little doubt that he would be accepted by the SMC, and he was duly elected to membership on 2 December 1896 in the company of twelve other men, most of whom were also to become active and distinguished members of the Club.

Then, as now, there was nothing unusual about a fit and active mountaineer becoming a member of the SMC. Of course, you had to know someone in the Club to propose you and to gather three other members to second you, but Raeburn's path was smoothed by his friendship with Willie Douglas, who introduced him to other members and invited him to meets. What is rather unusual is that Raeburn seems to have gone from being a non-member to being a leading member almost immediately.

The Proceedings of the Club section in the *SMCJ* reports that the day after the AGM and Dinner of December 1896, 'a large party were on Arthur Seat and the Salisbury Crags, the "steady guides" being Messrs Raeburn and

[Fig 1]

---

1 Douglas's letters remain available through the National Library of Scotland.
2 See photograph by Gall Inglis of Raeburn and party on Liathach in April 1900 (Chapter 5). See also, this chapter, photo of the Yacht Meet where he is wearing a cap.

Fig 1

Possibly the first ascent of Cracked Slab on Salisbury Crag. Raeburn given a hand by J Gall Inglis. Photo: SMC Image Archive

Brown' (*SMCJ*, 1897). Raeburn indeed had intimate knowledge of Salisbury Crags, as is shown by the fact that his first actual article in the *SMCJ* (as distinct from 'Excursions' pieces), was about climbing on those crags. It could be considered the first chapter in the SMC's Guide Book,[3] which made its official appearance in Volume Nine of the *SMCJ* in 1907. Whether Willie Douglas actually asked Harold to write a contribution for the Guide Book is not known, but the two were friends and both were interested in literary matters. It seems at least plausible that Raeburn's article was thought of as a possible Guide Book contribution.

However this might be, the article functions as a guide to the crags and is meticulous and comprehensive; from the amount of detail Raeburn gives, one gets the impression that he has spent a lot of time climbing there. But from the perspective of trying to understand Raeburn the man, we learn more. There is his affection and respect for his native city: 'Favoured in many respects by nature as is the city of Edinburgh, in none is she more favoured from a scenic point of view than in the possession of her bold crags and hills' (*SMCJ*, 1897). Raeburn sees these features: 'Rising like the Castle Rock from waves of greenery, or, like the Calton Hill, above a grey slate sea of houses, as lending a picturesque strength and impressiveness to her scenery.' The imagery of the sea, something wild and untameable, is contrasted with the abiding strength and solidity of the city mounted on its crags and hills. Born, bred and educated in the city, Raeburn was always an Edinburgh man; he lived there all his life. Edinburgh people are famed for their reticence and understatement, and these traits are found in Raeburn's character, but there is a tension between this essential stolidity and the lover of Tennyson and Coleridge whom we glimpse from time to time, the man who could describe a winter scene on Ben Nevis as having 'a fairy-like loveliness'. These disparate traits are part of what makes him such an intriguing figure.

Although the highest point in the Queen's Park, the top of Arthur's Seat, the Lion's Head, measures only 822.9 ft, and:

---

3   The SMC was keen to publish a Guide Book to the mountains of Scotland, but realised that they didn't have the necessary resources. The answer was to publish the Guide Book in sections in the *SMCJ*. This was very successful and the Journals containing this material were much sought after.

This to an Alpinist, or even to a bagger of native Bens, may seem truly insignificant; [but] ... a half-sovereign is smaller than a five-shilling piece, and many a Highland Ben of ten times its bulk has less of the real mountain about it than has Arthur's Seat.

This tells us something important about Raeburn's mountaineering values: he is not interested in mere size but in the form of the mountain and, by extension, the line and position of the climb. The routes on Salisbury Crags 'nowhere exceed 90 feet in height, yet even these gain a wonderful impressiveness from being placed on the summit of a steep talus slope of over 200 feet.' Nor is it just a question of the climb's line or position; atmosphere, too, is vital:

In a dense mist, when the North Sea 'haar' hides the city and the green slopes below, and exaggerates and distorts the rugged basaltic ribs and buttresses, one feels as far above the world as on some splintered crag in a wild north-eastern corrie ...

Raeburn is inspired by his local crags and mounts a strong defence of them; he also praises the view from Arthur's Seat: 'It is the supreme height in its neighbourhood, not cribbed and confined, as are so many hills of superior altitude, by jealous rivals pressing on their flanks, but kingly by name and shape ... it lifts its head proudly to the sky, the chiefest mark and ornament of Scotland's capital.' Fine rhetoric: not content with echoing *Macbeth*, and perhaps *Hamlet*, Raeburn even contrives to sound like Shakespeare.

Now a member of the Club and with a good contribution to the SMCJ in the pipeline, things were going well for Harold. He attended the 1897 New Year Meet at Loch Awe. In his meet report (SMCJ, 1897), Hugh Munro [Fig 2] notes that Douglas, Munro, Raeburn and Rennie ascended Cruachan. He also records that on the 2 January, 'Raeburn and Maclay made the third ascent of the Black Shoot', Bell and Napier having made the second ascent the previous day. It seems that the Black Shoot, the bane of so many earlier attempts, was at last losing some of its aura.

Better things were in store at the famous Easter Yachting Meet, which [Fig 3] took place in April 1897 aboard the steam yacht *Erne*[4]. Despite rough weather,

---

4   The West Highland name for the sea eagle.

Fig 2

Raeburn, left, at the Lochawe Meet of 1897, standing next to his proposer Willie Douglas. His pose could hardly be more awkward, one foot up, one foot down, headgear awry and staring determinedly at the ground, in contrast to the confident gaze of the three members at the back. The other well-known face is Hugh Munro in trademark beret (standing right). Photo: SMC Image Archive

Fig 3

Raeburn, left, wearing most unusual headgear, looking slightly more relaxed at sea on the 1897 Yacht Meet. Photo: SMC Image Archive

which from time to time kept people to their cabins and made landing on Skye impossible, it sounds like a truly memorable occasion. There was music and dancing, with Hugh Munro distinguishing himself by dancing the Highland Fling 'to frantic applause', and although Skye could not be approached, members and guests climbed and walked on the island of Rum and in Knoydart. Professor Lodge wrote the Meet Report (ibid.), and several members, including Raeburn, wrote up their experiences later in the 'Excursions' section of the *SMCJ*.

The *Erne* anchored safely in Loch Scresort. Taking their cue from an article by Munro (*SMCJ*, 1891) in which he describes 'a steep part on the N. Arête of Askival', John Bell, William Brown, Herbert Boyd and Raeburn headed for that mountain.

Raeburn wrote:

After mounting some 800 ft from the beach, we struck a very fair track, which skirts the spurs of Allival to the E., and takes one to the foot of Corrie nan Grunnd, a fine wild rock basin with a small tarn in it. We worked through the boulder-strewn desolation of this corrie ... gained the ridge connecting Allival and Askival, and reached the foot of the steep part leading up to the summit of Askival.

They discovered an avoidable but intriguing 'almost vertical cliff of over 100 ft', which 'forbade the slightest variation'. However, it transpired that the gabbro made the ascent easier than it looked, and, to the annoyance of the photographer who wanted an action shot, 'Bell and Brown rapidly scrambled up it and disappeared'. They excused themselves by saying they couldn't hear him because of the sound of the wind. Raeburn and Boyd then ascended to the summit by the ridge—'ropes not required at any point'. There was soft snow on 'the last few hundred feet, and near the very summit [at] 2,659 ft, a little ice was met with'.

Bell and Brown descended the east arête while Raeburn, always seeking the most knowledge and excitement from every outing, descended the south arête 'for about 300 ft ... and then traversed round the east side of the mountain till close to the east arête, ascending to the top again by a steep gully, thinly floored with soft snow'. No mean feat as the flanks of Askival are steep and rocky; Raeburn's little extra would certainly have involved at least high-grade scrambling in exposed situations. The whole party went back over Allival, and Raeburn says the weather was 'not bad ... though storm clouds from the west were continually obscuring the outline of the higher peaks'.

From Loch Scresort in Rum, the *Erne* sailed back to the mainland and anchored in Loch Hourn. This gave the assembled mountaineers a wonderful chance to explore the remote mountains of the Knoydart peninsula and its rough bounds. In particular, there was the exciting prospect of exploring the impressive Coire Dhorcaill on Ladhar Bheinn.[5] Then, few hill-goers would even have seen this corrie, and nobody had climbed in it. However, the club grapevine proved useful, for Willie Douglas and John Rennie had made a recent trip to Ladhar Bheinn, and Douglas had written about it in the very same number of the *SMCJ* (1897).

[Fig 4]

On Saturday, 17 April, Raeburn, Brown, Boyd and Bell set off to explore. John Bell describes their day (ibid.). They landed from the *Erne* and followed 'a stalkers' path which leads very easily up into the corrie'. The visibility was poor, but they could see, at one point, 'steep rocky buttresses ... projecting below the clouds'. They made two 'ineffectual attempts to climb the rocks' which were 'plastered with snow' but then managed to make 'an ascent ... by a great gully which descends straight down through the whole height of the cliff'. Less than halfway up, they encountered 'a vertical pitch of smooth rock approaching 100 ft'. This had to be turned by the rocks on the left: 'When free of snow', Bell thought, 'they would probably be quite easy, but ... it was only after a considerable struggle that Raeburn, who was leading, piloted the party up them and into the gully above the pitch.' The modern guidebook (SMC, 2007) says:

> *This gully is quite straightforward as far as the enormous chockstone at half-height. Circumventing this huge monolith can prove surprisingly difficult. It involves climbing awkward slabby rocks on the left wall, by two pitches totalling some 60 m.*

So perhaps not so easy *unless* coated in hard snow. Bell concludes his note: 'The gully can be easily identified, as it is the most prominent on the cliff, and has throughout its length on its right (west) side a very striking

---

5   No doubt attempting to copy local pronunciation, they called it 'Lurven'. Nowadays we say 'Larven'.

Fig 4

Coire Dhorcaill on Ladhar Bheinn.
Raeburn's Gully is just right of centre.
Photo: Noel Williams

vertical wall of rock.' How emblematic of Raeburn's career this day is: he walks into an unknown corrie in misty conditions and climbs the most prominent gully on the mountain.

On Sunday, 18 April, William Brown writes:

Two parties made a complete circuit of the Lurven ridge ... Bell, Garden, Gibson and Raeburn struck up through Corrie Dhorrcail ... to the point where the NE ridge of Stob a' Chearcaill rises up, as the Editor puts it, like "a slate set on edge". The ascent of this slate edge was a little troublesome ... it rises at a considerable angle, and care is necessary owing to the character of the rock. [With Bell leading] ... a zig-zag route was followed along various snowy ledges and up several steep slabs, where the holds were the reverse of satisfactory.

A fine day on Rum, two good days on Ladhar Bheinn, and Hugh Munro dancing the fling—Harold was having a good time.

A feature of Raeburn's mountaineering life was his willingness to go out on the hill with various companions. Before the successful Yacht Meet of April 1897, we find a pleasantly written record by Walter Smith of a trip he made with Raeburn and Willie Douglas to Stùc a' Chroin in Perthshire (SMCJ, 1897). With an overnight stay in the aptly named *Dreadnought Arms* in Callander, this was a one-day escape from routine in Edinburgh.

As Smith remarks, 'the weather had been unsettled during the week', the rivers were in flood, but as they set out in the morning, they had 'an hour or two of hope and sunshine'. How well one knows days like this. Raeburn spotted 17 different kinds of birds, while Douglas 'spoke of rocks and "rocky" reminiscences'. Smith himself 'smoked the pipe of peace. It was Sunday morning in the Highlands!'

Needless to say, the weather deteriorated completely. They had lunch 'under difficulties' in a snowstorm and deliberated. The outcome was that they made 'a steep and slushy scramble for 500 ft ... up some gullies', which brought them to a grassy terrace running along below the upper crags. Roped up, with Raeburn leading, they struck 'sharply to the left up a short succession of steep gullies, rocky corners and slippery grassy "bits" concealed in snow'. This brought them onto the ridge 'a short way north of the top'.

On the descent they walked into the teeth of the gale and driving snow but found a wire fence, which 'fortunately' took them towards Ben Each: 'It was wild work, and bitterly cold, fighting our way through the storm along that fence!' Once they knew where they were, they left the fence and traversed 'along the N. side of Ben Each', getting down at length 'to the ruined cottage at the very head of Glen Ample' where 'the soaking remains of the last sandwich were conscientiously washed down by something else'. They got back to Callander at 7 pm, 'tired and hungry, but with good appetite and minds at rest'.

A challenging day out in the Scottish hills. It is not easy to tell exactly where the party went, but it sounds as though they climbed some variation of Stùc a' Chroin's North-East Buttress, nowadays regarded as a grade 1 or 2 scramble (Thow, 2017). It is possible that they took an even harder variation of this route and, in either case, no small achievement in atrocious weather. Clearly, Smith felt it was well worth recording the day in the *SMCJ*.

In autumn Raeburn was back on Ben Nevis (*SMCJ*, 1898). He reports what was becoming for him and some of his clubmates an almost routine ascent of North-East Buttress followed by a descent of Tower Ridge with Douglas and Fraser. They left Fort William at 6.45 am and took three hours to the foot of the buttress, using the recently preferred route by the halfway hut. With his habitual accuracy, Raeburn records that the ascent took 2¼ hours and the descent 3½ hours, of which the Tower, unsurprisingly, took 1¼ hours. There was no time to traverse the Boulder for 'want of light'. They took the same route back to the Station Hotel, arriving at 7.40 pm. Raeburn concludes: 'The conditions of weather and rocks were, as one member of the party remarked, A.P.[6] —absolutely perfect!'

These late-Victorian climbers travelled light, were very fit and were technically capable of moving together on many sections of these routes. No time was wasted in 'looking for protection'—most of the time there was none—the leader never fell, and, as Ken Crocket (2015) points out, 'Not one fatality was recorded in Scotland to any mountaineer during these early years.' Of necessity, the Victorians moved together or climbed in much shorter pitches than we do nowadays. This, one suspects, had psychological advantages. If the leader has a stance relatively near the second, he can give advice and encouragement as well as direct help with the rope if

---

6   AP usually meant 'Absolutely Perpendicular'.

need be. Communication and the giving of support were easier. Factors like these, allied to the skills of the leading climbers of the day, perhaps help to explain the remarkably short times taken on long routes like Tower Ridge and North-East Buttress. It is also worth noting that usually, the best climber in the group led the whole route. This was crucial when a mistake by the leader could have disastrous results. When he was a member of any such group, that climber was almost always Harold Raeburn.

Deeper into the autumn, in November, we find Raeburn on the Cobbler with Willie Naismith; the male members of the Inglis Clark family were also there. According to a note by Naismith (*SMCJ*, 1898), he and Raeburn:

> *Found a short new climb on the Northern Peak. Starting from above the bottom pitch in the prominent gully on the Arrochar side of the peak, they scaled the rocks to their right, and after crawling on "all-fours" round a corner where hold there was none, and negotiating some easier places farther up, they emerged from the face at the head of the said gully.*

On top, they met William Clark and his son Charles, who had just completed Right-Angled Gully, and together they traversed the Central and Southern tops 'taking a look at every rock and cliff that seemed to offer the prospect of a scramble'. Mistress Jean 'was approached by the route discovered by Mr Bell's party in 1895' (*SMCJ*, 1896). How was the weather? 'Lovely everywhere excepting on the Cobbler, where a wet mist made the rocks cold and slimy'.

As to climbing on slimy rock, the Victorians had a distinct advantage over modern climbers. Nailed boots adhered much better than rubber to wet rock. This does something to explain how willing Raeburn and his companions were to climb in the wet; the other part of the explanation is just that they were very tough and prepared to climb in poor conditions, taking the weather and the state of the rock in their stride. Tweed jackets and breeches were warm so long as they were dry but absorbed water readily, becoming heavy and losing insulation. Soakings were frequent, and in winter conditions, if your clothing got wet it tended to freeze solid, especially if you were standing on a ledge waiting for the leader to solve a problem. All of this was accepted as part of the day's work and rarely dwelt on in the mountain writings of the time.

3. GLENCOE, TARMACHAN, SKYE CONTROVERSY 1897–1898

On Saturday, 25 September 1897, Raeburn cycled with John Stewart Napier[1] from Bridge of Orchy station to the Clachaig Inn in Glencoe. Apparently, this was Raeburn's first time in Glencoe, and he described their trip in an article in the *SMCJ* (1898). Napier said that the Buachaille had never shown up better; on the way down the glen, Harold spotted Ossian's Cave.

Good weather in Glencoe is a transient phenomenon, and the following morning they looked out 'upon a landscape limited by mist and streaming with water'. It was also blowing a gale. 'Despite these little unpleasantnesses' and by now thoroughly soaked, they headed up to the unclimbed Church Door Buttress. On a previous occasion Napier, Edward Green and John Bell had got quite a way up, but on this attempt, unsurprisingly, Raeburn and Napier did not get as far. They reached a committing move and Raeburn admitted to 'a preference for keeping a line of retreat open', so they descended. They climbed Collie's Pinnacle—'quite simple'—and had a 'shivering and chittering' lunch before going on up Bidean nam Bian by 'the big gully'. Having looked at the top of Church Door Buttress they went on over Stob Coire nan Lochan and descended via Aonach Dubh.

Still not content, they visited Ossian's Cave: 'hardly a desirable anchorhold for even the hardiest of anchorites … a most inhospitable cave indeed, telling visitors with the mute eloquence of gravity to "get out".'

They got back to the hotel about 6pm, the weather, as Raeburn wryly

---

1 John Stewart Napier is not to be confused with his brother Robert Graham Napier. Both were involved, on separate occasions, in the attempts on Church Door Buttress. Graham Napier was on the successful ascent.

remarks, 'having ... much improved, merely violent squalls of hail and rain at frequent intervals in place of a continuous downpour'. On Monday, they had to cycle back to Bridge of Orchy and, of course, the weather was fine.

Gullies are one of the most obvious mountain features. Great rifts in hillsides, like Clachaig Gully in Glencoe, or deeply-cut channels in long cliff faces, like the Black Spout on Lochnagar or the gullies on Ladhar Bheinn, to one of which Raeburn had already given his name, they have held a perennial fascination for mountaineers. They seem to provide easier and less exposed ways of getting up the mountain than tackling steep and exposed walls and ridges. This appearance can, however, be delusive. Climbers at the turn of the century, including Raeburn, returned again and again to what was to become known as Douglas-Gibson Gully on Lochnagar only to be comprehensively defeated, and some 40 years passed before Clachaig Gully was climbed. Classic lines like Zero and Point Five Gullies on Ben Nevis were regarded with awe until the late 1950s and early '60s. But, in general, gully climbing suited the Victorians. Their ropes were short—60 or 80 feet—and they climbed in shorter pitches. Gullies frequently provide long stretches of relatively easy climbing combined with a chockstone, an ice pitch, an abrupt wall or a cornice; these were things the early climbers were equipped to deal with, and none more so than Raeburn.

In an article in the *SMCJ* (1898) entitled 'Two Climbs on the Tarmachans', Raeburn describes a winter gully climbing trip with Harry GS Lawson on 19 and 20 February 1898 from the Loch Tay village of Killin. They had originally planned to make a traverse of the Tarmachan group in order to find the best climbing areas, but as Raeburn points out in his article, they were saved the trouble of a reconnaissance because AW Russell and his brother had recently visited the area and supplied details and photographs. This was just as well, for Raeburn and Lawson might not have seen much as the weather was rough and snowy.

Acting on a hint in Russell's note, the pair headed for a cliff face on Creag na Caillich where they found a 'Great Gully'. There was a north-west wind and soft, new snow. The Gully 'proved under the conditions fairly stiff, but went all right for about half the height'. But then the way forward was deemed 'impracticable' because of fringes of icicles on the 'overhanging edges' of the upper crags. They tried to the right, disturbing 'a pair of ravens, which flew around croaking uneasily'.² No joy that way, so they came back left and reached the top of the crag 'a few yards to the left of the line of the gully'. By this time, it had been snowing for several hours and when they came out on the ridge they 'were at once smitten by a piercing blast full of driving snowflakes'. Raeburn notes that they departed 'as hurriedly as we could' without even bagging the top of Creag na Caillich. It didn't matter because this top had not attained 'the mystic elevation' to be included in Munro's Tables; he was rather dismissive of mere peak-bagging.³

The following day the weather at least was better, and Raeburn and Lawson went to the crag above the south end of Lochan na Lairige. 'Close to the highest part of the face—here perhaps 600 ft high—a narrow and wonderfully straight chimney ran right from near the foot to the top ... we christened it upon the spot the "Arrow Chimey".' At first, they underestimated the climb, 'reckoning without the black overhanging pitches concealed under the fair white surface'. Even getting onto it was difficult; they had to rope up just to gain the foot of the chimney, 'as several ice slopes ha[d] to be cut across'.

Here Raeburn's language becomes decidedly military.⁴ Three times they were 'beaten back at the point of the bayonet of ice ... in our attempt to storm the first pitch'. The position 'was only carried by a strategic flank movement up steep grass ledges ... a determined assault with the ice-axe on the screen of icicles at the entrance [to a cave] and we mounted the chockstone through a hole behind it, and the outworks were won'.

In the upper part of the chimney, Raeburn found the climbing 'distinctly severe', and he had to clear quantities of snow to uncover holds. Lawson, bombarded below, shouted up to him, 'Make the blocks smaller!' Harold did his best to comply, cutting holds for the left hand and toe in 'the thin and rotten ice' on the left wall. His position sounds difficult and perilous—he had to do this with a long axe in his right hand, an unbalanced, dangerous and exhausting procedure. It sounds as if Raeburn was also severely constricted by the overhanging right wall of the chimney. They climbed four

2 Ravens play a small but interesting part in Raeburn's history. They appear on the Black Shoot, on Scafell Pinnacle and the Meije, exciting different reactions.
3 Great Gully was completed in 1902 without deviation by GW Young, A Mackay and S Gillon in better conditions.
4 Oddly enough, prefiguring the sort of language he uses about his famous ascent of Green Gully on Ben Nevis. See Chapter 15.

pitches in this fashion, and two were full runouts of 60 ft, long enough to be mentally and physically draining. There were no adequate belays. After continuously cutting steps for over four hours, Raeburn got cramp on the last pitch and had to stand on Lawson's shoulder to complete the climb.

From the account Raeburn gives, never seeking to exaggerate the difficulties, Arrow Chimney sounds much harder than the modest grade II/III it was given by earlier guidebook editors. In the SMC Guide to *Arran, Arrochar and the Southern Highlands*, Ken Crocket gives it grade IV. As climbers of the calibre of Graham Little and Crocket himself have put up routes of an equivalent standard on Arrow Buttress and on neighbouring crags, this grading should be respected. Raeburn himself thought that the Chimney would be 'fairly easy in summer' but that 'under the conditions met with, it proved quite sufficiently exciting'—a masterly understatement. To date, there is no record of a summer ascent. JHB Bell[5] must have passed it by.

Hugh Munro's report on the Easter Meet of 1898 sounds slightly grumpy. He complains that 'while there were climbing parties at Banavie, Fort William, Clachaig, Kingshouse, Inveroran, Kinlochawe &c., only ten members and two guests put in an appearance at Ballachulish' (*SMCJ*, 1898). And we have to search in 'Excursions' to discover some of what these renegade parties were doing.

Writing a brief report (ibid.) on the doings of those at the Kingshouse, John Bell wrote:

Raeburn and Green ascended the gully just on the right (west) of the Crowberry Ridge [on the Buachaille]. At the very top, where the gully forks, they were forced to take the branch farthest from the Crowberry Ridge. The gully gave a fine climb, with one sensational traverse, and the scenes throughout, with the tremendous overhanging wall of the Crowberry Ridge, were very striking.

Bell goes on to comment that:

Although the quantity of snow was exceptionally small for the time of year, it was sufficient to give a good deal of assistance in the gullies,

---

5   James HB Bell, who speaks up for 'vegetatious schist and granite', is not to be confused with Raeburn's contemporary, John H Bell, and they were not related.

which will probably be found more difficult in summer. In particular, the climbers in the great gully to the west of the Crowberry Ridge would expect to find a series of very formidable pitches when the gully is clear of snow.

Bell's comment demonstrates that these early climbers wanted to get the most 'sport' they could from every climb. If accumulations of snow made the route easier, then dry rock and the absence of snow were to be preferred.[6] The distinction between summer and winter climbing was in its infancy at the end of Queen Victoria's reign.

Raeburn himself did not write about Crowberry Gully until 1911, by which time he had ascended the gully three times. In the meantime, he continued to establish his reputation in the SMC. His aspirations were considerable, but, like his fellow mountaineers, by no means all of his expeditions were successful.

After stressful climbing on the Tarmachans and the Buachaille, the change to pleasant sunny conditions in the summer of 1898 must have come as something of a relief. Raeburn is in a relaxed mood as he describes a trip with John Rennie to The Cobbler on 3 July (*SMCJ*, 1898). For once, they enjoyed a pleasant cycle, this time from Helensburgh. Raeburn's delight in the ride and the beauty of the scenery is very apparent. He thinks Lomond is 'Scotland's finest loch', and comments on 'the screen of trees on this beautiful road'.

Once on the mountain, they follow the lead of 'the party which visited the hill' on 20 November 1897. Raeburn omits to mention that he was in that party: characteristic self-effacement. In fact, he does not seem to have spotted some specific goal to be attempted in future, so they started by investigating the north face of South Peak. They rejected a shallow chimney, 'steep and … destitute of holds', but gained the face by a sloping ledge which 'leads out on a very steep face, composed of moss and grass rather loosely adherent'.

They worked across this ghastly ground and 'gradually ascending, …

---

6   Whether Crowberry Gully is harder in winter or summer is a moot point. It was graded III in winter, rose to III/IV and is now IV,4; it is Severe in summer, roughly equivalent grades; but winter conditions vary vastly. Perhaps in thin, icy conditions the route is harder in winter. In any case, nowadays, no queues form in summer.

turned the angle of the northern face, about halfway up, below some overhanging rock, and entered the gully on the east leading up to the junction of the east ridge with the face'. Raeburn's comment is judicious: 'Our route has little to commend it, with few and bad "hitches" and treacherous mossy ledges.' It certainly sounds more than 'slightly dangerous', and it isn't really a proper, independent ascent of the face as it joins 'the ordinary route a good way below the summit' (SMC, 1997).[7]

However, better things were in store, for when Raeburn and Rennie started to explore the North Buttress of the Central Peak, they found 'a very interesting little climb'. They followed a sheep track which gave 'access to a large patch of grass about one-third up the face'. The first 100 ft were 'an easy scramble, then the gully passed into a large cave'. The cave walls were far apart and the roof projected considerably, but Raeburn spotted a small ledge running along the upper right wall. With a struggle, he gained the ledge and passed round the right edge of the cave into 'an upper and smaller one'. This cave had a window, but even 'a medium-sized mountaineer' couldn't get through. 'However, the window sill gives a grand hold, and an interesting traverse, where the arms have to do most of the work, led us round by our right and up a small chimney where the holds are small but good, into the upper continuation of the main gully.' From there, a 30 ft scramble took them out near the highest point of the buttress, and Cave Route, a 200 ft Difficult, was born. From a climbing perspective, it saved the day from mediocrity, and the pair were well satisfied as they made a beeline for the Arrochar Hotel across the head of Loch Long, where the tide, conveniently, was out. After slaking their thirst, they had a pleasant cycle back to Helensburgh.

In a more serious vein, Raeburn teamed up with John Bell for further attempts on Church Door Buttress on Bidean nam Bian. Bell recounts their efforts (SMCJ, 1898). After a preliminary reconnaissance at Easter, William Clark and Conradi Squance arrived from Ballachulish and were persuaded to make up the party. Because of the late start and 'the snow-covered rocks' they could not attempt the climb that day, but devoted their time to prospecting the route from above. By judicious down-climbing they managed to reach the point at which the earlier attempts of Green and Napier had failed. While this was going on, and it must have taken quite a while, 'Squance

---

7   Grassy Traverse is described as 'a vegetated and exposed moderate in summer' but as 'a very scenic route in winter' at grade III.

danced about on the summit to try to keep warm', and inadvertently caused perplexity on the Glencoe road, where Naismith and Maclay 'imagined that it was a dance of triumph, but were puzzled by there being only one man, and by his prolonged gesticulations'. But now they had the whole route prospected and, given better weather and conditions, felt confident of success.

On 15 July a large party gathered at the Clachaig. Bell and Raeburn were joined by Herbert Boyd, Willie Douglas, Robert Graham Napier and GT Parker. The following day the weather looked threatening but 'it steadily improved, and by the time [they] were on the buttress the sun came out, and the rocks were fairly dry'. Never mind the weather, one accepted the rocks in the condition in which one found them. After all, the equipment and even the clothing hardly varied with the season, and ice-axes were often carried in summer; they were long, made good walking sticks and were often used to clear holds and ledges of superfluous mud and vegetation. The climbing party was eventually reduced to four, as Parker and Willie Douglas, always modest about his climbing abilities, agreed to 'watch proceedings'. Bell and Raeburn tossed for the lead. Bell led up to the ledge reached before by diverse parties and Raeburn tackled the crux chimney above it. Bell gives a blow-by-blow account:

[Fig 1]

> *There are three jammed blocks close together in the chimney, and three or four feet above the highest of them is a big, jammed block with a hole behind it. The lower blocks shove one out very awkwardly in the attempt to get over them. Raeburn climbed up to them, measured the difficulty, and then retreated for a rest. The place was evidently very stiff ...*

So stiff indeed that they even tried to gain some protection by attaching a stone to 100 ft of string and attempting to throw the stone over the big, jammed block. If this had worked they could have attached the rope to the string and, by pulling it through, manufactured a top-rope to see them over the difficulties. But after half an hour's stone throwing, they gave up, and Raeburn took off his boots to try the pitch in stocking soles. Bell went to the end of the ledge 'to try to field him if a slip should occur', while Napier, jamming himself in the hole in the ledge, worked Raeburn's rope over the small hitch and anchored Bell at the same time. Fortunately, none of these rather desperate measures was put to the test because Raeburn's strength

Fig 1

Church Door Buttress is right of centre, with Diamond Buttress on the left and Collie's Pinnacle at the foot. Photo: Noel Williams

and skill took him safely over the crux, 'and wild cheers broke out from us on the ledge and from Douglas and Parker, who were watching ... from the top of the eastern buttress'.

Bell followed, and then the rucksack with Raeburn's boots and their one axe was sent up on the string. As Bell remarks: 'The string was not very strong, and the weight considerable, so that Raeburn naturally got somewhat excited at the thought of his boots taking a plunge to the foot of the buttress. However, they arrived safely.'

There only remained the 15-foot corner, which 'proved difficult'. Raeburn elected to climb 'a chimney close beside the corner', which he thought quite as difficult as the one below, 'but not in so sensational a situation'. Once up, he traversed to the top of the corner and brought the rest up that way, presumably including Herbert Boyd, whose name is never mentioned on the climb. A further outburst of cheering greeted them at the top of the buttress some 30 ft above: 'a very obstinate opponent had been overcome' (Taylor, *SMCJ*, 2014).

Thus far, Raeburn's membership of the SMC had been marked by success and popularity, but a whiff of controversy arose over something Raeburn was reported to have said to his friend, the Secretary of the Club, William Clark. In an article entitled 'A Day on Cir Mhor' (*SMCJ*, 1898), Clark quoted a remark Harold had made to him when, on a former occasion, they had been trying to climb the boiler-plate slabs on the lower part of the Ben Nuis precipice in Arran. According to Clark, Raeburn had said: 'I would not trust a climber who had only climbed in Skye', and he had gone on to amplify his remark by saying: 'Skye climbing, as far as my experience goes, is ridiculously easy, with the exception of the gap on the Alasdair-Dubh ridge and the lower portions of the rocks near Coruisk.'

William Brown, another distinguished member of the SMC, was offended by these remarks and wrote a long letter to Editor Douglas, which he published with replies by Clark and Raeburn (ibid.). Brown was a good climber who claimed to have begun his apprenticeship on Skye; he had climbed extensively there, on Ben Nevis and notably on Lochnagar, where he and William Tough pioneered their famous Tough-Brown Traverse. Raeburn had been a member of the Club for two years and had a growing reputation.

It seems to have been the phrase 'ridiculously easy' that really annoyed Brown. He calls the remark 'neither particularly relevant nor well founded'.

Brown concedes that, unlike climbs in Arran, 'Coolin climbs are generally much easier than they look', and he also admits that 'Coolin gabbro ... is exceptionally good and reliable, broken up so as to admit in most places of an almost infinite choice of routes, and "weathered" into most magnificent foot and hand holds.' (Both points made by Clark in his article.)

Again, Brown concedes that, with obvious exceptions, most of the Cuillin Ridge is straightforward, but since Clark is championing Arran, Brown scores a good point by asking if the Cuillin Ridge is 'easier than the circuit of Glen Sannox, or the A'Chir Ridge ... how does it compare with the horseshoe ridge of Cruachan or the circuit of the Ladhar Bheinn tops?' With some justification, Brown argues that these are the sorts of climb one must compare with 'ridge wandering in the Coolins'. It is not fair, he claims, to compare this with 'a gully on the Cir Mhor face, the Ben Nuis precipice, the Tower of Ben Nevis, or the cliffs of Lochnagar'.

Brown makes the valid point that apart from the main ridge on Skye, 'there is no limit to the difficulties a bold climber may find himself confronted with'. And he asserts that 'for variety and interest of climbing, from the "ridiculously easy" to the extremely difficult, there is no finer climbing ground in Scotland than the Coolins'.

Brown also notes that gabbro is not the only rock type in the Cuillin: there is 'a form of trap [rock] which is smooth, treacherous and very much shattered'. He says that he has come across every 'condition of rock'—he is careful not to say every *kind* of rock—'except thoroughly rotten and vegetable rock' (i.e. vegetated). He argues that the slabs of the lower slopes of Coruisk or Harta Corrie on the Mhadaidh side are 'worse than those of Arran'. He gives further examples of hard climbs in the Cuillin: the Water Pipe of Sgùrr an Fheadain, the 'Corrie Labhain face of Sgurr Alasdair' and 'the Coruisk faces of Dearg, Mhic Coinnich and Mhadaidh'.

Given all this, Brown concludes that the suggestion that 'this infinitely rich centre' is not a good school for the climber 'is profane, close to nonsense' and 'a slander' on the Cuillin.

Clark plainly does not wish to be involved in the argument but still manages to be critical of Brown—'much cry and little 'oo'—and also of the Editor by suggesting that in publishing all this, he must have been short of copy; rather barbed remarks from a habitually equable man.

By contrast, Raeburn's reply is playful but polite:

Is it the echo of a Coolin south-wester that I hear, howling and shrieking up the great chasm of Coruisk? ... no; after all, it is only a storm in a teacup ... raised by your correspondent over a couple of remarks of mine regarding the general character of Skye climbing ...

In a deft hit at the indignant tone of Brown's letter, Raeburn regrets that these remarks should have touched 'the "Skyeatic" nerve of any climber', and he offers 'a few words of explanation'. He and Clark were not really discussing the Cuillin; they were discussing the mountains of Tyrol, which seem, like the Cuillin, much more difficult than they are. Raeburn had mentioned the Dolomite guides and suggested that the latter might be dangerous if 'working out new climbs' in Arran, for example. Similarly, he argues, he would not trust 'the judgment of an entirely Coolin-trained mountaineer in such an enterprise'.

Raeburn argues that nobody is denying that there are difficult climbs in Skye, but this does not invalidate the point that, in general, the gabbro, with its plentiful hand and foot holds and its super-adhesive qualities, makes climbing there generally easier than elsewhere. He is at pains to compliment Brown on his 'lightning-like adaptability'; plainly *he* is a Skye-trained climber who *can* be trusted. However, he continues, 'even the best professional climbers of the Tyrol or Switzerland sometimes express diffidence as to their powers when transferred to unfamiliar conditions'.

Whether or not Raeburn is tongue-in-cheek at times, he maintains a light tone, but still insists at the end of his letter that 'the gabbro of the Coolins is *too* good, it makes one discontented with one's powers on other rocks'. This is why, in a nutshell, it is better not to begin a climbing career in Skye but rather on a rock type which will teach you not to put so much trust in friction. If you go from gabbro to mica schist and try to climb that in the same way, you may put yourself and your partner in danger.

Brown certainly does enough to show that there are difficult climbs in Skye and that Raeburn was wrong to characterise Skye climbing in general as 'ridiculously easy'. But Raeburn argues effectively that gabbro is not the best rock for a beginner to learn on. One could say that the argument ends in a draw, but Raeburn preserves a calm and balanced tone which contrasts with Brown's rather heavy, angry rhetoric.

4. CASTLE ON NEVIS, RAEBURN'S GULLY LOCHNAGAR

1898

1898 was a fruitful year for Raeburn. In late August and early September he was on Skye where, among other things, he traversed the Basteir Tooth by way of the newly climbed King's Cave Chimney with George Bennet Gibbs (SMCJ, 1899), and visited the Storr Rock (Ibid.) in Staffin. On his way back from Skye, Raeburn landed at Arisaig and cycled to Fort William, where he had arranged to meet Tom Gibson,[1] who was cycling from the train at Kingussie. They planned to climb the following day, but both found their respective cycle rides so exhausting that all they felt fit for was 'a stroll up Glen Nevis and a little bouldering' (ibid.). It is rather nice to see that Raeburn was, after all, human like the rest of us, and it tells us something about him that he can admit the fact in print.

[Fig 1] Feeling better the following day, they set off from the Alexandra Hotel at 7.35am for Ben Nevis. They wanted to climb the Castle, the prominent buttress south of Castle Ridge framed by the deeply recessed North and South Castle Gullies. It has a lower-angled slabby area which rises to the steep rock feature at the top from which it gets its name. The slabby area is cut by a barrier overlap which runs across the face.

Raeburn tackled this overlapping cliff and 'with considerable exertion' managed to ascend the steep wall. Gibson seconded by climbing 'a small chimney' running with water. As the leader placed no protection, the second was free, within limits, to choose a different line. Easier climbing followed for a while. The crest of the buttress is off to the right, and they tried to gain it, but failed 'ignominiously'. Raeburn complained that 'The whole

---

1   Tom Gibson was another talented climber who, like Harry Lawson, died young as the result of illness.

Fig 1

The Castle on Ben Nevis. Photo: Noel Williams

character of the rock here is somewhat exasperating'—slabs one above the other at 'an angle often just too steep to walk up, holds and hitches poor or awanting'. They were forced to go left and enter 'a line of trap-dyke' leading to a chimney 'which the leader found decidedly difficult'. All the holds 'had the same downward inclination'. A way was finally made 'out to our right on to the slabs, here at an uncomfortably steep angle and wholly destitute of holds'. Raeburn's language is moderate and controlled, but every climber knows the situation he is describing: gradually getting higher and higher on steepening slabs with no adequate belay below, no protection and no holds; one slip means catastrophe. However, Raeburn and Gibson refused to panic. They made progress by 'kneeling on the steps'—with tweed-covered knees—and 'utilising every ounce of friction on the edges of the "risers"' they made ground tenuously until they found a mercifully 'good hitch' some '50ft above the chimney'. Imagine their relief.

From there, the climbing was easy, and they gained the top 'about 30yds N. of the highest peak' of the Castle. They celebrated by having tea in the Hotel and visiting the Observatory, and then occupied the next two hours by descending the NE Buttress and getting what Raeburn describes as 'a real taste of Skye in a perfect waterspout which broke upon the ridge'. He seems really impressed by the volume and violence of the event: 'in every gully plunged and roared huge waterfalls, the white spray flying in dense clouds far into the air'. Just as well this was postponed until after their ascent of the Castle; nor can the descent of North-East Buttress have been straightforward in these conditions, but typically no mention of any difficulty is made.

When Raeburn got home, Willie Naismith pointed out that the first ascent of the Castle was made by himself, Brown, Maclay and Thomson in winter conditions at the Easter Meet of 1896, at which Raeburn had been a guest (not having joined the club until December of that year). There is a slight puzzlement about why Raeburn was not aware of this, but non-members are not entitled to a free *SMCJ*, and Harold may have missed the opportunity to buy one. Again, even if he did, the report of the climb is very brief and almost buried in the Easter Meet Report.[2] However, Raeburn's and Gibson's

---

2 In fact, Naismith's party had been trying to do a route on Càrn Dearg Buttress, failed, and climbed the Castle as a consolation prize; it's given one sentence in *SMCJ* 4, 20, 1896; 130. Equally, because they had failed in what they set out to do, they might not have been keen to talk about their day at the hotel afterwards.

sterling efforts did not go unrewarded, as they are credited with the first summer ascent.

As previously mentioned, a feature of Raeburn's climbing life in his early years in the SMC was his willingness to climb with a variety of partners, most of whom seemed quite content to let him lead. In this way, he gained a lot of experience in a relatively short time.

In the company of Harry Lawson and John Rennie, he visited Lochnagar in the dark month of November in 1898. They were keen to attempt a gully prematurely named 'Tantalus' by William Clark, who had attempted it with a partner named Shannon in August 1896. Clark and Shannon were eventually defeated by a massive boulder high up the gully. Raeburn was determined to do better.

On 12 November, Queen Victoria travelled back to London from Balmoral a week earlier than planned, causing disruption to the train timetable in the north-east of Scotland. Already four-and-a-half hours late, Raeburn's party then had trouble with their bicycles, as Raeburn recounts in an article in the SMCJ (1899). To make matters worse, there had been a clammy mist all day. The conditions aside, Raeburn was impressed by the mountain:

> *We had some rough scrambling over the Titanic screes which here clothe the hillside, gradually descending. Pausing for lunch, to our ears was borne the sound of many waters roaring in the depths below.*
>
> *This we imagined must proceed from waterfalls in the corrie, but some time later we came to the edge of a vast precipice, and there, some thousands of feet vertically below us, a great inland sea rolled its huge breakers against an ironbound coast. Lochnagar! and to our shouts the cliffs above gave back a guiding sound.*

Raeburn's description is deliberate romantic hyperbole: 'Titanic screes', 'thousands of feet'—he uses the same kind of imagery as in his description of Salisbury Crags, but here, of course, the scale is much larger.

What had actually happened was that they had got too high on the mountain and had to descend into the corrie. Navigating by map and compass, they managed to correct the error and find the Black Spout: 'a vast gloomy ravine'.[3]

---

3 In more prosaic terms, the steep grade I gully dividing Pinnacle Buttress from Black Spout Buttress.

They reckoned that going east 'for 100 yards' would 'place us at the foot of our gully', and their navigation worked.

All went well until they reached the first obstacle: a huge overhanging chockstone. This was overcome using combined tactics, but it was already 3.15pm and the short November daylight was fading. Undeterred, they made 'good progress for a while' but then came 'to a halt in a small cave under a great overhanging block', which choked 'the whole width of the gully'. Considering the difficulty and the time, not to speak of their lack of knowledge of what lay above, many would have retreated, but dooming themselves to a candle-lantern descent, they persevered.

There was a small block trapped between the gully wall and the chockstone. Again, they employed combined tactics. This reduced the gap between Raeburn's reaching hand and the promised hold on the small block to 2ft. He used the ice-axe to clear away earth and stones from the upper edge of the block. What followed has a rather contemporary aspect:

> [T]hen the pick was hung on the edge, the right hand of the leader found a crevice which admitted of its being inserted and half clenched, then pushing down with the right arm and pulling hard with the left [on the axe], the body was raised high enough to allow the left hand being thrown up to catch the edge of the jammed block; instantly the right hand joined it, then a pull, and the right knee was thrown up on the slope of the overhanging chockstone, the body thrust for a second against the slope of the left wall, while the hands were transferred to an upper block; it proved firm and a hitch was found 10ft higher up the gully.

The axe fell and was lost, but the rest of the party managed to follow Raeburn, '... the last man by the gentle moral suasion of the rope'. As Ken Crocket (2015) points out, 'Raeburn's techniques to overcome the crux have a modern feel about them, involving, as they did, hand-jamming, a dynamic move, and a hooked ice-axe.'

The fun was not quite over, for above there was 'a series of gigantic boulders, crowned by a great projecting mass, which seemed utterly to bar escape'. This may have been what stopped the earlier attempt by Clark and Shannon. Happily, Raeburn's party found that they could crawl underneath 'where a small chimney left a gap in the defences'. From there, they could 'toil up deep soft snow and over an incipient Bergschrund ...' The whole climb, crowded with incident, had only taken about two hours. Despite the presence of snow in the upper part of the gully, they had made the first 'summer' ascent of Raeburn's Gully (600 ft Severe). Seldom (if ever) ascended nowadays in summer, it is a very worthwhile winter climb on which conditions determine the degree of difficulty, often grade III.

The descent took much longer. After a struggle with the wind and, no doubt, damp matches, they managed to light John Rennie's candle lantern (taking us back to the 19th century with a bump), and they struggled down the Glas Allt. They had an impromptu stop for afternoon tea in the dark consisting of bread and jam, chocolate, raisins and acid drops, then made it down to the east end of Loch Muick and trudged along the loch to their bicycles. The descent of the steep nine miles from Loch Muick to Ballater must have been 'interesting' in the dark. They eventually sat down to dinner at 10.45pm. The largely upper-class climbers of the day seemed welcome to eat in hotels at almost any hour of the day or night—a privilege not enjoyed by anyone in Scotland nowadays.

Raeburn and Rennie went back the following day to find the lost ice-axe, but couldn't. Not to be outdone, Harry Lawson, despite having an injured foot, walked up Lochnagar from Ballater and got back before the other two.

Having joined the SMC in 1896, it is clear that Raeburn had thoroughly established his reputation as a climber. He also seems to have been a popular member who, as we have seen, was prepared to climb with a wide variety of partners. He was on friendly terms with Willie Douglas, the *SMCJ* Editor, and with William Clark, the Club Secretary. It was no surprise that in December 1898, he was elected to the Committee. At the very same meeting, Willie Ling, George Glover, Alexander Kellas, Alexander M Mackay and George Sang, among others, became club members, and Raeburn was to share mountain adventures with all of them, particularly Willie Ling, who would become his most often preferred partner. Alexander Kellas accompanied Raeburn on the Everest Expedition, and George Sang, who became Raeburn's solicitor, tried to help him deal with the aftermath.

***

Up to this point, we have concentrated mainly on Raeburn's major ascents in Scotland, and there are many more to come, but we should not ignore the minor notes that Raeburn contributed to the *SMCJ*, as these help to paint a more rounded picture of a man who had a genuine curiosity about striking natural phenomena. His interest in ornithology, of course, is well known, but in the very same section of the SMCJ in which he describes his ascent of the Castle on Ben Nevis, Raeburn publishes two other notes: 'The Narnain Caves' and 'The Storr Rock (2,360 feet) and the Old Man of Storr' (SMCJ, 1899).

John Napier made Raeburn aware of the Narnain Caves by pointing them out to him from a train window near Arrochar. Harold was intrigued and went to learn more. He gives us a careful description of how to find them and an equally detailed description of the caves themselves. It seems that the caves are really 'cracks or crevasses ... formed by a great landslip'. He was especially taken by the largest: 'now completely open to the light of day, [it] forms a small canyon cutting off a small cliff from the hillside'. The edges:

[A]re covered with long heather, and with a few rowan trees growing from its sides. At the bottom of this, a crack goes down an unknown depth, but the aperture is rather narrow. On the upper side of the great crevasse lies a small plateau, which is ... shivered by cracks running in different directions, but generally parallel to the canyon.

[Fig 2] Raeburn notes, perceptively, that some of the cracks have been covered by slabs, 'probably to prevent sheep falling in'. He estimates that the deeper of these cracks 'may be about 40ft', and there is climbing interest because 'some interesting back and foot work may be found in them'. We are told that the caves were 'discovered' by 'Green and M'Gregor in October 1895'—something that the shepherds who placed the slabs to prevent their sheep falling down might have disputed. Raeburn's interest here is mainly geological. Little did he think that at a future date the Narnain Caves would play no small part in the development of climbing in Arrochar, or feature in a classic of mountaineering literature, Alastair Borthwick's *Always a Little Further* (1939). A World War and a social revolution were needed to bring these things about.

Harold plainly studied his SMCJ carefully, for he notes that 'There does not appear to be any mention of the Storr [Rock on Skye] but these rocks are well worth notice, not so much in a climbing sense—though ... they ... would repay investigation—as for the extraordinary rock scenery they present.' Arthur Russell and he cycled up from Sligachan to Portree and then walked up to the Storr by way of the Storr Lochs. Raeburn was impressed: 'the bizarre

Fig 2

Raeburn practising back and foot work in the Narnain Caves. This picture was eventually used for instructional purposes in his book *Mountaineering Art*. Photo: SMC Image Archive

and eccentric in rock form ... a multitude of the most strange-looking rock pinnacles in Scotland'. All of this on 'a green slope below a ... wall of almost vertical rock, seamed with great chimneys of most formidable aspect'.

Raeburn describes the Old Man of Storr, the largest of the weird pinnacles, as 'a wonderful obelisk of trap rock 166 ft high and about 40 ft in diameter. It ... overhangs its base almost the whole way round, so that it has the appearance of dangerous instability ...' Will it ever be climbed? Raeburn's opinion is judicious: 'We will not venture to assert that the Old Man will never be ascended,' he says, 'but we were quite content to look at him.' In fact, the Old Man was not ascended for another 57 years, when Don Whillans fought his way up in 1955; the rock is appallingly loose, and the current grade is E4. The Staffin Face, climbed in 1988 by Mick Fowler, Tunstall and Lincoln, and graded E3, is described in the 1996 guidebook as 'another horror show'. Raeburn and Russell were wise just to look. They did, however, ascend 'a small pinnacle near the Old Man', and this is recorded in the guidebook in just these words. The day was windy, and Raeburn comments that 'it was no easy matter to hold on'. One wonders if this might have been the Old Boy, now graded Severe. Raeburn also takes note of the Old Woman, the 'ruined castle' and the pinnacle like 'a begging dog'. They didn't have time for a 'close examination of the great chimneys of the Storr', but here again Raeburn's remarks are prescient, for he thinks that 'some of these might "go" if properly investigated'. Sure enough, over fifty years later, these gullies began to attract the attention of winter climbers, and the grades now range from III to V.

Another curiosity is Raeburn's note on the Maiden Rock, 'a small isolated "stack" about a mile along the cliffs to the east of the ancient city of St Andrews'. Raeburn spent half an hour exploring it 'on the occasion of a visit to St. Andrews'. He found that it is steep on all sides, that the 'tourist route' is very polished, and that the traverse of the arête 'gives a nice little climb'. He found no marks of previous ascents except on the tourist route. 'The rock is sound but the handholds somewhat rounded' (*SMCJ*, 1902). Alas, like the Buddo Rock further down the coast, on which there are recorded routes, and Craig Lug crag at Dairsie,[4] the Maiden seems now to be ignored by the climbing fraternity of St Andrews, but these outcrops have helped many former generations of students (including the author) to take their first steps in rock climbing.

4   See Phil Gribbon: 'Craig Lug Lost in Translation' (*SMCJ*, 2018).

5. LIATHACH, BLACK SHOOT, GARDYLOO, OBSERVATORY BUTTRESS

1899–1901

1899 seems to have been a quiet year for Raeburn, and a quiet year for Scottish mountaineering, all told. However, Raeburn had days on the Scottish hills (and in the Alps) of which we are completely ignorant. Nevertheless, it is encouraging to remember that we probably have more third-party written evidence about Harold Raeburn's life than about that of William Shakespeare.

Things looked up in 1900. At the Easter Meet, held in Kinlochewe, a party of six set out to explore the Northern Pinnacles of Liathach. Initially, the party contained Raeburn, Willie Naismith, Alexander Mackay, James Gall Inglis, Willie Ling and Hugh Munro, but Munro chose to make a solo ascent of an adjacent ridge. Mackay recorded the day in an article (SMCJ, 1900).

They approached from Coire Mhic Nòbuil in the west. Mackay climbed with Naismith, and Raeburn with Inglis and Ling.[1] The ascent went smoothly, as one would expect, especially in reasonable conditions. After all, a grade II/III ridge was hardly likely to hold back some of the best climbers of the day. They met Hugh Munro at the top and the party posed for a well-known photograph by Gall Inglis, which contains the unusual sight of Raeburn wearing a balaclava helmet, perhaps purchased on Douglas's recommendation. They continued over the Am Fasarinen Pinnacles and the rest of the Liathach ridge. Mackay's article contains another photograph by Inglis: a classic shot of the eastern face of Mullach an Rathain and the Northern Pinnacles taken from further along the main ridge to the east. It was not a technically difficult day, but it was a long one, as Mackay records in his

[Fig 1]

---

1 Significantly, this could be Raeburn's first ascent with Willie Ling, who would play such a prominent role in his climbing career.

1899–1901: Liathach, Black Shoot, Gardyloo, Observatory Buttress

Fig 1

The Northern Pinnacles party: (L–R) Raeburn and Ling (sporting balaclavas), Naismith and Mackay. Hugh Munro makes up the numbers, although he came up a different ridge, technically of the same standard as the Pinnacles but not so committing, further west. Photo: James Gall Inglis, who was also part of the successful party

account of the Meet: 'We stumbled to the road at nine,[2] and the welcome hotel at eleven o'clock'. Doubtless, they got their dinner even at this late hour.

The late Victorians developed a strange fascination with a gully on Beinn Eunaich called The Black Shoot, first climbed by Naismith, Douglas, William Lester and John Gibson on 19 May 1892. Apparently, that was Lester's fourth attempt. Raeburn was not immune to this fascination, and he also made a summer ascent. One says a 'summer' ascent, but in fact this was at the Winter Meet of 1897, the year after he joined the SMC, and it only qualified as a summer ascent because it was wet rather than frozen (see Chapter 1).

In trying to account for the relatively few ascents the Black Shoot has had, Raeburn acknowledges that this is 'probably owing to the somewhat discouraging account of its wetness and dirtiness as experienced by the conquerors of its mossy waterslides, curious twisted chimney, and steep pitches' (*SMCJ*, 1901). However, the conditions under which Raeburn, Alexander Mackay and George Sang approached the Shoot on 30 December 1900 were quite different because there had been heavy snowfall overnight. As Raeburn remarks, the conditions 'could not be said to render the climb any easier, [but] they probably accounted for the comfortable cleanness'.

The party set off for the Shoot 'through ankle-deep slushy snow', but conditions improved as they gained height, and as they approached the rocks, three ravens sailed out from the face of the crag and circled 'around with airy wheelings and loud croakings'. This might have been taken as a bad omen by 'the superstitious forefathers, who saw in the movements and appearances of bird and beast only reference to themselves and their affairs, [but] the incident passed for what it was really worth'. Raeburn again demonstrated his bird knowledge by pointing out that the ravens would soon be looking for nest sites and would find this crag, north facing and out of the prevailing south-west weather, most suitable. His dismissal of superstition[3] is a fairly typical Victorian attitude, but the way he expresses it furnishes more evidence of a reflective quality of mind.

The initial pitches of the climb required a 'good deal of digging with the axe to make stands or find hitches'. Trying to stay dry, they straddled

---

2   Nowadays, getting down to the road in Glen Torridon ends the day; Raeburn's party had to walk the additional six miles down to Kinlochewe.
3   He is not quite so dismissive of an ominous chough on the Meije much later in his career—see Chapter 30. Ravens also disquiet him on Scafell Pinnacle in the Lakes—see Chapter 12.

up the sides of the gully and came to a very steep little pitch 'covered with green, slimy moss'. Raeburn tackled this by going out on the left wall and surmounting 'a rounded overhanging sloping ledge of moss and grass', which required 'cautious treatment, especially in snow'.

Presently they came to the 'Twisted Chimney'. It is this feature which gives the Black Shoot its name. Raeburn said of it: 'The gully walls project far on each side and overhang as does the chimney itself, and the next 12 or 15 feet is the hardest part, gymnastically speaking, of the climb. There was a good deal of ice now on the rocks, but this was fortunately very loosely adherent, and finger and toe holds could be cleared out with comparative ease.' Above the 'turn' of the chimney, where it is narrowest, 'the holds are poor for a bit, but they suffice'. Raeburn found a good place to 'jam' while bringing up the second. They were climbing on a 60 ft rope, and he thought that 80 ft would have been better.

'It was very amusing ... to listen to the puffings of the upstruggling second and third men, and to see their breaths like clouds of steam come drifting up the narrow crack.' Raeburn even wondered if they were actually smoking their pipes but discovered 'that only bronchials were in use'.

Ten feet above the 'jam', the left wall 'breaks away', and they found 'a considerable ledge, with good hitches and ample standing room'. Above, there seemed to be a choice of three ways, but the direct line was the only way so far climbed. This led to an 'adverse sloping small ledge on the right (north) wall of the chimney'. According to Raeburn, only John Stewart Napier had climbed this without resort to combined tactics, on the second ascent in December 1897. Harold used the second man on the rope 'who lean[ed] across the gully as a ladder'. In this way the step was:

> [P]erfectly safe and simple, but from here to the top of the overhanging part is ... especially with snow and ice about, the portion of the climb which calls for the greatest care and caution on the part of the leader ... who will find, in snow, a deal of hard one-handed burrowing work to find holds in the bank of loose stones, earth, and moss overhanging the exit of the pitch.

Above this difficult pitch, 'the gully resumes the character it exhibits lower down and the angle eases off'. Raeburn claims that it is from here that:

The "Black Shoot" looks most impressive, and might easily be pronounced ... impossible—the steep black walls projecting far on either side, and restricting the distant view to a narrow strip of snow-clad hill and green-brown valley, while at one's feet the pitch drops with an abruptness so great as to prevent a view of the hundred feet or so immediately below.

The whole climb from the lunching place took '1 hour and 35 minutes'. Astonishingly, Raeburn apologises for their slowness: 'The large amount of snow caused the pace to be slow, and a longer rope would also have assisted in shortening the time.' Two modern climbers, using proper main belays and runners, would probably take at least double the time.

It was undoubtedly a first winter ascent but, it has to be admitted, in very poor winter conditions of unconsolidated snow and insufficient ice. Holds had to be uncovered rather than being cut. It was nothing like Raeburn's earlier ascent of Arrow Chimney in the Tarmachans, or his ascent of Green Gully on Ben Nevis, but given this, it presented technical difficulties of its own, and the time taken for a party of three was remarkable.

For quite a time, the left branch of Observatory Gully on Ben Nevis—which came to be known as Gardyloo Gully—defied the attempts of the pioneers, but Geoffrey Hastings and Walter Haskett Smith succeeded in 1896. The difficulty of this gully varies enormously with the conditions: it can, in modern terms, be either Grade II or IV,5 or any grade in between, depending on the build-up or sparsity of snow and ice. Hastings and Haskett Smith struggled with the cornice, but when Raeburn and Harry Lawson visited, they found 'the ice pitch harder'. Raeburn recounts their ascent on 6 April 1901 in 'Excursions' (*SMCJ*, 1901).

In certain conditions, one of the prominent features of Gardyloo is an ice cave which forms around a massive chockstone. Raeburn and Lawson found this in situ; Lawson chopped the ice away and they gained access to the cave. The floor was of drifted snow, but 'the back ... ribs and columns of glistening blue ice covering the rock'. With Lawson secure in the cave, Raeburn tackled 'the ice-fall'. In order to get out of the cave and on to the fall, he needed 'pulling-in handholds'. Eventually, he got 'far enough to get a good undergrip for the right arm, below a great spout of ice that shot over the overhanging lip'. From this position, he managed 'to cut a handhold and toestep for the left hand and foot out on the face of the ice-fall to the left'. The strain was severe, but after two rests Raeburn was able to step out onto the face of the fall, and he began to cut holds with the axe now held in his right hand. Here he had some luck: 'Breaking right through here into a hole behind the ice, I thrust my hand in and felt with satisfaction the magnificent hold given by a clenched fist.'

The next 18 ft were 'hard work' but easier. Lawson followed and they thought they'd cracked it, but there was a sting in the tail as the cornice proved troublesome. The stance below it was unsatisfactory soft snow 'sticking to hard icy stuff'. Lawson offered the leader his shoulder, but the angle was all wrong: 'As he was already at an angle of 90°, I explained that if I stood up on him the bulge above would certainly reduce the angle, but it would be on the wrong side, and the ice-pitch 80 feet below was rather too big to jump comfortably; and anyway, we wanted up not down.'

With this rather Pooterish rejoinder, Raeburn went on hacking at the cornice. He got his famous hat 'about level with the edge ... when we heard the voice of an eloquent legal member of the SMC ... I expressed a desire to shake hands with one [of the party], so Workman kindly extended his arm, and I was so glad to see him that I did not let go till landed on the top'. Even the great Harold Raeburn was glad of a helping hand and able to joke about it.

This chapter has seen Raeburn in action on climbs of widely varying characters in winter. His performance on Gardyloo shows an increasing mastery of the techniques available. From his account, it sounds as if the gully on this occasion was near the top end of its grade, high III if not IV. Plainly he cuts steps and clears holds with economy of effort and precision: his times make this clear. He also seems wise and doesn't persevere when the odds are stacked against him. Crucially, he never falls. His next climb, often overlooked and undertaken only two days after Gardyloo, demonstrates these qualities to a high degree.

In his report (SMCJ, 1901) on the Easter Meet in April of 1901, which was held in Fort William, Lionel Hinxman makes brief mention of an attempt on Observatory Buttress by an unnamed party who were very late back. This party comprised Raeburn, Ling, Douglas and John Rennie. Ling contributed an account of the day to the next edition of the SMCJ (ibid.), beginning his report by saying: 'To some, it is given to achieve success lightly; to others, after strenuous efforts, to fail nobly is the reward.'[4] Ling says that the morning was pleasant and warm and they 'found miniature avalanches of snow pouring off the rocks'. They started to climb 'just opposite the commencement of the Tower Ridge climb', i.e. above the Boulder. There is no doubt that they are on Observatory Buttress. Ling tried the first pitch but was repulsed, so Raeburn took over, and the first 30 ft 'consisted of very steep rock sheeted with ice'. They had to uncover rock holds. Raeburn got up to a ledge where 'the snow was sufficiently deep to afford anchorage', presumably an ice-axe belay. From the ledge, the party went 'diagonally to the right by ledges' and gained about 200 ft; then they traversed 'left by an ice slope, where steps had to be cut' until they reached 'the edge of the arête', but here they had to turn back. Ling does not say they were defeated by technical difficulty, but rather because 'the task of clearing the holds from snow would have taken so long that, as it was now well on in the afternoon, there was no chance of our reaching the top before dark'.

All Ling says about the retreat is that 'we retraced our steps, got into the gully, and waded down in soft snow'. Not content with what must already have been a very demanding experience, they climbed the Ben by way of the Càrn Mòr Dearg Arête, faced 40-mile-an-hour winds on the plateau, had an epic descent, missed the Red Burn route and staggered down into Glen Nevis at 9 pm, by which time, according to Hinxman, fellow members were inventing excuses not to join the search party!

From the modesty of Willie Ling's report and the lack of attention this effort has received, it would be easy to miss the significance of what Raeburn and party attempted and what they achieved with their skill and courage. To climb the first 200–300 ft of Observatory Buttress in full winter condition, and to retreat in good order in rough conditions, was an achievement decades ahead of its time. As Ken Crocket (2015) remarks: 'Observatory Buttress was not climbed in winter until 1960, and the easiest route is still a Grade V. The 1901 party was a strong team but even so the boldness of the attempt and the fact that they managed 200 ft in poor conditions with the minimal equipment of the day is impressive.' Nowadays, when climbers think of Raeburn in Scotland, they tend to think of Green Gully and Observatory Ridge, but the attempt on Observatory Buttress ranks with these.

4   This sounds like a quotation from the classics, but it has not been possible to identify it.

6. OBSERVATORY RIDGE, DOUGLAS-GIBSON ATTEMPT   1901

In the article in which Raeburn writes about his ascent of Observatory Ridge (SMCJ, 1901), he begins by lamenting the fact that, as he sees it, Ben Nevis is falling out of fashion with his fellow climbers. Scottish mountaineers are in 'Switzerland, the Tyrol, Dauphiné or even in Canada or Kerry'. Given the long and continuing history of Ben Nevis as we know it, to us this seems fantastical. With the benefit of hindsight, we know that the Victorians had only begun to scratch the surface. However, we need to remember that the climbers of the day had climbed most of the more obvious features of the Ben: The Tower Ridge, North-East Buttress, Castle Ridge, The Castle itself and most of the easier gullies. Perhaps what a climber sees on a mountain is relative to what he or she is capable of attempting.

What Harold saw, and what others missed, was the third of the three great ridges of the mountain, Observatory Ridge. Rather confusingly, he mentions two Observatory Ridges in the article. One, of course, is what became known as Observatory Buttress. It was while failing on this in winter that Raeburn decided that Observatory Ridge would give 'not only a better climb, but one considerably longer and better defined'.

The climb took place on 22 June 1901. Raeburn got to Fort William at 10am and set out from the Alexandra Hotel at 10.30. He had no partner—apparently, someone 'failed at short notice'. On his way up to the North Face, he deviated 'to visit the nesting rock of a pair of buzzards'; they were not around and he hoped they had not become victims of 'the £.s.d. game trader'. This deviation on the morning of a serious climb is another indication of his self-confidence and lack of anxiety.

There was a heavy shower as he entered the corrie, but as he got to the foot of the ridge the mists lifted, and he was delighted by 'magnificent transformation scenes of gleaming snowfields, jagged ridges and pinnacles, black frowning cliffs and long white deeply receding couloirs ...'. Raeburn is not naturally effusive, but he says, 'there is nothing finer in all "braid Scotland", lovely Lakeland, or rugged Skye, to surpass or even equal the splendid north-east face of our highest mountain'.

He didn't have an ice-axe with him—interesting and unusual—but he says that if the bergschrund at the bottom of the ridge had been any deeper or broader he would have needed one. As so often, the Ben surprised the summer visitor with its capacity to hold snow late in the year.

Raeburn's estimate of Observatory Ridge is fair and balanced: initially, the angle is not severe 'but on rocks distinctly slabby, and poor in holds and hitches'. It is a 'well-defined arête' which 'throughout its whole length affords less opportunity for deviation from the exact ridge than does its north-east neighbour'.[1] In a surprisingly colloquial phrase, Raeburn says he remembers 'three distinctly good bits on it. First, the slabby rocks near the foot'. Second, a hand-traverse 'a few hundred feet up', which is 'begun by getting the hands into a first-rate crack on the left, then toe-scraping along a wall till the body can be hoisted on to a narrow overhung ledge above'.[2] From here 'a short *crawl* to the right finishes the difficulty, at the top of an open corner chimney', which he thinks might be 'a more direct and possibly preferable route'.

The third 'good bit' is 'more than halfway up where a steep tower spans the ridge'. He tries 'directly up the face, but judge[s] it somewhat risky'. He goes to the right and discovers a route 'which after a little pressure "went"... a slightly sensational corner, as the direct drop, save for a small platform, is several hundred feet'.

'The ridge now eases off', and Raeburn thought it would be possible to traverse 'on to the N.E. Buttress on one's left, or to the upper or S.W. Observatory Ridge to the right'. He notes that 'The gully on the left [Zero] holds heavy snow drifts.' He carried on directly up the ridge where 'numerous steep or slabby bits engage the climber's vigilance; but at length the last rocks are gained, where the crest of the ridge plunges under the great

1 North-East Buttress.
2 Possibly the move about which Frank Goggs writes so feelingly on the first winter ascent some 19 years later; see Chapter 31.

Fig 1

William and Jane Clark having breakfast in the Summit Hotel with blankets round their shoulders. Pictures of Victorian climbers doing ordinary things like having breakfast are very rare. The Clarks are using the old-fashioned method of eating porridge: Jane is dipping her spoonful in the central bowl of milk; the porridge stayed warmer and it used less milk. Note also the long ice-axe hanging on the coat hook to the left. (The white cups look suspiciously like those which infested the CIC Hut for many years.)
Photo: Possibly Raeburn or George Glover, SMC Image Archive

snowfield that girdles the face of the mountain, still at midsummer presenting in places icy cornices twenty feet high'.

After building a cairn, Raeburn sat down '... to bask in the sun ... and to drink in the grandeur and beauty of the surroundings'. These, he rightly says, 'are apt to be missed by the climber ... if engaged by the problems that confront him when engaged on a new ascent'.

'But what is that note? A bird song strange and new!' Raeburn was entranced by the song of a male snow bunting 'in full summer plumage, singing sweetly with utterly unbunting-like notes'. He had only heard the bird before in winter and the mating song was new to him. 'Heretically' as he puts it, if forced to choose between hearing the bunting's song and the climb, he might have chosen the song, but he adds with a smile, 'no such invidious choice was forced on me and the snow bunting's song was an additional pleasure to a most enjoyable scramble'.[3] Observatory Ridge was to hold a very special place in the history of Raeburn's Scottish climbs, but his famous first winter ascent was two decades in the future and separated from this innocent, happy day by a terrible war.

In the very next article in the *SMCJ* (1901), it is revealed that a telegram from William Clark brought Raeburn to Fort William 'to give us the benefit of his skilled leadership'. William and Jane Clark had been enjoying, or enduring, a very stormy holiday in Skye and had decided to try their luck on Ben Nevis on the way home. Even here they were pursued by a thunderstorm as they made their way to the Summit Hotel.[4] Their night's repose sounds [Fig 1] most uncomfortable: 'The storm raged fiercely all night, and so saturated was the atmosphere, that even in bed one's hair dripped with moisture, and the walls and ceiling streamed with water.'

However, as we have seen, the following day was much better, and at

3   'Scramble'? Partly a reference to Edward Whymper's *Scrambles Amongst the Alps*, published in 1871, but perhaps also Raeburn's final comment on the summer route. The author has heard the one-time Custodian of the CIC Hut, Bob Richardson, refer to Observatory Ridge as 'the best scramble in the country'.
4   Brainchild of Robert Whyte, owner of Fort William's Imperial Hotel, the Summit Hotel opened on 7 July 1885. Construction took just ten days: it had four bedrooms and was originally called the Observatory Hotel because it was annexed to the summit Observatory which had been collecting weather data since 1883. In summer the charge was 10/- per night, including dinner and breakfast. Two ladies ran the operation. The hotel did not serve drink and was known jokingly as the 'Temperance Hotel'. It closed in 1916 because the War made its operation uneconomical (*The Scotsman*, 2017).

the top of Càrn Dearg they met Raeburn, 'who had added to his laurels by a first ascent of the Observatory Ridge alone'. After enduring another stormy, and presumably damp, night in the hotel, they descended Tower Ridge to the Douglas Gap, ascended the short side of the Boulder direct and, via 'an excellent, though perhaps sensational hand traverse' gained the wall overlooking the eastern gully. Several 'rotten pitches' took them to the bottom. All this was just a way of getting into position 'to attack the Western Observatory Ridge' (i.e. Observatory Buttress). They made some progress on this, but torrents of rain and a cold north wind foiled the attempt. They climbed down and sheltered in a 'huge bergschrund and then decided to 'make for the summit by the North-East Buttress'. All the while the storm showed no sign of abating.

Raeburn led the party up partly by way of Slingsby's Chimney with deviations to the side; '... the temperature fell to near the freezing point, so we put on full steam to keep up the circulation'. Clark gave Harold and Jane a shoulder up the Mantrap, but then couldn't get up himself. After some delay, trusting Raeburn to hold his rope from above, he made 'full use of the somewhat rickety holds of the overhanging chimney above the gully to the left'. Only the 40-foot Corner remained, 'and with so good a man as leader what mattered if the hands and feet had little feeling, and that the teeth chattered with the regularity of an electric clapper'. Raeburn became a good friend of the Clark family (including Mabel and Charlie), and he met them by design on many subsequent occasions, notably after yet another solo ascent on Ben Nevis.

In the meantime his focus shifted to the north-east and a further tussle [Fig 2] with *dark Lochnagar*. In this venture he was joined by George Duncan and William Garden on 14 July. Duncan describes the action in his article, 'An Eight Hours' Day in a Lochnagar Gully' (SMCJ, 1901). Intriguingly he begins by recording the fact that he, Raeburn, Garden and Crombie (a non-member) had attempted what became known as Douglas-Gibson Gully in winter conditions in April but had 'got no higher than the earlier explorers of 1893', but there seems to be no other record of this attempt.

Even though it was July and the party was intent on making a summer ascent, they found a long tongue of hard snow coming from the gully's mouth. They had an ice-axe and soon gained the top of the snow, only to find 'what turned out to be probably the most difficult pitch ... ascended

Fig 2

This painting of the corrie of Lochnagar by Neil J Barlow shows the start of the gullies which Raeburn attempted and succeeded in climbing: Douglas-Gibson Gully is left of centre with a dark line coming down the snow and Raeburn's Gully is right of centre with the slabby 'Mound' outcrop at its foot. The Black Spout is the long strip of snow to the right of Raeburn's Gully. West Gully, climbed later, is off to the right. Photo: Gordon Ross

during the day'. Above them was 'a huge, jammed block' forming the roof of a cave ... and above that again, another huge stone similarly blocked the way'. To make matters worse, water was pouring over these obstacles. Raeburn traversed out onto the left and managed to get on top of the cave. It took 'some time and not a little skilful direction' to get Garden and Duncan up.

After many pitches of 'wet, waterworn rock with rotten bits intermingled', they came to the 'smooth black rocks at the top' which had defeated all previous parties. To the right was no good. Raeburn tried to the left, crossing the gully as he did so. He got about 60ft up and found 'a firm hitch'. After 'some involuntary gyrations', Duncan got up to Raeburn's stance by taking what he thought was an 'apparently easier route' up the left side of the gully. Raeburn and Duncan had a bite to eat—they had the rucksack—while the unfortunate Garden below had to make do with water.

Raeburn went 'on to prospect a traverse still more to the left'. As Duncan notes, it seemed 'perilous' and much loose material was dislodged. In the end, Harold had to admit defeat, and they agreed to descend. Duncan gives few details but says that 'The descent resulted in damage not merely to the clothes but also to the persons of some of the party.'[5] And when they came to the cave pitch there was no safe way of climbing down, and they had 'to lower [them]selves on the rope'. Raeburn and Garden found a 'firmly fixed boulder' and they either abseiled or came down hand over hand; Duncan doesn't say which. The rope jammed and they had to cut it. Famished, particularly poor Garden, they devoured their sodden sandwiches. With steely Victorian determination, they ascended the Black Spout to the top of the mountain and inspected the upper reaches of the gully. The top part of the 'chimney', which Raeburn thought he had spotted, looked 'easy', but mist descended at this point, and nothing further down could be seen.

The biographies of famous mountaineers sometimes read like catalogues of glorious successes, but Raeburn's history is not like this. In fact, he made yet another attempt on Douglas-Gibson, this time in winter, and failed yet again, but his repeated attempts showed ambition and determination. Many of his efforts ended in failure, but his climbs always showed skill and perseverance and another priceless quality in a top-class mountaineer: prudence. On almost all the routes Raeburn undertook in Scotland he was

---

5   One assumes the 'damage' was not serious.

the acknowledged leader; he went first to explore the best way, and with every upward move his personal danger grew greater, but not only are there no recorded instances of his falling,[6] he successfully protected the party behind him, patiently encouraging them over difficulties by which they might be otherwise discouraged. Crucially, Raeburn knew when to stop, when to say the next moves were too dangerous to attempt. And not only did he know this, but his concentration was unbroken whether climbing up or getting a retreating party down. So far as we can judge from what he wrote, and what others wrote about him, Raeburn was level-tempered; one can imagine him coaxing a nervous second along with a nod or a smile. He seldom got excited or angry: he was good to be with on the hill. With almost no exception, those who climbed with Raeburn were pleased to do so again.

---

[6] Except when jerked off his stance on Stùc a' Chroin by falling companions.

7. ARRAN, SGÒRAN DUBH GLEANN EANAICH   1902

Talking of trips on which not a great deal is achieved, Raeburn's trip to Arran with Harry Lawson and Alexander Mackay is a case in point, but the efforts they made in almost unremittingly foul weather cannot be faulted (*SMCJ*, 1902).

This trip started on 22 February 1902. Their chief aims were to have a close look at 'A' Gully on Cìr Mhòr and to explore a fine chimney on 'Cleibheinn' (now Beinn a' Chliabhain), which they had heard about from Raeburn's friend William Clark. Landing on the island, they set off at once in wind and rain and got onto the ridge of Beinn a' Chliabhain 'by an easy snow gully'. After several 'false casts', they thought they had found the chimney and descended behind 'two jammed stones and over a third'. Raeburn sardonically notes that Mackay's clothing was better for this job, for Mackay was wearing a gabardine suit which slid over the rocks, whereas tweeds tended to stick. At the foot of the third descending pitch, the chimney opened out into a 'face crack', and 'as the whole place was sheeted in ice and running with water' they went back up, varying their route by going west and climbing 'a second deep black cut' which 'gave a little sport'. After all this, they retreated the way they had come, thoroughly soaked. History does not relate why they started at the top and worked downwards, but there must have been a reason. As it turned out, they got more climbing that way than they would have done from the bottom up, given the condition of the 'face crack'.

Raeburn has a nice line in mordant weather humour: 'Next morning was rather more promising ... in fact, it did not begin raining till fully two hours after our start.' But it made up for it 'by raining extra heavily all the rest of the time', and he adds, 'I should think it is probably raining still.' It was one of those trips. Heading out again, they spent some time on the Corrie boulders, leaving skin and bits of clothing behind, but as they entered Glen Sannox, Raeburn was impressed by the visual effect:

The air below was clear as crystal, but a few hundred feet up hung like a roof, the solid-looking mass of grey mist extending from bank to bank. In this deep hollow was caught and concentrated, as it were, the light that poured in through the gap where the glen opened eastwards to the sea. Under this deep-toned light, the grass and heather took on a most vivid dark green, and the patches of dull burnt heath shone resplendent in rich purple.

As in his description of the eerie light seen while descending Ben Nevis, Raeburn responds sensitively here to an unusual effect. He is not there just for the climbing and the achievement; he is there also to experience and record. The detail in these descriptions makes one think that he must have recorded his impressions in writing soon afterwards because visual experiences like this tend to fade from memory rather quickly, but no diary of this period survives.

In Coire na h-Uaimh, on the North-East Face of Cìr Mhòr, the party arrived at the foot of 'A' Gully. Dimly visible above was 'the enormous black cavity of its upper pitch', which 'looked very formidable'. Raeburn's description here has to be read carefully: 'The lower pitch … was partially covered by a fine icefall, up which it might be possible to cut a way.' This does not mean the bottom pitch, just the one below the cave.

They roped up to climb the 'sloping ledge that leads' through steep slabs above and below, to the foot of 'the lower pitch' (the one referred to above). As they climbed, they were bombarded by chunks of ice released by 'Jupiter Pluvius'. Yes, it seemed possible to cut steps up this pitch, but no one wanted to because they were cold and still reasonably dry, while the ice was washed by 'a well-grown river of snow water'. They climbed down the gully a little and attempted to climb the steep slabs beside it, but it became holdless and their fingers were 'paralysed with cold', and they very reasonably agreed that 'it would be better as a summer climb'.[1]

1   Both in the 1997 SMC Guide *Arran and Arrochar* (p.114) and in *Scottish Winter Climbs West* 2022 (p.402), 'A' Gully remains unclimbed.

After having a look at B1 and B2 gullies—both were solid ice from top to bottom—they found and ascended B1/C Rib (now recorded as B2/C Rib, V. Diff. in the 1997 SMC guide); it is the buttress between B and C Gullies. This, as they knew, was climbed by John Bell and partners in July 1895, but surely Raeburn and his friends were making the first winter ascent? (*SMCJ*, 1902) This seems not to have occurred to them; they did not think like that at that time. Raeburn simply says: 'It is a capital climb of decidedly over-average difficulty.' They rounded off a very wet trip by ascending Cìr Mhòr 'the easy way'.

After they got home and compared notes with William Clark, they found that the chimney they explored was not the one he meant: 'That is a much larger and more formidable one.' And Raeburn concluded: 'It still remains, therefore, to reward the searcher after the beautiful or obscure, who seeks it diligently among the Arran mists.'

From the swirling mists of Arran, Raeburn turned his attention east once more to a little-explored part of the Cairngorms. The September issue of the *SMCJ* (ibid.) has an article contributed jointly by William King, Alexander Mackay and Raeburn describing, in detail, a series of first ascents made by SMC members on Sgòran Dubh, 'which has the great merit from a climber's point of view of possessing a very fine eastern face, where a long line of crags look steeply down on the dark waters of Loch Eunach [Eanaich] lying between the Sgòran and the rugged slopes of Braeriach'. The article goes on to point out that until February of that year, no successful ascent had ever been made, so the tale the writers are about to tell 'possesses all the dramatic unities of time, place and action'.[2] The SMC parties, the writer goes on, have now climbed all the 'main arteries of traffic'; the many climbs left will be 'variation routes'.

Number 5 Buttress, also known as the Pinnacle Ridge, was first ascended by Raeburn and Harry Lawson on 8 March, just a few weeks after their Arran trip, and Lawson wrote an article about it (*SMCJ*, 1902). They climbed over grass and slabs and gained 'a big gully which cuts up the buttress, striking the ridge at a col about 200 feet above the pinnacle'. The climb was 'treacherous rather than difficult' owing to vegetation on the slabs.

On reaching the base of the needle, Lawson 'somewhat impetuously' suggested that they should attempt to go straight on up the longer northern

---

[2] A reference to Aristotle's view that great drama should possess these qualities which have become known simply as 'the Unities'.

side (the side away from the col). Plainly this gave Raeburn the chance to give him a lecture about safety. As Lawson put it: 'Raeburn has frequently told me that he is quite misunderstood in the Club, and that he is really a good Salvationist[3] ... and for the next few minutes he beat the big drum, and held forth in a way that would have gladdened the heart of any member of that militant body ...' In fact, Raeburn could clearly see that Lawson's proposed route was ill-thought-out and dangerous. Instead they made a descending traverse of the north flank of the pinnacle and gained the upper col 'by a steep and rather treacherous chimney'. From here, they climbed the needle 'by clamping the narrow edge with hands and knees, but as the top proved too narrow to stand on, and the sleet and wind were damp and chilly, we pretty quickly returned to the col'. They descended on the south side and made a complete traverse round the needle, finding no evidence of a previous ascent, before going to the summit of the mountain and thence, in the continuing rain, back the long miles to Aviemore. Lawson ends by saying that 'with anything like moderate luck regarding weather, the forthcoming meet at Aviemore would be highly successful'. Raeburn, of course, was no 'Salvationist', but he did not believe in taking uncalculated risks and he strongly believed that saying someone was 'safe' was the highest compliment one could pay to any climber.

The east face of Sgòran Dubh is described in the multi-authored article as being like 'four gigantic funnels or wine fillers ... let into the rock'. There are five rock masses which take the reverse shape: broad to narrow going upwards. These buttresses are numbered 1–5.

Number 4 Buttress is described by Mackay, and he does not give the names of the first ascent party. The buttress is 'seamed by many snow gullies'. It was not climbed on the Easter Meet but rather on 21 June by 'a member with two brothers and a friend'.[4] After a struggle, they got up in

---

3   Roughly, the terms 'Salvationist' and 'Ultramontane' refer, respectively, to climbers who confine themselves to easier routes and hillwalking, and those who like hard routes with a spice of danger. See Helo Almond's article, 'Ben-Y-Gloe on Christmas Day' (SMCJ, 1893).

4   In 'Excursions' (ibid.), Mackay does not reveal the names of the party. He mentions two brothers, presumably his, but the fourth member, the 'friend', is a mystery. He mentions 'ladies'; and 'a lady' was in his party on Ben Macdui on 19 June. Mackay is seldom dull: he adds several verses of doggerel to the 'Excursions' piece, beginning: 'Five little Buttresses, Cliffs of Sgòran Dubh/Laughing puny man to scorn, and all that he can do ...'

five hours which, the author says, was a fast time. Mackay makes a useful point about the general character of the face. All the buttresses have 'a lower division of heather-clad slabs, where neither heath nor rock is so easy as it looks', and 'an upper division presenting a granite wall of very steep angle, but breaking away somewhat to the final ridge'. We cannot rule out the possibility that Raeburn was involved in the ascent of Number 4 Buttress, but it seems unlikely.

Number 3 Buttress was climbed on 28 March by Boyd, Gillon, Mackay and Raeburn. They ascended the lower slabs on snow, which made them easier, but then were stopped by a formidably steep wall with only 'shaky flakes' for holds. They tried to force a way up a chimney and failed, but traversed a little to the right and gained the ridge 'by means of a small snow-paved gully'. From there, it was 'a ridge walk ... landing one close under the summit of Sgòran Dubh Mor'.

Number 2 Buttress was tackled simultaneously by two different parties. William King, Alfred Maylard and Godfrey Solly, all the 'married men', took 'a shorter but sporting ridge to the north of the main ridge'. Meanwhile, the 'bachelor party', Willie Naismith, Sandy Mackay, Conradi Squance and Raeburn, started 'at the foot of the main ridge just at the bottom of the gully dividing No.2 from No.3'. They took a chimney on the right to avoid a big wall; this contained two pitches, the lower harder. The upper one passed through a cave below a huge, jammed block and looked worse than it was. After this, the climb was steep and interesting until it eased off near the top. In the opinion of the writer (Raeburn? The confident assertion sounds like him), 'the whole gives the best-defined route on the Sgòran'.

On 30 March, Raeburn climbed Number 1 Buttress with H. Kynaston and Arthur Mounsey. Throughout his development as a climber, we see Raeburn quietly trying out new partners.[5] Mounsey obviously passes muster because, years later, he was with Harold and Frank Goggs as they made the first winter ascent of Observatory Ridge on Ben Nevis.

On this occasion they started at the foot of the 'great gully' and traversed onto the buttress to the left. Deep snow made progress tortuous. They climbed a small chimney with difficulty to a subsidiary arête which went

---

5   In passing it is also worth noting Raeburn's continuing faith in Henry GS 'Harry' Lawson; but for his untimely death in 1902 in his mid-30s, he would have remained one of Harold's favourite partners.

up to the usual band of steep slabs. The slabs were impossible, but 'a short traverse to the south', and they climbed 'a shallow but steep and slabby chimney'. The snow helped, and once they gained the edge of the arête the difficulties were over. They saw 'a fine golden eagle' and descended by glissading down the 'finest gully on the whole range of cliffs'. That certainly sounds like Raeburn.

The 'Sgòran Dubh' article ends with a mention of Glover's 'glorious exertion and defeat' on 'the great bluff to the north of the prominent gully ... And so ends a plain tale from the hills'. The echo of Kipling is likely to be either Raeburn or Mackay, but we'll never know.

This article is in places a little dry but it is worth noticing Raeburn's unstated ambition: he is not an egoist but he is glad to be first on the scene and comes up early with Lawson to reconnoitre and bags the plum route. He is definitely on four out of the five ascents made. In all his years with the Club, he seems to enjoy the meets. He is there primarily for the climbing, but he seems to be someone who appreciates the company of fellow enthusiasts, and he's popular; people want to climb with him, perhaps not just because he is skilful and safe, but because he is a good, encouraging companion.

8. OBSERVATORY BUTTRESS, RAEBURN'S ARÊTE LOCHNAGAR

1902

On 28 June 1902 Raeburn returned to Ben Nevis, which had not, after all, been quite exhausted. The article he contributed to the SMCJ (1903) is remarkable in many ways, not least for the brevity of his account of the action. Raeburn, from time to time and notably later in his life, suffered from depression, but this article is positively ecstatic.

He begins in an exalted mood: 'Ah! Those days in Coronation week,[1] that brilliant oasis of sun and warmth in the Arctic deserts of an almost sunless summer,' and this mood continues throughout the article. He feels that 'Nothing is impossible today,' and quotes Tennyson's 'The Eagle':

> *He grasps the crag with crooked hands,*
> *Close to the sun in lonely lands …*

Then, as if to reassure his prosaic readers, he says, 'Is it not a sober account and description of the ascent of a hitherto unclimbed buttress that I have to write?' But this he does not even attempt.

He starts by discussing a possible distinction between 'climbing and mountaineering'. He thinks the distinction does not exist, but he never says why. No doubt we are to assume that climbing is part of mountaineering, just as hillwalking is, but this is not made explicit. He goes on to define mountaineering as 'the noblest of sports', and argues that it has its root in the 'love of nature as expressed in its grander manifestations'. There is a 'combative element … a delight in pitting our skill, knowledge, and strength

---

1 Actually it was to have been Coronation week, but that had to be postponed until August because King Edward had appendicitis.

against the rocks, the ice, and the snow'. He quotes Mummery: 'to fight some grim precipice, or force some gaunt ice-clad gully, is work worthy of men'. And Raeburn adds that 'these are contests that leave no bitterness in victory, no humiliation in defeat'.

It is certainly true that Raeburn loved nature, particularly birds, but also animals and plants. He responds to the grand scenes of nature with heartfelt emotion. He likes Romantic poetry, particularly Tennyson and Coleridge, but his religious position is shadowy. His view of mountaineering seems romantic, but it is also practical. In some ways one could, with caution, call him a forerunner of WH Murray without the latter's mysticism. For someone who left his name on so many Scottish crags, he seems free of the urge to compete with other climbers. One cannot imagine him sneaking up to a crag to climb the plumb route while others slept: that is just not his style. He has ambition, but it is only to climb fine routes. So far as one can judge, he seems to do it for its own sake. Very few people are completely free of egoism, but Raeburn seems freer than most. These, of course, are provisional conclusions; as always, one must see the end to judge properly.

Almost as a comic interlude in the article, Raeburn discusses the relationship between golf—'That insidious epidemic'—and mountaineering. The golfer's 'bergschrunds are shrunk to bunkers ... and his vaulting ambition, which once led him to place his whole desire upon the high places of the earth, is now sunk so low that only depressions, yea, holes, attained by the "easiest route" will satisfy him'. So much for golf.

Yachting fares better. This is Raeburn in a lighthearted and exalted mood: 'there is nothing inconsistent with scaling in sailing'. At sea, there are mountainous waves with snowy crests and glassy slopes and 'enough "rocks" and "pitches" to satisfy the most ardent face and gully climber', indeed 'probably more than enough', he adds sardonically. Joking aside, there is a real comparison too, for: 'To beat to windward against a strong wind and heavy sea' is rather like 'the feeling of fighting one's way up the ice-pitch in a narrow gully, or difficult traverse on a steep rock face'.

Raeburn wittily links his discussion with his current situation on Ben Nevis: 'The yacht is keeping us, as is only natural ... far away from the rocks.' In fact, that Friday he had been taking part in a yacht race in the Firth of Forth. He had arranged to meet his friends the Clarks on the Ben, at the bottom of Observatory Buttress at 2pm on Saturday, but as luck would have it, the wind drops and he doesn't make Granton Harbour until 1 am. However, true to form, he still manages to catch the 4.30 am train to Fort William.

He is so warm going up the Allt a' Mhuilinn that he actually takes off his boots and stockings and loosens the rest of his clothes as much as is 'consistent with their staying *in situ*'. A good symbol of the article: Raeburn unbound. He is tempted to bathe, but, determined to keep his appointment, ploughs on. He is on time, but nobody comes.

There is another semi-comic aside in which he discusses 'My Lady Nicotine', but as he does not smoke he has to be content with semi-dozing. 'Lying in the sun' he 'steeps [himself] in the spirit of the rocks and snows of this lonely upper corrie'. He hears the deep-toned musical 'cronk' of a raven and the 'clear sweet notes of the snow bunting, like silver bells …'. He notices fox tracks in the snow and 'the tiny footprints of the wee field vole' that feeds on herbage and berries on the ledges of the steep cliffs. 'Every tuft and crevice pulses with the life of the myriad forms of the insect world.' He is alive to the flowers also: 'yellow clusters of the golden saxifrage', the starry saxifrage and moss campion.[2]

A figure appeared on the Great Tower of Tower Ridge and Harold thought someone might be coming at last, 'but a few minutes dispelled that hope, so I turned my face towards the grim-looking slabs of the Observatory Buttress. Below was the fast-flowing shadowtide; above, the blaze of sunlight, and oh, blessed thought, perhaps afternoon tea'. With absolute economy he describes his solo first ascent of an important, unclimbed buttress: 'It was enough, I went up, and, fifteen hours from the Sea, stood on the Summit.' The sheer energy and ecstasy in this article are in stark contrast to the deep depression Harold encountered later in life.

Quoting one of his earlier articles with irony, he says: 'One should drink in the grandeur of the view and dissect the unhappy points of the compass.' But, says Harold, 'I did none of these things.' He eschews dull convention and makes a beeline for the tea table and his friends.

The Clarks, meanwhile, had been making the first ascent of Pinnacle Buttress of the Tower. William Clark writes (SMCJ, 1903): 'looking down we espied a moving speck on the rocks of Observatory Buttress, … It was that solitary climber, who amid the great immensities of the place

---

2   Raeburn actually uses the Latin names for the latter two: *Saxifraga stellaris* and *Silene acaulis*.

seemed to traverse invisible ledges, and to climb where foot and hand holds could not be seen.' When they finally met at the tea table, Raeburn told them 'about "pulling in holds" and "overhanging pitches" and such like mountaineering delicacies'. One can readily imagine the excitement of that conversation.

Raeburn's solo ascent of Observatory Buttress took place on Saturday, 28 June. On the Friday, Glover's Chimney (then called Tower Gap West Gully) was climbed by George Glover, and Jane and William Clark. On Sunday 29th, Raeburn climbed Pinnacle Arête and Number Three Gully Buttress with the Clarks. As already noted, Glover and the Clarks climbed the Pinnacle Buttress of the Tower as Raeburn was climbing Observatory Buttress. All these routes are either described or mentioned in William Clark's lengthy article.

It is intriguing, however, that Clark does not even mention in his article his ascent, on Monday 30th, of Raeburn's Arête with Jane and Harold. The Arête, on the buttress below the First Platform of North-East Buttress, is reckoned to be one of the best climbs on the mountain at its grade (Severe). The most plausible explanation for Clark's silence is that he had already written about this route in the SMC's Guidebook, which was published as part of the SMCJ in September 1902. It is also possible that he felt that his article was already long enough. Raeburn likewise is silent about this route; there is not even a note in 'Excursions', but he probably knew that Clark had written about it and simply left it at that. [Fig 1] [Fig 2]

Clark says that 'The angle was very great, but the rocks were of superb description.' He finds that 'the whole climb consisting of vertical slabs requires careful attention'. He comments particularly on the 'very interesting traverse ... made to the left, crossing the arête by a sensational corner ...'. Clark concludes that the climb 'ranks among the steepest on Ben Nevis and would be impossible but for the magnificent nature of the rock'. The time taken on the first ascent—no doubt noted carefully by Raeburn— was '2 hours 40 minutes'; a comparatively slow time for Raeburn on a route of this length, indicating difficulty. There is a tradition which claims that Clark and his wife climbed roped while Raeburn soloed alongside, but Clark had actually come on this trip to recuperate from illness and might not have been in good enough form to lead a climb like this. One cannot rule out the intriguing possibility that Jane led the climb. We'll never know

Fig 1

This photo is not of Raeburn's Arête, but Raeburn and the Clarks might just have climbed that route and be making their way up North East Buttress from the First Platform. Raeburn is leading, Jane is belaying and William's initials appear on the border of the picture. Photo: William Clark

for sure, but Raeburn was likely on the sharp end of the rope, as usual. The weekend was one of notable achievements.

Another person with whom Raeburn struck up a friendship was Frank Goggs, who eventually took over from Willie Douglas as Editor of the SMCJ. Like Douglas, Goggs, in his writing, always tends to underplay his own talents as a mountaineer. In a witty article entitled 'A Salvationist on Lochnagar' (SMCJ, 1903), he describes a trip to Lochnagar in the company of 'two well-known Ultramontane members of the Club', Harold Raeburn and Alexander Mackay. The climbers of the day seem to have had a penchant for visiting Lochnagar at odd times of the year when it was likely to be in neither summer nor winter condition, and the events Goggs describes took place on 18–20 October 1902. The crags were 'lightly covered with snow and ice'.

On the first day of the trip: 'A delicate gossamer veil of white seemed to have been thrown over the crags, not altogether hiding their blackness, but transforming it into a silvery grey.' A sight which probably appealed to Harold also, given his appreciation of such scenes.

Naturally the main goal of Raeburn and Mackay was the recalcitrant Douglas-Gibson Gully 'which, for ten years has eluded the grasp of its votaries'. But much to Goggs's relief, it was too late to start on that. Instead, he persuaded his companions to let him 'bag' the summit before they headed round the corrie for the, by now, almost ritual inspection of the top of the gully. On this occasion Mackay and Goggs lowered Raeburn down on two 60ft ropes tied together, and 'after he had given us sufficient time to get quite cool', he came up saying that he could 'see his way up' the 30ft that baffled him before. They must try from the bottom the next day. Goggs said nothing, 'but ruminated on the uncertainty of human plans'.

Next day Raeburn got them out of bed at 6am and they were at the foot of 'that gully' by 10am. Goggs looked up and saw 'a fairly wide couloir, with smooth black sides glistening with ice'. The first pitch, some 50ft from the foot, seemed to overhang, and a healthy-looking stream was 'tumbling over it'. Imagine his relief when 'Raeburn suggested that perhaps the conditions were hardly good enough to give much chance of success'. Goggs gave Raeburn's opinion his 'warmest support'.[3]

The gullies out of condition, they switched attention to 'the ridge forming

3   Most modest climbers will know exactly how Goggs felt.

the east side of the gully'.⁴ After sending down a great deal of loose rock and turf, Raeburn got the party about 250 ft up, but 'Above [their] heads was a mass of sloping rocks, with no apparent holds or route.' Raeburn and Mackay consulted, and the decision to retreat was made.

Back on *terra firma*, Raeburn launched 'a fresh thunderbolt by suggesting a new route to cut the Tough-Brown Ridge'. As Goggs says: 'I had a hazy idea that the Tough-Brown Ridge was something desperate, but I preserved a quiet outward demeanour.' But once again, his luck held. Raeburn went up about 40 ft but could get no further. Disgruntled, he descended, saying one of them should write an article entitled 'Failure on Lochnagar'. Except that Raeburn started west of Parallel B Gully, the route he attempted is not clear. However, all the routes on this facet of the Tough-Brown Face are HVS or above, and the earliest were not climbed until the late 1960s. To get even 40 ft up, and down again, in semi-winter conditions was no mean achievement and yet again demonstrated Raeburn's ability and sound judgment.

As a last resort they climbed West Gully, where Goggs 'felt comparatively happy and cheerful'. Even after Raeburn and Mackay had dislodged most of the helpful vegetation from a steep slab leaving holdless granite, Goggs did not mind shouting 'lustily to be hauled up, which I promptly was, to the detriment of my garments'.

After a tussle with a cave pitch they found a through route on the last difficulty, but as Goggs endeavoured to pass up his rucksack on an ice-axe, 'the head of the axe turned over and the sack slipped off', vanishing down into the darkening corrie. What Raeburn and Mackay thought one can only wonder, but Goggs reports no remark.⁵

Goggs's trials were still not over, for on the following day, after an unavailing search for the rucksack, Raeburn and Mackay turned their attention to the Black Spout Pinnacle. Their initial plan was to leave Goggs to ascend

---

4   Shadow Buttress B, as it was later named. Severe or grade IV and not climbed until 1934 by Symmers and Ewen. 'The line Raeburn attempted on the left of the Buttress was climbed in winter conditions in 1986 and named Raeburn's Groove (VII,7) by those latter-day Raeburns, Dougie Dinwoodie and Andy Nisbet.' (Greg Strange in a personal email.)
5   West Gully has come to be mainly regarded as a good winter climb, grade IV if the lower icefall is climbed, if not, grade III. According to Greg Strange, veteran climber, author and authority on climbing in the Cairngorms, 'The summer grade, Diff, assumes that the party misses out the lower pitch and starts from the terrace, as Raeburn's party did.'

Fig 2

Raeburn's Arête, North East Buttress
Ben Nevis. Photo: Noel Williams

the Black Spout and meet them later, but Goggs belied his Salvationist tendencies and insisted on being one of the party. His thoughts on the climb are worth quoting at length:

> *Halfway up the Black Spout, a similar gully branches off to the left, and just at the junction of the two routes, on the left, is a steep green recess carved in the north flank of the Pinnacle. The angle was considerably steeper than anything we had done yet, and, as the climbing was not easy, I had a considerable amount of leisure to spend on turf ledges, whilst our Ultramontane leader revelled in the difficulties presented. Being unable to think of nothing, I began to speculate—supposing Raeburn fell, which under the circumstances I considered a most natural thing for him to do, could Mackay hold him, and if Mackay went also, could I hold the two, or must we all three be precipitated headlong? A glance downward was not encouraging, nor was a similar glance upward ...* (SMCJ, 1903)

Goggs had just decided never to get into this sort of position again when the call came, and very nobly he banished his gloomy thoughts and struggled up to join the other two 'on a fair-sized ledge some 150 ft from where we had started'. Raeburn made a valiant effort on the pitch above. Goggs describes the action:

> *On his left was a rocky face without holds, but he managed to get a hold for his right hand inside the chimney, and by levering his left foot against the rock face and getting the benefit of its roughnesses, he wedged his body well into the narrow fissure.*

But that was as far as they got. After another look at the problem after lunch, Raeburn decided that 'even if he got up a little way, the overhang at the top would not be overcome'. The upshot was that they lowered Goggs off to a point where he could scramble down to the Black Spout and then Raeburn and Mackay climbed down by the route of ascent—a considerable achievement. They met at the top of the Spout, scrambled down the slabs and up the short side of the Pinnacle. It seemed to be virgin and they built a cairn.

The route Raeburn attempted on Black Spout Pinnacle was Twin

Chimneys Route,[6] 'an impressively steep line, Very Difficult in summer' (SMC, 1985) and Grade IV in winter. This route was not climbed until 1952 by the strong team of Tom Patey and Mike Taylor. In making these attempts on Lochnagar, Raeburn was pushing himself to the upper limits of what he could achieve. It is only by failing on a route that is too hard for him that a climber can establish what he can and cannot do. It is clear that in Raeburn's attempts he leaves a margin of safety; he does not commit himself beyond the levels of his own skill, and, just as important, he considers the strengths and weaknesses of those climbing with him and does not endanger them.

This chapter has featured wonderful success on Ben Nevis and what was more like honourable failure on Lochnagar. These two trips also capture the two sides of Harold Raeburn: in the sun on the Ben, ecstatic; in the misty corrie of Lochnagar, gloomy. The deep wells of a person's emotional life spring from who knows where—just as we are not responsible for the colour of our eyes, we are not responsible, for different reasons, for our emotional make-up. We can, though, affect our actions through willpower, and Raeburn was an outstandingly dogged and resolute mountaineer.

6   Information supplied by Greg Strange.

9. BEINN AN LOCHAIN, SKYE, GLENCOE 1902–1903

Like many adventurous mountaineers, a feature of Raeburn's life was his continual quest for new things. On 29 November 1902 he combined forces with his friends the Clarks to explore the climbing possibilities on Beinn an Lochain in Arrochar. Raeburn was inspired by an article in the *SMCJ* by Scott Moncrieff Penney to try 'the Old Man'[1]: 'I saw, at what appeared a considerable distance away, a splendid snow peak, which I thought at first was Beinn Ime …' It wasn't; it was Beinn an Lochain. Penney duly climbed it and was delighted when he found it was in Munro's List.[2] He doubted 'if even our crack climbers could follow the outline of [the Old Man's] profile and step over his nose on to his chin' (*SMCJ*, 1902). What more challenge was required?

In order to have a good look at the cliffs, Harold, William and Jane formed a 'committee of enquiry' and climbed the north ridge. This, they found, 'well defined, steep in places, but involves no climbing'. Raeburn reckoned that the cliffs in the corrie to the right of the ridge were fully 300 ft. They traversed onto the face by a narrow ledge some 80 ft up from the bottom and started to ascend 'in a slabby gully or chimney a good way to the right [west] and 300 ft below the pinnacle' (a distinctive feature of the corrie). In the 1989 *Arran and Arrochar* guidebook, Ken Crocket wrote: 'Right again from the Monolith the face becomes easier angled, very vegetatious, and broken by grooves and ledges. Raeburn and the Clarks pioneered two obviously loose and vegetatious routes here, including one taking in the obvious pinnacle on the right of the face (Raeburn's Route, 120 m, Moderate).'

1 Tom Prentice, Editor of the 1997 *Guide to Arrochar*, has never heard this nickname, but Penney must have had a reason to call the hill this.
2 A splendid hill, but now demoted: a Corbett, not a Munro.

Crocket comments that successive editors have not been able to determine these routes with precision and says that the face might be more suitable for winter climbing.³ From Raeburn's description in 'Excursions' their route sounds in places sensational, involved and 'not recommended for climbers with new clothes' (SMCJ, 1903). They finished by 'an easy ledge ... close to an upright slab of stone, placed for some purpose near the edge of the cliff'.

From the 'land side' they climbed the Pinnacle without difficulty and, seeking another climb, descended 'the eastern arête of the Pinnacle's pedestal a short way, and traversed onto the face again by easy ledges'. The party climbed 'slanting up, always to the left, till brought up by an impossible drop cutting across the ledge'. Raeburn thought it was possible to avoid this impasse, but the days were short and there was no time. Instead, they went right and scrambled up a 'rotten gully' between 'two prominent beaks of rock', gaining the summit '600ft above the foot of the lower climb'. At this point it started snowing, and after visiting the cairn they descended.

It sounds as if Raeburn and the Clarks completed at least one route and climbed the Pinnacle, but this is not mentioned in the 1997 Guide to *Arran and Arrochar*. The guide describes the north face of Beinn an Lochain as being now largely of interest in winter, but the author concedes that some very fine rock climbs have been made on the mountain, despite the damp and lichenous condition of the rock. All the more reason, one would think, at least to note the efforts of the pioneers in the historical section.⁴ Raeburn himself adds that 'The committee's report on the "Old Man" climbing is decidedly favourable.' [Fig 1]

The New Year Meet of 1903 found Raeburn returning to a steep chimney on Creag na Caillich in the Tarmachan range with Dundee cousins Charles and Harry Walker. The latter contributed an account of the climb to 'Excursions'(SMCJ, 1903). As we know, Raeburn had partially climbed the chimney with Harry Lawson, the day before their successful ascent of Arrow Chimney on the buttress of the same name. The Creag na Caillich climb had been completed by Alexander Mackay and party, including Geoffrey Winthrop Young on a rare visit to Scotland.

Rather than repeat Mackay's climb, Raeburn's party chose the arête

---

3   In fact a route in this area of the face was climbed in the winter of 2008 and recorded as Footsteps of Giants IV,4 (SMC, 2021).
4   An omission the editor regrets.

Fig 1

The north face of Beinn an Lochain
showing the Monolith and the Pinnacle.
Photo: Tom Prentice

forming the right wall of the chimney, as 'it had the additional attraction of being something new'. 'The first 200 feet consisted of a series of snow couloirs', and then Harold took over in front and 'a series of steep faces were successfully tackled'. According to the clinometer, one was 73°. The hitches were excellent and the 'decidedly interesting' climb is given grade III in the modern guidebook—the same grade as the chimney. Climbs of this grade, roughly the equivalent of the summer grade Severe, were becoming routine for Raeburn and some of his contemporaries during this period, and Harold was well capable of tackling grade IV climbs like Arrow Chimney.

The Easter Meet of 1903 was held at Sligachan on Skye. WC Smith, the President, wrote that 'perhaps the best expedition ... was done by Raeburn, the Walkers and Ling [on Friday 10 April]. They left Sligachan early and reached the foot of Sgurr Dubh by the long glen, over all the tops of Sgurr Dubh, crossed the famous gap, over Alasdair and Sgurr Sgumain and down to Glenbrittle' (*SMCJ*, 1903).

In the September issue of the *SMCJ* (1903), Willie Ling fleshes out Smith's brief account. The party took a mere six hours to get from the hotel to the top of Sgùrr Dubh Beag, where they put on the rope to descend to the col with Sgùrr Dubh Mòr. This 'afforded a sporting climb. The holds were not superabundant, and of the fingertip order, and the position was sensational'. Most modern climbers abseil. By this time the weather had deteriorated and it was 'rather cold'. After lunch on Sgùrr Dubh Mòr they scrambled onto Sgùrr Dubh an Dà Bheinn and round to the Thearlaich-Dubh Gap: 'It was very cold here and the snow was being blown through the Gap, plastering the rocks and obscuring the holds.' Ling and the Walkers descended, protected by Raeburn, who then came down 'with the rope hitched'. They tried to throw a rope 'over the hitch on the [long] side' but could not make it stick, and Raeburn solved the difficulty 'by climbing without it', despite the atrocious conditions. Ling says the climb was 'thoroughly interesting'.

Scrambling onto Sgùrr Thearlaich, they descended directly to the col, finding it higher than usual because of the depth of snow.[5] On over Alasdair and Sgumain 'the peaks were falling almost as fast as the rain'. The technical

---

5   From the excellent full-page photographs in the *SMCJ* by Lamond Howie (p.301) and AE Robertson (p.305), the Cuillin appear to have been plastered with spring snow. Heavy snow showers are characteristic of the north-west in April; snow can accumulate very rapidly in these conditions.

difficulties were behind them, but Raeburn made a false cast in the mist: he thought he remembered 'an easy rake leading down ... to Coire Labain ... but presently ... came to an exceedingly perpendicular place and decided to try elsewhere'. They found 'a stone strewn gully' which got them 'down below the slabs' and proved in daylight next day 'to have been the best line we could have taken'. In all, it took them twelve hours and ten minutes.

Ling was a very able climber and the Walkers likewise, but one wonders if they would have completed this day without Raeburn. Ling's typical understatement cannot disguise the fact that leading the long side of the Thearlaich-Dubh Gap in wind and driving snow, without protection of any kind, is a very considerable achievement; bad enough to second. As for losing the way momentarily on the descent, Raeburn is not the only member of the SMC who has done that in the Cuillin, and the most recent won't be the last, but it is comforting to record that he too was fallible.

On Tuesday, 14 April Raeburn and Willie Douglas escorted the President and presumably his son, Bennet, up the tourist route on Sgùrr nan Gillean, which from the way he writes about it gave the elderly William Smith a lot of pleasure; they were out for some nine hours. One guesses this was the sort of pleasant action the Club had come to expect from its leading climber, and indeed from his friend Douglas, the Editor.

William Inglis Clark contributed the unusually titled article, 'The Motor in Mountaineering', to the September issue of the *SMCJ*.[6] The article is sub-titled, 'A Visit to Buachaille Etive Mòr' (*SMCJ*, 1903), and two important climbs featuring Raeburn are documented here: Crowberry Ridge Direct and The Chasm, tackled on 14 and 15 June 1903, respectively.

Raeburn had again been yachting, but he caught a very early train to Tyndrum and cycled to the Kingshouse. After a 'few hours' sleep' he set off with William and Jane at 10 am. The direct pitch on Crowberry Ridge had been climbed only once, by the Abraham brothers, who contributed a note to the *SMCJ* (1902). It was regarded as perhaps the hardest climb in the British Isles at the time. Needless to say, the Direct pitch was what Raeburn was after. Clark was apprehensive and felt that this might be beyond his capacity and that of his wife. However, 'the party turned to the left and braved the dangers of that awful precipice'.

---

6   Clark was the first person in Edinburgh to own a motor car.

Fig 2

Headless or not, given the bulky equipment he had, this is a significant photo by William Clark. It captures the delicacy of Raeburn's footwork and the imperturbability of Mrs Clark. Unlike the famous picture of Frank Goggs belaying William Morrison, it seems that here a proper belay has been contrived by driving a hammer shaft into a crack below a boulder, bottom right. Raeburn has changed into Kletterschuhe, whereas Morrison attempted the climb in boots.
Photo: William Clark, SMC Image Archive

Clark notes the 'reliable hitch, the safety of which is somewhat problematical'. He was right to be dubious. If this is the same hitch as that featured in AE Robertson's famous picture of Goggs's and Morrison's attempt,[7] it looks absolutely useless, and it is probably just as well that, after being immortalised, Goggs and Morrison wisely decided not to press on. Clark tried to take a photograph but only succeeded in capturing 'Raeburn's headless body climbing the vertical corner'.[8] However, he bravely followed Raeburn and his wife, and he describes the pitch thus:

[Fig 2]

> *Stepping off the ledge, the left foot seeks a 2-inch foothold round the corner. This consists of a narrowing ledge sloping steeply upwards and outwards, and affording further out grip for the nails only. The right hand retains a rough grip, while the left is rested on a slender pinnacle projecting some ½-inch from the face. Having fairly balanced on these slender supports, the body is taken round the corner, and the fun begins. The nearest available hold was some distance from our leader's reach and he had to forego the little pinnacle and trust to mere hollows for support.*

As Raeburn led the pitch there was 'an anxious and silent interval' as the rope inched out, but then its pace quickened and 'after 35 feet were out', Jane Clark followed. Nothing, typically, is said as to how the lady fared. At all events, when Clark followed, he was 'not ashamed to call out "Hold me firm"', presumably the Victorian equivalent of 'Tight rope!'. It is significant that Raeburn changed into Kletterschuhe to tackle the main pitch. Expecting an absence of positive holds, he knew enough about this new form of footwear to prefer it to his habitual nailed boots. Clearly he had to concentrate hard, as the silence and slow progress indicate, but does not seem to have been over-taxed and no doubt his footwear helped. Here and elsewhere, one gets the impression that he was a calm, unhurried leader who weighed each move with care, but when he had worked out the proper sequence of moves, did not hesitate.

Anything above the direct pitch 'pales into insignificance'; they joined Naismith's Route higher up and completed the climb, then descended to

---

7 See, for example, the cover of Ken Crocket's *Mountaineering in Scotland—The Early Years* (2015).
8 Although Clark was appalled by this result, the picture he took is very worthwhile.

the east and looked into the Chasm, where they saw 'a hundred-foot pitch, apparently impossible'. As they were running down the screes, Clark realised that he had left his expensive Dallmeyer lens on the summit.

'Next day, instead of going up by the easiest way, what should Raeburn suggest but that we should endeavour to ascend by the Chasm'. 'With commendable prudence', they began their attempt above the pitch they had investigated the previous day. Clark gives us the flavour of their route:

> [T]he climb up to the branching of the Chasm was extraordinary and weird ... Now we were cutting steps ... or treading the sharp seracs, or crossing by snow bridge. Anon hemmed in by vertical walls, we traversed in a crouching position perhaps 50 feet through a snow tunnel ... Emerging, a forbidding pitch confronted us, and ... only succumbed after a severe struggle. It was ... a most strenuous climb, and demanded constant strain.

At length they came to the last two 'severe pitches leading into the cauldron' and saw 'a final triple pitch of at least 150 feet, well decorated with waterfalls'. They decided to escape to the left. This 'escape' was by no means without its difficulties: 'Here at the forking of the Chasm rises a magnificent 200 feet pinnacle, the angle very steep.' They backed up between snow and rock, 'to reach the bottom of a severe ... chimney leading up some 40 feet'. A grass ledge was gained, 'overhung by a difficult and dangerous wall ... the ascent of this slightly overhanging portion proved difficult ... Above this another wonderful chimney led to the top ... which is separated by a neat little col from the mountain'.

William Clark thought it was 'the most prolonged piece of difficult climbing' in his British experience. Very properly, considering Jane's involvement, they christened the pinnacle 'Lady's Pinnacle'. Not surprisingly, they were glad to relax their muscles after four hours of intense activity. Then William and Jane said farewell to Raeburn and watched him 'scamper down the screes like a chamois'. The Clarks lingered at the Clachaig for a couple of days, but they 'seized various excuses for doing nothing striking'.

In the SMC's selective guide to *Scottish Rock Climbs* (2005), The Chasm is graded Very Severe and given three stars. It is described as 'Scotland's best gully climb'. Raeburn would return to it in 1906.

10. CREAG MEAGAIDH, GARBH BHEINN, BEN NEVIS 1903–1904

Having visited Creag Meagaidh in 1896, Raeburn returned seven years later in the autumn of 1903 with the Walker cousins, Harry and Charles, from Dundee. He contributed to the SMCJ a substantial article on this visit entitled 'The Cliffs of Corrie Arder' (1904).

Raeburn begins by describing Creag Meagaidh: 'formless and dull as a whole', it exceeds Ben Nevis in bulk. It cannot, in his opinion, be ranked with the Ben from a climbing point of view, but 'it possesses in the 1,200 ft rock of the Pinnacle of Corrie Arder a cliff whose steepness is equalled by nothing on our highest Ben, and a face with gullies and buttresses well worthy of the climber's attention'. Modern climbers might quibble with the first part of this sentence, but surely most would agree with the second.

Raeburn recalls his earlier visit to the corrie. Then, with Tough and Douglas, he had been repulsed from Centre Post by avalanches, but they had climbed the Pinnacle from the short side and built a cairn. This time Harold, Harry and Charles set out from Dalwhinnie Station on 30 October to cycle to the Loch Laggan Hotel. The road was good as far as Laggan Bridge, and Raeburn enjoyed this part of the trip, as his atmospheric account reflects:

> The sudden cry of a plover … shatters the outer silence of the night with almost painful loudness. The murmur of a distant fall is now heard, now lost as we sweep round the hollows and over the shoulders of the moor. The whisper of the night breeze through the heath and sedge is scarcely audible above the soft rush of the wheels on the smooth damp sand …

A sensitive description which is then contrasted with what follows after Laggan Bridge:

It was a nightmare of a ride ... We slid, and skidded, and squelched, and side-slipped ... and sweated ... and walked, and waded, and jerked, and joggled, and vibrated, and fought, and muddied, and fell—the last five times ...[1]

Fortunately no one was injured, and they arrived at the hotel by 9.15 pm. After rain during the night there was the promise of better weather, and the trio cycled down the lochside and left their bikes at the farm. By 11 am they were at the lochan and had the whole corrie in view. Raeburn thought its 'most impressive piece of rock scenery is ... the "Pinnacle"', bounded to the south-east 'by a long gully of easy angle' (later 'Raeburn's Gully'). 'To the north of the Pinnacle Cliff opens out a wide gully ... which serves to separate it from the main mass, in which are situated the "Posts".' He notes the 'Snow Bridge' which often forms at the foot of what we know as 'Easy Gully'.[2] Even at the end of October, 'all the gullies of any size held masses of old hard snow, testifying to the cold, wet summer of 1903'.

Raeburn was interested in Centre Post, which had defeated him last time, but the lower pitches were awash with water, so they turned their attention to the Pinnacle Face. The first 300 ft were impossible, however, so they went round to 'Pinnacle South Gully'[3] and tried to get on to the face from there. Despite making three attempts, 'the comfortable green ledge by which [they] got out of the gully would invariably ... drop off in a smooth and impassable gap ...' and 'the rock, where not actually overhanging, was comprised of many holdless slabs'. In the end they gave up and kept on up the gully 'all the way'.

It must have been a rather dirty, mixed ascent, as 'CW Walker, who led throughout, excited the envy of his followers on their precarious dirt

---

1 Readers might like to compare this description of an inglorious cycle ride with Norman Collie's celebrated article on climbing Tower Ridge for the first time in Winter. Collie's piece may have influenced Raeburn to write its comic antithesis. (For Collie's article see *SMCJ*, 1894. The author's name, 'Orlamon Linecus', is a partial anagram of 'Norman Collie'.)
2 Raeburn calls this 'Snow Bridge Gully': a better name, surely?
3 Raeburn's Gully, as it became.

slope below by the ease and abandon of his reposeful attitude on a sloping, lovely, green, mossy slab' until 'The sudden appearance of a vigorous jet of water spouting from the lowest knee of his knickers, soon convinced them ... that the position was too absorbing for their taste.' A nice flash of humour on a less-than-successful day. It is worth noting that he also speaks of the 'Colossus-like attitudes' of the chimney climber—almost certainly an echo of Shakespeare's *Julius Caesar*.[4]

They reached the Pinnacle 'from above as in '96'. They had seen an eagle 'aslant the face' and 'here on the Pinnacle was his "Tower of Silence"'. Bones and remains were strewn about, 'victims of this "Angel of Death"'.[5] Raeburn noticed that in 1896 the eagle had been feeding mainly on ptarmigan, but now 'the Alpine hare had been the chief sufferer'. Like so many climbers after them, they didn't feel like 'groping in fog' for Meagaidh's elusive cairn, so they followed the cliff edges to the Window and descended.

Ever the naturalist, Raeburn looked out of his bedroom window the following morning and watched a heron glide down to the edge of Loch Laggan where it stood motionless, 'her shadow adding another picture to those of the hills and trees and clouds already mirrored on the surface of the water'. He delighted in the bird song: 'the Robin, the Wren, and the Hedge Accentor showed they were rejoicing in the calm and sun of this rare November day'. He revelled in the bike ride back to Aberarder:

> [E]very shade of yellow and brown to dark red and flaming crimson was painted on the withered foliage. As we rode through the birches, the long, nearly level rays of the yet low sun lit up their trunks and foliage till the one seemed silver and the other gold ... No season save late autumn can show a colouring half so rich and splendid.

There is so much more than the determined climber to Harold Raeburn. On the first day of November they tackled 'the central Post'. Quite surprisingly, Raeburn says, 'Climbing began almost at once on clean, steep rock with splendid holds.' Not the usual story told about Creag Meagaidh's rock. For several hundred feet they found the climbing easy 'though

---

4 'Why man he doth bestride the narrow world / like a Colossus...' *Julius Caesar*, 1.2.133-134.
5 Possibly a reference to a picture of 1895 by British artist, Simeon Soloman.

decidedly steep'. At first, the gully was merely 'a shallow scoop', but halfway up, it cut more deeply into the mountain. Here there was what Raeburn describes as:

> [A] triple pitch above a large mass of old hard snow. High above this opens out a great pot or chasm, with overhanging walls apparently on all sides, from which fell numberless streams of water. The whole air of the place was filled with the drifting smoke of the shattered spray. It was certainly a wonderful piece of rock scenery, but ... it was a fine day, all of us were still quite dry.

The modern winter climber, remembering the Grade III escape from under the great ice pitch, would guess that they went to the right here, but not so: 'We therefore sought and found a way out on to the buttress wall on our left.' The next part was difficult: 'It involved crossing to the left of a steep, rotten, dirt slope, and round a projecting corner. Here a slanting, narrow, green ledge led to a corner of easy though steep grass.' A passage of 'easy grass and rock' led to 'a broad grassy ledge', above which they had to tackle 'a remarkably steep and rotten wall, the whole 70 or 80 feet of which appeared to be on the point of falling in ruins into the corrie'.

After this nasty sting in the tail, their buttress became 'more of a ridge'; they climbed 'a steep little rock tower' and found themselves at the summit 'two hours and a half from the foot'. It was bitterly cold; they built a cairn and made off.

Having climbed a new route, they were still intent on enjoying the whole day and returned to the farm 'by the ridge above Loch Laggan'—presumably the Càrn Liath ridge. It was 'a splendid scenic walk', and they were further rewarded by seeing Brocken spectres, which Charles Walker tried to photograph. Among later mountaineers one can imagine WH Murray or JHB Bell completing a day of achievement like this, but not Tom Patey or Dougal Haston. Raeburn's mountaineering ethos was different.

The following day they cycled to Kingussie, 'taking Creag Dhu *en route*'. Another hillwalk, perhaps? Not a bit of it: they put up two routes on this forbidding crag, and went to the top on each occasion 'by steep and rotten grass ledges, which, but for the ice-axe we could not have ventured upon'. As Ken Crocket (2015) notes: 'One of the routes climbed in 1903 was later

Fig 1

The Reverend AE Robertson relaxing in Skye. Raeburn is never pictured like this. He usually seems tense and self-conscious if he knows he is being photographed.
Photo: SMC Image Archive

recorded in 1965 as Fred (100m Very Difficult).'

When they descended from the second climb they rescued a rabbit from a stoat: '... poor Bunny was completely palsied by fear, its small heart beating like a sledgehammer, and its eyes literally starting from its head. It gradually recovered, however, and by the time we had returned with our cycles repacked, was sufficiently recovered to hop away'.

Unlike the Arran trip, the first rain was just starting as they entered Kingussie Station.

Earlier in 1903 Raeburn had a trip to Ben Nevis with the Rev AE Robertson (*SMCJ*, 1904). On 5 July they made the first *descent* of a climb that Raeburn was keen to know well: Observatory Ridge. They had trouble at 'the hand traverse' and lost almost an hour in reascent. 'Torrents of rain' fell all day, and they ascended North-East Buttress as the quick way back to the summit hotel, gaining the first platform 'from the foot of Slingsby's Chimney and ascending slabs to [the] left to first platform'. This was 'done without hurry in eighteen minutes'. And so Raeburn's 'Eighteen Minute Route' was born. [Fig 1]

Having dried out in the hotel, Raeburn and Robertson ascended the Staircase Climb on Càrn Dearg the following day. Again the weather was foul: 'it rained, sleeted and snowed nearly all the time'. They made two variations on the route followed by the first and second parties. Raeburn admits that 'the second of these is more properly an evasion of difficulty, but was found grateful and comforting in the saturated condition of the rocks and the clothes of the climbers'. He had no need to excuse himself, prepared as he was to climb in weather like this. The details of the variations can be found in his 1904 *SMCJ* account.

The SMC New Year Meet of 1904 seems to have been a jolly and well-attended occasion. As John Bell remarked in his meet report: 'Thirty men were climbing for four days, and there is no record of anybody having even got his feet wet' (*SMCJ*, 1904). Not that snow conditions or weather were perfect, 'Throughout the Meet the clouds clung obstinately ... to the upper thousand feet of Ben Nevis, and a strong south-east wind made itself rather too keenly felt on the upper rocks.' There wasn't much snow, but 'what there was, was so hard that it was only possible to glissade standing'. But at least it was good for climbing.

On Friday, 1 January Raeburn, James Maclay and the Walker cousins made the first ascent of North Trident Buttress. Raeburn says that 'the rocks low down were in splendid condition'; for him, this consisted in their being free of snow with 'the crevices full of black ice'. Modern climbers would have much preferred a good covering of hard névé, but this just shows the difference between nails and crampons. At least the loose rocks 'were all firmly frozen into position'. They climbed by a trap dyke in the centre of the buttress, 'in places steep though not difficult. Towards the top it develops into a ridge crowned at the summit by a steep tower'. Their climb finished 'within a few yards of the cairn on Carn Dearg'.

After watching another party cutting steps up No. 3 Gully, they visited the Observatory Hotel where they received 'the usual hospitable welcome from Mr ... the Cook, [sic] and the famous cat'. Did Raeburn forget the name of the Observer, or mean to say 'Mr X and the Cook ...'?[6] Or is it an unusual typographical error in one of Douglas's SMCJs? One suspects, however, that Raeburn was pleased to see the cat.

John Bell describes the second ascent of the Great Ridge of Garbh Bheinn in Ardgour, made on Saturday, 2 January with Raeburn, Graham Napier (Robert G) and John Rennie. Given what he had said earlier about the lack of snow below 3,000 ft, this seems likely to have been a rock climb with a wintry feel rather than a first winter ascent.[7] The party did not tackle what became the Direct pitch at the foot of the climb but took the easier option of 'a backward traverse from a point higher up the corrie'. Like most climbers, 'once on the rocks the "preposterous" holds and hitches' gave them 'a delightful sense of security'. A security not found on the return journey across the Corran straits, where, having missed the ferry by an hour, they were rowed across in adverse conditions. Bell remarks with Edwardian stolidity: 'It was just about as rough as was pleasant on a dark and cold night, and I for one was by no means sorry to be safely across.' Had they capsized, the history of Scottish mountaineering might have been very different. The Raeburn family had already lost one son by drowning; perhaps they were fortunate not to lose another.

Raeburn was out again the following day with Rennie and new member

---

6   Two possible names may have escaped Raeburn's mind: Messrs Rankin and Mossman, both of whom were observers at this time.
7   The first winter ascent is now credited to Raeburn and Ling on a later occasion, in January 1908; see Chapter 18.

John Wigner. They went up to the Ben intent on North-East Buttress, but the ferocity of the wind made them think of going up 'Observatory Gully–Tower branch' instead. However, they changed objective for a third time when Rennie said he would like 'some rock-climbing for a change'. An odd remark, considering he had had plenty of rock climbing the day before on Garbh Bheinn. No matter, they traversed 'rather steep and treacherous snow to the foot of the Tower Gap Chimney', which they climbed and finished by the 'usual Tower Ridge route'. It was Raeburn's turn to understate, saying, 'The conditions were not ideal.' No indeed, with a howling gale and driven snow, Tower Gap is not very amiable, but there was a consolation: 'The traverse, and perhaps the lower part of the chimney, [were] apparently new.' Note the, albeit restrained, pleasure in doing something new, and the caution and modesty present in 'apparently': all typical of Harold's personality.

Having climbed with one new member, Raeburn went out again with another two on the Monday. William Newbigging and James Burns accompanied him on an ascent of the 'big gully of Meall-an-t-Suidhe, the second which is passed on the way up the path'. Newbigging, who wrote the brief account, had not quite got into the way of impersonal, modest understatement: 'Most of the leading was done by myself, except at one or two places which Raeburn took.' One can imagine Willie Douglas's eyebrow twitching just a little as he read this; Harold probably had a quiet smile also. Something here of the tolerated cheek of the young pup to the leader of the pack? As we have seen, Newbigging did not scruple later in his career to satirise Harold's attention to time. He may have felt a need to challenge the master, but in no way was he a serious rival. There does not appear to be any record of Raeburn climbing with Newbigging again.

On 5 March 1904 Raeburn, Charlie and Mabel Clark caught the very early train from Edinburgh to Tyndrum to join Willie Douglas and the younger Clarks' parents, William and Jane, in yet another ascent of Ben Lui. Douglas describes the action in an article entitled 'Ben Lui Revisited', which begins by asking: 'What can be said of Ben Lui that has not been said already?' The answer seems to be: not much. However, it is interesting that the party split into two, and Douglas refers to Raeburn, Charlie and Mabel as 'the younger and more energetic members'. The young Clarks were certainly younger, but Raeburn was ages with Douglas himself, so at 39 he obviously maintained a high level of fitness.

[Fig 2] There is a delightful photograph by Clark the elder of the silhouetted forms of three (or perhaps four) of the party standing near Cononish with the mountain in full winter condition in the background[8]. Raeburn seems to have got ahead with Jane and Mabel at this point. At a distance, it is not easy to tell the ladies apart, but Raeburn's image is unmistakable.

The 'younger party' actually looked for difficulty near the top 'over steep and fog crystal-covered rocks which led almost to the summit cairn'. Raeburn and company were merely on a day trip and descended the great corrie by a rather too icy glissade. Harold seems to have come on this excursion largely for the pleasure of enjoying a day with his friends. One needs always to remember that he is an amateur: he climbs because he likes doing so. It is interesting from the transport point of view that Douglas thinks that Ben Lui and Cruachan are two 'of the most delightful mountains within easy reach of Edinburgh'.

---

8   Adjoining Douglas's article (*SMCJ*, 1904, p.94).

Fig 2

The unmistakable profile of Raeburn at Beinn Lui. Photo: W Clark. Photo: William Clark, SMC Image Archive

11. SGÒRR RUADH, AONACH BEAG   1904–1905

The Easter Meet of 1904 was held at Aviemore from 31 March to 4 April. On 1 April Raeburn and William Garden took new members George Almond and A Roth to Coire an t-Sneachda and made the first ascent of Pygmy Ridge, graded Moderate in Summer and now reckoned to be III/IV in winter. DS Campbell, who contributed a short account of the excursions of 1 and 2 April (SMCJ, 1904), says that Raeburn carried his 'skis up to the snow' and used them to the foot of the buttress and down again, but the icy conditions were very unfavourable for skiing. At the time, Pygmy Ridge was the hardest climb recorded in the Cairngorms, and one of the first two in Coire an t-Sneachda, the other being a gully recorded on the same day by another SMC party.

For reasons unknown, the day after the Cairngorm climb, Raeburn and Euan Robertson (not to be confused with Rev AE Robertson) took the train, presumably to Inverness, and changed there for Strathcarron. Decamping from a meet like this was not Raeburn's usual habit, and speculation is fruitless. William Clark, who wrote the main report of the Meet (Ibid.), gives brief details of their doings in the west. Raeburn did not contribute an account until much later, indeed not until January 1905 (SMCJ, 1905); again, this was unlike him. It transpired that he was acting on the advice of Lionel Hinxman who, in a previous SMCJ (1895), had praised the climbing potential of the Achnashellach area.

Like a punishment for their truancy, the weather was dreadful. They put up at the Strathcarron Hotel, which they found to be small but comfortable. Having arrived at Strathcarron at 12.52pm on Saturday, they set off at once to explore Corrie Lair in 'dense mist, a howling sleet-laden gale, and underfoot eight to ten inches of slush'. They could dimly discern 'a fine series of cliffs on the east face of Fuar Tholl', and they climbed over the col between that hill and Sgòrr Ruadh 'against the gale', returning to Strathcarron via Coulags Glen and the road. For the benefit of future hill-goers, Raeburn described which path to take and where to find the bridge. He noted the 'fine falls in a deep picturesque gorge'.

On Sunday the weather was 'if possible, worse'. Raeburn and Robertson approached An Ruadh Stac's north-east ridge by the col with 'Meall a' Chinn Dearg'. They saw many deer. They traversed the Ruadh Stac's north-east arête, which was 'in places narrow' but 'affords no climbing', and then descended by the south-west face into the valley of the Amhainn Bhuidheach and so back to Strathcarron. A fair day's walking in foul weather, which took over six hours. Thus far unlucky with the weather, they had been exploring new ground, but on Monday, 4 April they took advantage of the Kyle to Inverness train, travelled a few miles up Glen Carron to Achnashellach and went up into Coire Lair by the track north of the station they had used on Saturday. The weather had turned colder, with a NW wind and the snowline down to 1,000 ft. A second breakfast was taken in the shelter of a boulder 'in comparative peace'. Wonder of wonders, after several days of murk, the clouds lifted and gave 'fair views of the fine NE face of Sgurr Ruadh'. Raeburn describes the cliffs and notes Rev AE Robertson's ascent 'with a friend' of Robertson's Gully/Buttress in May 1898 on the south side of the little corrie formed by Easy Gully. This was the only route that appeared to have been done on the crags.

Raeburn and Euan Robertson selected the north-east buttress for attack. 'Looked at *en face*, the rocks seemed hopelessly steep, and the gale blew with undiminished violence against the N face, but the snow in the chimney showed the angle was not so great as appeared.'[1] They hoped to avoid the wind 'by keeping below the crest of the ridge as much as possible', roping up at 10.30 am.

To avoid 'the extremely steep and slabby' iced rocks at the foot of the buttress, they went up the slender gully to the left for about 80 ft and followed a ledge back onto the ridge. Here they found that the wind was 'deflected by the rock wall'. Raeburn says:

1 Raeburn was developing fairly determined ideas about the angle on which snow will lie, see Chapter 13.

The climbing in places, owing to the conditions, was not very easy, but the icy snow usually adhering to the steep grassy walls gave good hitches, and handholds could also be cut where required. Below the tower we crossed a beautiful little col with sharp snow arête. Here we were exposed to the full violence of the wind, and it was extraordinary with what force the rope between us flew out to leeward like a drawn bowstring.

It reminded them of a 'picture by Willink in the Badminton volume on mountaineering'.

They completed the climb, visited the summit of the mountain and glimpsed 'Leagach[2] with the Fasarinen' in Glen Torridon. Instead of going back by Corrie Lair, they descended the endless south-west face of Sgòrr Ruadh into Coulags Glen, where the rain became a deluge. Even so, Raeburn had his eye on the Mainreachan Buttress of Fuar Tholl, which 'appeared extremely steep'. He agrees with Lionel Hinxman 'that the district is a fine one, and some excellent climbing is to be got here'.

[Fig 1] It is difficult to give a grade to Raeburn's Buttress as he climbed it. The modern guide gives the Buttress via Narrow Gully grade II, but Raeburn and Robertson left the gully after some 80 ft and traversed the awkward ledge onto the ridge. This is harder than continuing up the gully and perhaps a grade of II/III would be more accurate. It was certainly a winter ascent of what the modern guide describes as 'a good, natural mountaineering route' (SMC, 2007).[3]

After the conclusion of the Easter Meet in the Cairngorms, William Clark was not long in heading for Fort William, where his wife and daughter were being taught skiing by Herr Willie Rickmers. Raeburn was then involved with two climbs: an ascent of the North-East Ridge of Aonach Beag (described by William Clark) and an ascent of what was to become known as the Central Gully of the Trident Buttress on Ben Nevis. It is not clear, at least to the author, which of these came first. William Clark helpfully dates the North-East Ridge on 18 April. Jane Clark, contributing the first

---

2   To this day, nobody seems to know how to pronounce 'Liathach'; Raeburn's approximation is as good as any.
3   Interestingly, an earlier version of *Northern Highlands South* gives Slender Gully as Grade III, possibly assuming that the harder route on the buttress will be taken.

Fig 1

Sgùrr Ruadh from Beinn Liath Mhòr;
Raeburn's Buttress is on the right.
Photo: Roger Robb

article by a woman to the *SMCJ*, says only that the climb was done in April and modern guidebooks repeat this vagueness. The only rather dubious enlightenment to be found is in Graham MacPhee's 1954 guide, which claims, on unknown authority, that the Trident climb took place in 'early April' (SMC, 1954). This at least seems plausible and receives support of a kind from Mrs Clark's mention of skis being thoughtfully left for the party by Mr Rickmers, their ski instructor (*SMCJ*, 1904).

With this slender support, let us treat the Trident climb first. Mrs Clark takes it that their goal is the unclimbed 'central ridge' of the Trident Buttresses. One supposes that this is why she calls the route the 'Centre Grid'—a 'grid' at least being something with bars or prongs.

William, 'the photographer', accompanied them to the base of the climb and then is heard of no more while Raeburn led Jane and Charlie up the route. The crux was the turning of a large ice pitch, deemed 'absolutely impossible', by a traverse 'round to the left, across and along a steeply sloping ledge below overhanging ice-covered rocks'. Mrs Clark says it 'was an awkward and dangerous traverse'. Apart from the obvious fact that he led the climb, nothing is said about Raeburn who, with Edwardian rectitude, is styled 'Mr Raeburn'. In a nice human touch, she records that Charlie's hat blew away: 'It was a historical hat that had safely surmounted Monte Rosa, the Matterhorn, etc, but the Ben claimed it and it had to obey ...'

The 'Centre Grid' is now called Central Gully, graded III,4, and is described in the modern guide as 'A fine climb with an Alpine feel' (SMC, 2007). 'It was glorious,' says Mrs Clark,[4] 'to step up into the sunshine, and to feel that we had successfully accomplished a new climb under wintry conditions.'

For reasons unknown, Mrs Clark did not accompany her husband and son as, with Raeburn, they headed for the North-East Ridge of Aonach [Fig 2/3] Beag. This was not a new route, having been climbed on Saturday, 13 April 1895 by James Maclay, Willie Naismith and Gilbert Thomson. To this day it is a route to which most winter climbers aspire, though few there be that do it. It has the charm of remoteness but the way to it is arduous. Raeburn

4 One would call her Jane, but the conventions of the day forbid it; the lady would have been scandalised. Mrs Clark was a formidable mountaineer in her own right: she had a long list of ascents in the Alps with her husband and their family. Among other feats, she ascended the Meije alone from the Promontoire Hut. She was a founder member, and the first President, of the LSCC.

had wanted to go there in 1902 from the Summit Hotel on Ben Nevis, but had to wait another two years.

Raeburn's party started from Glen Nevis (no gondola then) in good weather. Clark wanted to photograph Sgùrr a' Mhàim and took too long about it. Eventually 'relentless Raeburn calls "Time's up" and we shoulder our packs and strike up for the sloping skyline which will lead us round the south-east shoulder of Aonach Beag to the col between that peak and Sgorr a' Choinnich Beag. It is new ground for us all' (*SMCJ*, 1904). And, one might add, a truly frightful slog, especially as 'deep snow lay in beautiful wreaths and rendered the going heavy'. But at least they were travelling light, the rope and Clark's camera being the heavier items. Their plan went well, 'and with scarce a waver we rounded the shoulder and found ourselves on the same level as our col'. They were perplexed by the number of ridges they could see, none of which was the one they were aiming for—in fact, Maclay and party had started up the wrong ridge on the first ascent—and they were keen to avoid this mistake.

They glissaded down 'into the level corrie, now dazzling with deep snow. Through this a vigorous stream turned and twisted, covered deep by snow bridges ... some circumspection was necessary to avoid immersion ...' The party was actually crossing an avalanche cone when they saw and heard another avalanche: 'As we looked, a puff like smoke, and down thundered ... masses of ice and snow, riving deep furrows in the steep slope', fortunately not near them. With uncertainty, they toiled 'northwards to the great slope of Aonach Mor', and 'it was evident that our ridge must be still farther round to the left'.

As Clark's account makes plain, 'the snow was knee deep and in bad condition' but they persevered and there at last 'towered up for 1,600 ft the object of our search'. They rightly thought that the sooner they got onto the ridge and out of danger from avalanche, the better, so they ploughed their way 'up a steep snow slope leading to the arête'. For the first 500 ft they were lulled into a false sense of security: 'Was it then ... to be merely a pleasant stroll?' No. Because, 'on the now narrow ridge ... several gigantic rock needles barred the way. On either hand the icy slope disappeared at a steep angle' just like 'a first-class Alpine ridge'. Raeburn was undismayed, according to Clark: 'One after another difficulty was vanquished by our leader, and the sensational passages yielded safe handholds to the rest of the party.' He goes on:

Fig 2

The North-East Ridge of Aonach Beag on the day of the ascent, this one taken at Raeburn's instigation with Clark's last plate (opposite). Photos: William Clark

Fig 3

> At length the ridge is reduced to a steep narrow overhanging edge, and our choice is over this, or on holdless slaps [sic] to the right ... Neither seems justifiable, but over to the left a fine traverse leads to an icy slope, and then right up over steep rocks to the ridge again ...

They were almost there and Clark wanted to take more photographs, but he had only two plates left and saved them for higher up. Clark expended his second-last plate picturing Raeburn and Charlie moving circumspectly up towards huge cornices. They wondered if they would be able to surmount them, but the tracks of a mountain hare led them to a passage through. Here again Clark was torn between several possible landscapes. Charlie wanted him to picture Ben Nevis 'like some gigantic form rearing its hoary head for one last look around ere night fell'. Raeburn agreed, 'but added with sweet simplicity, "This would make no doubt the finest picture, but you have a duty to the ridge, and even though the result be only topographical, the plate must record the ridge for the benefit of others."' And Clark's picture does give a very clear view of the North-East Ridge, despite being ever so slightly overexposed in the strongly reflected evening sunlight.

They went over Aonach Mòr and glissaded some 1,500 ft down a steep gully to the valley, feeling 'that a red letter day had been added to their mountain experience'. One suspects that in the matter of taking the useful rather than the beautiful picture, Raeburn's thoughts were with their friend Willie Douglas and the Guide Book project, which was continuing in successive volumes of the *SMCJ*. It was typical of him, however, to think how a photograph might be useful to other climbers.

Raeburn attended the New Year Meet at Loch Awe, but the weather was foul and not much climbing was done, though one nameless party ascended the Black Shoot. Raeburn is mentioned by the anonymous reporter as one of a small group who entertained the company by using the magic lantern and speaking about 'their respective summer holidays in the Alps'. His friends Clark and Douglas also contributed. Raeburn seems to have been at least a competent public speaker, which makes it all the more likely that his eventual refusal of the Club Presidency was not because of shyness in this respect.

The Easter Meet at Sligachan went much better in April 1905. The anonymous reporter recorded (*SMCJ*, 1905) that on Friday 21st, 'Mr Raeburn led a party up the east face of the Castles,' and on Saturday 22nd he 'traversed Garsbheinn, Sgurr nan Eag, Sgurr Dubh na Dabheinn, Alaisdair-Dubh Gap, Tearlach, Alaisdair, Sgumain, on his way from Camasunary to Glen Brittle'.[5] Apart from the omission of the main Dubhs, this strenuous expedition was very like one he had done before.[6]

---

5   For a full account of this trip see Chapter 14.
6   See Chapter 9.

12. LAKELAND FORAYS BY MIKE JACOB 1897–1919

Raeburn was a frequent visitor to the English Lake District, which in those days lay in the historic counties of Cumberland, Lancashire and Westmorland, but is now part of the greater region of Cumbria. His first visits, in the early 1890s, were spent fell-walking and coincided with the so-called 'golden age' of rock climbing that was pioneered by a small group of adventurers in the last two decades of the 19th century. Although Raeburn was not one of these pioneers, he most certainly was an adventurer.

Once he became aware of them, he could not possibly have failed to be challenged by Lakeland's test-piece rock climbs, all concentrated in a relatively compact and easily accessible area. The total number of rock climbers in Britain at that time was very low, the activity a preserve of a prosperous minority with time on their hands. It was inevitable that they would meet each other at the various inns and hotels they patronised and exchange details about the latest routes to be climbed. This was an exciting period of high-spirited exploration by young gentlemen more than willing to test their athletic prowess, balance and nerve on the steep gullies and rock faces of central Lakeland. They climbed for fun, thrills and in a spirit of comradeship typical of the time.

One of the members of this elite group of pioneers was the distinguished and magisterial Norman Collie, a passionate mountaineer and an inveterate collector, who started out with birds' eggs (although with less dedication than Raeburn) and moved on to minerals, Chinese porcelain and Indian embroidery. He is remembered particularly for his love of Skye, but he also climbed in the Alps, the Himalayas and the Lofoten Islands of Norway, and pioneered many routes in the Canadian Rockies.

At Christmas in 1897, Harold made a short visit to the Wasdale area because he was unable to attend the SMC's New Year Meet at Fort William over the holiday period. He was following a recommendation by WW Naismith, who had made a similar trip with W Douglas at Whitsuntide in 1896 and who delighted in the warm, dry conditions, ideal for rock climbing. Naismith wrote a short account of the visit in the SMCJ:

At Whitsuntide [in] 1896, Mr Douglas and I paid a first visit to Wastdale Head, where were gathered a large number of climbers. We received a kindly welcome, which made us feel at home at once, and added greatly to the pleasure of our trip ... Now that we have seen this climbers' El Dorado with our own eyes, we both confirm heartily all that has been said or sung in its praise. Indeed, the half was not told us. As compared with Sligachan, Wastwater Hotel has a great advantage in being placed in the middle of the best climbing ground, instead of on the edge of it; and as most of the finest climbs are within an hour or an hour-and-a-half of the hotel, one can enjoy a grand day's scrambling, and get back in time for tea, and have a swim in the "beck" before dinner "forbye ..."

... If I might venture to compare the Wastdale climbing with the rock-work one usually gets in Scotland, I should say that the English standard of difficulty seems to be a little the higher. Steep passages, which in Scotland would likely have been left alone, have here been reconnoitred, and studied, and worked out, until they were made to go; and now everybody does them, ladies included. (1896)

Raeburn had caught a train from Penrith to Keswick on Christmas Eve and then walked through Borrowdale and over Styhead Pass to reach the distant valley of Wastdale, or Wasdale as it is now more usually spelt. He wrote:

A couple of most enjoyable days were spent in sampling Great Gable and the Pillar Rock ... a climber is sure of a hearty welcome from the first-rate climbers and thorough sportsmen who make Wastdale Head Hotel their Headquarters at Christmas or Easter. (1898)

It was probably on this occasion that he met the pioneering Abraham brothers, George and Ashley, from Keswick, and OG Jones himself. Jones

Fig 1

Climbers on Napes Needle. Early in his career Raeburn made a daring solo attempt but wisely backed off the awkward moves onto the summit block. Naturally, he returned and completed the climb in 1897. Photo: FRCC Archive

was staying at the hotel for the final week of December. One of the climbs that Raeburn repeated was the famous Napes Needle on Great Gable, first soloed by W Haskett Smith in 1886. Raeburn found the top part sufficiently difficult to require help, in the form of the head of an ice-axe used as a supplementary foothold. [Fig 1]

In 1900, after his summer fortnight in the Dolomites with W Douglas (see chapter 21), Raeburn repeated his trip to Wasdale in November, this time in the company of Harry Lawson:

> *Leaving Edinburgh by the 2 pm Express to Carlisle, one can dine on board and be deposited at Keswick in time to walk up to the head of Borrowdale by 9 pm the same night. This we did, and were surprised to find how quickly and easily the nine-mile walk was reeled off.* (1901)

They climbed on Gable Crag on the northern face of Great Gable, finding the rock smeared in ice, and descended Eagle's Nest Arête to reach Napes Needle, which they climbed, before making an ascent of Needle Ridge. On the Needle, Raeburn gained some assistance from Lawson's shoulder at the awkward spot where he had previously used the ice-axe for aid.

The following day they were joined by William Ling and George Glover, English members of the SMC, who in July 1899 had made the first ascent of Engineer's Chimney (Very Severe), a deep cleft on Gable Crag. Ling wrote: [Fig 2]

> *Left Seathwaite at 8.30 on one of the few fine days of this month. On reaching Scawfell [sic] we found all white with fog crystals and the rocks all glazed, and a cold N. wind blowing. Many of the more difficult climbs were out of the question, so we tackled Deep Ghyll, which proved quite sporting in ice. Raeburn and Glover were not content until they had done Professor's Chimney and the short route of the Pinnacle, Lawson and I going on to the summit for the view, which was very extensive in the strong sunlight. We descended by the N. Climb and hastened back to Seathwaite [at] 3 pm and left at 4 pm to catch the evening train from Keswick.* (Ling's Diary, Book 2)

Two other leading English climbers of the period, William Cecil Slingsby and Godfrey A Solly, were well known to Harold Raeburn, as they were also

Fig 2

Glover, Ling, Raeburn, Lawson. Seathwaite, 1900. Photo: Alpine Club

Fig 3

Raeburn's smart headgear marks him out at the FRCC Dinner where he was the guest speaker. George Abraham is seated second left, his brother Ashley at the opposite end of the front row. Godfrey Solly, bearded, is in the front row behind the coiled rope. WC Slingsby is behind Raeburn and JR Corbett two spaces to the left of Slingsby. Photo: Alan Craig, courtesy of the FRCC

[Fig 3] members of the SMC; indeed, Solly was the Club President from 1910 to 1912. Slingsby was a spirited Yorkshire squire who completed many Alpine routes but whose greatest love was the exploration of the mountains of Norway, where he eventually accumulated over 50 first ascents.

In October 1901, Ling records that he was joined by George Glover, John Bell and Raeburn for a wet day on Great Gable. Rock climbing was curtailed, but they ascended Doctor's Chimney on the gloomy Gable Crag and then descended the left-hand branch of Central Gully in the mist. This was also the year when Raeburn joined the Edinburgh Skating Club and the new Raeburn brewery opened at Craigmillar.

In October 1903, Ling and Raeburn repeated a couple of Lakeland's hardest rock climbs. After days of continuous rain, they were fortunate to have fine weather for their walk from Seathwaite Farm to Styhead Tarn and thence to the Napes cliffs on Great Gable where they ascended Arrowhead Ridge (Very Difficult). They then descended the top part of Eagle's Nest Ridge where Raeburn put on his kletterschuhe and, in Ling's words, 'went down to prospect', with his friend giving him a top-rope: 'I paid out 70 ft of rope and then he returned, coming up without the slightest assistance.' Solly regarded the Direct start as having such a narrow margin of safety that 'no-one should climb it unless he had previously reconnoitered it with a rope from above'. Undaunted, Raeburn now accepted the challenge of leading the Direct route. They descended a gully to reach the foot of the climb and roped up:

> *Then Raeburn started off to the left to the very edge of the arête. The holds are minute but the rock is good, and he was very soon in the Eagle's Nest. A pull up on the hands to a platform higher up is the next proceeding and then comes a nasty bit, very sensational with scanty holds sloping the wrong way. However, they did not seem difficult to my leader, who simply romped up. I followed in boots with the security of the rope, but there is no doubt that klettershuhe are the correct footgear for the climb. It is very straight up and sensational and is only justifiable under good conditions, such as we had.* (Ling's Diary, Book 5)

Solly's ascent of this route has been described as the 19th century equivalent of Johnny Dawes's first ascent of the terrifying Indian Face on Clogwyn

Du'r Arddu in 1986, and it was the first British climb to be given a grading of Very Severe. To lead this climb without protection required nerves of steel and a cool head, as well as technical ability. Clearly, Raeburn possessed all of these. It remains a stunning and airy line, although these days it can be protected with small wires.

Then the pair traversed to the foot of Kern Knotts where Ling took a belay at the foot of Kern Knotts Crack.

Then, half-kneeling, I took Raeburn on my shoulder and straightened up. He then mounted onto my head (the scarpetti were quite soft) and pulled up into the crack above. He ascended some distance and I followed. I tried hard to get up by myself but it was no use and Ling had to submit to the help of the rope. (ibid., p.12)

They then made their way back to Seathwaite 'after a capital day's work'.

Although Raeburn made a habit of regular rock climbing trips to the Lake District, it has proved impossible to comprehensively catalogue his visits, particularly for the next few years, as he tended to give the *SMCJ* editor details only about his alpine excursions.

He was there in October 1906 with Ling and TE Goodeve, climbing Keswick Brothers' route in icy conditions on Scafell and down-climbing Collier's route. Ling wrote that 'over the last bit Goodeve was lowered first, I followed and was pulled in by him, and Raeburn came last with the rope hitched'(ibid., p.12). Although Raeburn usually spent his winter months in Scotland, during January 1907 he visited Great End with the same party and they ascended an icy SE Gully in snowy conditions.

One of his regular venues was Pillar Rock in Ennerdale. The altitude and northerly aspect of the climbs here, particularly in anything but the most benign of weather conditions, add a serious feel to any undertaking, and the summit of the Rock can only be reached by the use of hands as well as feet. In the early days, there was a double tin box on the summit of Pillar Rock in which climbers would deposit their cards. In *Heart of Lakeland* (1908), LJ Oppenheimer records that this was blown away in a storm and the cards distributed about the nearby fells. However, it was replaced by a book into which climbers recorded their names and some assiduous research by the Fell and Rock Climbing Club's (FRCC) modern guidebook

Fig 4

Pages 4 and 5 of the Pillar summit book.
Photo: FRCC Archive

editor, Stephen Reid, shows that Raeburn was there alone on 5 May 1907. [Fig 4]

Unusually, he gives no details about his climbs, but it was perhaps on this occasion that he made a solo descent of the North-West Climb (Very Severe), perhaps with the purpose of an inspection prior to a later ascent. More about this below.

Raeburn's signature appears again on 21 October 1907 with Natalia Yovitchitch and a Miss Brown. They ascended by Central Jordan Climb (graded Difficult and first climbed by Haskett Smith in 1882) and descended the Old West Route (Moderate). Raeburn often climbed with Natalia (whose middle name was Rutherford after her great-grandfather Robert Rutherford, a Scot).

The last entry in the book is dated 11 July 1908, after an ascent of the North-West Climb in wet conditions.

Ling describes this ascent in gripping detail. What a difference there is between a delightful ascent of warm, dry rocks and the same climb in cold, wet, intimidating conditions. The notional grade counts for nothing as your resolve chills and you lose trust in the holds. Imagine, then, that you have no nuts, no camming devices, no nylon ropes, no harness, no helmet … just a thick, hawser-laid natural-fibre rope knotted round your waist and the rocks 'greasy and slippery':

> *Raeburn called me and I traversed along to him. Standing on a small ledge where, however, I had good handholds, I gave him a shoulder, but it was no good. The rocks were impossible and he returned … After some time he called, and I followed with the two sacks. It was extremely steep, but I climbed up to a square corner with a sloping floor. This was overhanging above and it was necessary to traverse to the right … There was practically no hold and I should have been off if it had not been for the rope. I had to go back and reconsider.* (Diary, Book 7)

With the assistance of the rope, Ling managed 'with great exertion' to reach Raeburn's position. 'How he got up this place I do not know, nor is it a place to be repeated.' Then, after an 'ingenious variation of delicate balancing', and after five hours on the rope, they emerged on the top of Low Man. Ling's summary was that 'the wet state of the rocks had made the climb much more difficult and dangerous', and that neither of them wished to repeat the climb. They finally reached the Wastdale Head Hotel at 6.30 pm, 'wet through'. They walked over the fells back to Keswick the following day.

On 11 October Ling and Raeburn, accompanied by Ruth Raeburn and John Bell and his wife, had another wet outing when they climbed Oblique Chimney (Very Difficult), on Gable Crag. On 5 September the following year (1909), Ruth, who was eight years younger than Harold, again accompanied her brother, Ling and Frank Goggs for an ascent of Scafell's Moss Ghyll. Formed by aficionados in 1906, the FRCC is historically linked with the Lake District, and Harold Raeburn was invited to represent the SMC at their third annual dinner at Coniston on 20 November 1909. After the Great War, he was made an Honorary Member of the Club.

Raeburn, Vice-President of the SMC at the time, was called upon by George Seatree, President of the FRCC, to propose the toast of the evening's affair. In the FRCC *Journal* it was recorded that Raeburn received loud and warm applause for his speech, during which he commented on the compact nature of the Lake District and said that the SMC was not quite in the same happy position because of the relative inaccessibility of the Scottish mountains and the 'sporadic' nature of their climbs.

He went on to say that he had a deep regard for the Lake District and, indeed, it had been the location of his first introduction to climbing for its own sake. In those days he was a hillwalker (which he hoped he always would be) and knew nothing about rock climbing. One day, on the top of Great Gable, he met a clergyman and asked him if he knew anything about the Needle Rock. Encouraged by the response, Raeburn made his solitary way down to find the famous Napes Needle. It was near dusk but he attempted it anyway, succeeding as far as the shoulder below the top block where, he was bound to confess, the rest of the way looked rather unattractive. He dithered; it was getting darker and a nearby raven seemed to be croaking, 'Don't, don't,' so he took the bird's advice[1] and climbed down, somewhat chastened by the experience. All this occurred several years before his ascent in 1897.

Harold also commended the FRCC on the quality of their *Journal*, which appeared with great regularity, contained a large amount of valuable

---

1   Raeburn also takes the Raven's advice on the Meije in 1919, but he refuses the ill-omen on the Black Shoot.

material and was finely illustrated, and which he rated the best of all such publications. In conclusion, he proposed the following tribute:

> *You are a young club, only 3 years old. My club is practically of age and I am very glad indeed to be able to convey to you—a baby, but a very active baby—the fraternal greetings of an elder brother, and I shall convey to the members of my own club when I meet them, the very cordial way in which you have received me. I wish long life and prosperity to the Fell Walking and Rock Climbing Club of the English Lake District.* (FRCC Journal, 1910)

The following winter, 1909-10, Harold had his serious accident on Stùc a' Chroin (see chapter 19); however, he did not allow it to curtail his summer Alpine season and, later, another formidable excursion to the Lake District with Ling and George Sang. On that occasion, in October, after catching trains from Edinburgh to Penrith and Keswick, and hiring cycles, Raeburn's account for Sunday 23 says:

> *L. proposes to take us to Raven Crag. Went up the slopes of Glaramara ... right up to Great End almost ... Sprinkling Tarn to Styhead ... to Kern Knotts ... we did not try the crack ... went along to Napes ... there Sang led up the top stone very well, a horrid wind blowing. I also went up. I had a look at ... [the] traverse, which has no nail marks on it. It could be done fairly well in kletters but would be best tried with a rope thrown over ... came down the long side of it and then Sang led up the Needle Arête.*[2] *S. and I went down the Eagle Nest Ridge Ord. ... went down to Wastdale Head Hotel having a look first at the Church ...*[3]

Raeburn was meticulous in recording, often in the margins of his journals, all sorts of small details, usually relating to time. For example, the following morning:

---

2   At this point Ling left the party, presumably to return home.
3   From Raeburn's notebook in the SMC Archive. This particular notebook has survived because it was found among the effects of W Ling when he died in 1954. See also Ling Diaries 9, 22.

Breakfast promised for 7; not ready till 7.50. Left 8.30 and crossed footbridge ... Brown Tongue in 45 mins ... 10.20 foot of Deep Gill [sic]. Mists swirling round summits and crags ... Scafell cliffs look very severe ... I surprised a fox. It was within 1 yard, a big and very light yellow beast. It was watching a shepherd and his dog on the other side of the cirque. Fine moraines here, one might easily expect to see a little glacier clinging round the base of the crags of Scafell and the Pikes.

They climbed Slingsby's Chimney from Steep Ghyll with mist swirling round, Raeburn remarking that 'It seemed a good deal easier than when I did it alone, and I understand new holds have been found and developed since that date.' They then descended Moss Ghyll, Raeburn commenting that this was his first descent after two previous ascents, considering it much easier and safer coming down, although the Collie step (an infamous hold chipped by Norman Collie with an ice-axe on the first ascent), was perhaps a little harder coming down. They then went to the top of Scafell, taking 10 minutes to go both up and down Broad Stand before returning, over the hills, to Seathwaite and thence to Keswick where they missed the train. It cost them 35 shillings to hire a motor car to drive the 18 miles to Penrith to catch the train home to Edinburgh. All the fine detail of times of ascent might suggest that Raeburn was rather obsessive, but it was by no means an unusual practice. Geoffrey Winthrop Young did exactly the same in his own journals, for example, recording times for each stage of his ascent of the West Face of the Zinalrothorn in 1910; it merely provides a yardstick to gauge personal performance over the years.

It is known (Perrin, 1993) that Raeburn also stayed, when in the beautiful valley of Buttermere, at Lower Gatesgarth, the holiday home of the eccentric Arthur Cecil Pigou (1877–1959). It is thought that Raeburn explored on Eagle Crag, Birkness Combe—one of Cumbria's biggest cliffs with the promise of large raptors, an attraction that Raeburn could scarcely ignore.

Pigou, the son of an army officer, began lecturing at Cambridge University in 1901 and was awarded the Chair of Political Economy in 1908. The idiosyncratic Professor Pigou appreciated the beauty of mountains and men, as proclaimed by the photographs round his rooms. Conventional honours were regarded with humorous contempt; during the War he had acquired various medals and ribbons, which he used to confer on visitors to reward achievements, such as *distinguished incompetence*, in hillwalking and rock climbing (Champernowne, 1959).

In a diary entry for Saturday, 14 September 1912, Raeburn describes another visit to the Lake District which started when he 'left [Edinburgh] with motorcycle on board coal train for Carlisle'. He then used the motorcycle to ride to the Buttermere Hotel where he rendezvoused with Ling. On 15 September, 'a beautiful day', they made their way to remote Pillar Rock, [Fig 5] where the fine north face provides some of the longest and most exposed routes on the mountain. The altitude and northerly aspect of the climbs, particularly in anything but the most benign of weather conditions, adds a serious feel to any undertaking, perhaps comparable with one of Glencoe's north-facing buttresses.

Their target was North-East Climb (Mild Severe), first climbed by the Abraham brothers a few months earlier and which Ling had already ascended a couple of times. Raeburn described it as 'a very good and ingenious climb'. Ling notes that, near the top of the route, 'after doing the wall above the groove we went straight up the corner instead of taking the usual route'. At this point the pair separated as Ling had to return to Buttermere, and Raeburn decided to solo another climb.

Most climbers would feel a knot of apprehension in their stomach as they consider the wisdom of proceeding. Being alone at this point is a true test of character for, when doubt starts to niggle, there is no one to turn to for discussion and reassurance. The first few feet of climbing might seem reasonable but, as the ground recedes below your feet, your courage is tested ten-fold as an invisible wall of fear bars your progress. Now, you stand or fall entirely on your own resolve and route-finding and, hesitant and unsure, it is only too easy to find multiple reasons to avoid the challenge. Never have you felt so alone or in need of a word of encouragement. How you miss the welcome sight of a rope, that friendly umbilicus of safety. The battle now is within your mind.

To press on requires a unique willpower, a steely control of nerve, and Harold Raeburn, conditioned by many such solitary ascents, was, in this sense, on familiar territory. Although solo climbing was roundly condemned as extremely foolhardy by the traditionalists (and implicitly by Harold himself in *Mountaineering Art*, though probably with tongue in cheek), Raeburn would have been acutely aware of both his own abilities and the risks that

Fig 5

Pillar Rock basking in sunlight: scene of Raeburn and Ling's ascent of NE Climb which Raeburn described as 'a very good and ingenious climb'. Photo: Stephen Reid

he was taking, but the elevated danger also induces absolute concentration of the mind. In turn, the 'adrenalin rush' brings about a heightened state of euphoria—a powerful drug indeed. He records that he then ascended the West Climb, by which he probably meant that from the top of Low Man he joined what is now called the Old West Route (Moderate), to the summit of High Man.

The topography of Pillar Rock is complicated and route-finding, particularly in mist, requires competence and experience as apparently encouraging descent lines end above vertical gullies. Walker's Gully, for example, is not a route of descent for walkers but was named after a youth called Walker, who plunged down it to his death on Good Friday in 1883. However, Raeburn was familiar with the terrain, having previously declined to descend Walker's Gully on 9 July 1905. On that occasion, he and Ling had just climbed an unnamed route (which, from the description, sounds like Savage Gully, graded Mild Very Severe). There is a rock feature on this part of the cliff called 'The Nose', and the pair descended to it, where Raeburn then completed the Hand Traverse (Hard Severe) 'quite easily in scarpetti' while Ling secured the rope.

On the present occasion, he chose to down-climb Central Jordan Climb to reach the Shamrock traverse and rejoin the High Level Traverse and Black Sail Pass back to the hotel. Also staying at the legendary Wastdale Head Hotel were Siegfried Herford, a rising rock climbing star, HB Gibson and WB Brunskill, among others. Raeburn wrote that: 'They all have rather more than a respect for the NW, however. Had heard of my descent alone and seemed to think it a bit risky. It was not, of course, as I did it.'

Raeburn must have been referring to an earlier solo descent but what did he mean by the initials NW? It could have been either Botterill's 1906 North-West Climb or the easier New West Climb. Stephen Reid, who has an unrivalled knowledge of the mountain and its history, is of the opinion that the New West Climb was never abbreviated to NW and, even if Raeburn himself had done so, it was highly unlikely that Herford and company would have had 'more than a respect' for it. Having done the route several times himself, Stephen is sure that Raeburn did indeed descend the North-West Climb, one of the hardest routes of the day. It should be remembered that climbers were very aware of, and comfortable with, the necessity to be able to down-climb to extricate themselves from tricky situations and Raeburn himself wrote in his book that 'for the expert, climbing down is easier, much quicker, and very much less fatiguing. If the climb is steep and difficult, climbing down is also much safer, as a rope can be used for security'. It is open to conjecture whether he was able to use a rope for security, but this would have had to be at least 100 ft.

As for risk, some might question Raeburn's logic and the dogmatic nature of his assertion. The assessment of risk is a very personal business and he was accustomed to solitary wanderings on dangerous ground, something that was perhaps not appreciated by the others. However, these climbs were on a steep, isolated rock face, and any slip would inevitably have been fatal. This was one of his last visits to the Lake District before First World War intervened and many young climbers (including Herford) lost their lives.

During the War Raeburn managed some trips with his old friend Ling. In August 1915 they visited Gable Crag again. They rejected Smuggler's Chimney (Very Severe) as 'wet and slimy' before climbing to the Westmoreland Cairn 'by a steep chimney and face with excellent rock. Then we went down the ordinary Eagle's Nest climb,[4] lunched and then went up Abbey Ridge.[5] 'This is extremely steep but the rock is fine'. They then went down to Wasdale for tea.

The following year, in September 1916, he made an attempt on Birkness Chimney (Hard Severe), having approached Buttermere by rowing up Crummock Water with a party that included Ruth. It ended in retreat, but with RP Bicknell he climbed the strenuous Birkness Gully (Severe), which was 'wet and difficult'.

[Fig 6] In July 1917 Ling and Raeburn enjoyed good weather for more rock climbing. What follows is largely taken from Ling's diaries (Book 12):

> *July 14, Raven Crag Gully, Glaramara. Very fine morning. With H Raeburn from Thorneythwaite. Up into the Combe to Dove's Nest. Into the crack and up to the main cave. We had a candle but no lantern so did not explore to any extent. Up buttress to finish. Then across Combe Ghyll to Raven Crag Gully, which was wonderfully dry and we were able to do some of the pitches in the gully itself. At the top pitch, HR traversed to the chock stones while I went straight up.*

---

4   Eagle's Nest Ridge via the West Chimney, Hard Difficult.
5   Presumably, Abbey Buttress, V. Diff, first ascent 1909 by F Botterill and J De Vere Hazard.

Fig 6

Raeburn and Ling on the slopes of Glaramara, October 1910, one of few unselfconscious photos of the pair. The accidental light penetrating the lower right corner of the image gives it an ethereal feel. Photo: G Sang, SMC Image Archive

The FRCC 1968 guide to Borrowdale describes Dove's Nest as 'unlike anything else in the Lake District … a great rock face has slipped bodily forwards and downwards; instead of crashing into scree at the base of the cliff, its fall was arrested and it now leans back against the main face, leaving cavities of all sizes …' providing the opportunity for unique rock climbing akin to Crypt Route on Church Door Buttress in Glen Coe, although less committing.

> *July 15, Mouse Ghyll & Buttress. Same party. Another fine day. Through the woods almost to Grange then up to foot of Ghyll. We climbed up the main pitch but did not like it so went down and made a new route up the buttress. Very steep rock and heather and quite difficult. We then came down the gully and traversed in to the top of the main pitch. HR went down and came up again without difficulty, and we then both went down and returned to Thorneythwaite. (Ling, Book 12.)*

Mouse Ghyll is on a broken crag on the NE slopes of Maiden Moor and was first climbed by Slingsby/Topham in 1897; the direct finish by the Abraham brothers became the first recorded VS in Borrowdale, and it would seem that it was easily within Raeburn's ability.

> *July 21, The Screes. C Gully (part) & buttress. With H Raeburn from Wastwater Hotel. Leave 10. Foot of gully via Wasdale Hall 12.15. In spite of the dry weather the gully was still wet and slimy and water was coming over most of the pitches. We started up the left wall and after a number of pitches which were not easy and required care we came to the seventh, a cave which had to be turned on the left by a crack with much water. We had a good look at it and then went out up a slide on the left on to the buttress, where we had some steep heather. We traversed back off the buttress above two pitches but the next one looked very severe so we lunched (2.15) and then went out this time on our right (true left) on to the buttress, where steep heather and rock took us to the top. A fine view and fine rock scenery in the gully. A good walk along the top (fox and cub) down to the Burnmoor track, a bathe in the river and to the hotel 6pm. (ibid., p.67)*

The 1996 FRCC guide describes the crag as 'generally disappointing but does provide some traditional wet and dark gully climbs' typical of the period. Graded VS, OG Jones and HC Bowen made the first ascent in 1897. Jones described it as 'a deadly place'.

July 22, Scawfell. N Climb, Pinnacle from Deep Ghyll. With H Raeburn. Fine morning. Leave Wasdale 10.30. Styhead 11.30. Leave rucksacks by Sprinkling Tarn. Lunch 12.50. Pikes 1.50. We climbed up by N Climb, I leading, and then on to Pisgah where we watched three men on Slingsby's Chimney. Then down Deep Ghyll to Jones' Climb [graded Severe in 1996]. HR led and went up easily in rubbers [presumably an early use of plimsolls]. I brought the boots in the sack but sent them up on the rope over the hard bit above the belay. The rocks were beautifully dry and warm and I got up more easily than last time. The climb took us 50 mins. We went down the Broad Stand and had a hot walk back to our sacks. Then went down Grains Ghyll and a fine bathe in a pool near Stockley Bridge and on to Thorneythwaite 7.40. (ibid.)

August 25, Birkness Combe High Stile. With H Raeburn from Buttermere. We joined a large party from Gatesgarth, five Bicknells, two Challoners, Miss Nielson and R. Graham. We went up to the combe. Bicknell, Peter and I on one rope, Raeburn & Graham on another did the Mitre. Then the four did the slabs and the three seniors the Oxford & Cambridge buttress by the ridge finish, very hard, while I went down and took two heavy sacks to the top. After a meal we separated. HR and I by Bleaberry Combe to Buttermere, the others over High Crag to Gatesgarth. Next day was terribly wet and all we could do was to walk to Warnscale Bottom to the falls. (ibid.)

Raeburn was back in the Lake District on at least one occasion in 1918, as a letter[6] to Godfrey Solly indicates:

---

6 The letter to Solly can be found in the Raeburn Archive in the National Library of Scotland, Acc 11538/122.

> 18 Bruntsfield Avenue
> Edinburgh
> 9th Feb. 1920
>
> Dear Solly,
>
> I have yours with Meldrum's application form for the SMC, which I have signed with pleasure and return herewith. I climbed with him in Skye in 1913 and also met him in 1918 when he led the ascent of the Engineer's chimney on Gable. I consider him one of the very best rock climbers I know. In normal and former times of course his Scottish snow climbs, or rather lack of them, would bar him, but I do not think the Committee will bother about that for a year or two at any rate. If he tackles Nevis at Easter under your auspices he begins high up on Scottish Snow.[7]
> I do not know if I shall be at the meet. Everything depends upon the Himalayan Expedition.
>
> I am
> Yours Sincerely
> Harold Raeburn

On one of these later visits to Lakeland, Harold met a young woman called Mabel M Barker. She wrote in the *Pinnacle Club Journal* (1932–4) of how she yearned to realise her 'wild and impossible dream' of rock climbing. She was an extremely keen fell-walker but 'met with no rock climbers in those days. I knew that they existed, but they were as the gods, and far beyond my ken'. Then:

> [O]nce, in an inn, I don't know when or where, I met a Mr Raeburn, and he, finding that I knew the fells, told me a thrilling yarn about a rock climb. Now I know that this was an incident on the first ascent of Central Buttress. Which of us would have been the more surprised, I wonder, to know that I myself should feel those rocks one day, make, in fact, in two hours, with CD Frankland, its fourth ascent? (In August 1925).

---

[7] Bernard Meldrum's application to join the SMC was successful.

Central Buttress on Scafell was first climbed in April 1914 by a party led by Siegfried Herford, fresh from a trip to Skye, and it immediately became the most difficult rock climb in Britain.

On 19 October 1919, Raeburn, Ling and W Crowder climbed Stack Ghyll (Very Severe) on the 400-500ft Warnscale face of Haystacks, another of the area's hardest climbs and which is no doubt rarely climbed in summer these days. The first ascent was made in December 1900 by LJ Oppenheimer and party, at a time when chimneys and gullies, rather than open faces, were the focus of attention. Ling describes the first pitch as 'very hard' and led by Raeburn 'in stockings ... seven pitches in all, all giving good climbing with much variety'. This was another remarkable tour-de-force by the 54-year-old Raeburn, particularly his lead of the final pitch on dubious rock. This was akin to soloing, given the lack of equipment at that time, but he seemed to thrive in these situations; it demonstrates his physical fitness and driven nature, and it would appear to be Raeburn's swansong in the Lake District.

SCOTLAND PART 2

13. 'SCOTTISH SNOW'   1905

[Fig 1]

By 1905 Raeburn had been a member of the SMC for nine years and had established a formidable reputation. Given this, it is not surprising that Willie Douglas was prepared to give him considerable space in the *SMCJ* to discuss the topic of 'Scottish Snow' (1905).

Part of Raeburn's aim was to bring the subject up to date, because Willie Naismith's article, 'Snowcraft in Scotland' (*SMCJ*, 1893), had been published 12 years earlier. Raeburn pays tribute to it but notes that it is 'long out of print'. He aims to explore 'the results obtained' from the advice offered by Naismith, and also try to summarise the experiences of the Club during 12 years 'of snow work and snowy conditions … scattered throughout the articles and notes … in the *Journal*'; an ambitious project involving considerable scholarship and analytical ability.

Raeburn acknowledges his debt to Naismith who, unlike Claude Wilson in *Mountaineering* (1893)[1] or the unnamed author of the Badminton volume (1892)[2] on mountaineering, does not adopt 'an apologetic tone … with regard to this country as a possible school for real Alpine climbing'. Naismith, Raeburn says, 'claimed for British winter climbing that it … approached to good summer work in the Alps', but Raeburn wants to go further and say that:

> [W]inter mountaineering in Scotland is in many respects a better training and a more strenuous sport than most of the ordinary Swiss

---

1   Wilson was President of the Alpine Club 1929–32. His book was an instruction manual for novices.
2   In fact authored by Clinton Dent, who made the first ascent of the Grande Aiguille du Dru 1878; he also climbed in the Caucasus.

Fig 1

Raeburn cutting steps up a slope on Beinn Achaladair. Photo: SMC Image Archive.

Fig 2

Raeburn demonstrating good balance on Spearhead Arête, Beinn Narnain. Harry MacRobert was in the party but details are lacking. Photo: SMC Image Archive

work, where one plods behind a guide up a well-known route by what is often a plainly marked track.*

This view is a considerable development in thinking about Scottish winter mountaineering, which was then starting to be seen as a unique form of mountaineering in itself and not just as training for the Alps. Raeburn admits that Scotland doesn't have glaciers, icefalls, crevasses and seracs, 'but the ever varying condition of the snow on slopes, on rocks, and in the gullies provides plenty of exercise for study and skill …'

There follows a diversion into the 'great spike-versus-pick controversy' which emerged from Naismith's article. Naismith (op. cit. p.165) maintained 'that in crossing a piece of unmitigated ice, where it is preferable to prevent a slip than hope to check it after it has occurred, it is better to hold the axe as if in glissading, and dig the spike firmly into the ice about the level of the thigh'. Raeburn (op. cit. p.286) endorses this view. Here it is obvious that the lesson to be conveyed to the novice on ice '… is the necessity for *balancing out*'. In other words, if the climber leans forward to use the pick of his axe for balance this will adversely alter the angle of his boot on the step and make a slip more likely. The important point Raeburn is making here is that 'balance is the fundamental of good, i.e. *safe*, climbing … on ice or rocks'. [Fig 2]

Raeburn says that his article is not written 'for the expert' and that he does not wish to pose as an authority on the behaviour of snow, but he is concerned by the number of young climbers who go out in winter 'and do not know what can and what cannot be attempted in safety on the snow-clad face, or in the snowy and icy gully'. He urges caution in glissading gullies: one must know that the gully does not contain pitches and that it has a safe outflow free from boulder danger. If one cannot be sure that the slope is of the right angle and uniform, one should glissade in pitches using ice-axe belays between each. All good advice echoed by modern authorities (apart from the axe belays).

Concerning gullies, Raeburn is certain that 'attempting the ascent of an avalanche grooved gully, on a warm, muggy mid-day in late spring is not an advisable proceeding …' Here the crucial factor is really the temperature; the fact that the gully has been the scene of an avalanche might actually make it safer.

At that time, as Raeburn points out, 'there are no records of accidents through the breaking away of cornices in this country; still we have heard rumours of narrow escapes due to this cause'. The fact that there had been no fatalities due to cornice collapse was probably due mainly to there being relatively few people climbing in winter in those days. The sight of a cornice at the top of a gully tends to deter climbers anyway. One suspects that this and luck played a part in keeping the statistics free from serious accidents, and the anecdotal evidence of near misses suggests this. The burden of Raeburn's discussion here suggests the avoidance of cornices, particularly on warmer days, and his advice is sound.

Talking about avalanche risk when climbing, Raeburn is careful to distinguish between solid snow avalanches and downpourings of hail or spindrift on slopes and in gullies: the former being very dangerous but the latter 'though perhaps unpleasant', 'not at all dangerous'. Here one might beg to differ: heavy and repeated downpours most certainly are dangerous. A really heavy downpour can sweep one away and less heavy downpours can make progress impossible.

However, Raeburn is right to suggest that the frozen, rock-hard slope is a much more prevalent source of danger; and he claims that it was 'probably this condition that caused the fatal accident to an ice-axeless tourist on Ben More [Crianlarich] ten or a dozen years ago'.[3] Raeburn accurately describes the freeze/thaw cycle which leads to the creation of hard, icy snow (névé), and he is correct when he says that, without an axe, 'Even the ascent of an easy angle becomes under these circumstances difficult, and if the angle is steep ... becomes well-nigh impossible.'

'Angle' bulks large in Raeburn's discussion of Scottish snow. He claims to have 'examined and read every article and note in the ... *Journal* since its commencement' in January 1890. 'Averaging all the recorded angles of snow slopes on faces and in gullies' (and ignoring obvious exaggerations), he claims 'the figure of 47°... as the average angle of a steep snow slope'. Raeburn guesses that 'without a clinometer', the inexperienced would

---

3   In the 1949 edition of the *District Guide to the Southern Highlands*, JDB Wilson notes: 'Many years ago one of a party without ice-axe slipped over some small rocks on the north side of this bounding edge and was killed. The place where the body was found is marked by an iron cross'. Oddly enough, Willie Douglas, writing in 1894, says that the incident happened 'some 20 years ago' (*SMCJ*). Wilson's vague 'many years ago' is better than Raeburn's '10 or 12 years ago'! Writing in 1905 he is approximately 20 years out, an unusual lapse in accuracy.

probably guess at 57°. He believes, presumably on the authority of his own experience, that snow will not 'stay long on any extent of slope at an angle exceeding 55°'. But, he goes on, 'under a cornice or in a narrow chimney … any angle up to 90° may be found but only for a few feet'. Whether Raeburn is right about this is not the present point. From the perspective of trying to understand the man, what is interesting is that Raeburn is taking a scientific interest in snow's propensity to lie on steep slopes. He has not merely thought about his own considerable experience, but has taken the time and trouble to look through fourteen years' worth of SMCJ material, so that his conclusion can be as broad as possible; he has a scientist's respect for evidence.

One would have thought that Raeburn would go on at once to discuss the topic of avalanches, but perhaps guided by Naismith's article, he deviates briefly to mention snow formation on 'arêtes'. Naismith says that he 'has never succeeded in finding a satisfactory specimen [of snow arête] in Scotland' (op. cit. p.163). This, according to Raeburn, was because in the 1880s and early '90s, arêtes 'were not usually climbed in winter'. This has all changed by the time Raeburn is writing: there are plenty of snow arêtes in Glencoe, Nevis, Skye and Torridon, for example. He thinks that these are often soft, but sometimes hard, and 'do not usually present any difficulty except when a violent wind is blowing'. Here Raeburn seems to ignore what he himself has said about the freeze/thaw cycle. He is right about the existence of snow arêtes, but partly mistaken about their consistency. There is no reason why the snow on sharp edges should not behave in the same way as elsewhere, so this passage seems less convincing.

Returning to the much more important topic of large, dangerous masses of snow, Raeburn discusses avalanches. These, according to him, are not often seen, but some parties have provided anecdotal evidence. Raeburn himself saw a large avalanche on Aonach Beag while climbing the NE Ridge with the Clarks,[4] and much earlier he also saw and was nearly caught up in a serious avalanche on Creag Meagaidh. In any case the presence of debris confirms the fact that 'large and dangerous avalanches do often fall'.

---

4 See Chapter 11. One can't be quite sure about when Raeburn composed his thoughts on Scottish snow.

He notes that 'In the upper corrie of Nevis, the avalanche debris at the beginning of June cannot be much less than 100 feet in depth'; an estimated figure but one which at least gives an appropriate sense of scale.

Raeburn thinks that these dangerous avalanches, on Nevis, Meagaidh and elsewhere are 'usually caused by the breaking away of cornices', but he also notes that 'sometimes a surface layer of the snow will suddenly peel off a face'. And he goes on to give a classic description of the formation of a windslab crack—he doesn't call it this and his description ignores the action of the wind—but that is what is described. The climber in these circumstances should take Naismith's advice and cut footholds in the underlying surface. Raeburn seems to pay too little attention to causes of avalanche not related to cornice collapse, but at least he is aware of the danger of layers of snow cracking and breaking away.

Probably for the sake of completeness, but also perhaps because he cannot quite shake off the influence of the Alps, Raeburn includes bergschrunds and crevasses in his discussion. There are no 'ice bergschrunds in Scotland' (because we have no glaciers), 'but very colourable imitations' caused by 'the melting of snow, or ice, in immediate contact with the heated rock'. Raeburn has seen one at the base of Observatory Buttress 'at least 40 feet deep by 8 to 10 feet wide'. The implication is so obvious that Harold doesn't point out the moral. As to 'crevasses', plainly there are none of the glacial type in Scotland, but they are referred to in a less formal sense in the *SMCJ*. For example, Gilbert Thomson (*SMCJ*, 1895) mentions the sort of deep crack one finds behind a cornice which has partially broken away; Fraser Campbell mentions the bergschrund type (ibid.) and Naismith mentions what is, one assumes, a cleft in a snow bridge over a gorge, the weakness in the bridge being concealed by soft snow, in the manner of an Alpine glacier with concealed crevasses.

Turning to a more important matter, Raeburn notes that cornices 'of great size and exquisite beauty' may be found on any Scottish mountain 'possessing a steep rock face'. Size varies according to the height and aspect of the cliff and the quantity of snow in any winter. Analysing reports in the *SMCJ*, which are only estimates, gives an average dimension of 20 ft in height with a ten-foot overhang. These dimensions are sometimes exceeded, but if so, they make an ascent virtually impossible. Raeburn mentions the case of two Alpine pioneers making the first ascent of Tower Gully on Nevis who actually burrowed through a huge cornice, taking two days to do it, and descending to Fort William at night between shifts. But as he drily remarks: 'such a feat is too heroic for most'. For a scientific view, one of the observers at the summit observatory told Raeburn that he had measured a cornice at the head of Observatory Gully which was 40 ft in height; and here again we have the contrast between hearsay and actual measurement, which Raeburn rightly thinks important.

Climbers of Raeburn's era seemed fixated on glissading. Almost every article about climbing in winter mentions the glissade with which the day ended, and the disappointment felt by the writer when no glissade can be got is almost palpable. Raeburn wonders why 'the apparently simple and childish pastime of sliding down snow should possess such fascination'. The answer is simple: try it and then 'explanation is no longer asked for'. He says it is the same with tobogganing and 'the highest development of the glissade—skiing' (to which, nowadays, we must add snowboarding).

Raeburn categorises the glissade: sitting and standing. He dissects every aspect of what is like a sport within a sport. He kept records: longest standing glissade in Scotland: 700 ft in Coire na Ciste, July 1903. Ten thousand feet of glissading in Norway—better than the Alps 'in the ordinary climbing season'. He provides instruction: don't lean too heavily, if possible not at all, on the ice-axe, 'which is extended behind like a third leg'. Standing like this he has gone for 'hundreds of feet' in Norway, where he 'has seen young Norwegian ladies gliding down a steep snow slope on their feet, with ease and grace, with nothing at all in their hands', 'the result of long practice on skis'. He gives advice to beginners: 'select easy places at first'. He understands gullies: 'the snow in a narrow gully is ... usually hollowed out in the centre by the stream below and ... the place where the snow roof will be weakest will be just at the top of a steep pitch or concealed waterfall'. Glissader beware: here is the place to use rope and belay if unsure. Raeburn is patently keen to teach safe methods. The safest method of braking is to have the spike of the axe behind one with the forward hand holding the shaft palm up, and the rear hand palm down. Like this, 'immense brake power may be obtained by widening the space between the hands and raising the body on the lower arm' (remember that Raeburn is assuming the use of a very long axe). This method is much better than using the pick, or worse, the blade [adze], the use of either being prone to result in the axe being wrenched from the slider's grasp. Raeburn supports his advice with instructive photographs. Above all, his instruction and advice are based on extensive experience.

As to length of glissades in Scotland, 'these are often better and longer than can be obtained in the Alps in summer'. The longest recorded being an estimated 2,500ft on the descent of Ben More. Raeburn also documents all the examples he gives with accurate references: 'Easter 1895, on Nevis: 2,000ft; Vol II, p.80; Ben Doran: 1,000ft; Vol II, p.83 etc.' He claims there are 'numerous instances of from 500 to 800ft'.

Out of glissading comes skiing. Raeburn refers to Rickmers's well-known article (*SMCJ*, 1904).[5] There are very few mentions of skiing otherwise in the *SMCJ* to date. Naismith is the pioneer. Raeburn mentions Vol 2 p.89, in which Naismith describes his experience of 'long snow skates on 12 March 1892 on the Campsie Fells'. After that, there is no mention until 'Herr Rickmers took his party to Nevis at Easter, 1904', that party including Jane and Charlie Inglis Clark. JH Wigner 'has a note of an ascent of Ben Chonzie on 12 March 1904 (Vol. 8, p.133)'.

Raeburn himself had 'brought a pair ... from Norway' and had made several ascents in the Pentlands, the Braids and the Blackfords. He also notes that skis have been used by some North of England members in the Crossfell district. However, rather oddly, considering skiing's relationship to his beloved glissading, Raeburn considers that 'skis will but seldom be used in Scotland with advantage and enjoyment'. Why? Essentially because, he thinks, we don't get the right quality of snow often enough. On low ground, he argues, we get hardly any snow, while 'on the hills it is usually, if not soft and sticky, hard and icy'. What is needed is the sort of snow common in Norway: 'compact white powder'. He reckons we get this every ten years or so. But 'to become adept and enjoy this most interesting and fascinating sport to perfection', we need to go to 'countries less under the influence of Atlantic mildness and moisture'.[6]

It would be easy to think Raeburn's view very dated, and in a way it is, but we need to remember when he was writing. The Scottish ski

---

5 'Aquatic Sport on Ben Nevis'. Herr Willi Rickmers was a German member of the SMC (joined 1904) and the forerunner of a considerable tradition. Alas, as Campbell remarks: 'his membership was interrupted by WWI and terminated by WWII'.
6 Raeburn's comment might divide opinion among modern Scottish skiers.

industry in all its many manifestations did not really take off until after the Second World War, so for some 40 years Raeburn was not so far out. Most skiers at that time went abroad to ski. What Raeburn would have made of ski centres like Cairngorm, Glencoe, the Lecht and Aonach Mòr we shall never know, but he was certainly no spoil-sport; for example, he seems to have looked on the prospect of tourist development in the Caucasus with equanimity—a controversial view perhaps, but Raeburn was a businessman as well as a mountaineer. He also had an interest in and cared about the people who lived in mountainous areas; then, as now, they needed means of livelihood.

Glissading and skiing are not essential parts of mountaineering, though both can be employed to advantage. The topic of ice is different. Any four-season mountaineer has to come to terms with it. We have no glaciers in Scotland, but 'ice ... in many and varied forms, and its presence, or absence, may often mean the impossibility or otherwise of the climb'. The nomenclature which we use to discuss ice, Raeburn says, is in the process of being solidified, but 'ice in gullies is usually termed an icefall, but ... that term has quite a different meaning' in the Alps. 'Here the gully icefall is really a frozen waterfall' (which we would call an ice-pitch). Such 'icefalls' can give 'grand practice and experience in ice work, but should be attacked with discretion, and all precautions taken to guard against a slip'. Here again the emphasis on safety is apparent. For further reading he suggests Collie's article on winter climbing on the 'Screes' near Wasdale Head (SMCJ, 1895). And he gives another three references, including one to Snowdon (ibid.).

In order to climb ice or hard snow in Raeburn's day and for some 40-50 years after, one had to be able to cut steps. Raeburn thinks that step-cutting is easier in Scotland than the Alps: 'Although our slopes may be hard and steep, still they are only snow after all.' The trouble with his discussion here is that he makes only the crude distinction between 'ice' and 'snow'. He needs more categories. There is snow which one can kick steps up; there is névé which, if hard enough, can't be kicked up; there is water ice as discussed above; and there is glacial ice in the Alps and elsewhere abroad. Basically, Raeburn is arguing that Scottish snow is usually softer than that found in the Alps. This is a wild generalisation. Alpine snow in summer varies with the time of day: hard in the morning, soft in the afternoon.

If anything, one would think that Scottish snow is more constant. But of course, we are comparing the Alps in summer with Scotland in winter, and the comparison does not hold.

In the section entitled 'Snow General', Raeburn acknowledges that as climbers we spend a lot of time complaining about the snow conditions. What the climber wants, he argues, 'is snow fairly hard for the upward journey, fairly soft for the downward'. Again, this seems like a throwback to his Alpine experience and, in any case, is a dated view applicable to the climber without crampons. However, he is right in claiming that 'the same climb is never the same twice running'—even the grade may alter 'with astonishing celerity'—and that the time taken on a route is no guide to the ability of a party 'unless conditions are equal'. Editors of modern guidebooks would endorse this view.

'For six months of the year' the Scottish climber 'may find practically Alpine conditions': a debatable claim. Raeburn is thinking of the Alps in summer. Days of storm and spindrift from November to March are hardly the kind of Alpine experience he has in mind, but certainly towards the end of winter in Scotland there is a recognisable time of hard snow and sunlight very like a good Alpine summer. Raeburn thinks that at any season of the year, if one is attempting 'some of our highest north-east gullies, the ice-axe will be found indispensable'. And this accords with his own extensive experience.

Raeburn is well ahead of the general view of the time that saw winter climbing in Scotland as training for the Alps. He definitely sees it as a different experience in its own right. However, it *is* still good training for the Greater Ranges. The Scot 'will find that his expeditions on his native hills will stand him in good stead'. He will have learned how to use his ice-axe properly, and he will have learned 'a good deal about conditions on steeper slopes'.

Concerning technique, balance is everything: 'to stand up straight and to plant the feet firmly in the steps'. This prefigures WH Murray's 'standing foursquare to the slope and swinging from the shoulder'. Balance is the most valuable quality because it conserves energy—particularly important, according to Raeburn, on routes demanding the 'endurance of long continued exertion'. The climber has no need of 'coconut-like biceps'; 'man ... is not a monkey and ... the mountaineer travels, even though the angle approach 80°, mainly by means of his feet. We need to educate feet, hand, eye and brain'. There is, Raeburn insists, 'No better field for this education, apart altogether from the aesthetic joys to be obtained, than our Scottish Bens in their wintry garb of snow.' Balance, endurance and caution equal safety, and 'safe is the highest qualifying adjective we can bestow upon a mountaineer'. A vital sentence for understanding Harold Raeburn: his mountaineering life epitomises this.

14. THE COBBLER, CUILLIN EASTER MEET 1905–1906

Harold's friend William Clark gave him space at the end of his own article about 'The Mystery of Crois' (*SMCJ*, 1905) to record how he and Frank Goggs ascended the Central Buttress of that mountain. Raeburn said it was 'a steep and interesting little climb ... A good deal of time was spent trying to force the "absolute arête" near the top but eventually an escape was found to the left by a narrow, overhung grass ledge'.[1]

Turning from A' Crois to another Arrochar hill, Raeburn, writing an account in 'Excursions' in the *SMCJ* (1906), notes that in 1896 he and William Tough had been stopped about halfway up in the attempt to make a new route up the North Peak of the Cobbler.[2] However, 'on 30 October 1904, a large and merry party, including [Raeburn himself, John Rennie and] two ladies, had the pleasure of completing the climb'. Routes on this part of the Cobbler seem to criss-cross each other in a rather bewildering fashion. Raeburn's 'merry party' found that from the high point previously reached on the Halfway Terrace, gained this time via the easy start of Ramshead Gully at the left end of the terrace, they were able to climb 'a steep and difficult crack or chimney at the top of which the route meets the finish of Maclay's Crack'.[3] A short scramble led to the summit of the peak. Raeburn thought this was 'one of the longest and best climbs on the Cobbler' (referring, of course, to the whole route: the lower part climbed in

---

1   Raeburn's description appears word for word in the *The Arran, Arrochar and Southern Highlands Guide* of 1997, but the date given is wrong: it should be 23 May 1905, not 1895.
2   See Scotland Part I, Chapter I.
3   J Maclay and W Naismith, 25 May 1895.

1896 and the upper part just ascended). What Raeburn's party had done was to complete Recess Route by the addition of 'the steep chimney/groove of 'The Fold' which starts at the right end of the terrace', as previously noted by Tom Prentice. As Ken Crocket (2015) notes, when Jock Nimlin made the first complete ascent of Recess Route he was unaware of Raeburn's earlier ascent.

In the same note Raeburn draws attention to the 'Maclay/Workman Route'[4] on Central Buttress which joins the Raeburn/Rennie chimney [i.e. The Fold] just below the beginning of the interesting part'. It seems that the Maclay/Workman Route, traversing in from Great Gully on the right, actually climbed the upper and 'more interesting' part of the upper pitch of The Fold. However, Raeburn and his various companions do appear to have made the first complete ascent of Recess Route, but in two visits eight years apart. Nowadays, Recess Route is regarded as a classic Severe.

Turning to a more prolonged expedition, Raeburn has a long article in the January 1906 edition of the *SMCJ*, retrospectively describing his activities on the Easter Meet in April 1905 on Skye (*SMCJ*, 1906).[5] One suspects that experiences on Skye were special for Raeburn and that he wanted to do them full justice in a more fully developed and reflective article.

Raeburn thinks that the southern 'Coolins' are among the 'least accessible' Scottish hills. He thinks that there is no 'real rivalry between Mont Blanc by the ordinary route and the ice-clad Coolin arêtes in April'. He has previous experience of winter mountaineering on Skye and he recalls being spread-eagled on the 'Inaccessible' in 1903, and expecting 'to be converted to icicles' with his three companions and 'like the crew of the "Hesperus"[6] ... hurled away into Coruisk'. This year Easter was nearly a month later, but despite longer daylight and higher temperatures the wind blew 'with almost its old violence' and the snow and ice conditions were 'even more severe'.

The 1903 Meet was held at Sligachan, but this time William Clark had

---

4   Presumably Maclay/Workman Route is a variation of Maclay's Crack. It is not mentioned in the 1997 guidebook, but the SMC Guidebook article in *SMCJ* May 1901 p.186 and p.184 (diagram) clearly indicates that Maclay's Crack has two lines, but it does not mention Workman. He did climb with Maclay but their recorded route is on Central Peak (p.191). Perhaps Raeburn knew more.
5   The Meet took place from 21–24 April and is mentioned briefly earlier.
6   'The Wreck of the Hesperus' written by Henry Longfellow in 1842. Raeburn loved Romantic poetry. He was recalling the point at which 'a whooping billow swept the crew / Like icicles from the deck'.

arranged that they could also stay at Camasunary, then a 'shooting lodge', and in Glenbrittle, thereby making it easier to plan extensive ridge crossings. On Friday, 21 April, setting out from Sligachan, Raeburn, his Norwegian friend Erik Ullén,[7] Godfrey Solly and William Slingsby enjoyed 'a first class climb[8] ... up the Harta Corrie face of the Castles'.[9] Skye mountaineering expert Noel Williams comments:

> [O]ne of the most impressive outings that Raeburn did in the Cuillin was the Central Buttress of An Caisteal in April 1905 ... It was the first ever route done on the East Face of the mountain and the top half of the route was in full winter condition. (A fierce north-west blizzard blew all day!) ... For a party of four to frog march from Sligachan, climb the Bloody Stone, make a probe up South Gully, regroup and start up Central Buttress, change in to kletterschuhe, then breach the imposing headwall in icy conditions, find a way down into Lota Corrie, and then descend to Harta Corrie and frog march out via the Bad Step to Camasunary by 8.15pm is really quite mind boggling. (2023)

They had 'an excellent dinner' and a night's rest.

On Saturday Raeburn and Ullén set out with James Parker and Charlie Clark, who were heading for the Banachdich Pass to Glenbrittle. They had 'squalls of hail, brilliant periods intervening': typical April weather. Arriving at the Bad Step on the coastal path, Raeburn feelingly describes the scene:

> We were at a sufficient height above the calm transparent waters of Loch Scavaig to look down into the depths and see the long fronds of the tangles fringing the rocky shores slowly waving in the current, to see the colour of the water change from dark green to yellow above the shoals of brilliant sand. Flocks of common gulls with their sharp double

---

7   Eric Ullén was an authority on the Hörunger (Hurrungane) mountains in Norway: 'gabbro peaks ... like the Coolins but two and a half times as high'. Although proposed by Raeburn for the SMC, for some reason Ullén was refused membership. He climbed with Raeburn in Norway, Scotland and the Alps.

8   Now called Raeburn's Route, 360m, Diff. and IV. A day which occupied over 12 hours and included one pitch of slabs on which Raeburn wore kletterschuhe. Raeburn wrote a separate account in 'Excursions', *SMCJ* (1906).

9   An Caisteal and Sgùrr na Bàirnich were together known as 'The Castles' (N&S), according to Noel Williams.

note, "Klee-ah, Klee-ah", drifted about in the air between Scavaig and Coruisk, their snow-white bodies taking on an almost rosy tint as the sunlight struck through their semi-transparent wings. Out among the little rocky islets several parties of eiders were playing, their low guttural call, "oo-oo, oo-oo, oo", intensified by the towering rock walls above, the drakes resplendent in the full glory of their nuptial plumage. (op. cit. p.62)

One can see the scene and hear the bird calls; 'all was peace, warmth and sunshine at this the entrance to the Coruisk chasm'. But 'looking up ... in the direction of Greadaidh and Mhadaidh, nothing could be seen of these peaks. Great masses of black and threatening vapours boiled furiously over the precipices ...'[10] And of course they were caught in another brief but violent shower of hail and rain.

Raeburn's attitude to the Bad Step is enlightening—he is far from dismissive. It is easy enough in good weather, 'but in the dusk and with a rainful gale blowing this is not at all an inviting spot, and the rope is called for, at least should be, by prudent mountaineers'.

While Clark and Parker set off for the Banachdich col, Raeburn and Ullén headed up the NE ridge of Garsbheinn. They were tempted by 'a very attractive pinnacle', but because of the wind, they kept in the lee of the rocks to avoid buffeting. On the summit they found an 'eagle's feather quite recently dropped, and some fragments of prey'. Rare visions of beauty rewarded their toil: 'Rum, Eigg, and Canna, and the mainland about Loch Hourn across a sea flecked here and there by flying squalls.'

At this point Willie Ling, recovering from illness, coo-eed up from the depths of Coruisk. Raeburn tried to yodel in reply but learnt later that 'it was, of course, unheard below'. Ullén and Raeburn took in 'double reefs' and prepared to fight the wind on the ridge to Sgùrr nan Eag, but for unknown reasons the wind did not trouble them and they made good progress. On the descent from the north peak of Sgùrr nan Eag to the col with Sgùrr Dubh an Dà Bheinn they even found some 'neat standing glissades in very steep gullies'. They made the steep scramble up the 530ft of Dubh an Dà Bheinn

---

10   One wonders if George Mallory ever read Raeburn's articles. If he did, surely his opinion of Raeburn could not have been so mistaken? See the Chapters on Everest.

and rested for a few minutes, 'our visible world now confined to our top and the spectral, white-sheeted crags of Dubh Mòr, a short distance away to the east'.

After 'bread and jam, washed down with new snow' the friends came 'to the awkward corner or tower leading up to the "Gap"', and Raeburn called for the rope, which Ullén was carrying 'as a negligé scarf'. The Gap 'did not look an inviting spot under present conditions'. By now it was snowing very heavily, which particularly troubled Ullén, who wore spectacles. Raeburn says that if he had not done the Gap before in 'weather little better' he might have thought of avoiding it altogether, but 'that would not be playing the game. We held the trumps and knew how to bridge the "Gap"' (game, trumps, bridge—slick wordplay). They abseiled down and, of course, the rope got stuck and Raeburn had to 'swing up again' to free it.

Raeburn succeeded on the Gap, as one would expect, despite the awful conditions. In a brief interlude he dilates on the times taken by parties of various sizes—as always, he is very keen on timing—thus, when he crossed the Gap with three companions they took an hour; as a two they took 30 minutes. A soloist, he reckons, would only take ten minutes because no time is wasted on rope work. This leads him to discuss the ideal number for a climbing party: 'all climbers are agreed in condemning solitary climbing'. Well, not quite all ... what about Observatory Ridge and Observatory Buttress? First ascents: H Raeburn solo. Ironic humour, perhaps? He continues: 'Three is allowable when all are good climbers, but four or more means defeat in many cases where time and difficulty are involved.' His conclusion aligns with contemporary thinking: if there are no glaciers two is the ideal number.

It would surprise no modern winter climber that they wore gloves while crossing the Gap. Raeburn notes that 'many cases of frostbite in the Alps are due to the neglect or inability to wear gloves when climbing difficult rocks in bad weather',[11] another example of the difference between then and now. Few today would dream of going bare-handed, and temperature, not 'weather', is the determining factor. Winter climbing is in its infancy in Raeburn's earlier career.

---

11   Raeburn and Ling had to help a misguided German without gloves on the Aiguille Verte in 1909, see Chapter 24.

Continuing, the pair climbed Thearlaich and Alasdair, and took the rope off only to need it again for the step on the descent to the Sgumain col. 'Everything was covered with a thick coat of new snow which sometimes concealed plates of ice; the rocks are rotten and the ground steep'. Raeburn even records the five minutes it took them to climb from the col to the top of Sgumain, their eighth peak of the day. They descended by 'the first wide couloir which runs down to Coire Labain', glissading through 'a *tourmente* of snow rushing up'. As the snow thinned beneath their feet 'so thinned the mist and snow above ... and for the first time for several hours [we] could see some of the surrounding country, the grey-blue indentation of Loch Brittle with its flat sandy beach, fields, and the trees around the welcome oasis of Glenbrittle Lodge'. The descent took 36 minutes. Not only was this day a fine feat of mountaineering skill and endurance, but it was also a fine example of sound navigation in poor visibility. Raeburn was getting to know the ridge and had learned from his previous mistake on the descent from Sgùrr Sgumain. Anyone who knows the Cuillin Ridge understands that in thick weather there are many places one can go wrong.

Down in Glenbrittle they were greeted by Hugh Munro and Charlie Clark, with whom they were to climb the following day. Raeburn had a long-standing 'arrangement' with Munro to 'conduct him over the Inaccessible Pinnacle', but they soon agreed that the current weather made this impossible.[12] However, despite continuing rough weather they planned to climb Banachdich 'and take in as much of the ridge as convenient' on their way back to Sligachan.

On the way up Banachdich they attempted but failed on a gully which, mistakenly, they thought was 'new', being defeated by the third and most formidable pitch. Munro, however, was proud of their efforts. They climbed Banachdich and traversed to Sgùrr a' Greadaidh. Raeburn's comment is revealing: 'In places the ridge is very narrow, and in its icy and snowy condition was in many places almost as sensational and decidedly more difficult than the east ridge of the Weisshorn as usually climbed.' High praise but probably justified.

On the way they met cornices and arêtes of hard snow (*pace* Naismith), and more ice than the previous day, which Raeburn cautiously put down to

---

12   Famously, Munro never did climb the Pinnacle and so never compleated the Munros.

a thaw the previous evening. As if to delight him, a golden eagle 'sailed out of a deep recess in the Coruisk or sheltered side of the peak'. They got one decent clearing to take a photo of the 'snow-clad peaks and ridges to the South as far as Dubh', but very soon they were again enveloped in 'driving blizzards of hail and snow'. The party enjoyed the traditional glissade and then ran down a hard snow slope into Coire a' Ghreadhaidh where they coiled the rope, ate, and headed for Sligachan by the Bealach a' Mhàim. In fact, Raeburn and Ullén had traversed a goodly portion of the Cuillin Ridge since leaving Camasunary: a considerable achievement in very adverse winter weather.

[Fig 1] Raeburn describes his last day of this Easter Meet as 'tamer'. With W and JJ Brigg, Willie Douglas, Eric Greenwood and John Rennie he visited Fionn Choire and 'nick[ed] a few steps' up to the ridge below Sgùrr an Fhionn-Choire where they ate their 'frugal' lunch in comparative peace. All the while they were threatened by 'the fearsome-looking pinnacle of the Bhasteir, with its uplifted and overhanging rock blade'. Raeburn likens it to 'the lady of the Frenchman's apostrophe; it was "pure ice from top to bottom"', great plates of fog crystals covering every available hold.

They crossed the ridge leading to Sgùrr a' Bhàsteir, 'and on a slope of hard snow walked across to the Bhasteir Cave'. No joy. 'Thin black ice on one wall, faced by snow and fog crystals on the other, forbade all ascent.' After a 'bumpy and hard' standing glissade into the Bhàsteir Coire, Raeburn 'timidly' suggested doing Pinnacle Ridge[13] 'to warm ourselves', but this suggestion 'was utterly ignored and we faced instead the much worse ordeal of Rennie's camera'. Presumably they had to pose interminably, something Raeburn did not enjoy. On the way back to Sligachan, Raeburn and Greenwood deviated to watch 'the beautiful evolutions of a pair of buzzards above the rocks of the Nid an Iolair'.

This day ended Raeburn's meet, but he contrasts the good weather days then experienced by those who stayed on, with his own battles 'on the blizzard-swept ridges'. His last remark is enigmatic but touches on a truth about mountaineering: he holds the days he has spent 'as beautiful days on the hills though they were *something more than only that*' [author's emphasis]. The shared experience of danger and the awe inspired by the

---

13   Now rightly graded IV,4 and harder than Tower Ridge on Ben Nevis.

Fig 1

Editor Douglas and Secretary Clark in playful mood at the Easter Meet of 1899 at Kinlochewe. Photo: SMC Image Archive

extremes of dramatic weather in spectacular mountains: these are perhaps something like Harold's 'more than only that'. There is little doubt that had the idea occurred to him, Raeburn could have traversed the Cuillin Ridge in its entirety, certainly in summer and perhaps even in winter condition. He must have been upset when Erik Ullén was rejected by the SMC.

On the Easter Meet of 1906 Raeburn made two important climbs: The Chasm with Willie Ling, and Crowberry Gully with Clark and James Parker, which will be described presently. This chapter, however, concludes with a couple of brief notes interesting for the flicker of light they throw on Raeburn's personality rather than for mountaineering feats. William Clark recorded the 1906 Easter Meet at the Kingshouse, and apparently Harold was enjoying parlour games again. Remember his very first meet as a guest at Tyndrum when he starred in 'Pike's Peak'? This time he introduced 'the peripatetic frogs in which the laws of inertia and momentum were alternately invoked to direct the frogs in their course'. Frank Goggs wins with ease and is 'crowned with acclamation as the "Frog King"'. The other goings-on at this meet included a version of Blind Man's Buff and an attempt by two members to secure for the Club-room a pair of china dogs from the hotel mantelpiece. Make of this what you will, but it certainly shows that in certain moods Harold was up for schoolboy games.

There was more merriment on the road to Schiehallion. The party travelled in two cars. William Clark and Charles Walker in the 6 H.P. de Dion, while Charlie Clark drove Raeburn and others in the 10 H.P. Humber. Needless to say there was a bit of competition on the drive. The de Dion stalled on the steep road to Whitebridge and the Humber 'came up the slope with a rush, its mob of jeering occupants headed by Raeburn', who, instead of descending to help, used 'their comfortable position to scoff and laugh at our member from Dundee'. It was all very light-hearted and taken in a good spirit. They had a pleasant ascent of Schiehallion, and Raeburn, Walker and Charlie Clark even found 'a difficult rock chimney near the summit' on which to exercise their muscles. This playful side to Harold Raeburn complements the touches of humour in his writings.

15. THE CHASM AND GREEN GULLY 1906

Late winter and early spring of 1906 were blessed with good, stable weather. Heading for the Easter Meet at the Kingshouse, Raeburn and Ling caught the dreaded 4.30 am train from Edinburgh on 12 April, and at 12.45 pm they set out from the hotel for The Chasm on the Buachaille, which they reached in a further 45 minutes.

Raeburn describes their day (SMCJ, 1906). They found that the lowest part of The Chasm was 'a uniform slope of hard snow'. Climbing down to this from 'the first rocky ridge on the left (N) bank', they walked up for some way and passed the first pitch 'on the left wall'. They avoided a bergschrund, caused by meltwater, by stepping across where the gap lessened to three or four feet onto 'a somewhat minute toe-hold on the rock wall'; easier climbing led to a crossing of the stream 'on fallen snow blocks to the right wall'. Here they removed their boots to get round 'a jutting corner, with non-existent holds'. Raeburn climbed vertically 'for a few yards' to where 'a capital hitch' protected both leader and second across the hiatus.[1] Ling got past this awkward place with the help of 'a hand to pull him past the push-out'—Raeburn was a sympathetic leader—and they put their boots on again.

Only about 40 to 50 feet of the '100 ft pitch' were not covered by snow, and these two remaining pitches were climbed on the left wall. Raeburn says: 'One was rather difficult, and we judged with a few feet less snow might have been pretty well impossible.' He is being typically modest here: 'rather difficult' by his standards could well imply Severe at least. However,

---

1 A very early example of the use of a running belay or runner.

having got past the formidable 100-foot pitch they gained 'a great mass of snow filling up the bed of The Chasm below the Tower ... and covering all the pitches', climbed by Raeburn and the Clarks in 1903.[2]

The snowfield slanted almost halfway up 'the great top pitch'. Raeburn estimated that the depth of snow here was little less than 100 ft. Alas, the remaining part of the pitch was a 'black slimy slit of smooth rock' pouring with enough water 'to furnish an ample supply to a fair-sized town', and even if they had 'thought of tackling this', which they did not, they would have failed because there was an enormous gap between the snow they stood on and the slimy walls—the sort of Scottish "bergschrund" mentioned in 'Scottish Snow'.

A crack on the left wall looked like the only hope. Raeburn climbed with difficulty up the wall to their left, and 'after a scramble on rather loose rock the crack was reached'. It must have been quite wide, more like a chimney, because Raeburn was able to jam himself in it so that he could protect Ling, 'who then traversed out to the left round a projecting nose to a good ledge'. From there 'a slanting overhung ledge was followed back to the line of the crack', and they followed the gully above to a little col. The little col, indeed, separating the 'Lady's Pinnacle' of the buttress climbed in 1903 from the rest of the mountain.

They basked in the sun on the pinnacle and then climbed to the top of the Buachaille. After a difficult and involved description of what they had done, Raeburn relaxes and describes the scene:

It was a lovely evening, warm and calm, so windless was it that a match burned unsheltered on the summit. Though clear at near hand, the countless moor fires all around veiled the distant hills in a blue-grey haze of smoke, and the leagues-long Moor of Rannoch with its myriad loch mirrors looked vaster than ever, its hill shores hid as if by many miles of distance. (ibid. p.151)

But, as Robin Campbell remarks in the '100 Years Ago' section of the SMCJ (2006, pp.402–3), WH Murray 'discounted [Raeburn and Ling's] ascent of The Chasm' in his 1949 guidebook to Glencoe. Murray (1949) says:

---

2   See the account of their partial ascent in Chapter 9.

'The climb has not been admitted as a first ascent, on the grounds that the extraordinary volume of snow robbed the gully of everything, apart from situation, that distinguishes it as 'The Chasm'. Exit was made by the South Wall.'

Considering Raeburn's earlier ascent with William and Jane Clark and the one recorded above, it seems that, at the very least, Raeburn and his partners on both occasions should be treated more generously by guidebook editors. It would seem reasonable now to treat both the ascents in which Raeburn was involved as exploratory, partial first ascents, but to this day RF Stobart, Noel and Mona Odell are credited with the first ascent in April 1920. Perhaps worse, CM Allan, JHB Bell and Miss V Roy are credited with the first ascent of the South Wall exit from the Devil's Cauldron in June 1934, and the description of their climb matches Raeburn's very closely: 'Start up the chimney on the left wall. Climb the chimney for 6 m to a runner, then make a very awkward move on to a ledge on the wall on the right. Traverse round the edge on to a broad ledge and take the line of least resistance to the top' (SMC, 2005) Readers will make up their own minds whether or not justice has been done here.

The following day Raeburn set out for the Buachaille again with William Clark and James Parker. According to the latter (SMCJ, 1907) they 'made an ascent of the North Buttress by a route which kept close to the Crowberry Ridge Gully, and which is new in its upper portion'. From the lower rocks of Crowberry Ridge they dropped 'on to the snow of the Crowberry Gully'. They traversed upwards, got on to 'the rocks of the north buttress' and had a 'pleasant scramble up the edge of the well-defined ridge which runs parallel to the big gully, and is separated from the north buttress by a shallow rock gully'. Enveloped in mist, they could not take photographs of the climbers on Crowberry Ridge, which must have frustrated Clark. They kept going up without difficulty until they had to turn 'a seemingly impossible pitch by keeping to the left' and so reach 'the broad band of snow which crosses the face of the buttress'.

From there they traversed back into Crowberry Gully, 'just above the big pitch at the junction of the Crowberry Main Gully with the Crowberry Tower Chimney'. They ascended the gully 'for a few steps cut in hard ice', crossed it and climbed the face of rock between the gully and the chimney, 'starting at a conspicuous crack'. Parker says, 'The rocks proved to be extremely rotten, and were also very steep. From the top of the crack we held to the left and soon emerged at the beginning of the little saddle which runs out to the Crowberry Tower.'

From Parker's description it seems that his party finished by regaining the upper part of Crowberry Gully, which was completed, possibly, by Crowberry Gully Centre Rib Finish.[3] At all events, the ascent of the crack sounds like a considerable achievement. Parker does not say who led it, but the strong favourite is Raeburn, who seemed to be in happy mood and excellent form. It was just as well, because nine days later, on 22 April 1906, his mountaineering skill was to be severely tested on Ben Nevis.

There is surely significance in the fact that William Douglas chose to place first in the SMCJ the article in which Raeburn describes his ascent of what we now know as Green Gully (SMCJ, 1907). Over the years, editors have liked to suggest to the reader that the SMC is not short of energetic, skilful climbers doing fine things, and putting an article like this in the shop window, as it were, is a way of doing this. At this stage in his career Raeburn was firmly established as the best climber the Club had, so it was natural for Douglas to treat his account in this way. The article probably also appealed to Douglas because it is dramatic and does not waste words. The fact that it was given prominence in the SMCJ makes it even harder to understand why future generations of guidebook editors[4] ignored Raeburn and Phildius's outstanding achievement in ascending what was to become for many years the hardest ice-climb on Ben Nevis, using gear which can only be described as rudimentary. Of course, Raeburn set out to climb The Comb—the very steep buttress which forms the left side of the gully—in this he failed and there is a slight air of defensiveness, even apology, in his article, but it does not mean that he failed to climb Green Gully. [Fig 1]

Raeburn begins his narrative by observing that Scottish climbers are not put off by bad weather. Readers of this chronicle will have seen as much. 'It is grand training, and teaches us how much bad weather can be endured with

---

3   First recorded ascent Robson and Ward at IV,5, March 1996.
4   As late as the Revised Edition of the *Climbers' Guide to Ben Nevis* (1979), Green Gully was still being credited to Bell, Henson, Morsley and Small in 1938, so this mistake was still being perpetuated seven years after Robin Campbell published his seminal article, 'The First Scottish Ice Climbers' (*SMCJ*, 1972). But for Campbell's tireless research and advocacy, Raeburn's magnificent ascent of Green Gully might have gone unnoticed.

Fig 1

The massive buttress to the left is The Comb; Green Gully is the sinuous ice-line to its right, now graded IV: a very severe test for a party cutting steps without crampons or any real protection. Photo: Simon Richardson

wonderfully little risk, *if properly clad and taking proper precautions against chill and frostbite*' [his emphasis]. A safe approach to mountaineering is typical of Raeburn. Not only do we need to be properly clad and equipped, but we must also be able to navigate, because mist is 'a normal condition of affairs'.

Raeburn called the article 'A Scottish Ice Climb', and indeed that is just what Green Gully is: snow and ice from bottom to top, but in Raeburn's mind there lingers the notion that all climbing is in essence rock-climbing—sometimes made easier by 'the plating of ice and snow which forms so thickly on our crags in spring'. This, he says, 'may be a means of overcoming difficulties otherwise insurmountable ... Possibly this is ... the case with the climb described below'. One gets the (to us absurd) impression that the optimum conditions for this ascent would have been dry summer conditions such as those in which he eventually made the first summer ascent of Crowberry Gully![5] And yet it is clear that Raeburn relished the conditions as he found them.

He was particularly delighted by the state of the snow:

As we ascended the steepening snowfield, here and there projected from the smooth slope large masses of half-buried fragments of cornice ... They exhibited in a high degree all the qualities of Scottish névé in late spring. Struck by the pick of the ice-axe no result is produced; the pick merely sinks in and remains. If levering out is attempted, the ordinary Swiss amateur axe, which ... is nearly useless for real hard ice work, stands a strong chance of being broken. The only way to make an impression on this toughest of snow is to cut a groove with the blade and then drive the piece out with the pick ... [H]andholds and footholds once made can be relied upon. They are practically as good as if cut out of rock.

---

5   Scottish mountaineering was in fact bedevilled for many years by a failure to make the necessary distinction between summer and winter climbing. For example, it was only decades later that a separate grading system was introduced for winter routes. This now seems incredible, but it was part of the natural evolution of mountaineering, not only in Scotland but elsewhere. It must be remembered that most Victorian and Edwardian climbers' conception of mountaineering came primarily from the Alps—Scotland was a training ground—and they climbed in the Alps in summer: warm dry rock was mingled with snow and ice. In his article on 'Scottish Snow', Raeburn is groping after the idea that Scottish winter climbing forms a separate genre. His 'Scottish Ice Climb' is another, not entirely conscious, step in the same direction.

Just imagine the labour and skill required to deal with this recalcitrant material for some 180m on slopes of up to 80°, cutting steps, for long spells one-handed, with a long wooden axe.

Frank Goggs remarks on the fact that Raeburn is prepared to climb with many different partners. He also sometimes pairs up with strangers at short notice. On this occasion he had planned to climb with AE Robertson, but when the latter pulled out 'owing to a slight indisposition', Raeburn was content to accept Robertson's suggestion that he climb with a young man from Geneva, Eberhard Phildius, who was a member of the Swiss Alpine Club. Raeburn had never met him before, but he 'proved a pleasant companion and a keen and capable climber'.

The weather was rough: 'a strong cold wind from the north-east' carrying with it 'flurries of snow'. In a brief clearing they paused in Coire na Ciste to get their bearings on The Comb. Looking down to their left they saw Tower Ridge:

... through the drifts the snowy clifts
Did shed a dismal sheen.[6]

Just like a great iceberg it was, or perhaps like a mass of rough marble, all the dark rock hid by a plating of ribbed and embossed dull, white snow-ice, with here and there streaks, ribs, and columns of pale green water-ice from a few inches to several feet in thickness.

By now they had got their fix on The Comb. One should remember that it was this steep rock tower that Raeburn wanted to climb. His plan was to ascend the icy lower slopes of Number Two North Tower Ridge gully (i.e. Number Two Gully), 'till under the great overhanging beak of The Comb, traverse across a narrow snow ledge below it to our right, and then cut up till we gained the foot of the slabby gully prospected in 1902. Then to cut up this, going out to our left to the arête whenever possible'.

From Raeburn's description it sounds as if he planned to traverse the ledge which forms the first pitch of what we now call Piggot's Route[7] on

---

6 From Samuel Taylor Coleridge's poem, 'The Rhyme of the Ancient Mariner'.
7 FA summer 1921, Severe; FA winter 1960, V,6.

The Comb, and then start up Green Gully and try to gain the arête from it. 'Soon leaving the gully [Number Two], we reached the rocks below the beak of The Comb, ice and snow covered as everywhere. The ledge noted was traversed, steps kicked and scraped, round to the right, then up a steep slope of soft snow, lying from one to two feet deep on hard icy stuff.' To avoid avalanche risk they had to cut steps in the hard lower surface. 'Now,' in spite of blinding spindrift, 'we found ourselves looking up … the steep gully which should give access to the ridge. Then began the real struggle'.

Raeburn's language becomes military here, reminiscent of the terms he used to describe Arrow Chimney on the Tarmachan:

> *We two, stormers of one of the salient towers [i.e. The Comb], felt the blast strike us … The worst was that the snow batteries were opened on us from both above and below. From above one could, to a certain extent, take cover beneath the shield of our cone-pointed, brim-turned-down felt hats, but occasionally the snow … that poured down the gully, was caught by the powerful ascending eddy and rushed up, thus taking us behind our defences. The pain of a stream of icy snow in the face is so great that work must stop, and the face [be] covered till breath is regained. Fortunately these underhand tactics were never long continued, and the … sapping and mining*[8] *was soon renewed.*

Raeburn knows that without accurate measurement by clinometer, trying to gauge the steepness of a slope is 'always dangerous'. However, he reckons that two pitches 'were what is usually known as perpendicular, i.e. probably 70° to 75°, with small portions approaching 90°', and his estimates tally with modern opinion.

It was only because of 'the snow-ice curtain hanging down these steeper portions that they were climbable at all'. In order to stay on at this angle, holds had to be cut so as to give an inward pull, and 'these icy curtains allowed of this being done. Frequently the pick broke through to soft snow or black vacancy, backed with green bulbs of ice, and "pigeon-hole" holds resulted'. As before in his career,[9] Raeburn complains that:

---

8   The metaphor is eerily prescient of the First World War, in which much sapping and mining was done to tunnel under and blow up enemy strongholds.
9   See the account of Arrow Chimney on the Tarmachan, Chapter 3.

Fig 2

Raeburn glissading on Ben Nevis the day after his ascent of Green Gully in April 1906. Photo: Rev AE Robertson, SMC Image Archive

Ice work of this kind is … particularly cramping and exhausting, and progress was slow. To hang on with one hand, while that long two-handed weapon, the modern ice-axe, is wielded in the other, is calculated to produce severe cramps, and did so now.

In fact it took three attempts for Raeburn to lead the second steep pitch, which is long and serious, and he then let Phildius go ahead up the steep snow leading to the final ice pitch, which, now as then, often contains a slight bulge.

Raeburn notes that at this point they could have traversed to their left and reached the arête of The Comb, but the sight of the 'unstable looking cornices' deterred them and they continued up the gully. Seen from below, the cornice in the gully had not looked very high, but now they could see that it was 'more than two-man height above the slope'. Raeburn says: 'Our only chance here was to traverse out to our right where a rib of ice-covered rock ran up to meet the cornice, reducing it to half the height'. Grappling with this last problem, Raeburn confesses:

[T]o a feeling of helplessness … as I stood on my ice-axe, driven horizontally into the vertical snow wall, some hundreds of feet of little less than vertical ice-plastered rocks stretching away down into the depths of the mist beneath, while my fingers slid helplessly from the glassy surface of the cornice névé, in the vain endeavour to find or make a hold by which I might haul myself up.

Below, Phildius was belaying with his ice-axe—a belay which would almost certainly not have prevented disaster had Raeburn fallen. Harold's solution to the problem was bold in the extreme: he climbed back down to within reach of Phildius, who passed him his axe. Now they had no belay at all. Raeburn climbed back up his steps, stood on his embedded axe again and managed to cut a handhold over the top. 'And with fingers well crooked in the tough névé a steady drag landed the body over the cornice lip, and Phildius soon followed.'

In terms of difficulty, Raeburn compares their climb favourably with the Zmutt ridge of the Matterhorn, which he climbed with Ling in July of the same year. On the other hand, he is rather defensive about it: 'Objection may be made to this climb that it is not the actual climb of The Comb. This is true, for we were never once on the exact arête. But what does this really matter?'

[Fig 2] Unfortunately it is crucial: you can't climb a buttress by climbing the gully next it. One suspects that Raeburn, honest man that he was, knew this perfectly well but was covering up his disappointment. Perhaps this apologetic tone and the fact that he records what he and a now recovered Robertson did the next day—kicking steps up North Castle Gully—serve partially to explain, though not at all to excuse, why the ascent of Green Gully escaped notice until rescued from oblivion by Robin Campbell, to whom should go the last word: 'It seems that by pretending to have climbed The Comb, poor Raeburn was later deemed not to have climbed Green Gully' (SMCJ, 1972).

16. CREAG MEAGAIDH IN JUNE   1906

In June 1906 Frank Goggs happened to be staying in Kingussie and, thinking it seemed a good idea to explore Creag Meagaidh while in the district, he contacted Raeburn. In the article (*SMCJ*, 1906) he wrote about their adventure, he begins half facetiously by saying that Raeburn should be appointed 'Honorary Guide' to the Club. Why? Because he was a bachelor and therefore available; 'he never seems to mind what kind of climber he has at the other end of the rope'; and because of his skill, which it was superfluous to mention. Goggs, like Willie Douglas (whom he was to succeed as Editor of the *SMCJ*), knew Raeburn well and had climbed with him on a number of occasions, notably on Lochnagar. Like Douglas, Goggs was very modest about his own climbing ability, but was much better than he made himself out to be.

When Raeburn arrived in Kingussie, the day was so warm that they spent it lounging in the garden of the house where Goggs was staying, something most unusual for Raeburn, who was normally off to the crag as soon as his feet touched the platform. They found each other's company congenial and, like club members who met infrequently, they would have had a lot of news to exchange.

In the cool of the evening they cycled to Laggan, hoping to find bed and board in the hotel there, but to their dismay they found that William Gladstone, then Home Secretary, and his entourage had occupied almost the whole hotel. There was one single bed left: if they occupied that room, could they get breakfast at 5am? 'No,' was the answer, as it would disturb 'the Liberal Government'! 'Finding once again that men were made for inns and not inns for men' they gave up, and, after having a drink and buying a loaf of bread, they cycled on to Aberarder, arriving there just before 10 pm.

The day had been hot and the evening rather frustrating. Presumably they had been expecting to have dinner at Laggan. Now it was getting late and they had no accommodation. At the shepherd's cottage 'Raeburn went forward to try his hand at diplomacy', but, says Goggs, 'his appearance was distinctly against him. He wore one of those soft slouch felt hats, which, in the popular mind, denotes an Italian brigand. I wished afterwards I had gone forward myself, as I happened to be wearing a most respectable cloth cap'. A woman came to the door, but 'after one glance at Raeburn she never looked at him again', and nothing he could say would procure accommodation, although they did manage to borrow a box of matches. In the end it seems as if Raeburn was actually downright rude. As Goggs puts it: 'Raeburn told her that we should put our machines in an outhouse … and leave them there till our return.' 'Told her'? The lady may have said nothing to this, but one suspects she thought it most impertinent. It isn't like the sort of polite, almost deferential, behaviour we expect of Raeburn from his own writings and from those of others, and is perhaps an example of upper-class bad manners towards the lower classes. Raeburn, of course, was high up in the brewing business and cannot have been used to his inferiors saying no to him. Heat and weariness may help to explain but not excuse Raeburn's abruptness here, and the pair seemed to make matters worse by trying to sleep in a hayshed uninvited. Perhaps they were lucky not to have the dogs set on them.[1]

At all events, sleep was impossible, and they set out for Coire Ardair shortly after 2 am: 'the moon was obscured by cloud but there was ample light to walk by'. The walk to the lochan was 'delightful' and birdsong was heard all night. Raeburn showed Goggs 'two nests of the titlark,[2] both containing eggs'.

They enjoyed a rest in 'a sunny spot at the foot of the Pinnacle' and ate their supply of jam sandwiches. The three great Posts were running with water, so they selected what Goggs calls A-Buttress; probably that to the left (west) of the three Post climbs. In order to get to it they scrambled up the lower section of the central buttress and traversed across South Post.

---

1   Goggs and Raeburn sadly recall AE Robertson's famous remark that: 'In all my wanderings I have never been refused a night's shelter.' But the Highland custom of hospitality does not confer rights on would-be guests. Hospitality may be expected but cannot be demanded.
2   A former name for the meadow pipit (Anthus pratensis).

Now embarked on their chosen buttress, Goggs describes the scene: 'The rough slope quickly increased in steepness, and we were soon on a very steep and much broken-up face composed of short ledges of mixed turf, rock, and heather.' It sounds rather precarious. At one point Raeburn stood on Goggs's shoulder 'to prevent himself being pushed out'. They reached a point at which further progress looked unlikely. Raeburn reconnoitred to the right, but there was a *mauvais pas* which could not be passed. A descent of some 12 ft 'to a longer ledge than most there, which we reckoned would bring us round to easier ground on the left' was contemplated but finally rejected. After all, they did not want to leave the 'direct ascent' to 'some second-hand expert'. With this in mind, Raeburn stepped round Goggs and wormed his way up to the left, and 'after a few more feet the [absolutely perpendicular] face decreases in steepness, and curving back to the right, the arête of the buttress, was struck at the foot of good rocks'. Up to this point their fingers had been getting 'grubby and black-nailed with digging into turf and heather, but now they 'grip the pure rock with delight'.

For 'some fifty feet' they climbed the 'well-shattered ridge at an easy angle'; then, as the rock became steeper and more compact, they went out on the face for about a dozen feet 'and up a steep and narrow chimney which we had seen from the breakfast place'. The chimney, Goggs says, 'is sensational—looking down between your legs, you see the long snow tongue of the gully apparently vertically below you—but at the same time perfectly safe as you can wedge yourself in capitally'. Their one complaint was that it is too short, about 20 ft. To get the most out of the climb they 'strolled across some thirty yards of snow to a well-shattered mass of rock which can be scrambled up anywhere', and this brought them to the 'summit plateau of Creag Meggie'. Raeburn erected 'a stone obelisk some four feet in height to inform future generations of climbers that buttress A had been conquered'.[3]

---

3   Robin Campbell notes: 'now South Buttress or South Pillar, and entirely suppressed in modern guidebooks'. (*SMCJ*, 2006). Not entirely suppressed but certainly disparaged as summer climbs in the SMC Guide to *Ben Nevis* (2022), South Pillar 250 m, 1906, is listed along with Central Pillar, North Post and the ominously named 'Amustoavoid' as: 'all poor climbs and to be avoided'. Campbell thinks Goggs's description 'sounds like a decent route'. The upper part maybe, but not, perhaps, the lower pitches. South Pillar, Central Pillar and North Post are all high-quality winter routes at grades IV and V.

Because Raeburn had not 'bagged the summit', they walked out to it, but the view was poor. They descended by the Window, with the obligatory, but rather wet, glissade.

Back at the farm, 'we called on our hostess to thank her for her hospitality'. They returned the borrowed matches and Goggs is at pains to point out that 'Raeburn also bore in his hands as a thank-offering the loaf we had bought at Laggan' but hadn't needed. Rather sententiously, Goggs says: 'Thus we repaid good for evil'. Perhaps Raeburn felt guilty at his rudeness and was really offering an apology? There is no record of the lady's response.

17. QUINAG, STOB COIRE NAN LOCHAN 1907

Strong and skilful climber though Raeburn was, he was not immune to injury. At the SMC's New Year Meet on 29 December 1906 in Arran, never really a lucky place for him, Harold struck his knee against a boulder and bruised it so severely that he had to forgo climbing during the Meet (SMCJ, 1907).

However, at Easter in 1907, the 39th Meet of the Club at Inchnadamph was the scene of a notable ascent by Raeburn, Willie Ling and Sandy (later Lord) Mackay. Their route on the Barrel Buttress of Quinag was described by Herbert Boyd in the Meet Report as 'The great climb of the Meet', and he gave only a brief description in the belief that it would be elaborated upon elsewhere by one of the participants. As it turned out he was right, but a full description of the day was not published until 1928, when Sandy Mackay wrote *Sail Garbh: its Barrel Buttress*, an account written partly as a tribute to Raeburn, who had died in 1926. We do not know why nothing was written before. Ken Crocket (2015, p.258) speculates:

> *It may be that Raeburn decided not to describe the route, being dissatisfied with the manner in which it was climbed ... he had been modest in the past, barely describing the actual climbing on his solo ascent of Observatory Buttress, or the first ascent of Raeburn's Arête.*

Crocket adds that Mackay himself could offer no explanation for this omission, but corresponding with Willie Ling and reading his diaries brought back much of the detail of the day to Mackay's mind:

[T]he buttress was a wonderful sight, in appearance unassailable, rearing up proudly to an apparently isolated and flattish summit; but in the middle regions, at every point, bulged, protuberant, disjicient,[1] *repellent, with a fine round belly that seemed to say to man: "Miserable fly without even a fly's suckers to aid, you shall but drop off if you try hither."* (SMCJ, 1928)

Mackay's style is idiosyncratic as ever, but he quotes the sober Ling, whose notes were made soon after the event: 'Raeburn had been much impressed by a fine buttress and we wished to explore it.' They gazed at the buttress for a long time from below. 'Nothing so like the upward cast of a hogshead, hooped and coopered at the middle, narrowing … to the top, could well be figured.'

Mackay led the first pitch, 'a steep staircase of alternate rock and grass', but Harold took over when the real difficulties started; Ling followed with Mackay on the tail. For much of their first attempt Mackay found himself 'clinging to something, under an ever bulging-out canopy, with no one in sight, while pants and groans, and grunted doubts and despairs came floating out of the ether'. When called on he climbed quickly but found that the angle of the rock was often overhanging, and that 'much prime climbing in the leader was needed'. Not for nothing did the climbers of this era have the unshakeable rule that the leader must never fall. If Raeburn had fallen here, the almost certain result would have been three fatalities. Likewise if either of the others had slipped while Raeburn was in certain positions. But Raeburn's leading remained as solid as ever and nobody did slip. As Mackay remarks of the exposure: 'Below was nothing even to hope to fall upon until one went out of this exhilarating world altogether.'

By this time, according to Ling, they had climbed some 150 ft. Mackay thinks it was much more. Ling speaks as if they are trying to climb a crack or chimney; Mackay thinks it was more like 'a sheer round open face'. Ling's account is likely to be more reliable, but whatever the case, they were trying to get to a 'corridor' formed by one of the hoops or 'staves' of the barrel—in reality, a ledge which might provide a means of avoiding the steep crack in

---

1 '"Disjicient"'? The author has no idea what this means, and cannot find it in any dictionary. A legal term?

the next tier. Mackay believed that neither Raeburn nor Ling realised how long they took to reach this ledge, while he, below, lay over a shaky flake, securing himself by jamming his arm into the crack behind it.

In order to reach the ledge, Ling describes 'A shallow chimney, angle against us, leader could not get purchase off the heather to raise himself ... [but] ... I passed up a stone which he put on the platform and just managed to raise himself. A nasty place without much hitch.'

From this point Raeburn and Ling could see no way of progressing, and they brought Mackay up. A debate ensued. Mackay thought that the only way ahead was to go back to the central crack, which at least 'afforded two splayed walls by whose help to utilise the subtlest of all climbers' arts— carefully distributed counter thrusts'. Mackay urged 'the attack' and even offered to try to lead it. He insisted that Harold could do it, but 'my more experienced leader said no' and Ling and he insisted on retreating.

However, acting on Mackay's urging, they went by some means to the east (one assumes along a ledge system), and climbed the gully 'which separates the Barrel from Buttress II'[2] and, after lunch, led by Ling, they climbed down 'abrupt' but 'open and broken' rocks. Some 300-400ft below they saw the narrow 'string corridor' by which they had retreated. They climbed down further and got into the central crack from the west by a 'perilous open traverse', this central crack being the feature which had daunted them in the first place. Now they descended it.

Once in the cleft they found 'a block belay of superlative workmanship', and they circled it with 'a separate rope ring' in case they had to retreat.[3] Using this ring as a handhold, Ling and Mackay swarmed down, 'first over a blob of rock split by the crack, and then down the perpendicular splay ... certainly not easy', but perhaps less difficult than they had imagined.

Mackay vividly recalls their separate styles. Supple Ling climbed 'close to the rock corner'. Mackay, by contrast, climbed primarily by balance, 'hands not used as hooks ... but balancing, distributing, controlling'. Crucially, 'In this form of rock work the arms are hardly weight carriers at all and do not tire.' But 'Harold disliked the method. His words were,

2   Now known as V Gully Right Branch II*** (no summer grade) in the SMC's *Northern Highlands North*, 2004.
3   This is the first recorded instance in Raeburn's Scottish career of the use of a sling as distinct from a loop of the main climbing rope.

"No, no, not that way. Keep close in".'[4]

They descended in their individual fashions, Raeburn last, protecting the others, and now he thought the climb was not quite so impossible as before. Details are lacking. All Mackay says is that once they began to ascend this crucial pitch, 'Raeburn led magnificently up'. (A phrase oddly reminiscent of Harold's 'I went up' in his article on Observatory Buttress.)

After the crux pitch, Ling and Mackay insisted on climbing:

[T]he black cleft throughout. It made a magnificent finish. At one point, [Raeburn and MacKay] having surmounted an overhanging chockstone, Ling, now third man on the rope, had to kick himself off backwards into space so that the others could 'haul him past the obstruction'.

They got to the top of the buttress 'by more grand open climbing', went over Quinag and down to 'great triumph at Inchnadamph'.

The ascent of this route was a singular achievement, and there is no satisfactory explanation of why Raeburn wrote no account at the time. Crocket may be right in thinking that Harold was dissatisfied with the manner in which the climb was accomplished. There was a lot of hesitation on the day, justifiably so, but it was a hallmark of Raeburn's Scottish climbs that once embarked on a route he either succeeded or decided to retreat. And in the latter case, his decision was always final. On this occasion he seems to have swithered and was finally persuaded to try again by his companions, notably the enthusiastic Mackay. As Crocket says, Raeburn was habitually modest; but he was also a proud man. It might have gone against the grain to admit that he had been in a state of uncertainty and had to be cajoled into making the successful attempt, but this is speculation, and we shall never know.

No other rock climbs were recorded on the Barrel Buttress until the early 1960s, and all other climbs now recorded are either Very Severe or Hard Very Severe. Original Route was graded Very Difficult, but there is little doubt that this is a gross under-grading: it is probably Very Severe at [Fig 1]

---

4   Raeburn's conclusion about rock climbing style remains something of a mystery. Much of what he says elsewhere, e.g. in *Mountaineering Art*, supports Mackay's view, and he always stresses the importance of good balance. However, it is also noted by others that he 'climbed close to the rock'. Like other Victorians he was not shy of making use of the friction generated by tweed. The answer may be that he did whatever was necessary to get up.

Fig 1

The Barrel Buttress of Quinag: Raeburn's Route follows the crack-/chimney-line in the centre of the face. The buttress faces north and has a forbidding atmosphere. The climb starts up the broken grassy ground below the chimney. The modern grading of V. Diff should be taken literally.
Photo: Noel Williams

least—an opinion supported by Andy Nisbet. In winter the route is graded VI,8. Like his climb on the Shelter Stone,[5] Raeburn's Original Route on the Barrel Buttress on 1 April 1907 was not years but decades ahead of its time.

Just a fortnight later Raeburn joined his friends William and Jane Clark and their son, Charlie, at the Kingshouse in Glencoe. They were intent on making a winter ascent in Coire nan Lochan. William chronicles their day (*SMCJ*, 1909).

They approached by Gleann Allt Coire nan Lochan and found the corrie in winter condition, 'ledge and gully now filled with glittering snow or ice'. Of the three great buttresses, 'The central buttress was the most attractive and would afford a longer climb.' They avoided the steep initial nose at the start and went into a recessed corner on the eastern side of the buttress, then Raeburn led up to the narrow ridge. The handholds at times filled with snow, and getting to this point took them one-and-a-half hours. [Fig 2/3]

A short stretch of easy snow followed. Raeburn exuberantly climbed a 'crazy pinnacle on the ridge' and jumped down into the snow. By now they had reached the tower: to the right it would not go, and looked formidable face-on, so, while the Clarks had lunch, Raeburn unroped and prospected to the left. After a rather anxious interval, he returned with the welcome news that he had reached the top of the tower. Clark says: '[W]e poor mortals … can only look on such a climber with astonishment, if not with envy.'

This pitch was the crux, and Clark was convinced that only a 'strong party' should attempt it. There was a little saddle of rock which had to be crossed 'to get into the corner between the tower proper and the big block' behind which they had been sheltering. The holds were excellent 'but the next step require[d] more care … a long stride round a slightly bulging rock, the ledge being of slender proportions'. A few feet along the ledge was a short, exposed chimney with good holds, 'which soon [led] one up beyond the tower and to the skyline'. Having completed the climb, they went due south to the summit of Stob Coire nan Lochan, and eventually descended to Coire Gabhail and followed the burn back to Glen Coe, the Study and 'the ever trusty motor'.

All the guidebooks consulted credit the Raeburn party with the first winter ascent. However, universal confusion reigns as to the people involved:

5   See Chapter 18.

Fig 2

Central Buttress Ordinary Route on Stob Coire nan Lochan; the route starts from the discoloured grassy ramp just right of centre. Photo: Noel Williams

Fig 3

Sketch map of Central Buttress by Mabel Inglis Clark published in *SMCJ* (1909). Photo: Noel Williams

five out of six guidebooks invent someone called *Mrs C Inglis Clark*—the initials of this fictitious lady should have alerted the editors to a mistake. Of course, Mrs Clark was called Jane (or Janie) and her son was Charles (or Charlie), who lent his initials posthumously to Scotland's most famous mountain hut. There were three Clarks on the climb: father, wife and son. Not one of the earlier guidebook editors bothered to ascertain the date of the climb (14 April 1907), contenting themselves with the month only.[6] The grade, of course, is to an extent debatable; it has never been less than III, and some now say IV,5. In *Scottish Winter Climbs* (SMC, 2008), Central Buttress Ordinary Route has been appropriately renamed Raeburn's Route, but the Cicerone Guide to *Winter Climbs Ben Nevis and Glencoe* (Pescod, 2010) retains the original name. Of the two, Raeburn might well have approved of the latter. The renaming, however, does avoid the confusion between Raeburn's climb on Central Buttress and the other 'Ordinary Route' by Kenny Spence and partner on the buttress to the left of Broad Gully.

---

6 The task of a guidebook editor is an unenviable one, and carping is uncalled-for, especially nowadays with a vast number of new routes every year, but it is a pity not to get the names of the pioneers right.

18. SHELTER STONE, BEN NEVIS, LOCHNAGAR, CÀRN DEARG 1907–1908

Having contributed a fine new rock climb in Sutherland and an important winter buttress in Glencoe, Raeburn turned his attention to the Cairngorms. Until this time relatively little climbing had been done here except on Sgòran Dubh Mòr and in the Northern Corries, but Raeburn was alive to the potential of this vast area:

> [I]n their deep recesses and far-reaching glens, circling the lonely hollows where sleep the dark waters of their alpine tarns, are many fine masses of steep bare rock. Such a mass is the Shelter Stone Crag at the head of remote Loch Avon. (SMCJ, 1908).

On 15 June 1907 Harold met with his friend Frank Goggs, who was again living temporarily in Kingussie. They were determined to visit the Shelter Stone. It should be remembered by the modern reader that in those days the Cairngorms had not been tamed by ski developments and there was no easy access. The Shelter Stone was really remote—probably more remote than the Garbh Coire of Beinn a' Bhùird is today.

Goggs and Raeburn set off by bicycle from Kingussie at 7 pm, past Coylum Bridge, and then on 'to the forest track that leads to the crossroads near Loch an Eilean'. They found that they could cycle with care except 'where the road was laid corduroy fashion' with rough pine logs over the boggy parts. Raeburn had an 11-year-old memory of there being a bothy at the foot of the Lairig Ghru, and by good fortune Goggs had been there the week before and found it open.

They arrived at the bothy an hour and 40 minutes after leaving

Kingussie—no mean feat—and spent time collecting heather to sleep on, drawing water and getting a fire going. Raeburn, a notoriously poor sleeper away from civilisation, found the bed 'a trifle spiky'. He was up at 1.30 am and 'looked out upon the forest night'. The weather prospects were good, the north wind 'rapidly driving the black pall of cloud southwards'. After rousing the fire and cooking a good breakfast they left at 2.40 am and headed for the Loch Avon cliffs by way of the tops above Lurcher's Crag. Up on the plateau the north wind was cold, and the pools covered with a film of new ice. 'Swinging round the west shoulder' of Cairn Lochan they 'entered that desolate country … where the Allt Feith Buidhe has its source'. The scene reminded Harold of the 'high Fjelde of Norway. Widespreading snowfields stretched away on all sides … névé, filling the hollows, terminated in miniature glacier snouts, from below whose steep snow gushed many a running rivulet of snow water'.

Making their way over to the top of the Shelter Stone Crag they had difficulty crossing the Garbh Uisge. It is fascinating that Raeburn and Goggs started their exploration of the crags from above. They had what Raeburn describes as 'a pleasant steep scramble of fifty-five minutes to the foot' of what we now know as Castle Wall (Diff in summer, III/IV in winter). 'Somewhat ill-defined at first, the climb lower develops into a definite arête.' Raeburn concedes that 'the lower part … occasionally develops portions of a mildly difficult kind'. There was also some rotten rock to contend with.

The friends descended to the Shelter Stone itself. Raeburn was not impressed: 'its interior is comfortless and damp in the extreme'. After lunch and a doze in the sun they roused themselves and discovered 'a well-defined very steep rib' to the right of the Castle Wall, and divided from it by a steep gully.[1] They tackled the rib.

After climbing for about 60 ft 'the direct route became so steep and slabby' that they had to make a traverse to the left almost into the gully. A neat little chimney with an overhang at the bottom and a difficult and exposed exit got them back onto the arête. Raeburn describes the rock as 'good' but the holds as being 'apt to be obscured by moss and earth, adhering in places at angles approaching the vertical'. The word horrendous springs to mind.

1   Now Breach Gully, grade IV.

Worse was to come. 'Then followed forty feet of slabby rockwork, which Goggs wishes me to label as dangerous'. It certainly sounds so, and even Raeburn had to concede that 'Possibly that label is no libel.' As he says, it was 'no place for the exhibition of chamois-like agility', rather they needed to combine moving delicately with 'the adhesive crawl of a remarkably sluggish lizard'. A slightly easier portion followed, and then they had to make another short traverse to the left and regain the arête by 'a short overhanging chimney'. Above were 'more steep ledges, and two "balance corners"', one requiring a mantelshelf. From that point they ascended 'a steep grass gully' for some 60–70 ft, eventually going right to regain the elusive arête yet again.

From here the drop to the screes appeared almost vertical for 400 ft. There was more scrambling but the real difficulties were over and they reached the top at 10.55 am. Goggs, perhaps high on adrenalin and doubtless glad to be alive, wanted to walk over Cairn Gorm or Macdui, but Raeburn pointed out that he had to be back in Edinburgh that night, so they retraced their steps, and after tidying up the bothy cycled back to Kingussie in the teeth of a strong south-west wind. They arrived at Goggs's place at 4.30 pm and Raeburn, remarkably, had 'ample time' for a bath and a meal before catching the 5.16 for Edinburgh.

[Fig 1] Goggs and Raeburn had descended, an awkward Diff., and climbed what was to become Raeburn's Buttress, which one modern guidebook to the Cairngorms describes as: 'Severe, vegetated and dangerous'. It was the hardest rock climb on the Shelter Stone Crag for some 62 years until Consolation Groove was climbed at HVS in 1969. As with his route on the Barrel Buttress of Quinag, the ascent of Raeburn's Buttress here on 16 June 1907 was several decades ahead of its time. Robin Campbell comments: '[O]nly a vague trace of this ferocious day remains in our current climbers' guidebook. I doubt whether there is any party in the present Club capable of repeating it' (*SMCJ*, 2007).

At the end of 1907 Charles Inglis Clark and his friends, Thomas Goodeve and John M'Intyre, arrived at the Alexandra Hotel in Fort William for the New Year Meet of the SMC. They set out early next morning for Tower Ridge and got themselves into all sorts of trouble through a combination of route-finding errors and inexperience. The story is told by Clark (*SMCJ*, 1908) and re-told by Ken Crocket (2015). The party was on the hill for a day

Fig 1

The Shelter Stone, on the right, is the scene of a famous long day by Raeburn and Goggs. Raeburn's description does not encourage modern summer ascents. Severe (and dangerous), IV,5 in winter.
Photo: Julian Lines

and a night, causing great anxiety, and several search parties were organised. Raeburn's part in the proceedings was significant.

To cut a long story short, Clark's party were unable to climb or find a way round the Great Tower on the ridge. They tried to traverse off to the right into what we now know as Glover's Chimney, descending that until they were stopped by the daunting appearance of its lower icefall. Deciding to escape the gully to the right (west), they found a way onto the steep ice and snow slopes, now home to routes of grade III and upwards, and heroically climbed these, with the usual lack of protection, surmounted the cornice and gained the plateau in the dark. By this time Goodeve and M'Intyre were both suffering from frostbite. They were unable to light their candle lantern because of the wind and so could not see the compass. Trying to avoid the corniced cliffs to their right they deviated too far left and headed down into Coire Eoghain. Climbing down a very steep slope, M'Intyre slipped, pulled the others off, and injured his head, but recovered enough to continue. As dawn came at last, they headed for the col between lower Càrn Mòr Dearg and the west flank of the Ben.

As they neared the col they saw:

> [A]n active figure bounding down to us at a very rapid pace. From his speed we surmised it could be none other than Raeburn, and a few minutes later he was heartily shaking hands all round, acting the kind Samaritan with sandwiches and other dainties ... Under his kind and able guidance, we were piloted through the narrow and difficult gorge which leads down into Glen Nevis.

They reached Fort William at 1pm on Sunday afternoon.

It says a lot about Raeburn that he seems to have made no judgments and offered no criticism of the young party and simply concentrated on cheering them up and getting them down safely.

Raeburn was out again on Monday, 30 December, and with Ling and Harry Walker climbed the Castle. On Tuesday he soloed a route on the north face of Castle Ridge—unfortunately his line is not recorded; nor was any other route until 1959.

On New Year's Day (Wednesday) Raeburn, Ling, Walker and John Bell hired bicycles and went to Garbh Bheinn in Ardgour by way of the Corran

Ferry. Raeburn, writing in 'Excursions' (SMCJ, 1908), says that it is possible to get to 'Garbhvein' [sic] from Fort William even at New Year, but one must start and finish in the dark. Accordingly, the party took the 6 am ferry.

Unfortunately the bicycles gave trouble, and the split boulder in the corrie was not reached until 8.30 am. Bell and Walker went off on their own and crossed 'below the ridge, climbed the opposite slope, and then returned to the split boulder' in order to help each other with the faulty bike. Pace M'Intyre, who wrote the official account of the Meet, it looks as if they did not climb any more that day and Ling and Raeburn were left to their own devices.

They looked at the Great Gully, but it was too severely iced, and they climbed the Great Ridge instead: 'the narrow little grass ledges on the very steep and slabby rocks were powdered with icy snow and too hard to be penetrated by an ice-axe'.[2] However, they enjoyed sunny weather and, remarkably, it was 'quite warm on the ridge'. They surprised an eagle which, to judge by the paw prints round about the summit cairn, Raeburn guessed was waiting for a hare to emerge from it. [Fig 2]

Raeburn and Ling followed 'the whole ridge of the mountain' and descended the north-east buttress. Near the bottom of this is a very steep and slabby section, and Raeburn casually mentions that they had to 'abseil' into a gully cutting the right wall to avoid this. They got back to the Alexandra at 6.30 pm. One wonders if the north-east buttress has had any more voluntary descents since. It was another very demanding day accomplished in exemplary time.

Good Friday in 1908 (17 April) saw Raeburn, Goodeve and Ling back on Lochnagar. Plainly, Raeburn had been impressed by Goodeve's performance on Ben Nevis and with him and the trusty Ling chose to make yet another attempt on Douglas-Gibson Gully. In the event they were 'driven back by the sudden thaw and consequent avalanching in the gully'. However, as recorded in the Proceedings of the Club (SMCJ, 1908), they went on to make what may well have been the first winter ascent of 'the north ridge of the Black Spout', which we now know as Black Spout Buttress (III,5), but this is credited to others in modern guidebooks.

On Saturday 18 April, Raeburn, Ling, Goodeve, William Garden and

2   Raeburn and Ling are now credited with the first winter ascent on 1 January 1908.

Fig 2

The Great Ridge of Garbh Bheinn in light snow conditions. Similar to those in which Raeburn and Ling made the first winter ascent. Photo: Neil Adams

Henry Watson crossed the Dee by the Inverchandlich Ferry, walked up the Slugain, climbed the north arête of Beinn a' Bhùird and descended by a steep snow slope to the left of this ridge. They lengthened their day by climbing a 'snow rake, running through rocks on the south side of the lochan', continuing to the south top of the mountain and so back to Braemar by the Slugain.

The weather on Easter Sunday was frightful with blizzards on the tops. Raeburn and Ling walked to Derry Lodge and spent the night there. On Monday they climbed a gully leading from the 'little upper Corrie' to the top of Braeriach, then went round the Garbh Coire, over Angel's Peak and back to Derry Lodge in soft snow. Overall the weather and conditions were not favourable during this Meet, but Raeburn and his companions had four days of continuous endeavour and activity. The winter ascent of Black Spout Buttress, a feather in the cap of any ordinary climber, is recorded as an afterthought. Also notable is their determination to go somewhere different each day.

Late summer of 1908 found Raeburn back on Ben Nevis. The article he wrote chronicles the day (*SMCJ*, 1909). On 28 September Raeburn combined with Harry MacRobert, David Arthur and others for a couple of days' climbing. MacRobert's party had already had a good day on Tower Ridge and on the 27th Raeburn had let MacRobert lead them all up Observatory Ridge. For the following day Raeburn promised them 'something new'.

Accordingly they foregathered 'about level with the foot of the Castle rocks' under 'a massive and well-defined buttress'. They made 'a direct attack' on this, but the rocks, greasy in the drizzle, were 'covered with very slightly adherent sheets of moss'. So they took to the waterslide on the left with some difficulty; it too was greasy, and also slabby. Once in, however, things improved; they found the holds better and quickly got up 100 ft. The gully divides at this point, the right fork 'running up in a deep chimney'. They took to this chimney, getting in 'over a chock-stone of doubtful stability', and encountered a 'very steep pitch, where the rocks were decidedly worn and slabby'. Raeburn thought this the worst part of the climb, especially in the wet.

In 80 ft the holds improved and the chimney became 'a black cave gripping between its jaws a far-out chock-stone'. They went by the right wall of the cave, which was 'slightly overhanging' but had 'superb holds'. The party gathered on top of the chock-stone and the second took 'a good stand' while Raeburn 'contoured some rather nasty slabs', eventually getting into another 'narrow gully, farther to the right'. The angle eased and they gained the arête by climbing the gully wall on the right.

The arête was gentle to begin with but 'soon narrowed and steepened, and in places [was] extremely rotten'. They threw down many blocks, one of which was 'over half a ton in weight, [and] caused a perceptible tremor to shake the whole of the great buttress'. As they made progress the arête became 'ever steeper and narrower, and at length ... overhanging and not more than a few feet' wide. To the right was 'a smooth slab, rushing down almost vertically, "straight as a beggar can spit"'[3] for several hundred feet. To the left was 'a steep drop into a black chimney'. An exposed and difficult situation. Raeburn says: 'there was one small foothold on the slab side of the arête, and another, very high and badly sloping, for the left foot on the chimney side, but the handholds at first appeared non-existent'.

At this crucial juncture Raeburn indicates a somewhat startling development in rope-work, mentioning that his companions were 'carefully belayed to blocks lower down'. This, one suspects, is the first mention of a 'belay' rather than a mere 'hitch' in Raeburn's mountaineering articles. The phrase 'carefully belayed' might suggest that they have actually tied themselves to the blocks and not merely run the rope behind them.

Be that as it may, 'with an effort the mauvais pas was passed, and the leader gained security astride a knife edge on the top of the slab'. The arête was now level and led across to the summit of the buttress. Raeburn reckoned that the climb was 700 ft and, characteristically, he is sure that it took 3 hours and 10 minutes. They built a large cairn and came down by Number 4 Gully.

Raeburn adds that he has never seen Ben Nevis's corries 'carry so little snow', and his closing remarks lament the fact:

To me, Nevis is much more familiar in snow and ice conditions, and I must confess to a feeling of something wanting, a gauntness and raggedness of the great crags. There is a flowing grace of line lent to their beauty by the far-flung drapery of the snow-fields, that enhances, to my mind, the pleasure of a visit to the north-east face of Ben Nevis in the early summer.

---

3   Quoted by MacRobert from the fifth verse of Rudyard Kipling's poem, 'Screw Guns'.

Fig 3

Raeburn's Buttress on Càrn Dearg, Beinn Nevis. The route follows a line out of the dark area at the base of the gully to the left and up the steepening rocks in the centre of the photo. The final slender prow which caused Raeburn some trouble is clearly visible at centre-right. Photo: Noel Williams

[Fig 3]   His climb is now called Raeburn's Buttress; it is entirely separate from the Walker Cousins' Buttress, and is graded V. Diff and IV,5.

Raeburn's year ended with his being made a Vice-President of the SMC in place of Willie Naismith, whose term of office had expired. Raeburn never became President. He was offered that honour later in his career but declined it, a fact we only learn from his obituary by his old friend, Willie Ling.

19. SOME TRIUMPHS AND AN ACCIDENT

1909-1910

The 1909 New Year Meet at Killin on the shores of Loch Tay found Raeburn skiing in a party of five from the watershed above Lochan na Lairige and over the Tarmachans, 'half the time on grass', according to the Meet Report by AD Smith (*SMCJ*, 1909). However, better things were in store, for on 2 January Harold drove with Willie Ling and Herbert Boyd to Luib and climbed Stobinian from the north-east corrie. What made this ascent special was that they accompanied seven members of the LSCC.[1] This is the first mention in the *SMCJ* of Harold being out with a group of women, though he had often been on the same rope with female members of the Clark family—most often Jane. In her report of the Meet, printed in 'Excursions' in the same edition of the *SMCJ*, Jane's daughter, Mabel Clark, says:

> *The ladies met Mr Raeburn, Mr Ling, and Dr Boyd on 2 Jan at Luib, and from there made the ascent of Stobinian by a snow gully. Three ropes were used and in each case the ladies led their party up the gully, aided by the advice of the members of the SMC who had so kindly arranged the climb. The descent was made to Crianlarich where the gentlemen were entertained to tea.* (ibid.)

It is interesting that the SMC seems to have 'arranged' the climb. William Clark of course was the Secretary of the Club at the time, and his wife Jane was President of the LSCC. One wonders if it was suggested to

---

1   The LSCC had been founded a few months earlier.

Raeburn—newly appointed Vice-President—that it would be a nice idea. We'll never know, but it certainly appears that Raeburn enjoyed climbing with women and chose to do so on many occasions.

After this pleasant diversion Raeburn, Boyd, Harry MacRobert and Austen Thomson went to Craig na Caillich on the Tarmachan Ridge on Sunday, 3 January. Raeburn, as we know, had climbed there previously with the late Harry Lawson. On that occasion they had failed to climb the obvious gully in its entirety. This time they found 'a fair waterfall to start with, but after the first plunge was over, things were not so bad. Very little snow was found in the gully, but some ice was encountered in the central pitch'. At the nasty grassy pitch about halfway up, a new traverse was made to the right and then back again before the final difficult section, which was climbed 'on the left side, gradually working out to the steep grassy face'. Still not completely content with the line, they then tried to top-rope the direct ascent of the difficult pitch they had circumvented, but came to the conclusion that it was 'impossible'.

On Monday, Raeburn, H Hill, Harry Walker and John Bell took the train to Crianlarich. From there Hill and Walker walked back to Killin, but Raeburn and Bell went up Ben More and again met the LSCC, this time near the top, but apparently no snow was to be found anywhere on the mountain. Presumably this was an unplanned trip, perhaps undertaken just for the pleasure of enjoying the ladies' company again.

Readers cannot have failed to notice that Harold Raeburn is reticent to the point of silence about his feelings for other individuals. He seldom voices any sort of opinion about anyone and never a bad opinion. He was a popular member of the SMC; other people sought his company and he had friends with whom he repeatedly chose to share his adventures. He liked literature. He had a sense of humour. He was good looking and dressed well, and he was a relatively prosperous businessman. In short there was no reason why he should not enjoy fulfilling relationships with women, and observing how he actively sought their company one senses that he wanted such relationships. That, so far as we know, nothing substantial ever happened, or if it did (perhaps with Natalia Yovitchitch—see Alps chapters), came to nothing, is an enigmatic part of his story.

However that may be, at the Easter Meet of 1909 on 8 April, according to Mabel Clark again, 'a large party of thirteen ... seven ladies and six members

[Fig 1] of the SMC, made three new ascents of Ben Dothaidh[2] by the north corrie, the ladies in each party taking the lead'. Raeburn was one of the six.

The Easter Meet in question was very productive for Raeburn. On Friday, 9 April, with Ling, George Gibbs and Arthur Mounsey, he climbed Tower Ridge, including the Douglas Boulder by its west arête. Apparently the rocks low down were in 'ideal condition' (for rock climbing, the preference still being for dry rock), but high up they were iced. Willie Douglas, looking down from the plateau, saw Raeburn 'working busily in the "Recess", the chip, chip of his axe being plainly heard, whilst every now and again a shower of ice could be seen to shoot out and rattle down the cliffs, indicating what was being done to get the road clear'. An accompanying photo by Mounsey of Tower Gap shows much snow. The party of four took twelve-and-a-half hours: a very good time given the conditions, the inclusion of the Boulder and the choice of Recess Route on the Great Tower.

Raeburn was out again on Saturday with Frank Goggs, Gilbert Thomson and Percy Unna. They climbed the North-East Buttress, approaching by the slabs to the right of Slingsby's Chimney. Thereafter the arête was closely followed. The only difficulty was at the 40-foot Corner 'where every hold was thickly caked with ice'.

After these two expeditions, both starting, not as nowadays from the proximity of the CIC Hut, but from the hotel in Fort William, Raeburn used 11 April to cycle to Glencoe, where the following day with English acquaintances, WA Brigg and H Scott Tucker, he made what can probably best be described as the first full winter ascent of Crowberry Gully. In his Meet Report (*SMCJ*, 1909), John Levack says that Raeburn climbed the gully 'under very bad conditions'. He rightly calls it a 'second ascent', the first having been made by Raeburn in 1898. Quoting Raeburn, he says:

> The old snow in the gully was good and firm, but it was snowing nearly all the time, and the fresh snow kept pouring down and was heavy enough to sweep out the party without careful hitching. The pitches near the top were difficult owing to ice on slabby rocks. The last pitch was

---

2   Robin Campbell has pointed out that these routes, two of which were subsequently claimed by other climbers, were quite hard, likely 'Stairway to Heaven' and 'Taxus', both III. Raeburn's party probably climbed West Gully. See Campbell's note 'Some Old New Routes' (SMCJ, 2009).

Fig 1

Six men and six ladies apparently en route for winter climbing on Beinn an Dothaidh. This took place at the Easter Meet of 1909. Standing from left: Anna Ranken, Mabel Clark, Raeburn, George Lissant Collins (AC), Alexander Mackay, William Garden, Willie Douglas and Willie Ling. Seated: Ruth Raeburn, Pauline Ranken, Joan Smith and Daisy Gillies. Photo: Lucy Smith

turned by a traverse which was somewhat difficult under the prevailing conditions. The climb took four hours and twenty minutes.

Raeburn wrote about this ascent in a later edition of the SMCJ (1911) shortly after he made the third ascent of the Gully, this time in summer conditions. The 1909 ascent is important because it is arguably the first ascent in good winter conditions. Raeburn notes that there was actually less snow in the Gully than in 1898 and the first serious pitch 'was very stiff. Fortunately the thick glaze of ice on the right wall allowed of steps and handholds being cut.' He says that most of the other pitches were 'greatly snowed up, and were not seriously difficult'. At the 'great pitch below the "fork", however, [they] were forced to make a long traverse out on the north wall, rather nasty with ice, and slippery with new snow'. They regained the bed of the gully above and found that the remaining pitches were so snowed up 'as to offer comparatively little resistance'.

Why, one might ask, if there was more snow in 1898 was that ascent not the first winter ascent? If there is an answer it is that the temperature in '98 must have been higher and there was no ice to speak of. By contrast, ice is the means by which the crux is overcome in 1909 and the weather is also extremely wintry. Plainly there will be ascents which are hard to categorise.

It is significant that Harold only feels the need to write an article about the Gully when he has climbed it in fully summer conditions; he still seems to think that this is the more complete form of ascent. (It is also worth noting that when Raeburn eventually climbs Crowberry Gully in summer, on 18 September 1910, Francis Greig leads the way except for a diversion which he and Raeburn make to explore the left fork. Here Raeburn takes over, but they eventually decide that it 'won't go'. Harold mentions that Greig had also led the 'Slanting Gully of [Sgùrr a'] Mhadaidh' in Skye and thought Crowberry Gully 'a finer climb than that'.)

In the space of four days in April 1909 Raeburn climbed three lengthy classic winter routes, cycling from Fort William to Glencoe on the 'rest' day. He was obviously very fit and full of energy.

Although Raeburn and Ling enjoyed an active season in the Alps in 1909, sources reveal no more activity in Scotland until 27 February 1910, when Willie Ling records a serious accident in his Diary. Raeburn, Ling, Edith Gray, Ruth Raeburn, Lucy Smith, John Bell and Robert Hope set out from

Strathyre Hotel and motored to the foot of Glen Ample. They walked up the glen, but at the shepherd's cottage Bell left and went home, for reasons unknown. The rest continued to the bealach and had lunch on the other side. The weather was warm and the snow was in good condition.

They wanted to climb a buttress to gain the summit of the Stùc a' Chroin, so Raeburn roped up with Lucy, Robert and Edith, while Ling and Ruth climbed on a separate rope. Lucy felt unfit, so on reaching the same height as the pass Raeburn's party decided to continue by an easier route. To the left was an open chimney above a steep slope of hard snow, which was topped by a stone without holds. Raeburn tried the stone but couldn't get up it, so traversed across the bounding slab by 'a frozen turf foothold, and from another foothold gained a platform above the slab'.

Clearly they were attempting to move together, for Robert climbed onto the grassy hold. Before he was properly established on it, Edith slipped and pulled him off, thereby dislodging Lucy. The combined weight of all three came onto Raeburn and he was jerked out horizontally from the cliff and landed on the snow with 'a sickening thud'. All four then slid down the slope, Raeburn in front.

Fortunately the falling climbers missed Ling and Ruth, who were just below where the first party had been. Ling untied, left Ruth, and dashed down the slope. The others were apparently unhurt, but 'Raeburn was lying helpless and head down'. When Ling reached him he was barely conscious, but he came round when raised, though his ribs were broken and he was in a bad state. Robert descended and they 'bandaged Raeburn with puttees, then slid him down the slope through a narrow gap between rocks'. Amazingly he then managed to stand up and, heavily supported, reached the bealach at 4 pm.

Ling left his coat and hat for Raeburn and raced down to Glen Ample Farm in 25 minutes. With shepherds Tam and John Hunter, they made a makeshift stretcher from two poles with a large wool bag nailed to them and two blankets. Ling sent off a message for a doctor and then set off back up the hill. Just before 6 pm they met Raeburn, almost exhausted, supported by Lucy and Ruth (they had met Lucy and Edith descending earlier).

Raeburn was suffering from the cold, so they wrapped him in coats and blankets and got him on the stretcher. The carry was exhausting and many stops were necessary. It was dark, and until Ruth, who had gone down, returned with a lantern, they had difficulty seeing their way. They eventually reached the cottage at 8.30 pm and got Harold into bed with hot water bottles. The doctor arrived just after 9 pm and bandaged him properly. With broken ribs (either from the fall or, more likely, by the sudden, heavy jerk of the rope), shock and cold he was in intense pain. Ling gives no account of the aftermath. We don't know if Raeburn was hospitalised, given morphine, or if an ambulance came to take him home. Ling says only that it was 'truly a sad end to a joyous day'.

It seems that as well as his more obvious injuries, Raeburn suffered some kind of internal damage. A letter he wrote to Geoffrey Winthrop Young, dated 13 April 1910, is worth quoting:

My accident though bad enough for me was less thro' the actual injury than to the digestive troubles ensuing. It kept me six weeks on my back however and of course I am still very weak and not able to get about much.

Of the incident, he says:

The place was not a definite climb and was not difficult and only about 25 ft high. My injuries were caused more by the fearful jerk of 30 stones' weight on the rope round my waist than by the fall.

He ends on a positive note, however:

One thing the accident has demonstrated to me ... is the kindness and consideration of my friends. I am profoundly grateful to all of them. I am glad to say that I am mending so fast that I have hopes of not only getting out to the Alps but of being able to do smaller climbs ...

And he did indeed get to the Alps that year and did much more than 'smaller climbs'. However, one cannot help wondering about the 'digestive troubles' his accident caused, and whether they played any part in the ill-health he suffered thereafter on the Everest Expedition.

The accident itself did not seem to make Raeburn reflect on the use of the rope in mountaineering. It seems to us obvious that the leader should attach himself firmly to the rock before bringing up the second, and that if Raeburn had done this the accident would probably have been avoided. Of course, taking a proper belay was just not the way things were done in those days: one hitched the rope behind a convenient projection and hoped for the best. We don't know if Raeburn even had this security or simply relied on having a good stance—probably the latter. After all, as he says, it wasn't really 'a definite climb'. If a demonstration of the dangers of this kind of belaying was needed, the accident could hardly have been bettered, but the message seems to have gone unheeded. Raeburn was said to be a man of very firm opinions. One gets used to doing things in a certain way and changing or even questioning engrained habits is notoriously difficult. Moreover, mountaineering had begun to develop its own code of conduct. Suggesting safer belaying methods might have been viewed by some rather as if a change in the rules of cricket were being proposed.

Raeburn cared about safety on the hill, demonstrated by his long article on 'Scottish Snow'. He even maintained that 'Safe' is the highest commendation that can be given to a climber. Plainly, however, he is primarily thinking of the intrinsic ability of the leader and not about what he might be able to do with equipment and belaying techniques. Safety, it seems, resides for him almost entirely in the skill and prudence of the leader, although he must select good hitches and know how to use an axe to belay with. Raeburn was a very intelligent and reflective person, but it never seemed to occur to him to question the orthodoxy of his age, and in this he was a man of his time.

20. PRE- AND DURING WAR PERIOD   1910–1918

We next encounter Raeburn on 25 June 1910, just four months after his accident, as he and Ling joined up with their old friend, John Bell, and his wife for a surprisingly wintry *descent* of Ben Nevis shortly after midsummer. The action is described by Bell in a *SMCJ* article (1911).

Bell and his wife, who remains nameless, are given credit for punctuality by Raeburn when they turn up at the Alexandra just after 8 am, but he complains that they should have started an hour earlier. The walk up is reasonably cool, and Ling and Raeburn produce their 'aluminium cooking apparatus brought in honour of [Bell's] wife' and provide 'a very excellent second breakfast'.

Bell admits that time has qualified his enthusiasm for serious climbing—perhaps that was why he turned back on the fateful day of Raeburn's accident. He was last on the Ben 12 years before, but he says that, 'in the case of my friends, constant stoking had caused the fire in them to burn more fiercely than ever'. This observation certainly fits with Raeburn's recent exploits on the Ben and in Glencoe.

Ling and the Bells roped up to climb Tower Ridge, but 'Raeburn roamed about unattached, sometimes in front and sometimes behind.' They climbed the Great Tower by the Eastern Traverse because none of them had been that way before, and must have been amazed at how much easier it was than the alternatives to the west. The ascent from Fort William took some eight hours. The Ben was in cloud and they spent the rest of the day in the Summit Hotel on 'tea, dinner and inspection of the visitors' book'. It got cold after dinner and they were invited to share the kitchen fire 'with the staff of the inn'. (The proceedings sound suspiciously like a jolly afternoon and evening in the CIC Hut.)

They awoke the next morning to a snowy gale and 'every rock covered with a frozen white coating'. Nevertheless, they decided to press ahead with the plan to descend North-East Buttress, and Raeburn partnered up with Mrs Bell while Ling and Bell climbed together. The best climber partnering the least experienced was clearly deemed to be the sound option. Bell notes that 'North-East Buttress offers numerous back doors, and almost all the difficulties can be dodged. Under the conditions it was not quite easy to find the way, and even by the easy route we had to go slowly and carefully on the upper three or four hundred feet until we got off the ice.' Bell makes this sound mundane, but one suspects it was really quite gripping, especially for Mrs Bell, who must have been a spirited and capable climber. Near the foot of the buttress they attempted to traverse off to Coire Leis but got too low, missing the easier way along the First Platform. Bell was glad they remained roped and ignored the suggestion of unroping made 'when leaving the ridge'.

Raeburn had to catch the afternoon train to Edinburgh, and anyway the cold and the wet chased them away. The experience left Mrs Bell wanting more, 'to see the legendary Ben of the photographs and the stories of Easter 1895 with a great snow mantle ... and the sun glittering on the ridges'.

James R Young,[1] the reporter at the New Year Meet of 1911 at Loch Awe, records the fact that 'a party of Ultramontanes essayed the buttress on the true left of the Big Gully on Beinn a' Bhuiridh's cliffs'. Apparently, its icy condition forced them to 'traverse off it into the gully, which was crossed, and the climb completed on the true right' (i.e. the left, looking up). The party was composed of Raeburn, Ling, Charlie Walker and Thomas Goodeve, who seemed by now to be firmly established in the circle of Raeburn's partners of choice. However, the weather was poor and nothing further seems to have been done on this occasion.

After this meet in 1911 it is rumoured that Raeburn had another accident of some kind. Indeed, *The Scotsman* obituary of 23 December 1926 reports that an accident took place, but there are no details. A medical report from the time of Raeburn's confinement in a mental hospital, after his return from the Everest Expedition, also states that he was treated at home for

---

1   Young would later accompany Raeburn to the Caucasus.

'melancholia' (depression) in 1911. It is certainly true, whatever the cause, that Raeburn missed an Alpine season through some form of indisposition.

Harold was back on the hill on 28 September 1911 when he and Arthur Russell attempted a first ascent of No. 2 Gully on Ben Nevis 'without the aid of snow', although their attempt was brought to a halt when 'a not inconsiderable weight of sodden snow' fell on the leader's head (SMCJ, 1912). They prudently retreated, avoiding 'rocks deeply covered with soft, fresh snow' and ascended to the plateau by what has become known as Raeburn's Easy Route, which gains a broad ledge above a line of steep cliffs and brings one to the plateau between No. 2 Gully and Tower Ridge. As Raeburn remarks, one only has to use one's hands in two places following this line; it is the easiest route to the plateau out of the Càrn Dearg and Nevis corries except for No. 4 Gully.

While Raeburn was climbing Easy Route he was probably reminded of the much more difficult escape from Tower Ridge made by Thomas Goodeve, Charles Inglis Clark and John M'Intyre in 1907, for he says:

> [A]ny party climbing the Tower Ridge as far as the Tower and finding the upper rocks ... in too icy condition, might make a safe descent to Coire na Ciste by this route. Crossing the Tower Gap Chimney [Glover's] about half way of its height, the upper ledge would be gained. Thence the upper snowfield above the "Garadh" is easily reached.

Raeburn called his 'Excursions' piece 'Ben Nevis – Coire na Ciste – An Easy Way Out' (SMCJ, 1912). Plainly he was thinking of the safety of other mountaineers when contributing this note.

On 22 September 1912 Raeburn, his sister Ruth, Harry MacRobert and James Young made a variation on the north-east face of Cìr Mhòr on Arran. Starting up B1 Gully they crossed over into the big cave on B2 Gully, which Raeburn (SMCJ, 1913) mordantly remarks, 'was, as originally, and probably almost always, wet'. They avoided the cave by a traverse on the right wall. Back in B1, a short distance up, they traversed Gully B2 and reached B-C rib 'above its steepest part'. From here they looked up 'into the great upper chasm of C gully'. Raeburn was impressed by the scale of its bounding slabs. 'Even the adepts of the most modern oromaniacal school, the "Naked-footed slab-crawlers" ... would find it difficult to make anything of such a place.'² On traversing back to the left the party managed to get onto and finish up B1-B2 rib. Raeburn adds that the top is level with 'the Bottle Dungeon Cave at the head of B2 gully' and this cave is now avoided 'by a new route'. Obviously in a good mood, he adds: 'Those ... who wish a neat problem in back and knee work, extending that expression to cover "shoulder and toe", may find keeping to the gully more amusing.'

In 1912 Harold contributed his last full article to the SMCJ, describing an ascent of Elephant Gully on The Brack in Arrochar. Raeburn's articles can sometimes be rather dour and technical, but on certain occasions they are suffused with sunny good humour. This article is not so ecstatic as his article on climbing Observatory Buttress on Ben Nevis, but it is a happy one, reflecting the simple joy and amusement of a satisfying day in the hills.

At the start Raeburn notes that the first ascent was by A Maclaren, SG and CP Shadbolt in 1906. He says they were unaware of this at the time, and only discovered their error when they found a cairn³ at the top of the route.

Elephant Gully contains two enormous chockstones. It got its unusual name when one early viewer wondered if there would be enough space to get past them, and another replied, 'an elephant, were he a rock climber, would probably be able to get through'. For his part, Raeburn reckoned that 'a seventy-foot whale would have no difficulty due to waist measurement'. He also thought the name much better than those usually given to climbs of this nature.

Evidently Raeburn's party had a very good day for their outing:

The day of our visit, 3 Nov. 1912, was a quite perfect one. Keen frost the previous night, and this morning an absolute dead calm, left the whole visible extent of Loch Long unruffled by the faintest ripple. The water was of extraordinary clearness, and more extraordinary still, seemed to possess in full the double capacity of perfect reflection and absolute transparency. At once every detail of the boulder-strewn shore, the bracken-clad lower slopes, the snow-tipped peaks, and the deep blue sky were mirrored in its polished surface. At the same time the rocks,

---

2   A joke at MacRoberts's expense: he was prone to climbing slabs barefoot.
3   The cairn, however, was built by James Wordie and partners on 23 May 1910, as he informed the editor in a note (SMCJ, 1913). Wordie, like Raeburn, was ignorant of the Shadbolt ascent at the time.

the sands, and the seaweed of the loch bottom were visible through the upper pictures of the surface. The effect struck one as though the water was not real. Something airier, lighter, more alive than the somewhat heavy and inelastic substance which we know results from the marriage of the fiery oxygen to the volatile hydrogen.

Raeburn was with his sister Ruth and Mrs Jane Clark with daughter Mabel and son Charlie. Jokingly, Harold calls Charlie 'the Cautious Chauffeur' because he had never been known 'by the Police' to exceed the speed limit. Charlie, not wanting to leave the family car by the road, took it down to the farm, but interestingly still beat the rest of them 'easily to the gully'. Was Raeburn slowing with age, or just being chivalrous and walking with Ruth, Jane and Mabel?

When they got to the base of the cliff they discounted the buttress to the left of the gully, because it was heavily iced. While the ladies waited, Harold and Charlie scrambled up under the first chockstone. They got about 80 ft up but retreated because 'the way got very narrow, slimy' and steep. With one accord they both thought, 'The ladies would not like this.'

On roping up at the bottom they got up the steep right wall despite the holds being 'loose and turfy'. A short traverse above led back to the gully bed. At this point Jane and Mabel discovered a small opening and, dropping a stone down it, they heard 'a faint rattling' for quite a time and concluded that this was the exit of the dark chamber below.

The party climbed up under another huge chockstone (some 30 ft across) and found a neat little ledge in the cave behind it. It was steep but straightforward and got all of them established on top of the stone. Then came the crux. From the turfy roof of the stone a narrow ledge, somewhat overhung, led out onto the right wall. Towards the outer end of the ledge, some five-and-a-half feet above, was a small flat-floored recess about 18 inches wide. At its back was a sharp-angled crack, which was 'the desired safety-key for the opening of this passage', but Raeburn could not reach it and had to use Charlie's shoulder. Contouring 'a rounded mossy rib' above, which demanded 'care and balance', they again entered the gully bed.

The third and last pitch was 'a long slanting tunnel', steep 'enough to render the stones with which it was superabundantly lined very restless ... One could almost think they could see real malignant mountain gnomes heaving and pushing behind the seldom ceasing stream of rock fragments'. At last they crawled out at the exit ... and found a cairn! 'However,' says Raeburn, 'we did not grudge it to the then unknown pioneers.'

In traditional manner they went on to the top of the mountain. To all the northern aspects the sky was clear, but to the south and west 'all the sun-bathed landscape was obliterated by a thin brown vale'. Smoke from Glasgow, 'it covered such an extent of Scotland as one could hardly have believed possible'. Ending on a happier note, Raeburn says: 'One could turn the back on this and gaze on the dazzling snows of Ben More, and nearer admire the almost Fujiyama-like outline of Ben Ime. This peak's form, framed in the black walls of the gully, had been one of our greatest scenic pleasures during the whole climb.'

It is fitting that Raeburn's fine series of articles for the *SMCJ* should end on this positive image, but his obvious disquiet at the pollution of Scotland's atmosphere in 1912 is also a significant characteristic of the man. In the same volume of the *SMCJ* he reviews the naturalist Seton Gordon's book, *The Charm of the Hills* (1914), in a very positive manner, demonstrating his deep affection for the natural environment, which runs like a motif through his work.

From this time onwards the echoes of Raeburn's activities become slighter and fainter in the *SMCJ*. At New Year in 1913 he was at the Meet in Killin. On 1 January he traversed the Tarmachan range, rather a favourite of his, and on the second he traversed Meall Ghaordaidh in Glen Lyon.

In 1914 he published three 'Excursions' notes in the *SMCJ*. The first two concern routes he knew on mountains in Skye. It seems that he wanted to alert other climbers to their existence as they might be useful.

The first is the East Ridge of Sgùrr Theàrlaich: 'a steep but broken buttress'. This, Raeburn says, is probably 'the quickest and easiest way of reaching the summit from Coruisk or The Dubhs, or even possibly from Coire Ghrunnda'. From the Bealach Coir' an Lochain, a short descent over scree leads to the foot of the ridge, easier on the north side 'and a straight line kept to the summit'. Raeburn holds that 'In a western gale this is a comfortable sheltered scramble, and avoids the somewhat difficult passage of the Theàrlaich-Dubh Gap.' The route is recorded in guidebooks as a 200 m Moderate, climbed in 1913.

The second note concerns a 'similar buttress' on Sgùrr MhicChoinnich, but it is 'unsatisfactory'—steep, slabby and overhanging. The climber has to traverse north on slabs which lead 'to broken easy ground without definite climbing'. Raeburn says, 'the first known ascent was in April 1903, under snow and ice conditions', presumably by him.

The third note is longer and concerns Sgùrr Coire an Lochain:

> *This splendid rock-mass, which may be described as a lower buttress of MhicChoinnich, presents to the north and facing Bidein a huge tower of steep and compact slabs. This tower is well defined by a remarkably straight-walled gully ... which cuts it off from the ridge separating Coire an Lochain from the upper part of Coireachan Ruadha.*

First climbed by Norman Collie in 1906, Raeburn thinks it probably has not 'been visited since' because of its inaccessibility—unless coming from Coruisk one actually has to 'descend' to reach it.

Raeburn, Meldrum and 'the brothers Wallwork' made what was probably the second ascent in 1913.[4] They approached from Coire a' Ghrunnda and crossed the ridge close to the foot of the tower leading to the Theàrlaich-Dubh Gap. 'An easy descent led past Theàrlaich's Coruisk face and across to the far side of the ridge connecting MhicChoinnich with Sgùrr Coire an Lochain': down here, slabby in places, to the foot of the buttress. They started to climb 'below the overhang of the very steep edge facing Bidein, but 'after a few hundred feet' they were 'forced to traverse, always on steep slabs, round to the south or left, and gradually worked their way up'. They 'failed to find an opening through the formidable overhang of the upper series of slabs till right on the corner of the tower facing the head of Coruisk'. They reached the top in 3 hours and 50 minutes, and despite being a party of four, 'no time was lost'. Raeburn says: 'It is an intricate and interesting climb, and as it is on a face, nowhere easy, it is difficult to describe a definite line to take.' He warns that 'hitches are not abundant, and great care is always necessary'. It is now simply called 'Raeburn's Route', a 300m V. Diff.[5]

It sounds like top-class mountaineering exploration on a little-known face and confirms one's impression that at 47, although Harold was perhaps

---

4   Raeburn does not give an exact date.
5   Probably under-graded.

a little slower on the hill, he was still undertaking very demanding routes.

At the Easter Meet of April 1914, he climbed Castle Ridge on Ben Nevis with guest and prospective member, Tyndale, on Saturday 11, going on over the summit and down by Càrn Mòr Dearg (*SMCJ*, 1914). On Monday 13 he climbed North-East Buttress yet again, with the same guest, obviously delighting in showing a prospective member what the Ben had to offer.

As related elsewhere, Raeburn was in the Caucasus in the summer of 1914 at the outbreak of the Great War, and he spent most of his time during the war working in an aeroplane factory in Glasgow. His recorded visits to the hills during this time are few, and he is not mentioned in the *SMCJ* as attending any meet until he and others are guests of the President Hugh Munro at Lindertis from 28 to 31 May 1915.

On that occasion, Raeburn, with Walter Reid and William A Galbraith, ascended 'the big Gully of Mayar', which began with a stretch of steep hard snow for which the leader (Raeburn?) had to borrow an axe. They went up the snow, 'over a bit of a rock face' and had to avoid a steeper, wet pitch on the right. They saw 'a tempting pinnacle' below and climbed it, then made a 'descent of the buttress of the Spout Gully'. As soon as they got to the bottom 'they made an ascent by the east buttress, thus making a clamber of 2,000 to 2,500 feet'. Reid (*SMCJ*, 1915), who wrote the report, says that Raeburn 'glissaded down the steep snow slopes towards the White Water' while he and Galbraith went on to Mayar and Dreish. The mention of glissading reminds one of Raeburn's almost childish fascination with this method of descent: how nice that he was able to practise a little in the middle of the war.

Undoubtedly more was done on this meet, but on the following days Reid couches his report in terms of Parties A and B without saying who was in each. However, strenuous exercise was had by all, and Raeburn was obviously still very fit and keen, and likely still the leader of any party he was in.

When Raeburn's friend Lt-Colonel Harry Walker, one of the Dundee cousins, was killed in the war, Harold wrote to the SMC committee suggesting that Walker's photograph should be hung in the Clubrooms in Edinburgh, and the committee considered this suggestion when discussing the issue of a suitable memorial to Club members killed in the war (*SMCJ*, 1916).

Raeburn attended the 56th Meet of the Club at New Year 1916 at Lochearnhead. Again, we do not know what he did because the hill parties are not named, but we are told that 'Raeburn, who arrived on motorcycle, reported that there was no Falls of Leny, but simply one rushing torrent of water, and that at one part the road was flooded to a depth of two feet or thereabout'. The weather seems to have precluded any serious climbing, but apparently at least two parties ascended Stùc a' Chroin, and it is natural to wonder if Raeburn went back to a favourite hill which caused him so much anguish (ibid.).[6]

Although he had some successful trips to the Lakes with Willie Ling, Harold's climbing activities during the war were relatively insignificant. Ling, by contrast, managed regular trips not only to the Lakes but also to Scotland, and he even managed to get to the Alps. It could well be that, in taking time off from work, Ling was wiser than Raeburn. After all, nobody knew how long the war was going to last and good health, mental and physical, requires relaxation and refreshment. So far as we can gather from the scant evidence provided by the war years, Harold, perhaps smitten by conscience—the feeling that as a fit man he should have been on active service—maintained his demanding tasks.

He worked in Glasgow, staying in Partick at an address which no longer exists, and it is probable, though not certain, that he worked for William Beardmore and Co. a few miles to the west and easily reached by tram or by motorbike. Beardmore and Co. manufactured planes and airships and eventually a remarkable range of war products, including ships, tanks and fuses for shells. This industry apparently provided work for 13,000 people at Dalmuir alone.

Given his experience, Harold probably worked in some supervisory or managerial capacity, but we do not really know what he did day by day. He has left no written records of this time, no diary, no letters, and he makes no allusion to it in his writings on mountaineering. This work was something he felt he had to do, and he undertook it, no doubt, with the same conscientiousness as he showed in his life as a businessman and a mountaineer.

What he did do during this period was write his book, *Mountaineering*

---

6 The only other wartime mentions are that he attended the informal Club Dinner on 7 December 1917, and that he was involved in work for the war effort for the duration of the conflict. The latter note probably did something to assuage Harold's quite irrational feelings of guilt that he was unable, because of his age, to take an active part in the fighting.

Art; indeed, the original manuscript was (inexplicably) lost and he re-wrote the whole thing in an astonishing three months so that the agreed publication date could be met. It is likely that writing the book, at least for the first time, gave him some sense of release and escape from what must have been an exhausting and tedious daily existence.

So far as he could, Harold obviously wanted to influence the war effort. Apart from his work, which was certainly his primary contribution, he wrote to *The Scotsman* with the advice for marching soldiers that they should wear a thin well-fitting inner sock as well as a thicker outer one to prevent rubbing and blisters, which in serious cases could turn septic. One doubts if any attention was paid to this well-meant advice by soldiers facing slaughter on an industrial scale in the horrors of the trenches. Like much of British society at the time, Harold seems to have been largely ignorant of the conditions faced by the troops in France and Flanders. (A fact which might have had a bearing on his relationships with some of the members of the Everest Expedition in 1921.)

In 1914 Harold also wrote to the SMC Committee suggesting that 'members of the club were in an ideal position to act as ... lookouts for enemy activities in the hills'. At the October Meeting the committee duly discussed this letter, which proposed that they 'circularise the keepers and shepherds in remote areas to report on any suspicious circumstances'. This sounds, now, like an episode of *Dad's Army*, but then, in a country just getting used to the idea that its borders could easily be crossed by aircraft, and given repeated reports of 'Flashing lights' seen in the hills, not to speak of attacks on coastal shipping by enemy submarines, it must have seemed much more serious.

Following Raeburn's suggestion, though not necessarily as a result of it, there was a well-documented spy hunting exercise carried out in the Galloway hills. Ling records in his Diary that several distinguished members of the SMC, including John Rennie, George Sang, Charlie Walker and Ling himself, trooped off into the hills to look for signs of suspicious activities on 19 March 1915. Ling records in his Diary: 'The burning heather interfered with our duty of watching for lights. At sea we saw 2 vessels signalling ... but we found nothing tangible.' A blizzard, perhaps mercifully, put a stop to this exercise. They tried again on 21 March, 'but heavy rain and mist rendered signalling out of the question'. Harold may have been involved in a similar exercise on the Merrick. It is known that he visited White Hill near Kirkcudbright on Wednesday, 19 May 1915 and 'acquired a shag's egg for his collection'. Presumably this visit also was concerned with monitoring enemy activities. There was probably a heightened sense of danger at that time because, only 12 days before, the *Lusitania* had been torpedoed and sunk with enormous loss of life 'as she entered the Irish sea bound for Liverpool'.

After the war ended with the Armistice of November 1918, Raeburn was swift in getting back to the Alps, traversing the Meije in 1919. In 1920 he made one final great Scottish climb: the first winter ascent of Observatory Ridge on Ben Nevis. Later that same year he visited the Himalayas to explore Kangchenjunga.

THE ALPS AND NORWAY

21. EARLY ALPS, NORWAY, SLOGEN

1901–1903

There are hills beyond Pentland
And lands beyond Forth ...

Raeburn's experience of the Alps began in 1900 when he had been a member of the SMC for four years. He and his long-time friend, Willie Douglas, spent the inside of a fortnight in the North-West Dolomites (*SMCJ*, 1901). Douglas was a good mountaineer and a splendid Editor of the *SMCJ*, but he was not in the same class as Raeburn as a climber and their brief trip was fairly modest. Among their joint ascents were the Grosse Fermeda, the Zahnkofel, the Fünffingerspitz and the Marmolada, and they employed guides, as was the custom of British climbers at the time.

They had 'broken weather', but Raeburn managed to include the summit of one of the Vajolet Towers. In the same 'Excursions' section of the *SMCJ*, other SMC members report much more successful Alpine trips. For example, Lawson, Ling and Glover climbed the Weisshorn, the Dent Blanche, the Strahlhorn, the Rimpfischhorn, the Rothorn and the Täschhorn. They too had rather poor weather, but more Alpine experience. Raeburn, however, was not one to rush things. He seems to have valued a gradual but steady approach to maturing as a mountaineer.

[Fig 1]

In August 1901, Douglas and William Garden spent three weeks in Switzerland and Raeburn joined them for their guided ascents of the Weisshorn, the Matterhorn and Monte Rosa. William Clark and his wife, Jane, spent five weeks in Chamonix. The weather was poor and not a lot was done, but Raeburn and James Parker joined them on an ascent of the Aiguille du Géant. After 1901 Raeburn, as he put it, largely gave

Fig 1

The Weisshorn from the Matterhorn. Raeburn climbed both peaks with guides in 1901 with Willie Douglas and William Garden. Photo: Roger Robb

Fig 2

Summit view from Skagastølstind. Photo: Barry Hard

up 'plodding behind guides'.

For two summer seasons he also abandoned the Alps for Norway, then as now a popular destination for British climbers. In August 1902 he visited Turtagrø with Howard Priestman and from there climbed in the Hurrungane group in Jotunheimen. The weather was bad: snowfalls interfered with the climbing, but Raeburn and Priestman traversed the Dyrhaugstinder and descended to Ringsbreen. With Herrer Tandberg and Pauss they managed to climb the 'face of the highest of the Soleitind', which they 'believed to be new'.

With Ole Berg (who was a guide), Raeburn made the first ascent of the season of Store Skagastølstind, the third-highest peak in Norway and one of the most highly prized among mountaineers. With Tandberg, Pauss and Lows he then made a complete traverse of all five Skagastølstinder from Turtagrø. The very next day, with Ole Berg and Fröken Berthau[1], Raeburn and Priestman went up to the Skagastol hut on Bandet, down Maradalsbreen and then up Midt Maradalstind. [Fig 2]

The South Dyrhaugstind from Bandet, with the ridge to Turtagrø, was climbed by Raeburn, Tandberg and Pauss. Raeburn delighted in this district, and thought it was like 'an enlarged Coolins with snow and glaciers'. Norway was a good place for him to abandon the use of guides, since there was less social pressure to employ them, away from the pervasive influence of the Alpine Club in the Alpine ranges. From this time onwards Raeburn's climbing was guideless.

In 1903 the weather was better in Norway. Raeburn and Priestman were joined by the experienced Willie Ling, by profession a grain merchant in Carlisle, who became Raeburn's most important partner, climbing with him in Scotland, the Lake District, the Alps and the Caucasus over some 15 years. Ling kept a remarkable climbing diary in which every expedition he ever made to the hills is recorded in considerable detail. Without this invaluable resource our knowledge of Raeburn's climbs would be much scantier.

In July 1903, Raeburn, Ling and Priestman got good climbs, mainly by new routes, in Sündmore. All three made a traverse—following an initial defeat—of the three peaks of the Sætretinder near Kolaas. Moving to Rise,

---

1   Thérèse Berthau was Norway's foremost lady climber for many years. She scandalized the bourgeoisie by wearing trousers on the crags (Campbell). One wonders what climbers might do nowadays to achieve similar notoriety.

Raeburn and Ling climbed the three peaks of the Grøtdalstinder, two of which were believed to be first ascents. From Hotel Union at Øye all three climbed Jakta (5,200ft), mostly by the North-East Arête. With the addition of Corder they also summited the first peak of the Brekketind Ridge in the Habostaddal.

Priestman and Corder then crossed the glacier to the Langesæterdal and followed the valley to Urke on the shore of the Norangsfjord. Meanwhile, Raeburn and Ling traversed the whole ridge of the Brekketind to Gjeithorn (about 5,200ft), which they thought 'a thoroughly sporting climb, the connecting ridge, extraordinary pinnacles, new'. Their account is in the Hotel Union guestbook:

24 July 1903 Grotsdalstinder [Grøtdalstindane]: These are the sharp peaks just above Rise & are a fine feature in the landscape from a short way down the fjord from Oie [Øye]. The most southerly has a surveyor's cairn on it. The other two do not appear to have been climbed before this date. The route followed was from Rise about 3km up the dal & up by the E side of the stream that comes in from the N out of the Glacier ... between Grotsdalstinder & Li ... horn. The route then went up the shoulder that comes down from the S peak to E and str up the .... to top. From the S peak the ridge was followed over the middle & N peaks—the latter has some not quite easy climbing taken this way & lies over in very slabby ridges. Fine views to N to Kolas, Saetretinder [Sætretindane] etc & S to Oie, Slogen etc.

Again, on 27 July they wrote:

27 July 1903 Brekketind & Gjeithorn [Geithornet]: These two peaks were completely traversed from the pass between Habostaddal & Velledal. The little peak lying on the watershed of Brunstaddal to S was ascended & the ridge followed round to Brekketind which was climbed from N. The ridge connecting B & Gjeithorn is a most cut up & pinnacled one & gives a very good climb. One or two of the pinnacles were traversed. After crossing Gjeithorn a descent was made to the glacier to N & Oie reached via pass between Slogen & Smorskedtind [Smorskredtinden].

On 28 July even better things were in store for Raeburn and Ling. Leaving the Hotel at Øye at 7am they set off up the unclimbed seaward face of Slogen (5,131ft), a magnificent rock peak, its face split by a huge gully. As Raeburn describes the ascent in the *The Yorkshire Ramblers' Club Journal* (1904), the conditions were absolutely perfect. At first, however, they had to retreat from 'holdless slabs' at 950ft. Descending to the screes they traversed below the falls of the great gully to gain the buttress 'which walls in the Armstrong-Vigdal gully on the South' and started climbing again to the west of the falls. [Fig 3]

The first part was 'a hot, stiff fight … by steep grassy ledges and through bushes and trees', often having to haul themselves up overhangs 'by roots and stems'. At 11am they crossed slabs on their right and entered the bed of the gully above the waterfalls. For half an hour they rested, had some lunch and admired the view, then they crossed the gully and got onto the ridge by a steep chimney. Raeburn says that for some 2,000ft it was 'interesting and varied' but not of 'special difficulty'. Twice they were forced into gullies and had to cut steps; once they had to use kletterschuhe. At 2,650ft they found a mountain finch's nest in a crevice—the bird flew out—and they took one of five eggs; sadly it did not survive the rest of the journey. Four hours later they paused for 'a second lunch, afternoon tea, or whatever it might be called'. The aneroid said 3,550ft.

'At about 4,000ft the great ridge began to merge in the almost vertical West face of Slogen' and 'the climbing became so crowded with interest and incidents'[2] that Raeburn confesses he can't remember them all. He frankly admits that they almost had to give up on several occasions 'and without kletterschue I do not think we could have gone on'. At one point both thought they must abandon the climb, but with Victorian stolidity neither 'hinted as much to each other'.

One crisis arose when 'Ling was … seated astride a spike of rock projecting from the vertical face, the snow of the gully being fully 1,200ft below' while Raeburn vainly endeavoured to drag himself up an overhanging bulge above. 'The difficulty was finally overcome by a traverse round a crazy corner, where the mining out of half a ton of rock alone allowed of a passage

---

2   An obvious echo of Oscar Wilde's Lady Bracknell in *The Importance of Being Earnest* (1895). Raeburn appreciated theatre; remember the 'transformation scenes' on Ben Nevis for echoes of *Macbeth* and *Hamlet*.

being effected ... the rock ... was decidedly rotten.' Raeburn remarks that the rocks they dislodged here 'went whizzing into [the snow in the gully] with the terrific velocity gained in a fall of 1,500 ft'.

At about 8 pm they 'reached a slanting ledge where a little snow was able to lodge'. The final line of cliffs appeared vertical but they found a chimney which 'thinned out into a deep crack splitting off a huge block from the face'. They scaled this crack and gained a ledge, above which 'another vertical crack sprang upwards' and at last they reached the summit 50 ft below and 100 yards east of the cairn at 5,200 ft.

> *The black shadows were creeping up the narrow fjords and dales, filling them with dusky haze; but still a good height above the jagged spears of the NW mountain ridges the glorious sun shone in hardly diminished radiance and at this hour the air was warm. From our feet fell down, almost to the laving waters of the Norangsfjord, the vast wall up which we had toiled throughout this long summer day ... we were happy, with the perfect and utter mountaineering happiness born of a long struggle finally ending in victory, though swaying at times in the balance towards defeat.*

After 11 hours of climbing they got down in one-and-a-quarter, mainly due to being able, no doubt to their delight, to make 'some fine standing glissades'. Raeburn says that their reception at Øye 'was so public and cordial that, as modest men, we were grateful for the gathering dusk, the more especially as certain essential garments had suffered considerably during our long wrestle with the rocks'. And even at 11 pm they got an excellent dinner from 'Fru Stub'.

Not content to rest on their laurels after this fine first ascent, Ling and Raeburn went by boat down the Hjørundsfjord to Bjørke and traversed Hornindalsrokken to Kjelstadli, crossed the 'Jostedalsbrae' Glacier[3] from Årdalstangen to Fåberg,[4] and went on to Turtagrø in the Hurrungane. They attempted Store Ringstind by the Solei ridge, but after ascending Soleitind were driven back by wind, snow and iced-up rock.

---

3   Now the Jostedalsbreen Glacier.
4   Ling: 'Erdal to Faaberg'—presumably an attempt to follow Norwegian pronunciation.

Fig 3

Slogen from Sæbø. The route taken by Raeburn and Ling follows the steep ridge just right of centre. Photo: David Stone

Fig 4

Thérèse Berthau seated 2nd row centre. Raeburn and Ling also pictured and Eric Ullén seated front left. Photo: Campbell Collection

Fig 5

Raeburn in an awkward position climbing on Kjerringa. Photo: SMC Archive

In the company of Raeburn's friend, Eric Ullén, they went round into Berdal and tried Store Ringstind again from the Solei col, once more without success. They also failed to force the ridge facing Austabotntind but found a traverse across the south face which gave access to the ordinary route, which they followed to the summit.

[Fig 4] Raeburn, Ling, Ullén and Thérèse Berthau then made an abortive attempt to traverse the Dyrhauger from the south. They also crossed Bandet, descended to the Midt Maradal glacier, and climbed Kjerringa. They wanted to try to bridge the great gap between Kjerringa and Mannen, the south side of which had previously been descended by Ullén, Berthau and Tanberg with the guides Ole Berg and Knut Fortun. On this occasion Raeburn struggled
[Fig 5] 200ft down the north side of the impressive gap on a rope but considered that both time and rope were too short to give a chance of success. That day lasted a gruelling 17 hours.

The heroic ascent of the Slogen face made up for Raeburn and Ling's numerous failures on this trip as a result of weather, iced-up rock and over-ambition. There had, after all, been very great snowfalls in Norway that spring, but Raeburn says this 'did not interfere with the climbing, and gave magnificent standing glissades'. After this trip he seems to have decided that he was now sufficiently experienced to make a real impact in the Alps, and in 1904 he did just this.

22. THE MEIJE, GRANDE CASSE, AIGUILLE NOIRE DE PEUTEREY, PETIT DRU
1901–1903

In 1904 Raeburn, Ling and Charles Walker had planned to make big traverses from the Meije to Mont Blanc, but Ling was ill with a nasty bout of influenza and couldn't go. Raeburn and Walker went to the Dauphiné, the Tarentaise and the south side of Mont Blanc, and had mostly 'magnificent weather'.

In the Dauphiné they climbed the South Aiguille d'Arves 'from a ruined hut on the south side', crossed the Brèche de la Meije and attempted the Meije 'from the wooden hut on the Promontoire'. Although not a 4,000m peak, the Meije is one of the most coveted peaks in the Alps and indicates a step up in Raeburn's ambitions. Plainly the experience gathered during two seasons in Norway was standing him in good stead.

On the first attempt they were turned back by an electrical storm 'at the foot of the Grand Muraille';[1] the ice-axes sang *'le chanson du Piolet'* [sic], and 'even Walker's rucksack had something to say for itself'. They retreated to La Grave then tried again, this time successfully, from the Promontoire Hut. Their time to the summit, always of interest to Raeburn, was four hours and 55 mins. The Meije was to play a significant part in Raeburn's life; he eventually completed a solo of the classic traverse after suffering defeats due to bad weather, but his cherished aim, the first ascent of the then unclimbed West Ridge, was not to be.

Moving on to the Tarentaise they went to Pralognan and climbed the Aiguille de la Glière from the Refuge Félix Faure (now known as Refuge du Col de la Vanoise). Next day they climbed 'Le Versant Nord' of the Grande

---

1 In his last encounter with the Meije, Raeburn used the Great Wall as his route of descent as darkness fell.

Casse (3,855 m), the highest mountain of the Vanoise Massif. Raeburn thought the 800 m North Face Route (now graded *Difficile*) 'a difficult climb up steep ice and very rotten rocks',[2] and they traversed the mountain into the bargain. The first ascent is credited to two Italian climbers in 1933. If Raeburn and Walker climbed the true North Face their ascent was almost three decades ahead of its time, but details are lacking.

Over the Little St Bernard pass to Courmayeur in Italy, Raeburn and Walker continued their programme by climbing the Aiguille Noire de Peuterey (3,773 m). As with the ascent of the Meije this marked another rise in Raeburn's mountaineering standard—the Aiguille Noire is a very serious rock peak with no easy way to the summit. After bivouacking at 8,100 ft in the corrie[3] known as the 'Fauteuil des Allemands', they set off at 4.15 am, reached the summit by 12.50 pm and got back to the 'Germans' Armchair' by 8 pm. They made a valiant attempt to descend the 2,000 ft of cliffs below the Fauteuil by candle lantern but found it impossible and spent the rest of the night 'on a broad ledge close to water'. When they got back to Courmayeur they had been out for 48 hours: the time alone indicates just how serious this ascent was. Unfortunately there are very few details of the climb, presumably some version of the South Ridge, now graded *Très Difficile* (the Alpine grading being roughly equivalent to the British Very Severe). [Fig 1]

The last two days of their trip were spent going over the Col and Glacier du Géant to Chamonix. Raeburn noted that because of the prolonged fine spell of weather, the icefall of the Géant was 'much more intricate than in 1901'.

In this Alpine season all Raeburn and Walker's expeditions were without guides. By now Harold had been tackling demanding routes on serious mountains guideless for three years, which distinguished him from many of his contemporaries, even some of the best-known, such as Geoffrey Winthrop Young.

---

2   See the account in *SMCJ* January 1905 p.218. Unfortunately this seems to be one of the 'Excursions' pieces which Douglas put together from Raeburn's notes, possibly to save space. It is not entirely clear what route Raeburn climbed: it certainly sounds like the North Face and the description fits, but Raeburn did not initial this piece, indicating that Douglas probably paraphrased his words.

3   Raeburn calls it a 'grass ledge', but the Fauteuil is actually quite a large corrie between the S and E ridges of the Aiguille Noire. It is also described as 'a detrital terrace' with the characteristic armchair form between Mont Rouge, Aiguille Noire S Face and Mont Noire.

Fig 1

L'Aiguille Noire de Peuterey. Photo: Grahame Nicoll

In 1905 Ling (now recovered), Raeburn and Charles Walker made the ascent of the Lautaret Col by 'steam automobile—a great improvement on the old diligence',[4] and came by the 'Sentier des Crevasses' to the Chalet Hôtel de l'Alpe. At 4am the next morning they set off for the new Écrins Hut going by the glacier pass of the Col Emile Pic, making a brief diversion on their way to climb the Pic de Neige Cordier (11,857ft), which must have helped their acclimatisation.

The hut was small but clean and leaving at 2.10am they ascended the Glacier Blanc by moonlight, got onto the north-east arête of the Écrins and climbed this by traversing the 'great tower near the foot of the final ridge, on the icy north face—angle of ice slope below north-east ridge, 54° by clinometer'. Descent from the summit (13,462ft) was made by the Pic Lory, over the great bergschrund and by the Col des Écrins, 'a steep rock climb' down to the Bonne Pierre Glacier, and 'a sporting passage of the bridgeless torrent of the Bonne Pierre'. They thought it 'a very repaying day', the only downside being the heavy rucksacks, which, being guideless, they had to carry themselves.

They continued their itinerary by going up to the Promontoire Hut, hoping to traverse the Meije, but bad weather put paid to that plan. They retreated to La Grave, as the previous year, by the Brèche de la Meije.

Shifting their ground by 'steam, auto, tram, rail and electric rail', the party eventually walked up to the Montenvers Hotel by the Mer de Glace at Chamonix. Ling and Raeburn had their eyes on the Petit Dru (3,754m). Les Aiguilles du Dru are twin rock spires belonging to the Mont Blanc Massif and are situated on its north side.[5]   [Fig 2]

Unfortunately Raeburn's party came down with severe food poisoning, apparently from eating 'bad fish' at the hotel. Charles Walker was so ill he went home directly, but Raeburn, and to a lesser extent Ling, managed 'to buckle their distempered cause within the belt of rule' sufficiently to drag themselves up to the Refuge Charlet, the new hut on the Charpoua Rognon. Willie Ling (Diary, Book 5) takes up the story on 4 August:

4   A horse-drawn coach.
5   1879 saw the first ascent of the Petit Dru (whose least challenging route is *Difficile*) by Jean Charlet-Stratton, Prosper Payot and Frédéric Folliguet. The first ascent of the Grand Dru (3,754m) was by Clinton Dent, James Hartley and their guides, Alexander Burgener and Kaspar Maurer, in 1878. The first traverse of both peaks was by E Fontaine with Joseph and Jean Ravanel in 1901.

We left the hut at 2.20, accompanied by M. Manod and M. Gos ... We roped in the hut and scrambled up the rocks to the glacier by lantern light. It was a fine morning. We crossed the glacier with care, going up a good long way, and then across a small ice couloir to the rocks [at] 3.50 ... Raeburn and I were rather ahead of the other pair. We crossed the rock couloir to the true R. side [i.e. left, looking up] to be out of the way of any stones falling from the Grand Dru, then ascended by easy rocks to the ridge ... Manod and his friend joined us here and we breakfasted together till 5.55. We did not see our friends again ... till our return to the hut.

They reached the cairn on the col at 6.20 am, took off their boots and put on kletterschuhe. Using Ling's shoulder Raeburn was able to reach a handhold and pull himself up the first difficulty. Ling followed with a little assistance from the rope. What followed was something most mountaineers have experienced:

The appearance of the mountain was now most forbidding. We first tried what afterwards proved to be the right way, but the place seemed so hopeless that we proceeded to exhaust all the other possibilities at much expenditure of time and labour. Finally we returned to our first point of attack, and throwing a rope over what we hoped was a good hitch, Raeburn struggled breathlessly up and a joyous note from above told me that we were on the right track. A decayed ring of rope and a rusty piton showed that others had been there before. The chimney was very difficult[6] and so was the climbing which followed ... we gained the arête at 11.15. Here we halted for lunch till 11.30.

As well as still feeling unwell, Ling had been very much hampered by having to carry both ice-axes and rucksacks while Raeburn wrestled with the technical problems, so he was delighted when they decided to abandon one axe and one rope.

---

6   When Ling (or Raeburn) describes a pitch as 'very difficult' it means just that; in modern terms it means well into the Severe category or beyond.

Fig 2

The Drus from Montenvers, the Petit Dru seen against its larger neighbour and distinguishable by a small blob of snow on its summit a short way down the ridge of the Grand Dru. Photo: Peter Macdonald

> *The climbing after this was very difficult [with] chimneys of rock, and a chimney of ice. In one place there was a piece of rope fixed, but we did not put much strain on it, as it appeared unsound. On a ledge on the N. Face we met the party traversing from the Grand Dru. I had been feeling unwell for some time but managed to climb on till we reached Charlet's ledge where the shaft of his bâton was still to be seen.[7] There I was so bad that I was quite unable to go on, so Raeburn took the thin cord, and climbing with difficulty the obstacle immediately above the ledge, managed to reach the top 300 ft above ... surely the first mountaineer to stand alone on the summit.*

Raeburn climbed down quickly, safeguarding himself by hitching the spare rope, and found Ling a little better for the rest. A painstaking descent made use of one or two pitons. They recovered their boots, the axe and the rucksacks, but found when they reached 'the top of the large stone couloir' that it was too dark to go further, so they put on their 'two Shetland sweaters, [balaclava] helmets and gloves' and propped themselves 'on a hard, strong and uncomfortably sloping couch, our feet braced against stones which we hoped would hold us up'. It was windy but they were fairly sheltered and 'though it was rather cold, the night passed wonderful quickly'.

Although they saw 'four magnificent avalanches falling down the Charmoz' the following day, they reached the hut at 5.30 am, some 27 hours after leaving it. Ling comments:

> *It had been a magnificent expedition, and my grievous disappointment at not reaching the top was mitigated by the fact that my companion was not prevented by my illness from reaping the reward of his skill, pluck and careful foresight.*

To complete the story of 1905, a couple of days later down in Montenvers they had a passing-through call from Willie Douglas, the Brigg brothers and Eric Greenwood. The day after that the weather was good and with Hilda Hechle[8] they went up the Petit Charmoz, and Raeburn ran up and down

---

7   Left by the first ascensionist, Jean Charlet Stratton.
8   One of many female climbers with whom Raeburn and Ling climbed. Hilda Hechle was a fine mountain artist whose work is still in demand.

the Aiguille de l'M in 15 minutes from the Charmoz Col. Wednesday was also fine and Ling and Raeburn 'went for the [Grand] Charmoz'. Ling, who was still suffering somewhat, waited at the top of the Grépon Couloir while Harold traversed the five pinnacles, including the weird 'Bâton Wicks'. Ling, in any case, had been that way before. Apparently they were 'a little late for afternoon tea' in the hotel.

Raeburn's great though unremarked triumph of 1906 was his ascent of Green Gully on Ben Nevis. As well as acting as an able partner on that occasion, Eberhard Phildius also passed on to Raeburn some tips from Marcel Kurz about what might be 'new' and worth climbing in the Alps. Acting on these in the 1906 season, Ling and Raeburn had three successful weeks (on the second of which they were accompanied by Eric Greenwood) visiting three regions: the Val Ferret, the Oberland and Zermatt. The trip was essentially about quality rather than quantity, 'few peaks were climbed, but all ... were, with one exception, also traversed, by routes, in directions, or by combinations of routes, never before followed, so far as is known, by any parties of amateur climbers'.

In the Val Ferret, acting on one of Kurz's tips, they 'made the first ascent of ... [an] Aiguille of the Rouges de Dolent', which they called 'La Mouche' (11,750 ft). 'The last 350 ft is steep and difficult; boots removed on ascent, and a rope ring left on descent.' Ling thought that the difficulty of the rock climbing on the last part of the climb accounted for the fact that nobody else had got there first.

In the same district from the Saleinaz Hut, Raeburn and Ling 'walked up the Saleina Glacier, climbed the ridge between the Aiguille de la Neuve and the South peak of the Aiguille d'Argentière' (a first traverse), then 'over the central to the west peak' and eventually by the *voie normale* to Chardonnet Glacier, Col du Chardonnet and 'down Saleina Glacier to Cabane': an exceedingly long day.

After this they made a 16-and-a-half-hour journey 'by foot, diligence, rail, diligence, and horseback' to the Hotel Jungfrau in the Oberland where Eric Greenwood was waiting for them.

They spent a night in the Concordia Hut and next morning crossed over the Grünhornlücke and across Fiescherfirn, arriving at 'the small new hut at the foot of the Finsteraarhorn'. The same day they discovered 'a way on to the great south-east ridge' of that mountain. Their night was horribly disturbed because 'a party of fifteen Swiss and guide' arrived in the evening to share a hut 'adequate for six to eight'. It was almost certainly with great relief that Raeburn, Ling and Greenwood left the hut at 3am, climbed to the south-east ridge of the Finsteraarhorn (14,026ft, modern Alpine grading: *Difficile*) and followed this to the summit. They continued by a traverse down the north-west ridge (*Peu Difficile*) to the Hugisattel and the Agassizjoch, down the rocks of the Agassizhorn, and then cut many steps in the ice of the great couloir. This brought them to the Finsteraar Glacier, from where they went through the Finsteraarjoch, straight down through the seracs of the Ober Eismeer and mercifully to the Schwarzegg Hut.[9] Next morning they went to Grindelwald.

It is not entirely clear when they left Grindelwald, but when they did, they went back up to Schwarzegg and traversed the Schreckhorn by going up the north-west and down the south-west ridge: the first traverse in this direction and the first descent of the south-west ridge. A 'lovely day and tea made on the summit, 13,386ft'.

Raeburn's and Ling's boundless enthusiasm and energy sometimes seems to have had the effect of burning off their companions; this was probably not so in the case of Greenwood as he went home at this juncture after another gruelling 16-hour day crossing the Grimsel from Meiringen to Fiesch. Harold and Willie went up to Zermatt where they 'found the wall lined with unemployed guides' because of a week's bad weather. At the Monte Rosa Hotel they should have met Hugh Munro but got a letter instead saying that he had had to 'go in a Pyrenean direction'.

In order to let the fresh snow settle, 'Saturday 28 July was devoted to a traverse of the Riffelhorn by the Matterhorn couloir', and they ended this easier day by 'dancing at the Mont Cervin Hotel'. This seemingly uncharacteristic activity was probably a more common feature of Raeburn and Ling's trips than the infrequent references to it might suggest.[10] Both were brought up in Victorian middle-class households and learning to dance was thought 'a good thing' by parents. It facilitated pleasant relationships between the sexes and both men were aware of the attractions of the opposite sex. They actively sought out female company when climbing, and it is a mystery why neither of them married.

9   It is not clear if this hut is in the same location as today's Schreckhorn Hut.
10 Discussing mountaineering clothing, Harold recommends the use of old dancing gloves under one's mitts (*Mountaineering Art* p.32).

On Monday 30 July, 'loaded with sleeping bags, provisions and wood, they went up to a gîte[11] below the Zmutt arête' of the Matterhorn.[12] The first ascent of this ridge by Alfred Mummery with three guides in 1879 was a daring exploit ahead of its time. Today it remains a challenging climb on which conditions need to be right. The ridge faces north-west and gets little sun, so snow on the rock can cause serious problems, as Raeburn and Ling discovered. They paid off the two porters and settled down for the night in their bags, which were comfortable enough, but they were on hard ground and didn't sleep. Ling says: 'It was very impressive lying there at nearly 11,000 ft hearing the avalanches roaring off the Dent d'Herens.'

The Zmutt Ridge, towering above them in the starlight, is fairly easy to start with, but a number of small towers in the middle section have to be turned on poor rock. More difficult but technically better climbing follows to near the Zmutt nose (a large overhang just left of the ridge). Here the route traverses right onto the West Face and gains a large terrace, Carrel's Gallery, from which the final ascent is made. The climb is long, and even in good, snow-free conditions, ten hours is often taken for the ascent alone. [Fig 3]

They set off at 4 am, leaving their 'sleeping bags for the next comers'.[13] They wore crampons and roped up at once. At 5.15 am, they ascended the ridge:

[E]asily, only about eight steps to cut and a few to chip to the foot of the first tower, 6.15, 12,600 ft. We had good climbing up the rocks, which were however loose in places. We climbed over the first two towers, skirted the third and gained the gap of the fourth tower at 7.40. After that we climbed on the arête 13,200 ft, a sensational position.
(Ling's Diary, Book 6)

Ling says that they now climbed on very slabby rocks, covered with much fresh snow, 'in fact in very bad condition, and we had to fight for every foot of height we made'. But Raeburn 'kept on and at 11.37 we gained the col',

---

11 When Ling mentions a 'gîte' he usually means a bivouac. Modern guides lament that even getting to this ridge from the Hörnli or Schönbiel Huts is a major undertaking. Raeburn and Ling solved the problem by bivouacking.
12 It is reported that the well-known Alpine guide Melchior Anderegg, standing on the summit of the Dent Blanche and looking across at the Zmutt Ridge, said: 'It goes, but I'm not going.'
13 Not a usual practice; one would like to know more.

The Zmutt Ridge of the Matterhorn
from the Obergabelhorn.
Photo: Peter F Macdonald

Fig 3

having taken two hours and ten minutes for 500 ft. They 'still had to take the greatest care up slabby rocks' and then they traversed into the couloir where they saw 'a Frenchman with two guides going down the Italian ridge'; Ling called to them.

They went 'some distance into the couloir but not so far as is generally done', or so they thought. They climbed carefully up some ice-covered rocks and then mounted 'diagonally back to the ridge, off which we had been forced'. Here the climbing was not 'quite so difficult', but the height and the hard work were rather telling, and the pace was 'not very great'. Ling says they could take no risks and that 'some of the traverses were very ticklish'. They reached the Italian summit of the Matterhorn (14,700 ft) at 3.03 pm. 'The sun was pleasant and the view gorgeous. We were not sorry to sit down and eat some bread and jam, for we had done neither for six hours.'

> *After an all too short half-hour of heaven on the summit we reluctantly turned to descend the Italian Ridge ... We went rather slowly because I was tired and the way needed a little finding. The ropes and ladder were a great assistance. We had not gone far before clouds gathered and we were in the midst of a snowstorm with thunder and lightning. Our axes began to hiss and Raeburn had a slight shock in his face from the point of his axe. At a gap in the ridge which we were crossing, we had a fine Brocken spectre and saw our shadows projected onto the cloud. This snowstorm made the way difficult to find and also made us very wet, but fortunately it ceased before we got down to the hut [at] 8.10, sixteen hours from the start. We were glad to find that, though not clean and ill provided, the hut was empty. Raeburn went for water while I got things ready, and we soon had some hot soup going which was very comforting. Our clothes were wet, but we made the best of it with blankets, and were soon stretched on the hard deal boards, for the sleep which we had really earned ... The expedition was a splendid success, and Raeburn's route-finding and leading up the snow-covered slabs were beyond praise. (ibid.)*

Modern guidebooks estimate ten hours for the Zmutt ascent in good conditions, and five more for the descent of the Hörnli; Ling and Raeburn took just 16 hours in poor conditions, tackling the more difficult descent of the Italian Ridge in a snowstorm. Ling adds, 'I went well to the top, but was tired coming down. Rucksacks very heavy.'[14]

The following day they crossed the Furggenjoch and made a leisurely way back to the Schwarzee Hotel where they felt they deserved the *Thé Complet*. As Robin Campbell (SMCJ, 2021) remarks:

> *It was the end of a very successful season in which four major mountains were traversed in novel ways, in all cases involving first British guideless ascents or traverses—thanks to the excellence of Raeburn's research and route-finding, his determined leading, and Ling's steadfast support.*

---

14   It is an odd fact about Willie Ling that in almost every photograph he seems to carry his rucksack rather uncomfortably halfway down his back.

23. MEIJE II, DÔME DE LA SACHE-POURRI TRAVERSE, MONT BLANC, DENT BLANCHE, DRU TRAVERSE 1907–1908

July and August of 1907, according to the account in the *SMCJ*, gave Raeburn and Ling a 'delightful' if somewhat stormy holiday in the Dauphiné, the Graians and Mont Blanc. First in the Dauphiné, they spent three days in bad weather at the Promontoire Hut on the Meije. Willie Douglas, the Editor of the *SMCJ*, paraphrasing Raeburn, says that they did 'a little exploratory climbing'—in fact they wanted to tackle the unclimbed West Ridge of the mountain, something Raeburn may have wished to conceal—but the weather and lack of provisions forced them to retreat via the Brèche to La Grave—a route they were familiar with—on 28 July.

After this they made an attempt to traverse the Meije in the 'reverse direction to that usually taken', but 'after a night on a rock shelf on the Bec de l'Homme' they found themselves, at 3.30 am, some 1,200 ft below the Pic Central, in a furious blizzard. Ling (Diary, Book 6) recounts the action:

> *The clouds did not look well but we persevered and ... we were high up on a slope of hard snow ... then a tremendous thunderstorm came on, much lightning, strong wind, hail and snow. We hung on, getting what shelter we could from the slope, but at 4.30 we saw it was no good and turned back. We glissaded sitting, and ran down the slopes—easy going but wet. We overtook our porter and all got back to the hotel together.*

Raeburn had mixed fortunes on the Meije. He eventually made a solo traverse of the mountain by the normal route, but the first ascent, and descent, of the West Ridge always eluded him. Unsurprisingly, on this occasion he and Ling gave up the Dauphiné and travelled to Val d'Isère. From there they traversed 'the whole arête, 3 miles, of the Dôme de la Sache (11,840 ft), [to] Mont Pourri (12,430 ft)'. They found the weather on the Sache quite homelike: 'cold and misty and reminiscent of the Bens'. Their descent of the North-East Ridge of Mont Pourri was believed to be a first. The traverse itself is now graded AD and the time required given as a day.

Leaving Val d'Isère for Italy on 5 August, Raeburn and Ling went 'via the summit of Tsanteleina (11,830 ft) along the frontier, over the peaks of the Cime de Quart Dessus (11,400 ft), Pointe de Bazel (11,305 ft), Pointe de Calabre, and tried the traverse of the Rocca Bassagne'. Ling again:

> *The summit ridge was narrow and very much disintegrated, and we followed it and descended some distance. We then found it extremely rotten, and when we came to an awesome overhanging precipice, we retraced our steps to the top ... and descended again on rocks and snow to the Col de Calabre. We were sorry to miss the traverse, but it was quite impossible.* (ibid.)

To conclude they descended to the head of the Isère valley, went over the Col de Galise and had 'a long walk down the wild and striking Orco Valley to Ceresole'. Their day had lasted over 20 hours and involved 10,000 ft of climbing.

After two days of relative inactivity, partly relaxation and partly because of bad weather, on 9 August Raeburn and Ling turned to Gran Paradiso (4,061 m, the only mountain over 4,000 m entirely within Italy). They started from a gîte under a boulder at 12.15 am. After halting 'to put in some ice nails',[1] they continued up the glacier 'with a fine view of a comet'. The upper glacier was 'rather steep up to the foot of the rocks'. Here they roped up and climbed 'screes and rock ledges with very loose stones to the col at 5.7'.[2] Ling says:

[Fig 1]

> *Then we got on to the appallingly steep South Face, traversing on narrow ledges and climbing difficult chimneys, most sensational and*

---

1   Not crampons, but nails adapted for penetrating ice, screwed into the leather sole of the boot.
2   Ling sometimes gives times in this abbreviated form. Here 5.7 means 5.07am.

Fig 1

A climber contemplates the ridge of Gran Paradiso. Photo: SMC Image Archive

technically difficult work, which our heavy rucksacks did not make easier. A shallow chimney with remarkably few holds was unclimbable, so we crossed it and made a desperate assault on the arête on the other side. Standing on a small platform, I gave him my shoulder while Raeburn climbed over the overhanging bulge above us, but higher up it got worse, quite impossible, so there was nothing less [sic] than to try elsewhere, though we were only about 200 ft from getting out. It was awkward work for Raeburn to descend on to my shoulder. We then retraced our course and prospected. We saw a ledge running round the face and if we could get along this, we thought we could ascend the rocks by the couloir from the Col d'Abeille. We started and on the ledge found chamois tracks. It was very narrow in parts but brought us to our couloir, though once or twice we had to hurry on account of falling stones. The rocks by the couloir were very steep but easy and the seracs in the couloir were splendid. We joined the ridge on the top of the buttress and, still guided by the chamois tracks, we climbed along a narrow ledge and joined the main ridge between the third and fourth teeth.

The ridge was long and the snow very soft, so we kept to the crest, climbing the pinnacles, then down a steep slope to the last gap before the summit. (ibid)

They reached the top at 2.15 pm, hungry and wanting to recuperate for a while, but 'a heavy thunderstorm was threatening' so, grabbing a mouthful, they began the descent:

Scarcely had we left the summit ... when the storm broke. A flash of flame and a deafening crash of thunder burst upon us giving us both a shock, in Raeburn's case nearly bringing him to his knees. It was no time for words, we must be off the ridge, so down the steps we dashed, over the bergschrund and on to the snow slope below. A hurried enquiry about injuries then on we sped, plunging in the snow, axes hissing, hair of the head and moustache sticking out and tickling while now and then a boring sensation was felt in the head. On the level glacier it was not so acute, but we had, lower, to follow an ice ridge and here it was so bad that we put our axes down and crouched below the ridge. (ibid.)

Eventually the storm passed to the south and they got down to the Victor Emmanuel Hut at 4.20 pm, having descended 4,200 ft in one and three-quarter hours. Ling says, 'We were a little dazed and head aching from the stroke but were otherwise no worse.' Despite Ling's magnificent *sangfroid* they were also, one suspects, very lucky to be alive. They had some tea—probably good for the shock—and continued down to the 'comfortable and clean inn at Pont by 6.20'. Ling concludes, 'The rock climbing on the south side was very difficult, but under ordinary conditions the ordinary route is perfectly simple.'

Still buzzing with energy, if not with electricity, the following day they set out with a young porter, Elisée Dayné, and crossed over the Col de l'Entrelor from Valsaveranche to Val de Rhêmes. They were again struck by lightning—'only a slight shock, however'. They spent the night at the Curé's house at Notre Dame de Rhêmes and from there set out to climb the East Ridge of the Bec de l'Invergnan, a striking rock tower (3,607 m) also known as the Grande Rousse North. As they started out, the south wind made the weather rather doubtful. In the dark they soon lost the path and 'did some difficult climbing up ... rocks, which became so bad that we waited for quarter of an hour for daylight'. When it got light they traversed to the right by a ledge and struck the path, turning off to a ridge on their left and paused for breakfast at 6.30 am. Taking their cue from some chamois higher up they descended slightly and came 'by snow and rocks to the foot of the final ridge'.

Ling was impressed by the appearance of the East Ridge. 'There is an immense step to start with and the ascent ... gives good climbing.' They found a cairn on the summit of the first tower with the name of the Italian climber and his guide who had made the first ascent by this route. Then they were faced with the worst part of the climb:

> *The arête ran up in a straight line and appeared to overhang above, so we traversed out on a ledge to our right on the side of the tower and tried to force our way up from there, but it was impossible. The rocks were horribly rotten and loose ... we had to traverse further out across a shallow couloir where a long balancing step led to a corner, which looked more promising.*

The normally phlegmatic Ling sounds anxious here:

The couloir fell away below us most appallingly. Leaving his axe and rucksack, Raeburn carefully made his way, while I watched, running the rope behind blocks which we hoped would stand the strain should any slip occur. (ibid.)

However, the blocks were not tested and Ling followed, carrying both rucksacks and axes, which 'took careful balance'.

Once round the corner they climbed steeply to the arête again. As Ling ruefully remarks: '200 ft in one and three-quarter hours'. Fortunately, although the arête was 'extremely narrow ... and shattered', it was not difficult, but they had 'some steep rocks to climb' just before they reached the summit at 12.52 pm. They were delighted with the ascent, the panorama and the exquisite cloud effects.

The way down the North Ridge was 'steep and narrow in parts, one piece rather difficult', but having made a descending traverse over the towers they were able to unrope and plunge down the screes to the glacier.

They expected to find accommodation in the village of Eglise in Val Grisanche, 'but the cantines were dirty in the extreme and had no rooms'. Perhaps remembering their good treatment by the last priest they had lodged with, they called on the local one and he 'kindly sent out one of his curates with us to a farmhouse ... the place was very primitive but clean, and after some soup and an omelette we sought our welcome couch'.

The following day, 12 August, they thought their walk was through the 'most beautiful valley we met in our wanderings'. After bathing in a glacier stream they went on to Liverogne and from there by 'automobile' to Courmayeur. Here they rested, bought provisions, 'arranged about porter', went for a walk with magnificent views of their next objective—Mont Blanc—and got their letters from the Poste Restante.

On 14 August Raeburn and Ling set off for the Sella Hut[3] on Mont Blanc with Ferdinando Melica, who 'had been with Workman in the Himalaya the previous year', acting as porter. They reached the hut at 1.55 pm, had some tea and paid Melica 22 francs. The little used hut they found very

3   The hut is now known as the Quintino Sella Hut.

comfortable. Off by 3.30 am the following morning, they found that the glass had 'fallen three-tenths' and there was a south-west wind. With occasional minor difficulties they got to the Tournette ridge by 8.10 am and had a breakfast stop. They followed the ridge, 'good going on rocks ... mainly sound ... the cloud effects were beautiful but the weather was looking worse'. They continued with 'no particular difficulty but long and steep traversing where one had not to slip, and on to the ridge again'. Steps had to be cut in an ice arête: 'it seemed a long way, and we could not see clearly what lay before us'. High-angled snow led from the top of the rocks, gained from the ice to the Bosses route (Dôme de Goûter). 'It was very cold, windy and thick mist along the ridge to the summit,' which they reached at 12.40 pm. Ling notes that there were a French lady and party and some others. He and Raeburn had tea and bread and jam till 'all had gone but two men staying in the hut'.

Ling and Raeburn had meant to descend by the Midi route, 'but the mist was thicker and thicker and the weather getting worse, so after an hour's waiting we started down the ordinary route at 2.20'. They got to the Vallot Refuge and went straight on into the teeth of 'a regular blizzard'. All the tracks were obliterated and they got lost for about 15 minutes before 'hitting off the right route on the Grand Plateau'. Going down this 'was not so bad' and they 'made good speed in the soft snow, avoiding crevasses to the Grands Mulets, 4.15', where they overtook the other parties from the summit. 'They stayed here, but we went on down the glacier ... to the moraine, 5.07, where we took out our Mummery Spikes, coiled the rope and trotted down to the tea chalet ... answering many anxious enquiries about the other parties.' They arrived 'at Couttet's at 7.30 ... 5 hrs 10 mins in all or 4½ hrs going time from the summit'. They were very glad that they had not attempted to descend by the Midi route, or stayed at the Grands Mulets. The night was one of fearful storm, with thunder, lightning and deluges of rain 'with snow above'.

As Ling says in his diary (Book 6, pp.46–82): 'Ten peaks, seven passes and much new country explored was the result of our campaign of 1907.' Despite very unsettled weather (and narrowly avoiding death by lightning strike), they had indeed 'enjoyed a very jolly holiday'.

The account in 'Excursions' (*SMCJ*, 1908) of Ling and Raeburn's doings in the Alps in 1908 begins by regretting that they, like everyone else, 'had their share of the bad weather'. They got to Zermatt on 27 July, and two days later, with William Brigg and Eric Greenwood, went up to the Trift Hotel where, according to Ling, a snowstorm meant 'we had a delightful off-day'. However, on 30 July they set off for the traverse of the Zinal Rothorn (4,221m), described by Robin Collomb (1975) as 'Probably the most popular rock peak in the Zermatt district, certainly with British climbers.' Now usually climbed from the Rothorn Hut, but then from the Trift Hotel much further down the valley.

Ling describes 'a fine cold starlit morning … Venus in particular being brilliant … we saw a wonderful meteor like a flash of lightning, leaving a trail like a comet'. They skirted the rocks and climbed a gully, stopping at the top for breakfast to witness 'a beautiful dawn … the Matterhorn glowing crimson in the rising sun'. They climbed snow to the ridge where they roped up. Being on the *voie normale* they encountered a couple of other parties, but they soon left them behind. Going over the saddle they went up to the rocks of the Gabel 'then up the slabs, which we found less difficult than we expected, to the ridge, round the sensational corner, and scrambled up to the top 8.15'. For once, this season, 'It was bright and clear' and they could 'spend an hour admiring the views'.

Descending the North or Zinal Ridge 'was very sensational but the rocks were good'. They surmounted the big gendarme, 'which gave good sport', traversed the side of the small gendarme and reached the end of the rock ridge by 11.30am. Down the 'sharp snow arête … in good condition … down the slope … over the bergschrund to the glacier'. Thus, according to Collomb, completing 'one of the finest expeditions of its class in the Alps'. They passed by 'the old cabane' and reached 'the new Mountet Hotel at 1.30'.

That afternoon was spent 'writing postcards'. To whom did Raeburn write? His sister Ruth? Willie Douglas? Frank Goggs? One of the ladies whose company he sought on the hill? We don't know, but it is significant that he made the effort to keep in touch with friends or family, and this fits with the general estimate of his friends that he was sociable and well-liked. They also enjoyed 'magnificent views of the Dent Blanche', a mountain [Fig 2] which Raeburn and Ling were soon to experience.

The following morning Briggs and Greenwood set off over the Dent Blanche col, while Raeburn and Ling enjoyed a lie-in, not leaving the hotel until 6.35am. Seeing their friends in the distance, they yodelled to them. In preparation for the Dent Blanche on the morrow, Raeburn made steps in the foot of the slope to the Col de Zinal, then they went back and had 'a sporting scramble along the ridge of the Roc Noir', a rognon which had 'a very ... sensational knife edge down to the glacier'. They were back in the hotel by 11.30 am.

The Dent Blanche, as Robin Collomb (op. cit. p.101) remarks, is 'One of the great summits of the Swiss Pennine Alps. A fairly symmetrical mountain, of bold outline, recognisable from afar. It has four ridges, forming a cross.' Robin Campbell (SMCJ, 2021) comments:

> *The configuration of the Dent Blanche is complex. Going clockwise from the normal South Ridge, or Wandfluh, there is next the steep west or Ferpècle Ridge, where Owen Jones met his death in 1899, then the steeper North Ridge, not climbed until 1928, and finally the East 'Viereselsgrat' or Four Asses Ridge, climbed by Ulrich Almer in 1882. But the East Ridge, after falling gently from the summit for 300 m, bifurcates into a North-East Ridge (used by the Four Asses) and a steep South-East Ridge climbed by two Swiss amateurs in 1900 and not since then.*

At 1.30 am the next morning Raeburn and Ling followed by lantern light the tracks they had made the day before. They got on to the rocks of the South-East Ridge above the bergschrund two hours later. Moderate going soon led to difficult rock and a rake, where they paused for breakfast. 'The weather looked settled', Ling records. 'Then came a very difficult bit ... partly iced, slabby and loose.' Raeburn abandoned sack and axe, which Ling brought up. By 5.55 am they were on the shoulder at 11,850 ft. 'The ridge was steep but not difficult', and they built a small cairn on the top of the first tower. 'After this we had some very steep climbing up to the tooth before the red tower ... we climbed along the face of the red tower, which was very difficult, and along the ridge, stopping at 11 o'clock for an acid drop.'

Ling's diary account (Book 7, p.46) continues:

> *We joined the main arête where the NE ridge runs in at 11.45. There was a lot of fresh snow and we had to proceed with the greatest care. The thin rock ridge was crowned by a thin, brittle cornice of snow ten to fifteen feet high, bending first to one side then the other, just thick enough to hold the axe, and we had to move in short rope*

Fig 2

The Dent Blanche from the Ober Gabelhorn. The ridge which caused Raeburn and Ling so much trouble is the upper left-hand skyline; only the upper part of this ridge can be seen; below is the bifurcation. The Wandfluh, the easiest route of ascent and descent, is to the right. Photo: George Sang, Raeburn's friend and lawyer. SMC Image Archive

lengths astride along this, flattening it down as we went ... We had about half a mile of this work to do, ... some of it ... necessitating the cutting of steps.

From time to time, for variety, they encountered slopes on which iced-in rocks helped them,[4] but Ling says they 'had to fight for every foot gained'. They reached the summit of the Dent Blanche at 5.35pm.

The view was fine but they had quickly to think about the way down, 'and after some zwiebacks and jam' they began to descend. The snow on the Wandfluh route was in good condition and they could avoid the cornices. They 'cut' the great tower on the side and tried to do likewise on the next one but had to turn back and climb over it, losing precious time. Of the afterglow, Ling says that neither of them had 'ever seen such beautiful colouring'. The snow and rock ridge seemed to go on endlessly as they descended by the light of 'a bright but small moon', by whose aid they 'went down the glacier to the top of the Wandfluh rocks' where for lack of light they were forced to bivouac. They got out the spirit stove and made tea, and Ling says, rather surprisingly, 'I changed my boots and socks, which froze during the night and had to be thawed out by the cooker in the morning.' (Presumably by 'changed', he means changed his socks and took off his boots.) Summer lightning over the Matterhorn kept them at least visually entertained during the long night. Fortunately it was not very cold, but 'every now and then a slight breeze made [them] shiver'.

After thawing out Ling's footwear they started down at 4.35am 'and had some trouble [finding] the way off', but they got over the small bergschrund and onto the glacier, down this, past the Schönbiel gîte and along the moraine. 'We followed the stream through Zmutt and reached Zermatt at 11.30 in time to bath, shave and change for lunch. A very fine expedition.'

After a week of bad weather at Montenvers Raeburn and Ling went to the Cabane d'Orny. From there they traversed the Aiguille du Chardonnet (3,824m), first to the Glacier du Tour, where they left their rucksacks before traversing below the Chardonnet to reach the normal route by the North Face and the West Ridge. They descended the East Ridge over the Aiguille

---

4   Collomb's guidebook (op. cit. p.106) speaks of 'huge cornices, separated by outcrops' and of the need to 'proceed delicately ...'

Forbes,[5] recovered their rucksacks and then, to quote Robin Campbell, 'ground back up to the Fenêtre du Tour and across the head of the Glacier de Saleina to yet another grind up to the Col du Chardonnet before descending from there to the Argentière Glacier and hut'. Campbell (op. cit. p.26) describes the day as 'absolutely brutal', but they accomplished it in a mere 13 hours.

After some delays caused by bad weather, which involved much disappointment going up and down to huts, Raeburn and Ling left the Charpoua Hut (Le Refuge de la Charpoua) at 4.40 am on 15 August, intent on a traverse of the Grand and Petit Drus. Once over the glacier they climbed chimneys of varying degrees of difficulty, in one place avoiding easier ground taken by the guided party which had left the hut after them. 'Steep climbing then brought us to the ridge at the col' where they and the others, including their friend Carry, had breakfast. Ling notes that the weather was fine where they were, but that 'it was snowing on the Jorasses'.

They climbed some steep chimneys and then up the side of a couloir, which they crossed by blocks at the top. There followed a traverse 'along a ledge to a block' with a piton, and they used this to abseil down to 'a cunning little corner where there was a short, fixed rope, which one took in one's hand and swung over to a foothold'. Further difficult chimneys were climbed, varied only by 'an awkward ledge like the stomach traverse on Pillar' (in Ling's beloved Lakeland). After this they climbed precipitous rock to the summit, 'neck and neck with Carry's party and twenty minutes ahead of the German'. Another climber called Winkler, who seems to have been soloing, was already across the gap and up the Petit Dru.

Raeburn and Ling decided to go on over the Petit Dru, and bade farewell to Carry, who promised to leave a bottle of Bouvier at the hut for them. They scrambled down snow-covered rocks to the top of the Z Chimney, 'which was full of ice', so they abseiled again and got down more easily than they expected to the platform at its foot. 'There,' Ling says, 'it was very sensational but there was a good hitch,' and they climbed down to a lower ledge, partly in the crack and partly on the face. After another similar pitch the angle eased, and they reached the Brèche between the Drus at 12.05 pm.

---

5   The Forbes Arête alone is regarded as one of the best routes of its grade in the Alps and one which is often underestimated. Most guides give it AD, with a time of 3-5 hours. For Raeburn and Ling it was simply part of their itinerary.

The descent took an hour. By contrast the route to the top of the little Dru was 'quite easy'. They reached the summit 'at 12.20 and stayed till 12.45'.

Unfortunately the snow showers seen earlier on the Jorasses had drifted across to the Drus, and as they descended Raeburn and Ling were 'enveloped in mist and softly falling snow'. They made 'free use of the doubled rope' and hurried down as quickly as possible. Ling was interested to see the ledge where he had been stopped by illness on his previous attempt. Charlet's bâton was still lying there.

Ling comments: 'The steepness of the rocks is almost incredible,' but they had 'the advantage of knowing the route and made good progress'. At one point in the thick mist they did go briefly off route, 'but were able to abseil down the rocks leading to the ridge'. The weather was getting worse, with heavy snow alternating with rain. They gained their former breakfast place near the top of the couloir at 6pm, where they should have had at least two hours of daylight, but the bad weather brought darkness on prematurely, 'the mist thicker and thicker and the snow heavier and heavier'. This made the slabby rocks they were trying to descend 'most unpleasant and more than a little dangerous'. They persisted, however, until they 'felt that it was time to traverse out by the ledge to the glacier … but all around us were huge slabs plunging down to unknown depths, coated with wet and slippery snow, nothing to see but a blank wall of mist, all landmarks gone'. At this point they 'heard a shout which we took to be from Winkler lower down the couloir, but as we afterwards found from the hut'.

Unusually Ling admits that their situation was serious. 'To press on in the dark with the dangerous condition of the rocks was risky in the extreme, but there was no shelter, we were already wet through, the snow and rain fell pitilessly … the dawn was far off and there was every probability that we would be frostbitten'. But, as he says:

> It was Hobson's choice, so putting on our wet sweaters and helmets we prepared to stand where we were until dawn … The time passed, though we were cold and very weary … We tried sitting on an axe, we held each other for warmth and support, and the time went on. At long last the dawn appeared and the fall of snow became less. A sip of Cognac each started the circulation—it had been a sore temptation to use it during the night—and the movement continued it.

The mist thinned and 'at last a swirl of wind enabled us to see the glacier below'. As they had thought, they were close to the descent ledge, now coated with new snow, and they escaped along it and gained the glacier.

Progress was slow because of the amount of snow now disguising 'the immense crevasses'. As they approached the hut they saw two men coming up the glacier who, they discovered later, 'were an incipient search party'. When they reached the hut their first thought was to breach Carry's Bouvier and they had an additional stroke of luck, for two kind ladies 'gave us of their chicken'. Their traverse of the Drus in 1908, only seven years after the first ascent, taken together with their earlier ascent of the Petit Dru, shows that Raeburn and Ling were climbing high-angled Alpine rock routes at a very good standard, and one should always remember that they were operating with only the barest minimum of equipment.

The rest of their season in 1908 was delightfully lighthearted. By 18 August they were joined by their friend Eric Ullén and three lady climbers: Maria and Persida, sisters of Natalia Yovitchitch[6] (with whom Raeburn was to climb later), and Miss M Johnston. It would not have been the first time that Raeburn and Ling climbed with women they met on their travels.[7] Their first day was spent 'making preparations and plans, bouldering, a traverse of a wooded rocky ridge' with a tea party and dancing thrown in. This sort of activity sheds a quite different light on Raeburn's personality; indeed, the evidence suggests that he was, in a mild and unspoken way, quite a ladies' man, and why ever not?

The following day they went up to the Cabane d'Orny, but Persida felt unwell and turned back. On 20 August, despite a little mist, they climbed the Aiguille du Tour without difficulty. Retracing their steps, the women recuperated in 'a nice little hollow', while Raeburn, Ullén and Ling went on to the Aiguille du Purtscheller, a striking rock peak, which gave much better climbing up a chimney Ullén called the 'Troll man's delight'.

When they met up with their female companions again and headed for the Fenêtre du Saleinaz and so back to the Cabane, Ling thought that they had 'gone very well and were not unduly fatigued, though rather sunburnt'.

The following day Raeburn, Ling and Ullén attempted the Petit Clocher

---

6   The Yovitchitch sisters were known to Raeburn and Ling: their mother was Scottish and had married a Serbian diplomat.
7   The artist Hilda Hechle and Miss C Campbell, for example.

de Planereuses, but could only climb the minor summit because of 'quite impossible slabs on the higher peak'. They retreated, and the whole party travelled down to Champex with the minor inconvenience of thunderstorms and 'a slip on the steep rocks', which Ling says 'nearly resulted in an accident'. He gives no details.

Down in the valley they had a great reception, and 'after dinner there was music and dancing and much drinking of healths'. Like most mountaineers, they were not puritans but people who knew how to enjoy themselves. Nor was it the last time that Raeburn and Ling would climb with one of the Yovitchitch sisters—next time it would be Natalia.

24. GRÉPON, AIGUILLE VERTE, MONTE ROSA, GABELHORN

1909

As the edited account in the *SMCJ* (1910) makes clear, Raeburn and Ling's Alpine season of 1909 had to be 'considerably modified' because of bad weather. Their first climb was an ascent of the Aiguille du Midi (3,842m) in the Mont Blanc massif after a very poor night in the half snow-filled Midi Cabane. Hugh Munro found the going too hard and turned back from the foot of the rocks.

On 4 August they thought to attempt the Grépon but only reached the Nantillons Glacier where they were stopped by a heavy snowstorm, getting back to Montenvers 'in a decidedly damp condition in body if not in spirits'. However, they later redeemed the day by climbing the Petit Charmoz and l'M, led, surprisingly, by one Miss CM Campbell, who, like the Norwegian Thérèse Bertheau, wore quite tight-fitting breeches. Whether she also 'scandalised the bourgeoisie' is not known, but she seems to have got on well with Raeburn and Ling and is pictured on one of the peaks with her hand on Raeburn's shoulder; from her expression and attitude one suspects she was quite a character, and she won praise from Ling for her competence in leading. Their day, however, had a sad ending as they had to deal with the fatal accident of one Herbert Tatham (*SMCJ*, 2021) on the descent path.

[Fig 1] Bad luck seemed to be dogging them, for when they attempted the Aiguille Verte[1] by the Moine Ridge (AD) on 6 August, they were followed by a German solo climber who used their steps and eventually had to be roped up to them. Ling says the German 'was not safe and occasionally

---

1   Somewhat of a misnomer, 'neither particularly needle-like nor green. It is a prominent golden wedge at the intersection of three needled ridges which descend to the west, south and east.' Sean O'Rourke.

slipped' (Diary, Book 8). Incredibly he had no gloves so of course his hands were numb. Neither had he supplies so Raeburn and Ling had to feed him. It was one of those situations which experienced mountaineers must deal with in order to prevent a serious outcome.

When they reached the tower known as the Cardinal near the top of the Aiguille it was heavily iced and they would have had to turn it. The German climber was plainly exhausted. At one point he cried out, 'Ich bin sehr müde.'[2] Raeburn and Ling found this disconcerting and made the wise decision to retreat. Manoeuvring skilfully with ice-axes and their barely adequate 60 ft of rope, they managed to lower the German from the cornice onto snow 'which looked as if it would hold'. It did, and after much tribulation they descended the South Face to the exit couloir and on to the glacier, reaching the hut by 7.30 pm. Ling was irate: 'I gave the German my views on his conduct.' If Raeburn made any comment it is not reported. One suspects it would have been typical of him to say little or nothing, even though they had had to turn back some 200 or 300 ft short of the summit.

On 8 August they resolved to make another attempt on the Grépon traverse. They left Montenvers on a fine moonlit night, but it was windy and the weather was suspect. They made their way across the glacier, over the bergschrund and to the foot of the couloir. By 7.10 am they had reached the Charmoz-Grépon col. 'The couloir to the Mummery Chimney[3] was glistening with ice and looked most forbidding'. Raeburn cut his way up, finding that the upper part of the couloir was slightly easier because there was some snow and he got 'some help from the rocks at the side'. By 8.30 am they were resting on the platform below the Crack. At the second attempt Raeburn solved the problem and Ling sent 'some of the spare rope and impedimenta up'. He found the Crack difficult but by 9.45 am they were both up. After food they crawled through what Ling calls 'the Canone's Lock' and up the face to a chimney. Avoiding the new 'through-route' behind the chockstone—'not for stout men'—they 'hotched along the bottomless passage and climbed up to the Grand Gendarme'. To ascend this they had 'to abseil into a corner leading to the broad ledge which leads to the highest summit'. The rope stuck on the abseil and had to be cut. The ascent from

[Fig 2]

[Fig 3]

2 'I am very tired.'
3 Referred to in French as the 'Trou du Canon', literally 'The Cannon's Hole', but more likely 'The Cannon Port', as in a wooden battleship.

Fig 1

The Aiguille Verte: The Moine Ridge forms the right-hand skyline, which Raeburn and Ling would have approached from the far side of the mountain. The Whymper Couloir is the prominent gully to the right of the summit. Photo: SMC Image Archive

the ledge to the summit was 'extremely difficult and severe work, swarming up the edge of a crack with nothing to lift from', and the rock was very polished, but by midday they were on the summit. While they lay in the sun they saw Captain Spelterini's balloon floating past: he was trying to fly over Mont Blanc but the wind carried him away to the Oberland instead. He did, however, take many excellent photographs of the Alps.

The descent went well. They used a 'rope ring' to thread the abseil ropes through—doing this on the ascent might have saved trouble. Ling says they 'only hesitated once about the route'. The rock was excellent and the 'traverse to the rock O.P.[4] was sensational and rather tricky' but 'once across the big block the difficulties [were] almost over'. By 2.40pm they were off the rocks. Their ascent was the second that season.

The following day the weather was bad and they went down to Argentière where another day of poor weather followed. Raeburn and Ling left Argentière on 10 August for Macugnaga where they put up at the Monte Rosa Hotel. In the morning the weather was improving at last, and they engaged Giuseppe Perazzi as porter, got provisions together and set off for Monte Rosa on the 'Glorious Twelfth'.

Monte Rosa is a massif in itself. It has numerous tops, from north to south the main peaks are: Signalkuppe (4,554m), Zumsteinsptize (4,563m), Dufourspitze (4,634m) and Nordend (4,609m). The Grenzgipfel is only of political importance, being on the frontier, and is an insignificant satellite of the Dufourspitze which is the second-highest summit in the Alps and the highest in Switzerland. The usual route of ascent, the North-West Flank and West Ridge, is described by Robin Collomb (1987) as 'One of the most frequented snow climbs in the Alps, a beaten trail in summer and indicated as such on the map.' It is graded F+. Raeburn and Ling were aiming for the East Face Route, AD+, sometimes referred to as the Marinelli Couloir Route, although the Couloir itself is sedulously avoided because of stonefall. The face is described as 'A famous ice climb with a big reputation ...'. And 'The face is one of the highest in the Alps ... the vertical interval of serious climbing up to the Grenzgipfel is nearly 1,600m' (ibid.).

From the Belvedere, where Perazzi got a supply of wood, they had

---

4 O.P.? Or is it A.P.? Ling's writing here is faint. A.P. stands for 'Absolutely Perpendicular'.

Fig 2

Not Raeburn and Ling, but similarly
equipped climbers on the traverse of
the Grépon. Photo: SMC Image Archive

Fig 3

The sharp pinnacle in the centre is the Charmoz summit. The Grépon rises to the right of the obvious couloir. It has a thin, slender pinnacle summit. Photo: W Lamond Howie, SMC Image Archive

'a splendid view of the S face of Monte Rosa' (Ling, op. cit., Book 8). Crossing the glacier they came to the rocks 'which were not quite easy' and they overtook three young Italians who arrived at the Rifugio Marinelli some time after them. Possibly fearing more troubles with inexperienced climbers, they persuaded the Italians to return with Perazzi, 'a good climber and a decent man'. Raeburn and Ling then prospected the dangerous 'Marinelli couloir, found the narrowest point to cross and made steps up to the edge of the groove'.

[Fig 4]

On 13 August they roped in the hut at 12.25 am and went quickly back to the groove. 'At this point it was about ten feet deep and fifteen across scored out of the snow by the rock and ice avalanches ... All was still. I drove [my axe] in and hitched while Raeburn hastily cut four or five steps and crossed the murderous funnel. He ran out the rope and I quickly followed and at 1.18, thirteen minutes in all, the first danger was behind us.'[5]

On the Imseng Rücken (now il crestone Imseng) the rock was steep and the snow patches hard but they made good progress 'for we had no time to lose'. At 3.40 am they reached the top of the rock and stopped for a second breakfast. Ling says, 'We had the most beautiful dawn we had ever seen, the Engadine peaks clear cut in the now crimsoning sky made a sight never to be forgotten.'

Climbing as quickly as possible, they were 'forced somewhat towards the couloir by the seracs'; they knew that such was the avalanche danger when the sun got on the mountain that 'they must not even be near the couloir'. They had to 'creep along the narrow pathway formed by the broken crest of the ice slope' below the seracs. In the distance they could see the Grenzgipfel rocks they were making for. They had to cut many steps up the snowfield to the bergschrund, above which 'a steeper slope still' led to the foot of the rocks.

These rocks were heavily iced and Raeburn and Ling had to move one at a time traversing under them. It was fortunate that the rope was behind something solid for Ling took hold of a rock which he thought Raeburn had used and 'it came away and still holding it in my arms we slid down the snow-covered ice for a yard or two till the well-hitched rope tautened and I left the rock to slide down itself to the bergschrund below'.

---

5   Modern guidebooks say that in good conditions 15 minutes should suffice for a pair, and they give serious warnings about stonefall and avalanche danger.

Fig 4

The East Face of Monte Rosa. The Marinelli Couloir is the slender strip of snow dividing the central rocks.
Photo: SMC Image Archive.

Fig 5

A modern photo of the Obergabelhorn. Wellenkuppe is the snow-capped peak to the right and the Grand Gendarme is obvious on the ridge leading to the Gabelhorn. The Gabelhorngrat is the central ridge dropping from the summit and was used by Raeburn and Ling to descend to the sunny glacier bowl and thence down the glacier to the Trift valley.
Photo: John Cleare

But for their good rope technique, this incident could have been disastrous. Ling passes it over almost humorously.

A little further and they were at last 'out of danger of anything falling' and could stop to eat and drink after nine-and-three-quarter hours of hard and anxious climbing. They got going again at 10.40 am but found that the rock couloir through the steep cliffs above was 'draped with glistening ice' and they were forced to climb 'the steepest [rocks] we could find where no ice could stick'. They persevered and 'at 3 o'clock exactly we stood on top of the Grenzgipfel'. At 3.15 pm they reached the summit of Monte Rosa, the Dufourspitze. They knew the way down was easy so they gloried in the view, made hot tea and ate jam sandwiches. They had plenty of tracks to follow on the descent to the shelter where they had coffee. Leaving there at 7 pm they reached the Riffelberg Hotel, after a long passage of glacier travel, more than 20 hours after leaving the Rifugio Marinelli. Ling says, 'It had been a magnificent expedition and we never had any danger from falling things.'

After a rest day in Zermatt, chatting with friends at the Monte Rosa Hotel, they arranged to go up to the Fluh Alp 'for the Rimpfischhorn' but only after they 'had been to church'.[6] Then Harold and Willie, accompanied by three ladies, Ruth Raeburn, Natalia Yovitchitch and Edith Gray,[7] set off up the Findelen path, making 'an imposing exit from Zermatt'.

The Rimpfischhorn (4,198 m), one of the big peaks of the line of summits between the Mattertal and Saas Fee valleys, was duly ascended in good order the next day and the party had a picnic lunch on the summit complete with freshly brewed tea. They got down to the Fluh Alp by 4 pm and back to Zermatt by 6.30 pm, having got wet in a thunderstorm that was tracking across from the Matterhorn. Apparently 'the ladies were delighted with the expedition'.

Coming towards the end of their 1909 season, Raeburn and Ling decided to go up to the Trift Inn, a favourite haunt, 'and make a dash for the Gabelhorn'. The Obergabelhorn (4,062 m), 'a shapely conical peak of four ridges and four faces, half snow and half rock', is sometimes overlooked in favour of its more famous neighbours, the Matterhorn, the Dent Blanche

---

6   No doubt St Peter's Anglican Church, the English Church, consecrated in 1871, with its numerous memorials to British climbers killed on the mountains.
7   The following year Edith Gray had the misfortune to slip while in a roped party being led by Raeburn on Stùc a' Chroin, an accident that had serious repercussions for him.

and the Weisshorn, but it is a fine peak 'with a lot of interesting climbing'. All the routes are worthwhile, and it is customary to combine different routes to make traverses.

On 20 August Raeburn and Ling set off for the East-North-East Ridge. They climbed Wellenkuppe (3,903m) without difficulty and traversed towards the Obergabelhorn.[8] 'The ridge was corniced but there was room for us to walk on the rocks under the cornice and with a little management we came to the big gendarme without much trouble.' But the Gendarme[9] was another story altogether: sheeted with ice, it could not be climbed so they had to traverse it. 'A rock saddle had to be swarmed up and then steps cut in almost perpendicular and very hard ice.' Ling describes the action: 'I got up on the saddle and hitched while Raeburn cut splendid steps with much toil in the ice. It made very sensational watching for the angle was tremendous. He cut his way back to the ridge and I followed.' Like his performance on Green Gully this traverse must have been a *tour de force*; Raeburn would have had to cut handholds with which to hold himself on to the high-angled ice while he cut the next foothold. Ling's description barely does justice to the difficulty. Robin Collomb (op. cit. p.83) says that the traverse originally involved 'two or three rope lengths on steep snow or ice'. Proceeding along the ridge they had to cut many more steps 'from rock to rock jutting out, sensational work, but the upper part opened out better and at 10.40 we each in turn stepped solemnly on to the corniced top of the Gabelhorn while the other anchored lest the cornice gave'. The descent by the Gabelhorngrat, the SE Ridge (PD+/AD), involved 'some very interesting and good rock climbing, ridge and face, some of it quite difficult and full of variety'. They had to be careful to leave the ridge at the Gabeljoch to descend to the Gabelhorn Glacier but they were off the rock by 1.10pm and glad of steps to lead them over the glacier with its 'rather complicated crevasse system'. Down at the Trift Inn they met Percy Unna[10] and stayed till 4pm before going down to the Edelweiss Inn for tea on the way back to the Monte Rosa Hotel. Despite the adverse weather, Ling describes their season in his diary as 'a very enjoyable one'.

8 Like the Zinal Rothorn, this route is nowadays ascended from the Rothorn Hut. The ascent from the Trift Inn is much longer.
9 Equipped with a fixed rope after 1918 and nowadays a cable.
10 According to Crocket (2015, p.309), PJH Unna, (1878–1950) made a major contribution to the purchases of Glen Coe South and Dalness estates which were donated to the National Trust for Scotland.

Fig 6

Raeburn had to cut traversing steps on the shadowed side of the Gendarme, the black pinnacle roughly halfway between Wellenkuppe (L) and Obergabelhorn (R). Photo: © John Cleare.

25. NORTH FACE OF DISGRAZIA, CRAST' AGÜZZA, SCERSCEN   1910

By late July 1910, Raeburn was sufficiently recovered from his accident on Stùc a' Chroin to travel to the Alps, where bad weather predominated. On what the account in the SMC *Journal* describes as an 'off-day' on the 27th, he and his stalwart companion Ling, in company with Ruth Raeburn and Natalia Yovitchitch, undertook a climb from Château d'Œx.

[Fig 1]

Although Natalia was not often in Scotland, it is possible that she and Harold had some form of romantic involvement; they certainly had a lot in common. She was a champion skater, having won the Challenge Cup at Gstaad four times, and she also won a prestigious skiing competition in Switzerland. According to her obituary (*LSCC Journal*, 1937), she exhausted herself with War work, for which she was decorated by the Serbian government and the Red Cross. Like Harold, Natalia became ill in 1921, and her activities were much reduced. She mainly climbed with Harold and Ling in the Lakes and the Alps, although there is a record of a visit to Arran in the autumn of 1910 after this trip to the Alps, but her companions are not known.

On this occasion they climbed the Satarma Needle in Arolla. Raeburn thought the climb 'underrated' and bordering on 'dangerous'. He removed his boots to deal with the questionable rock.

It may be significant that the party started in Arolla, traditionally held to be one of the easier centres in the western Alps. Although he had climbed Tower Ridge and descended North-East Buttress on Ben Nevis in a summer snowstorm since his accident, Raeburn may have felt the need to play himself in gently.

At all events, after 'a shockingly overcrowded' night in the Bertol Cabane, the party climbed the central peak of Les Bouquetins. On 30 July

Fig 1

Natalia Yovitchitch's penetrating but inscrutable gaze. Raeburn is almost smiling and looks relaxed: Arolla in 1910. Ruth Raeburn and Ling also feature.
Photo: SMC Image Archive

The North Face of Monte Disgrazia;
painting by Anthony 'Ginger' Cain.
Photo: John Cleare

they crossed the Col d'Hérens to Zermatt, enjoying fine cloud effects on the Matterhorn and witnessing a massive avalanche from the Dent d'Hérens. Bad weather pursued them to Zermatt, but on Monday, 1 August, Harold, Willie, Ruth and Natalia traversed both peaks of the Unter Gabelhorn 'direct' from Zermatt and, despite some snow on the rocks, 'got back to dinner'. With fitness improving it was obviously time for something more serious.

Leaving Ruth and Natalia to their own devices, Raeburn and Ling then attempted to traverse the Lyskamm into Italy. The weather was poor. Ling says: 'once or twice it looked like improving but afterwards got worse'. They toiled to the top of the first icefall and halted for a while but 'it was so cold and the wind so strong that it was impossible to make headway'. They retreated to the hut and back down to Zermatt in heavy rain by 3pm. 'The mountains were again covered with new snow.'

On 4 August Raeburn and Ling embarked on a long and complicated journey by train, steamer (on Lakes Maggiore and Como) and by 'diligence' to Chiesa in the Valmalenco. Raeburn (1911) described their objective in the *Alpine Journal* (*AJ*).

> *From several of the Engadine summits on the Swiss frontier, the beautiful Italian peak of the Monte della Disgrazia presents a splendid appearance … It turns to the spectator its icy N face. Down this streams, into the head of the Val Sissone, the great, much crevassed Disgrazia glacier … No one to our knowledge had attacked the N Face direct from the Disgrazia glacier. It looked formidable on the photograph,*[1] *but was worth close examination. We resolved to go and see.*

[Fig 2]

After a day spent resting and making arrangements, they set off with the guide Albareda Casimiro acting as porter and had a beautiful walk up a well-wooded valley to Chiareggio where they 'lunched at a primitive inn near the church'. Climbing on to 5,800ft they paid off the porter, who thought they only wanted to cross the Passo di Mello:

---

1 The photograph which had originally caught Raeburn's imagination was by AW Russell; it is reprinted by Raeburn's article in the *AJ*, 1911, p.690.

> To our declared intention of attempting the traverse of the Disgrazia by the N face, he evidently gave no heed. A torrent of Italian, in which the two words 'impossibile' and 'brutto' were the only two we could catch, was all we could make of his opinion of that project.

However, while entertaining doubts about his employers' sanity, Casimiro kindly found them a camping place by a boulder and cut wood for them before departing for the valley, no doubt shaking his head and muttering. Raeburn says that he too would have had doubts about their sanity if they had stayed on the site Casimiro had chosen, 'open to every wind', and he and Ling scouted around for a more comfortable spot. Some 1,400ft higher they found 'a grassy ledge, which we covered with fir branches'; they also lit a fire. As Ling has it, they didn't sleep 'owing to a drip of water from above'; Raeburn simply says it got rather cold, but they were 'fairly comfortable'. The night was fine with starlight.

Leaving the gîte at 1.10 am they climbed a rocky, grassy ridge, which Raeburn had inspected the night before, by lantern light to the glacier. They were making steady progress till 2.35 am (8,500 ft), when they paused to rope up.

> The going was good, fine crisp snow, not too steep, till we entered, while it was still dark, a more broken part of the glacier. Huge crevasses, overhung by steep séracs thinly covered with snow, loomed ahead ... I dropped the candle here, while doing some one-handed cutting up the wall of an ice wave, and we seized the excuse to call a halt until the rapidly waning moonlight was banished by the faint grey light of the coming dawn. Things gradually gained shape as the light grew. Problems of the unseen as well as the unknown glacier were slowly simplified. We found that our position was too advanced, as the French say, 'Il faut reculer pour mieux sauter'[2]. (Raeburn, 1911)

To do this, they descended one ice wave and made their way along the narrow crest of another where a narrow flake of ice formed a fragile

[Fig 3] footbridge, by which they 'escaped to the uncrevassed ice slope on the

---

2   'It is necessary to go back in order to jump forward better.'

Fig 3

Raeburn and Ling seem to have climbed the central rock rib dividing the snow face. Above that Raeburn cut many steps until they got to surmountable rock which had no cornice to the right of the couloir.
Photo: John Cleare

left'. Raeburn says, 'We kicked steps here in good snow, cutting across the polished avalanche slides when met with.' After another slight descent, 'a long, easily sloping snow valley was entered upon, leading straight up towards the N face of the Disgrazia'. This section was not difficult but was made laborious by soft snow. At 6.10 am they paused for food. Raeburn notes that:

The face presented a splendid if somewhat forbidding appearance from this point. Direct attack upon the highest summit was evidently barred. Some hundreds of feet above the 'schrund a great lunette-shaped overhanging bastion of ice stretched across the face of the mountain.

After enumerating all the difficulties which made a direct ascent of the face impossible, Raeburn says:

We had observed that the upper rocks formed a kind of incipient minor top on the NW ridge of the Disgrazia and that there was no cornice at the place where the steep rocks reached the summit. The idea, therefore, was to cut or, we hoped, kick steps up the snow on the ice wall to the rocks and climb them to the ridge.

He adds significantly: 'If we had known just how much of this we were going to have, it is possible no attack would have been made after all'.

'More laborious work up snow slopes of varying hardness' brought them to the bergschrund at 'the foot of the rib of snow and ice which we proposed to attack'. The slope angle above the bergschrund measured 62° (by Raeburn's clinometer). The snow was good and hard, and they kicked steps until it became necessary to cut them. They made towards the 'small island of [steep] rocks' that they had spied from below, protruding from the icy slope. From the summit of the rocks rose 'a very narrow snow ridge which led out into the general face' (angle 52°). To their left was 'a large massif of rocks but these proved quite impossible, icy and slabby with no hitches so [we] were driven out on to the face again'. They had to be extremely careful because they were on precipitous ground 'and the snow was getting very thin'. Most unusually, Ling admits that, 'A slip on the part of either would have been fatal.'

'We tried here and we tried there, but there was no easier route.' Cutting steps in hard ice, they came to 'a jutting out rock where we managed to clear out a hitch. Above this a very steep and dangerous slope led to the top rocks. Those above us were impossible and it was necessary to traverse diagonally upwards to see whether the rocks were better at their other corner'. Ling 'kept to the hitch as long as possible' but had to follow on to the face when the rope ran out. Raeburn cut on:

> *Occasionally a good lift was obtained up the long ribbon of snow piled upon the upper sides of various small rocks jutting out of the ice on the face. Hours of strenuous toil passed. The bergschrund by now had sunk far out of sight; the great cornice on our right loomed high overhead. It became necessary to make a way on to those slabby iced rocks on the left.*

The climbing was extremely difficult. Three times they were defeated and tried other routes.

> *At last, after an ineffectual effort to get up an overhanging chimney, baffled by the bulging ice at the exit, a neat traverse was discovered to the left. This led at once into rocks of quite a different character; though excessively steep, they were well broken up with cracks and chimneys, good holds and not excessively iced. We soon passed the chimneys and at last found ourselves on the summit ridge of the Disgrazia.*

They gained the first top by 3pm, some 14 hours after leaving the bivouac. After some much-needed food they left their rucksacks and followed the ridge to the summit of the mountain. Here they found tracks made by a party that had climbed the south-west route 'a day or so before'.

The weather was 'now not so good and the valleys were mirky'. They went back, retrieved their sacks and then descended by the South-West Face to the Preda Rossa Glacier which, though the snow was soft, gave easy going. In mist they reached the Capanna Cecilia.[3] They had with them 'the huge gun-metal key, lent us by our host at Chiesa'. At first the double lock proved stiff and their hearts sank, 'but after some coaxing … [it] yielded' and they got in, made tea, lay down and 'were soon wrapped in sleep'.

---

3   Now the Rifugio Cesare Ponti.

Like many of Raeburn's first ascents in Scotland, his ascent with Ling of the North Face of Monte Disgrazia was not repeated for a further five years, when it, or something like it, was climbed by Angelo Calegari and Gaetano Scotti. Ironically, Raeburn and Ling's route became known as the Via degli *Inglesi* or Lo Spigolo degli *Inglesi*.

Continuing on their way Raeburn and Ling crossed a 9,000ft col and came down in mist into the upper Val Pioda. There followed an engaging pastoral journey. They got milk from a shepherd who told them how to get round the spur which the Pizzo Torrone sends down. They had to climb steeply and then descend by a gully into the upper Val Torrone where they had lunch in a shepherd's shelter. Rather lost, they wandered about in mist and rain until it grew late and they decided to go back to the hut where they had had lunch. The rain came down in torrents and they were 'glad to get shelter'. A couple of shepherds came in and they had a 'disjointed conversation in Italian'. After the shepherds left they managed to get a fire going and made soup. They got in more firewood. There was some hay for a bed and they kept the fire going all night by taking it in turns to blow on it. By so doing, they managed to dry their clothes a little.

After a scanty breakfast they left at 5.30am, hoping to reach Maloja. Climbing grass slopes and a scree gully, they gained a col by 6.50am. From there they could see the Allievi Hut and made for it across rough ground and slabs. On reaching the hut they cooked up the last of their food: 'a tin of peas and an egg fried in butter, which were very good'. Things improved and the sun came out as they ascended to the Zocca col. They roped briefly to descend the Albigna Glacier and stopped to rest on a slabby spur above a curious hollow, on which the new Albigna Hut was being built. Here they made tea and had almost an hour's rest 'basking in the sun'. Descending by the track at the side of the 'magnificent gorge and Albigna waterfall', they reached the Maloja road at 1.56pm 'near an inn where we got welcome liquid refreshment'. Going on a mile they [Fig 4] came to Vicosoprano 'where a large omelette, coffee and bread put us on good terms with ourselves'. The long day ended at the Maloja Kulm Hotel. 'The weather had now turned cold and a bottle of Bouvier for the Disgrazia was a fitting close to the expedition'.[4]

4   References in this account are to Ling's Diary 8, 84ff and Diary 9, 1–5; and Raeburn's article in the *AJ* op cit.

Fig 4

Vicosoprano, where Raeburn and Ling had an omelette after their post-Disgrazia wanderings. Photo: Roger Robb

Fig 5

The ridge of Piz Scerscen centre, with Piz Bernina to its left. Photo: SMC Image Archive

Leaving Maloja on 12 August, Raeburn and Ling 'took electric train to Morteratsch ... and walked up to the Boval Hut'. The next day they attempted Piz Bernina in the company of 'several other (mis)guided parties', as Raeburn dryly puts it in the account in the *SMCJ* (1911). They got no further than a snow-filled bergschrund where they waited, fruitlessly, 'for the improvement promised by one of the guides'. They retreated to Morteratsch and went up to the Boval Hut again the following day.

On 15 August they set out to traverse the two sharp peaks of the Crast' Agüzza. Gaining the col between the Crast' and Piz Argient (Pizzo d'Argento), they climbed snow to rocks, which, Ling says, were easy at first but became slabby and iced. In one place Raeburn had to leave his axe and 'use his knife to clear some holds of ice'. The upper part of the ridge was 'slabby and steep' as well as being corniced and they had to take care. The summit, which was reached for only the second time that season, at 8.15am, was narrow and exposed so they went down the easier-angled ridge where they stopped for breakfast. They continued down this ridge, which was also corniced, using the rocks on the face where possible to finish down a gully between the main ridge and a projecting spur. After a stop for tea, 20 further minutes down the glacier took them to another small 'capanna' named in honour of Marinelli where they found 'several pleasant Italians and our Disgrazia porter with a German, Dr Müller, who were very interested in our Disgrazia ascent' (Ling's Diary, Book 9).

Despite being called late at 1.30 am, on 16 August Raeburn and Ling made good progress towards their goal, a traverse of Monte di Scerscen (now Piz Scerscen), at 3,971m one of the highest peaks of the Bernina Range. It is a satellite peak of Piz Bernina, joining it by its north-east ridge via a 3,382m pass. Raeburn and Ling, of course, were aiming to traverse both mountains. After gaining height rapidly on broken rock, they paused for breakfast. Continuing, they kept to the rocks, 'which were now snow and ice covered and became very steep' (Ling's Diary, Book 9). They were forced to avoid an ice-choked chimney by a 'very awkward traverse which was rather dangerous' across 'a very steep wall of ice'. Above this more rock led to the edge again 'and by this we ascended to the main ridge close to the SW peak. We were hailed by two Italians coming up to the SW peak from the other side'. From there they followed 'a narrow snow arête to the highest summit', where they paused for 20 minutes. Their troubles were only just

[Fig 5]

beginning. Ling describes a gripping struggle as they traversed the ridge:

> *It was now misty, but we could see the extremely narrow and badly corniced arête which led over the towers which cram the ridge. Below ... on either side the snow lay thinly on ice. Now followed a very exciting and difficult piece of work ... much time had to be expended in working along the cornices piled up on the narrow ridge; sometimes they had to be beaten down, then we would be astride, now balancing along the top, and now gingerly kicking steps while we pressed delicately for handhold on the top. It was exhausting work and the tension was great.*

Some of the towers on the ridge they 'cut on the north side ... and we took on the S side whenever the state of the snow would allow ... At 3.25 pm we reached the col before the last main [tower] at the head of the big couloir, from which the ascent to the Bernina springs'. There they took a much-needed rest. The weather had worsened and they found themselves in a thunderstorm with hail and snow. The ascent of Piz Bernina, which would have completed a notable traverse, was obviously out of the question and they took the only possible decision. They tried first to descend to the north, but after going down for some 300 ft they judged the snow too dangerous.

On the south flank of the ridge they were at least sheltered from the wind and 'got down to snow in the gully'. They descended for a way till they came to a steep ice pitch 'and had to take to some badly iced and difficult rock, which Raeburn managed with uncommon skill'. They got into the gully again and tackled 'a groove cut by snow avalanche ... as it was now evening [therefore cold] and safe ... we ... found the bed of this better than the snow outside, which was hard'. Pitch by pitch from ice-axe belays, they 'kick[ed] steps for 2,000 ft ... it required care for we came on ice from time to time'.

At the bottom of what must have seemed like an endless slope they found the bergschrund filled with avalanche snow. With deft understatement, Ling remarks: 'we were glad to be out'. They lit their candle lantern, descended the slopes below the 'schrund without further difficulty and trudged back to the Capanna Marinelli by 10.20 pm where they had soup and went to bed. As Ling says: 'It was a long expedition, 20 hours, but we were lucky not to be benighted'. In a revealing later comment, Raeburn remarked in his 1910 notebook that the Scerscen traverse 'was about as hard a climb as

I have ever had'. With his record that comment is significant.

On 17 August, as Robin Campbell puts it, 'meaning only to cross the col to the Boval Hut, they were seduced into detouring to the Piz Bernina by its E Ridge'. They had the mountain to themselves because the guides, fearing another storm (which failed to materialise), did not set out. Reaching the summit at 4pm, they then went down to the col and the Boval for coffee before going on to Morteratsch, where they dined before getting a carriage to Pontresina by 10pm, 'well pleased with our three days' work'. Indeed, considering the weather and the state of Raeburn's body after his accident, it had been another splendid season. By the end of it Raeburn had actually regained the weight he had lost during his lengthy spell of convalescence.

The successful visit to the Alps in 1910 was followed by two years during which, for some reason, Raeburn remained in Scotland and even there did relatively little mountaineering. The reasons for this are somewhat obscure. It is known that in 1911 he was 'treated at home for melancholia',[5] or depression as we would call it. In the obituary published in the SMCJ in 1927, Willie Ling stated that Raeburn had another accident, or perhaps more than one, in 1911 or 1912, and this information also appears in the obituary written by George Sang in the *Fell and Rock Climbers' Club Journal* (1926). *The Scotsman* obituary (23 December 1926) is categorical about a second accident having occurred. Details, however, are lacking. It is quite possible, of course, that Raeburn had an accident or accidents and also suffered from depression; indeed the one might cause the other. It is also possible that Raeburn's friends were covering up the fact that his trouble was psychological, given the stigma attaching to mental illness at the time. As so often with Raeburn, we don't know for certain. It is certainly true, however, that by 1913 he was full of life and making his first visit to the Caucasus. That visit was followed by a second expedition in 1914, which was cut short by the outbreak of the Great War.

Raeburn's last great climb in the Alps, the solo traverse of the Meije, came in 1919 after the Great War; like his winter ascent of Observatory Ridge on Ben Nevis in 1920, it was an ample demonstration of his fitness. Both were prologues to Kangchenjunga and Everest.

---

5   From a medical background report when Harold was a patient in Craig House Asylum after the Everest Expedition in 1921.

THE CAUCASUS

26. THE CAUCASUS EXPEDITION: CHANCHAKHI   1913

Whether Raeburn's relative inactivity in 1911 and 1912 was due to an accident or accidents, or depression, or both, there is no doubt that he seemed fully recovered by the summer of 1913, when he found that he had two months of leisure. With Willie Ling he planned an expedition to the Caucasus,[1] where they were joined by JR Young, a younger member of the SMC and a good photographer, and WG Johns of the Alpine Club.

When the party reached Vladikavkaz they recruited a young student called Rembert Martinson, 'who came as climbing comrade, interpreter and aide-de-camp' and proved 'plucky, able and competent in all respects'. As well as his native Russian, he spoke fluent French and German and some English, with which 'He was able to make, with a Scottish intonation, the necessary remark when he barked his shins!' They also recruited a cook, Militan Burjeladzé (called Melitan by Ling), who spoke the dialects, but that it seems was his only virtue, for 'His inability to cook was only equalled by his laziness ... and an unfortunate taste for vodka led once or twice to his fall ...' (Ling, *AJ*, 1914).

[Fig 1] Leaving Vladikavkaz on 8 July, they drove up the Mamison Pass to the mouth of the Tsaya Valley. From there they went with pack horses to the highest pinewoods below the snout of the Tsaya Glacier where they found a delightful spot to pitch camp. They wished first to explore the Adai Khokh mountains, which lie immediately west and north of the

---

1   As usual, the *SMCJ* (1914) provides a sketch of their doings in and Ling's Diary provides much more. Raeburn kept a diary at this time, and it is quoted at length on the attempt on Ushba's North eak. Raeburn also wrote a long article for the *Geographical Journal* (*GJ*), to which reference is made.

1913: The Caucasus Expedition—Chanchakhi

Fig 1

The idyllic camp in the Tsaya woods. From left: Martinson, Johns, Ling and Raeburn. Ling and Raeburn keeping up a good standard of dress for a camp in the woods: this habit caused amusement among the locals apparently. Photo: JR Young, who became the expedition's photographer

Fig 2

On the Tsaya glacier with some of the Aiguilles in the background. From left: Johns, Martinson, Raeburn and Ling.
Photo: JR Young

arterial Mamison Road. On the south the range is bounded by the Mamison hills and the Chanchakhi group, on the north by the Sadon Valley and the upper Urukh River. On the west one can say it is bounded by the line of the old native glacier pass of the Gurdsivzek leading from the Karagom and Urukh valleys to that of Rion. [Fig 2]

The pinewoods were a known place of pilgrimage. According to Raeburn (*GJ*, 1915), people came to 'drink goats' milk, breathe in the glacier air, and inhale the spiced breeze of the pines'. Raeburn actually quotes the famous first lines of Chaucer's Prologue to *The Canterbury Tales*:

Whan Aprilé with his showerés swooté
The drought of March hath perced to the rooté ...
... Than longen folk to gon on Pilgrimages.[2]

Reasonable red Caucasian wine and 'good Russian bread' were available. Raeburn knew his wines and, like Bill Tilman after him, he liked good bread.

To gain a grasp of the area's complex geography the expedition set out to tackle two of the so-called 'Tsaya Aiguilles'. They climbed up past the 'Koshes' of the tur (large mountain goat) hunters and shepherds with their savage dogs (they named one of these summer dwellings 'the doggeries'), got onto the glacier and ascended one of the rock peaks rising from it, which they named 'Tur Khokh' or 'Mountain Goat Peak'. Two days later they climbed another similar peak and named it 'Ullargh Khokh'[3] after the great rock partridges—rather like huge ptarmigan—whose whistling sounded all around the tents in the mornings. On these outings they equipped the porters with nailed boots as they were carrying loads to higher camps. Raeburn noted that the younger porters adapted well to this new technique for climbing ice but the older ones still tried to place their whole feet against the slope instead of kicking in. It is significant that in all Raeburn's wanderings he never abused porters or asked them to do anything unreasonable. He seems always to have enjoyed good relationships with the native people who served him. As for the dogs, he claimed that he had never heard of anyone being

---

2   Raeburn may have been quoting from memory or from a version current at the time; the quote is not quite in line with the received version now, but Raeburn's version has been retained here.
3   The names Tur Khokh and Ullargh Khokh still appear on Russian maps.

injured by one of them, but WH Murray tells a different story, reckoning that the hounds that attacked him in the Himalaya would have savaged or killed him without the owner's intervention.

The peak in this part of the Caucasus that Raeburn really wanted to climb was Chanchakhi. He also wanted to settle the vexed question of whether the earlier explorer, de Déchy, had climbed it. Still prospecting, they attempted a third peak, which Raeburn named 'Curtain Peak'.[4] In the event they were turned back by bad weather, but Raeburn had been able at least to rule out attempting the north face of Chanchakhi, which, viewed from the mountains they had climbed, looked far too formidable.[5]

When they got down from the failed attempt on Curtain Peak they found the camp in uproar. They had been burgled, and Melitan claimed that four men armed with revolvers had driven him off. One of the tents was cut, 'and a large basket containing precious jams and soups ... and several other items, including the groundsheet of our tent, had been stolen'. In his immediate annoyance, Ling speculates darkly in his Diary that the cook was probably in league with the robbers, but in his *AJ* article he contents himself by saying, 'we never got the full story'. 'With a retinue armed to the teeth', the Mayor of Tsaya village came out to hunt the robbers, but of course nothing was ever recovered.

They shifted to an upper camp at 9,300ft, and from here Raeburn set out to reconnoitre a way to Chanchakhi, the 'finest peak of the Tsaya group, also virgin'. He discovered that the north Tsaya icefall was at present too dangerous, being continually swept by boulders, stones and blocks of ice. Raeburn chose instead the southern glacier's icefalls—not considered difficult by the earlier explorer, Douglas Freshfield, or by Raeburn's friend and informant, Dr Ronchetti of Milan.

Accordingly, the following day, they climbed the icefalls of the southern glacier and entered 'an almost circular snow basin ... walled round with peaks of steep rocks and ice' (Raeburn, 1915). Nothing, however, was simple. On the right there was a 'long high-ridged mountain mass with two tops' up to over 14,000ft. Raeburn notes that this is marked in Woolley's photos

4   This peak is now named Mamison Khokh.
5   Raeburn also ruled out the possibility of Déchy having climbed Chanchakhi because it would have been too difficult. It is not clear, however, that he was right in thinking that Déchy had not climbed Uilpata.

as 'Mr Freshfield's Double Peak', sometimes called 'Bubis'. On the left are the well-marked peaks of Ronchetti's 'Triple Peak' (but seen from here, confusingly, as two), rising between the Mamison Pass and Tsaya. Below the lowest gap on their eastern side the 'Freshfield Perival' (or pass) of 1889, not easy to approach, leads up to the east Mamison Glacier on the north side of the Mamison Pass and Tsaya. There was no sign of the mountain sometimes referred to as Adai (but nowadays known as Uilpata). Crucially there was no sign of Chanchakhi.[6] They decided to attempt Double Peak.

With difficulty, they climbed by the rocky arête falling from the main ridge in a south-easterly direction. With many 'loose stones', the party of five went slowly to be safe. They got to a minor top at 2pm, realised that the summit 'was a long way off and about 500 ft higher' and, with snow and a cold wind, they turned back. But with the height gained, they had seen how to climb Adai and, even more importantly, 'a threatening vision of an enormous black cliff at the head of the north Tsaya basin'. This was Chanchakhi's north-east face. It looked quite hopeless and they decided to shift camp away from the Tsaya basin 'to the headwaters of the upper Mamison'. By the time they got back to their upper camp, packed up and descended to the lower one, they had been out for 22 hours. Without delay they marshalled their resources and set off for the upper part of the Mamison Pass.

Raeburn continues the story: 'Mr Young and I were the rearguards, somewhat temper-rasped and semi starving ...' They reached St Nikolai, which Raeburn thought would become 'the Visp of the Caucasus',[7] at 12.15. Later they had a meal 'at a *gostanitsa* of sorts below the ruins of King George of Georgia's castle'. Here they got two horses, which Ling and Johns rode up to the Kalaki Kazarma,[8] the highest permanently inhabited spot on the pass.

---

6   If the reader is not confused it is nothing short of miraculous. The naming of peaks in the Caucasus is bedevilled by Russian and Georgian languages, by visiting climbers casually naming mountains, and later by ideological re-naming, e.g. 'The Council of Trades Unions' Peak'. The mapping also is poor. Fortunately, the names of certain notable peaks like Chanchakhi, Ushba and Elbruz have remained constant. For a considered discussion, see Robin Campbell's article, 'The Caucasus Expedition of 1913' (*SMCJ*, 2013).
7   Visp being a mountain sport-orientated village near the foot of the Mattertal in Switzerland. For good or ill, St Nikolai has not developed to the same extent.
8   The names 'kazarma' and 'kazerne' seem to be used interchangeably. They are hostels with military backgrounds possibly used formerly by soldiers guarding roads.

Unfortunately Melitan had been drinking and had somehow procured a white horse. He 'continually charged up in the rear of the cart' and incited the driver to race. Raeburn, who was with Martinson and Young in the cart with the luggage, acidly remarked, 'The road is not adapted for this.' It had no parapets, no fence or wall and it was a great height above the river; also, the surface was 'about as bad as anything pretending to be a road could have'. Raeburn had almost decided to stun the driver with his ice-axe and take the reins himself when the driver, at this point leading the horses, slipped and went over the cliff—fortunately he had twisted the reins round his arm and the startled horses jerking to the side helped to drag him back up again. They reached the village of Tib after dark.

[Fig 3] Here Raeburn was beset by a mob wanting to guide them to the kazarma because 'the road was impossible'. Alive to Caucasian exaggeration, Raeburn imperturbably ordered the procession to move on at once, and sure enough they found the road in better shape than that already travelled. The Kalaki kazarma was very crowded so they put up their light tents. Even after such a day, Raeburn the geographer noted the sort of trade going on: timber from the south and salt and provisions from the north.

Next day they took two pack horses 'up to the highest earth patch— 10,000 ft—below the huge moraine of the Mamison west glacier'. Raeburn attempted to sort out the geography, but his attempt was vitiated by the fact that the names he used for the various peaks (e.g. 'Ronchetti Peak') have not been adopted.

From this camp they climbed the two highest summits to the west and east. The west summit is triangulated on the Russian 1-verst map as 1897 Sazhens (13,297 ft). Raeburn thought that the triangulation was on a lower point than the virgin summit. (Confusingly, Merzbacher called it 'Mamison Khokh' with a height of 4,048 m.) The mountain, anyway, is a 'long sharp ridge of rock with a great precipice ... over the south Tsaya side'. To add yet more confusion, Ronchetti apparently thought that this summit was 'not sufficiently important to bear the name of Mamison and would transfer ... that name to the next peak on the north-west. This is the great "Double Peak" already described from the Tsaya Valley'. (To be fair to Dr Ronchetti,

[Fig 4] his suggestion seems to have been adopted. Mamison Khokh is marked on current maps as a near neighbour of Chanchakhi, but considerably lower than it; in fact what Raeburn called Curtain Peak; see note 4 above.)

Fig 3

A vignette of life at the Kazerne. It looks as if Martinson, upstage, is chatting with the locals; Johns and Raeburn by the door.
Photo: JR Young

Fig 4

Chanchakhi, the sharp peak right of centre. Only the upper part of Raeburn's route on the right skyline is definitely visible, but the slender gully running up to the ridge may have been part of it. To the left is Mamison Khokh, called 'Curtain Peak' by Raeburn. Photo: JR Young

The night of 24 July saw heavy rain, wind and thunder. In the morning they ascended the east Mamison glacier to the Saramag col. From there 'the watershed rock ridge was climbed to the top dominating the east Mamison and also the Saramag glacier. It is triangulated on the 1-verst map ... but has no name'. They were surprised to find that a large cairn had been built on the summit. Raeburn says: 'The peak is easily accessible from the Saramag glacier and must have been reached from thence by a Russian survey party. It may be considered as entitled to the name Saramag.'

The following day they managed to hire an ox-cart to take their gear over the Mamison Pass to the Chanchakhi kazarma on the Rion or Asiatic side. The pass is the highest driving road in Europe at 9,800 ft and from it they had exciting views of Chanchakhi. Having purchased a loaf of bread from the shelter at the summit of the pass they unwisely left it in the ox-cart in the care of Melitan and the son of a Cossack whom they also employed, and the climbers descended directly to the kazarma where they waited 'hungrily' for the cart to arrive. 'Alas,' says Ling, 'the cook had got some vodka at the pass and had lost our bread. We loved him less than ever.' Now was the time to think of making a serious attempt on Chanchakhi.[9] The north-east face looked impregnable so they decided to try from the Tvilisa glacier on the south-west. Sunday 27 July brought mist and rain, and it was very cold, so they spent most of the day in bed. When they could see Chanchakhi's lower rocks they were 'white with new snow'. Raeburn said in his diary: 'Chanchakhi sends down to the south a huge rock ridge cut up with gigantic obelisks and pinnacles of black rock separated by steep snow and ice couloirs.' At the foot of this ridge a shepherd's track led over to Tvilisa valley.

On the 28th they left the kazarma at 10 am and crossed over to the Tvilisa glacier. They followed the left moraine to a rocky slope level with its first icefall. Here they bivouacked in some discomfort on loose blocks at 10,500 ft. Raeburn found an almost perfect eggshell of an ullargh (ptarmigan).

The following day a party of four, Raeburn, Ling, Johns and Martinson, set off at 4 am. Young remained at base to concentrate on the photographic record he was building. A party of five had, in any case, been found too slow on serious ascents. According to Raeburn's diary, they 'found a way, guided

---

9   The German spelling used by Raeburn and others is 'Tschantschakhi'. For ease of reference the English phonetic spelling is used.

partly by mouse and marten tracks', through the very complicated three icefalls of the Tvilisa glacier 'and attacked Chanchakhi by its south-west face'.

[Fig 5]
> *Here a steep ice couloir runs up between the first rocks on the face, and a very steep ice-slope leading to the col on the south ridge below the final peak of the mountain. We all wore crampons, but heavy cutting was necessary before the bergschrund was crossed at 9 am. First an ice-slope and then a steep rock chimney with [an] overhung exit led to a small rock platform. The rocks above were unclimbable, so return was made to the ice couloir.*

Raeburn's account of Chanchakhi is more detailed than Ling's, but Ling describes one incident which Raeburn omits. As they were nearing the top of the couloir, young Martinson 'nearly collapsed from the cold and the strain,' but a 'drop of cognac and promise of dry gloves heartened him up', and he was able to continue. Raeburn probably omits this incident out of sympathy with Martinson—he never highlights any weakness in his companions or makes any kind of criticism.[10] Ling, of course, includes the incident as it redounds to Martinson's credit. Ling also mentions that at one point Raeburn dropped his axe and he caught it. Raeburn continues the account in his diary:

> *After ninety minutes hard cutting the angle became hopelessly steep. Escape was effected through a crack in the overhanging ice of the couloir's left edge on to the open slope beyond. On this becoming too steep for crampons to hold, the party cut back north to a rock rib running far up the south-west face of the peak.*

The rocks here, though almost vertical, were 'good'. However, they kept their crampons on because of the fresh snow and ice on the rock. Good progress was made up the rock ribs. However, 'Higher the rocks died out, and steep ice thinly covered with new snow made the climbing both difficult and slow.'

At last the south ridge was reached not far below the top, and the climbing

---

10 In stark contrast to many other mountaineers.

1913: The Caucasus Expedition—Chanchakhi

Fig 5

Johns, Ling and Martinson, who is managing to smile—perhaps with relief— enduring severe weather on the ascent of Chanchakhi. This could be after the escape from the steep ice of the couloir.
Photo: Harold Raeburn

Fig 6

Chanchakhi with modern routes marked. It is difficult to be precise, but Raeburn's party gained the right-hand ridge, possibly by the couloir between routes 10 and 6. As the earlier photo shows, there was much more snow when Raeburn visited. Photo: Campbell collection

became 'relatively safe and easy, except for a fierce and very cold wind'. The summit of Chanchakhi, gained at 3.45 pm, comprised 'a narrow rock ridge capped by two feet of new snow'. Raeburn says: 'Because of the difficulties only fifteen minutes could be allowed for cairn, records and food.' Ling is more expansive:

> [W]e built a cairn and left our cards and the date in a tin; we also put up a miniature Union Jack and Raeburn produced a Scottish Lion,[11] after which we started down the route of ascent at 4 pm.

They agree absolutely about the timing, but where Ling provides only an outline of the difficulties they faced on descent, Raeburn's diary tells a fuller story:

> *In the gathering darkness the ice-crack giving access to the couloir of ascent was missed. However, all the party were safely established in another crack, and, fastened on to 140 ft of rope the leader was lowered over into the couloir. It is astonishing how time flies in such circumstances, but it must have been fully two hours later before a sufficient staircase was constructed to the steps of the morning in the couloir. The leader then came up to take the post of sheet anchor in the depths of the crevasse, and the descent was resumed.*

In other words Raeburn, after hacking out a safe passage of steps for the party to follow, climbed back up them and gave the others a top-rope down, and then descended again with no protection: a heroic feat. One recalls Mallory's sneering remark on the Everest Expedition: 'Was he always such a very stupid man? One wonders how he can ever have got a party up a mountain ...'

They got down to the rock platform by 10 pm and spent the hours of darkness there. Ling stoically remarks, 'Though cold enough it was not too bad.' Tea-making was unsuccessful but they 'sang many songs'. Ling's boots and socks froze, as they had once before in the Alps, and had to be

---

11   Raeburn is a fully committed member of the British Empire, as his attitude in the War makes clear, but he has a special affection for his native country.

thawed out by the spirit lamp. At about 4am they started down and managed to descend a difficult chimney 'and so to the glacier'. They reached their bivouac at 8.30am, having been on the hill for over 28 hours. They had a good meal and a rest and then, while descending to base camp, met 'Mr Young, who, somewhat anxious at our prolonged absence, had engaged a porter-shepherd and come to seek us'.

[Fig 6]

Ling thought 'the mountain first class. Raeburn led splendidly and refused to be turned even when further progress seemed impossible'. He had praise also for Johns and Martinson: 'The latter pluckily overcame his attack of faintness.' Indeed, given his youthfulness and relative inexperience, suddenly to find himself in the company of tigers like Raeburn and Ling must have been difficult for him, to say the least.

Raeburn's map of the Adai Khokh area gives some idea of the territory explored by the 1913 Expedition and is a good example of Raeburn's geographical acuity. Photo: Campbell collection.

27. NUAMKUAM, USHBA   1913

Why not try it by an entirely novel route?
— Harold Raeburn

Much to the party's regret, Johns had to depart at this stage, reducing the expedition's numbers to four. Ling's left foot was swollen and painful from minor frostbite so, as the expedition shifted on 31 July, intent on Ushba, he rode in the cart ('arba') to Ghurshevi, the next village after the kazerne from which they had launched the ascent of Chanchakhi. From Ghurshevi the party headed for Zhibiani, and the next eight days were spent on the awkward traverse from Ossetia to Svanetia, during which 'three 3,000 ft passes had to be crossed and everything had to be carried by horse, since the tracks were unusable by carts. On one pass the horses had to be belayed on the descent' (Campbell, *smcj*, 2021). Raeburn was interested in a three-topped peak called Nuamkuam on the frontier ridge 'east of Shkara and west of Ailama'.

[Fig 1]

By 8 August they were in position to set off for a bivouac 'on the virgin Nuamquam' [sic]. From the top of the moraine there were 'some steepish rocks and a gully above this and the porters refused to go any further'. They paid them off and took their loads up a steep gully, then grass and scree slopes to a small plateau at 10,120 ft, where they found a place for the tents 'and with a little work levelled it and put them up'. The weather, Ling says, had been 'peculiar, dull sky but tops clear, and not too hot'. They had dinner and turned in at 6 pm, by which time the weather looked more hopeful. However, the night was wet and cold, and the wind nearly blew the tents down. At 3.10 am, in starlight, they roped up and put on crampons at the

Fig 1

Belaying a horse down steep ground on the journey to Svanetia. Photo: SMC Image Archive

Fig 2

Shkhara to the left; Nuamkuam to the right. The latter's snows merge indistinctly with the sky. Ling, Raeburn and Martinson seem intent on bringing their diaries up to date. This is a rare picture of Ling with pen or pencil poised above his diary.
Photo: JR Young

On the summit ridge of Nuamkuam:
from left, Ling, Martinson and Young.
Photo: Harold Raeburn

Fig 3

bivouac and went up the glacier with only 'occasional serac trouble' to the start of the rocks. Here they halted briefly 'for jam and bread rings till 06.10. The morning sun was striking Shkhara and looked very fine.'

[Fig 2]

Above the icefall they climbed 'fairly steep slopes of snow and ice through the seracs [at] 13,200 ft [by] 7.15'. They had to cut some steps to the bergschrund and then they climbed 'to a snow and ice ridge (51° measured) which led up to the main ridge at 13,980 ft at 9.45'. This ridge was corniced in places and they followed it to the 'highest rock summit, 14,000 ft at 11.10'. They paused for jam and rusks.[1] By now the weather was fine and they had a clear view of Dych-Tau and Koschtan-Tau.[2] Refreshed, they 'contoured along the corniced snow ridge, over a snow top to the highest snow summit at 12.20'. The views of the 'mighty mountains on the other side of the Dych Su glacier' were splendid.

[Fig 3]

From the easily-reached third top they started to descend the 'south ridge, which consisted of broken rocks and gendarmes'. They climbed over one of these, 'but were not getting on well so we returned to the top of the couloir where we made tea'. Whereas 'there was an extraordinary overhung cut off on the rocky ridge', the couloir, too, looked doubtful. Ling went down first to prospect and found the route feasible, so they kept well in to the right where there was some snow and they were sheltered from 'anything falling'. They soon had to leave this shelter and kick steps down the edge of a ridge of snow, after which they got on to 'disagreeable slippery rocks with gravel on them and had to move very carefully as Young was not used to this work'. They finally escaped from the varied difficulties of the couloir and 'scurried across the glacier' to their bivouac site where they made tea 'and turned in after a good hard day'.

What Campbell describes as the 'short traverse west to Betsho' was nonetheless not devoid of colour and incident. Finding their packs too heavy, they got a herdsman 'to catch a horse and carry the luggage on it'. At Ushkul a funeral was in progress where 'the mourners in the brightest coloured garments chanted a dirge'. Young, intent on his photographic record, fell behind and became temporarily lost to the expedition, causing

[Fig 4]

anxiety and doubtless irritation among the others. Ling's mildly frostbitten

---

1. A form of dehydrated toasted bread popular in central Europe at the time.
2. Just to add to the confusion, according to Robin Campbell (2023), 'Dych-Tau and Koschtan-Tau swapped names after Raeburn's visit!'

Fig 4

Ling approaching one of the three summits
of Nuamkuam and looking towards Ailama.
Photo: SMC Image Archive

Fig 5

The priest of Ushkul, who gifted Raeburn's party a bearskin. Photo: JR Young

foot caused him some trouble, but he was distracted by walking:

[D]own one of the most beautiful valleys I have ever seen ... trees clothed the slopes, occasionally opening into fields of yellow corn, and from time to time, a view of the mountains. Strawberries and raspberries grew in profusion by the way. (Ling's Diary, Book 11)

At one point they put up in a courthouse and parties were sent back to seek the missing photographer.[3] It turned out that he had somehow gone past them and was heading for Mestia. Journeying thither they encountered another funeral and were offered 'bread and vodki as we passed', the onlookers much amused by their rather drab and formal clothes. Continuing this rather Chaucerian journey they fell in with a priest, 'a very pleasant man' [Fig 5] who gave them honey and lent them a bearskin—useful because of the theft of their groundsheet—but then had a violent row with the horsemen 'who discovered that he was cheating them'. In the midst of all this *couleur locale*, Ling, 'the unfortunate historian', went on metronomically recording mundane details: 'up at 6.00, breakfast and away ...'.

They had the good fortune to come across a man called Muratbi, 'now somewhat old-looking ... yet a tireless walker, whose "guide's book" went back to the early nineties, and included the names of Caucasian pioneers, personal friends of our own',[4] and who, as Ling notes, had been a porter for SMC members Godfrey Solly and Willi Rickmers on their expedition in 1903. They added Muratbi to the party. One gets the impression that Young had had enough serious climbing; at all events he elected to stay with the tents at Betsho—perhaps not a bad idea in view of the earlier burglary—and focus on photography. Raeburn's diary says:

On the 14th we set off, accompanied by Muratbi and two horses. The walk along the main valley, and up the steep, tree-clad banks of

3 Young, realising he was lost, ingeniously sketched the rest of the party and showed it to the natives. They applauded his art, and he thought they were saying, 'Yes, yes, go that way.' And thus, he ended in advance of the others.
4 This quotation is taken from Raeburn's own diary, an extract from which was published by the long-serving Editor, Jim HB Bell (*SMCJ* 25, 1955). In what follows it is good, though unusual, to be able to draw on both Ling's and Raeburn's diary accounts. The difference in style is very noticeable.

the Gulba glacier stream to the highest hamlet, Gul, ... was pleasant but uneventful ... Presently we arrived at a small grassy flat where slight walls of stone and the marks of many fires made it unnecessary for Muratbi to inform us that it was the usual camping place whence two successful assaults, and the other twelve or fifteen unsuccessful ones, on Ushba had been delivered.[5]

They reached a suitable bivouac site by mid-afternoon on 15 August, within striking distance of 'the stupendous twin-towered Ushba' (4,710m), perhaps the most famous and difficult mountain in the Caucasus.[6]
Raeburn again:

[Fig 6] *Ushba, from the south-east, takes the shape of a great cathedral with two towers of equal height at either end. A couloir, surely one of the greatest in the world, of very steep snow with a hanging glacier extends between the huge buttresses of the towers, which are connected some 500 to 800 feet below their tops by a narrow corniced arête, mostly ice. A more unpromising and frightfully dangerous access to a peak ... I have never seen. At this hour the whole space between the peaks was almost ceaselessly alive with falling stones and ice avalanches. Moreover, from the ominous glitter of the steep slopes, it was obvious that the greater part was composed of bare ice.*

To attempt this, he concludes, would have been to court almost certain destruction. Raeburn details the 1888 ascent of the couloir by Cockin and Almer, when conditions were quite different: 'heavy snowfall succeeded by frost', which made the climb up the central couloir 'long and hard, but not difficult or dangerous'. But now 'the face of the mountain was almost black'. Raeburn also mentions the ascent led by A Schulze of the South Peak in 1903. He says: 'I had studied this from a description ... Its lower part, at any rate, would present no serious difficulty, though long, steep and probably quite dangerous climbing.' However, significantly, Raeburn says:

5   It is worth noting the amount of research into the history of climbing on the mountain that Raeburn undertook, typical of his methodical approach.
6   Celebrated in RLG Irving's *Ten Great Mountains* (1940), which devotes a chapter to Ushba.

Fig 6

The magnificent twin-towered Ushba, one of the finest and, by almost all routes, one of the most difficult mountains in the Caucasus. Photo: Campbell collection

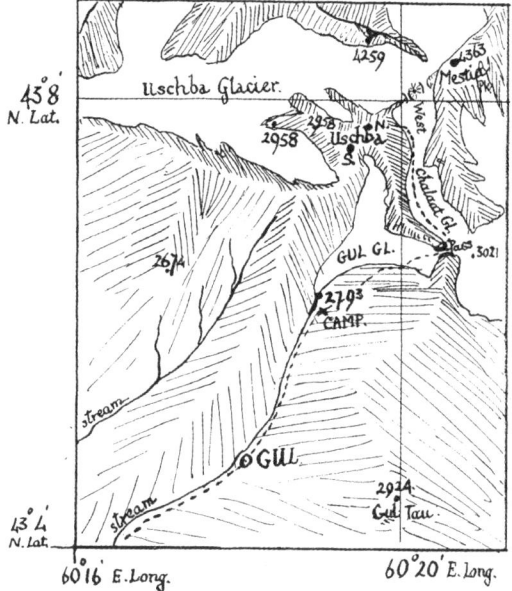

Fig 7

Raeburn's sketch map of the approach to the North Peak of Ushba. First printed in *SMCJ*. Photo: Robin Campbell

[O]ur expedition was not for the purpose of following in other parties' footsteps. Why not try it [the North Peak] by an entirely novel route, from a glacier hitherto unvisited and by a face looked on as hopeless—by the north-east face, from the Chalaat Glacier? This face is enormously large and is steeper than that of any great mountain hitherto climbed, the Meije not excepted; a much more formidable climb than the Matterhorn by the Zmutt.

This would be no death or glory attempt, however, for the canny Raeburn had also noted that the north-east face should be freer, because of its aspect, from stonefall and avalanches, and that 'the early morning sun would be largely kept off it by the high peak of ... Mestia, on the other side of the great Chalaat Glacier'. As always in Raeburn's mountaineering decisions, safety was crucial.

Ling, Raeburn and Martinson set out for an attempt on the North Peak of Ushba on 15 August at 4.15 am. They went up scree and easy snow slopes, reaching the col south of Gulba at 10,550 ft at 5.33 am, Ling paying his usual attention to time. Raeburn says the weather was perfect, but: [Fig 7]

> We were rather disappointed to find that there was a big drop (1,300 ft) to the Chalaat Glacier. Down steep but easy ribs of rather crumbling rock and a good snow couloir we gained the glacier at 06.30. This was the West Chalaat branch, which had never been trodden by human foot before. Its upper part pours down in huge, steep icefalls below the vast wall of Ushba's north-east face and the shapely peak of Mestia.

Raeburn's aim was to:

> [R]each a good sleeping place as high up as possible on Ushba's NE face, and start early on the final climb. We had first to find our way through a very broken icefall which stretched right across the glacier. At first the glacier was flat and almost free from crevasses. There had evidently been a tremendous rockfall recently from the cliffs of Gulba, just above us on our left. Great blocks weighing many tons had been shot nearly half-way across the glacier, here nearly a mile wide. We kept well out till past this place. It cost us four hours of hard ice-work before we won through the icefall.

Crampons proved their worth. Crossing a difficult bergschrund and ascending another ice slope, they finally reached 'the rocks of the north-east face at 11.55'.

Raeburn says that the rest of the day's climbing was:

> [V]aried and interesting; never excessively difficult, it was continuous, and, I judge, like that met on the Brenva face of the Aiguille Blanche de Peuterey, but with everything on a bigger scale and at a steeper angle. Owing to the aspect, the icy parts were still covered with snow, rather inclined to avalanche, and requiring great care. The leader often took out 60 ft of rope before the others moved.[7]

They spent a long time over lunch (with jam and rusks), 'enjoying the pleasant sun, which we should soon lose'.

They climbed on at 1pm. Ling says, 'The loads were horribly heavy and the sun very hot.' However, they had now gained steep but sound rock and they made good progress amid occasional snow flurries. At 5pm they came to an ideal spot for a bivouac at just 13,000 ft and almost on a level with the col to their north between Ushba and Little Ushba.[8]

Raeburn:

> A mass of rocks jutted out from the face; in these a cleft floored with ice and stones formed the only space level enough for three to lie down upon that we had seen for hours. The rocks overhung it ... and the sleeping berth had an inward tilt that would prevent anyone from rolling off in his sleep—very necessary, as a stone flung out from the edge of the bed touched nothing for 200 feet, and did not come to rest for 2,000. But it was quite a difficult climb to get into this bedstead!

His account continues:

---

7 It is worth remembering that in the absence of spikes behind which to 'hitch' the rope, 60 ft exposed the leader to a catastrophic fall in the event of a slip or a breaking hold, and in this scenario it is likely the others would also have been pulled off.

8 A small peak dividing the col between Mestia to the north-west and Ushba to the south-east.

The great feature of the upper regions of Ushba is a belt of real ... precipices which almost girdle both peaks and give them their tower-like form. Their height at this point was roughly 1,000 ft, and for a long distance they seemed quite impossible, soaring almost straight up in dark red slabs of granite or protogine, smooth, flawless, and more forbidding even than those upon the north face of the Petit Dru. Below the cliffs a sloping band slanted upwards to the north, and gradually the cliff broke down to meet it in that direction. Not far from the head of the West Chalaat Glacier a steep snow-covered edge came down to meet the band. We hoped to be able to work along till we gained this rib of snow-covered rock and ice which obviously led up to the possible slopes of the upper peak. But there was a major problem. The crux lay in a great couloir floored with ice which lay between us and the snow-edge beyond.

They got water from a minor couloir close at hand. A few minutes later 'there was a tremendous avalanche of ice and rocks' down the great couloir, the wind 'from which powdered us with snow' and almost blew away their hats. Typically imperturbable, Ling only says, 'We made soup and turned in at seven.' Raeburn elaborates:

This bivouac stands out as the most romantic and impressive I have ever known. It was not for its wide views; the outlook was rather restricted. The nearest I recollect was on the Zmutt arête of the Matterhorn ... rock, ice and snow alone composing the landscape. Nothing else is visible. Here the scale was greater, the horizon narrower ... the planets shone and the stars sparkled in a cloudless moonlit sky. Ling and I dozed or turned uneasily on our stony beds, but young Rembert, who had carried a heavy load, and been as sure-footed and steady as a veteran, slumbered peacefully and soundly. O happy privilege of tired and healthy youth!

On 16 August they had a good breakfast but had to wait for daylight before climbing because, as Raeburn says, it 'was too difficult, only one man being able to move at a time'. They had their crampons on and were away by 4.45 am. 'We crossed the avalanche-couloir nearby, and were disgusted to find that even at this height and on this aspect the snow was in bad condition: even at 13,500 ft it was already quite warm.'

They climbed rocks 'which were not easy'; they 'went up an arête and followed a crack and vertical face, which were hard climbing'. At 14,000 ft they:

[A]rrived at a point where it became necessary to consider very carefully the choice before us. We had come up a long slanting gully partly filled with snow and ice, which led northward up the base of the great precipice girdling the summit, now greatly reduced in height; we could see the edge of the cliffs and the ice-cap about 300 ft overhead.

Unfortunately the crack which they had been following 'diminished and died out in an expanse of granite slabs. The immediate surroundings resembled the cliffs and slabs above the Cioch on Sgumain[9] in snow and ice condition ... For heavily laden men without Kletterschuhe ... the slabs were impossible.' But, Raeburn continues, 'We were ... now level with the lower part of the ice-arête leading up to the summit ice-cap: this gained our difficulties would be over.'

Alas, between Raeburn's party and this 'Promised Land':

[S]tretched ... a canyon ... pitched at a very steep angle ... and floored with polished rock and glistening ice. This was, in fact, the bowling alley of the Jötuns[10] of Ushba. The game had just begun ... Missiles of rock and ice hurtled and crashed against the sides and against each other: masses of snow slid hissing down the groove, or overflowed high up on the surrounding slabs. The Marinelli Couloir on ... Monte Rosa is a tame and feeble place by comparison.

As Raeburn grimly remarks: 'It is no use playing with Jötuns if the game is skittles, and you are the skittles.'

They considered another place where they might be able to cross the couloir in the late afternoon when the avalanches might cease, but that would have involved a bivouac on the summit. Raeburn, as always considering

9   In the Cuillin on Skye.
10 Roughly, a tribe of Norse Gods representing chaos and natural disasters.

the party as a whole, remembered the problem of food. They had enough for one day. He says:

> Ling and I could go on little or nothing for a day or two. We had, however, to consider young Martinson. Big, strong, active and heavy, though looking 24 he was only 18 ... and required more food than we did. He could hardly be expected to climb at over 15,000 ft on air, fine though it was.

A gallant attempt on a singular peak by a new and difficult route ended with 'Defeat by the Demon Bowlers of Ushba,' and they started the long, difficult and dangerous descent at 10 am.[11]

One of the problems, especially on the lower slabs, was avoiding the line of least resistance, which on one occasion led to a 200 ft drop. Raeburn says: 'every faculty was strained to pick up the landmarks noted on the ascent, to watch every footstep of the men in front, and to look after the rope ... Where the route was doubtful the cairns I had erected the previous morning helped us'.

Ling, perhaps suffering diarist's fatigue, merely says: 'We hit off our previous route pretty closely ... and eventually got off the rocks on to the upper glacier at 7.45.' Crossing a snow bridge over a large crevasse they had to 'hitch carefully most of the way' down the glacier. Another crevasse was 'dodged by the rocks at the side'. They were helped by the light of the moon and had more rusks and jam on the glacier.

While contemplating the 1,200 ft of re-ascent to the col crossed on the approach they had to shelter behind a boulder as another avalanche thundered down a nearby couloir, 'an enormous fall of rock, fire and clouds of smoke'. Not surprisingly they chose a safer couloir to re-ascend. 'The 1,200 ft up to the col was very laborious', but they got back to their tent, where Muratbi was waiting, at 3 am.

JHB Bell, who climbed in the Caucasus in the 1930s, comments: 'It was not too easy to decipher parts of Raeburn's diaries, written partly in ink and partly in pencil ... it is certainly a dramatic story, even if they did not succeed

---

11 Faced with a retreat like this, modern climbers would undoubtedly resort, where possible, to 50 or 60 m abseils. Raeburn, at best, had about 100 ft (approx. 30 m) of rope and there is no mention of abseiling. It looks as if they climbed down the whole route.

Fig 8

This picture of the South Peak shows the 'Cravat' or 'lower snowfield' and gives some idea of Raeburn and Ling's route on their attempt. It is tempting to think they ascended by the obvious couloir but that is probably the one ruled out as being too dangerous. Their couloir of ascent is likely hidden. Photo: JR Young

in climbing Ushba' (SMCJ, 1955). Robin Campbell says: 'While it might be concluded that conditions on Ushba were just too difficult to have allowed any ascent in 1913 except by the North Ridge (which requires an approach from Russia), the attempt on Ushba's North-East Face was nevertheless an admirable and futuristic failure, and almost succeeded' (op. cit. p.361).

Possibly still overdosed on adrenalin even after 23 hours on the mountain, they were up again at 7.30 am drinking tea and eating sardines and bread and jam. It was decided to send Muratbi down to basecamp for provisions. 'Martinson, who was very tired, decided to go down with him, with many apologies for deserting us.' (Raeburn's wisdom in not prolonging the attempt on the North Peak was even more amply justified by Martinson's decision.) The old hands basked in the sun and dried their clothes till 5.45 pm, when the faithful Muratbi returned with 'ample provisions'.

The following day, 18 August, Raeburn and Ling set off at 5 am with heavy loads to attempt the South Peak of Ushba, previously only ascended by Schulze. They put on crampons to go up the Gul Glacier and climbed a 'big couloir on excellent snow', roping up near the top at 7.30 am. Even this couloir was not entirely safe for 'a big stone came down clear of us'. The last section was at a high angle and the snow hard. Without front points on their crampons and with straight-picked axes this would have meant a long, tiring spell of step-cutting, so they took to the rocks at the side. These were loose and required care. They went up 'a steep and stiff chimney', above which lay a narrow couloir full of soft snow lying on ice—'very treacherous'. Again 'the rocks at the side were very loose and the climbing difficult'. The top of this narrow couloir was overhanging, but they managed to climb the wall at the side and reached the col, 12,820 ft,[12] at 11.35 am. [Fig 8]

Elbrus was visible, and Ling was struck by the atmosphere surrounding it: 'A peculiar haze, almost primrose, distinguished it from the black and white of the other peaks.' They paused for the inevitable jam and rusks till 12.30 pm. It is not easy to follow their route from the description given, but Ling says:

---

12 The col and couloir Ling mentions are not, of course, the main col between the North and South peaks, nor the larger couloir already ruled out as too dangerous: it is a couloir rising from the north end of the Gul Glacier. Robin Campbell (2023) says: 'My reading of the attempt on Ushba South is that the col referred to is simply the Mazeri Notch.' He may well be right.

From the col we climbed down some rocks and scree to avoid ice and crossed to some very slabby rocks over which gravel was lying, and which were very unpleasant. This lower snowfield was now ice, and stones rattled down it as well as on the ridge on the other side.

This snowfield, now turned to ice, seems to have been Schulze's *Untere Schneefeld* or lower snowfield (now known as the Cravat). Above them was a ledge which they thought might lead round to the upper snowfield taken by Schulze on the first ascent. 'Raeburn went round a very sensational corner and then unroped to go further, but the ledge soon petered out into the sheer face, so there was nothing for it but to return.' They had reached 13,500 ft.

Getting back almost to the col they made tea 'and had some chicken on the screes'. By their standards they had a long rest—an hour and a quarter. Then they scrambled back to the col 'and Raeburn made a strenuous effort to get on to the (East) ridge, but it was impossibly overhanging'. It seems that they had reached what is now known as 'the Mazeri Notch'. A later explorer, Robin Hodgkin, 'found a way up from the Notch in 1937' (Campbell, op. cit. p.358).

Near the col they found a tin with Schulze's card recording his ascent on 27 July 1903.[13] They spent the night in a reasonably sheltered bivouac nearby, from where 'The moonlight on Elbrus ... was something to remember.'

They were descending by 4.45 am. 'The couloir was very difficult, icy and lower down stones fell ...'. The snow at the top of the lower, large couloir[14] was hard. They got back to the tent at 9 am. After relaxing for a while in the sun, they packed up and, leaving the baggage for Muratbi to bring down, headed for Betsho, reaching the tents just after 3 pm where they 'found the others at tea in which we were ready to join'.

[Fig 9]

Robin Campbell comments:

As for the second attempt, it seems remarkable that they should have attempted this exceptionally serious route with no more than a short day's rest. With more time for recuperation, perhaps Raeburn and Ling

13 Why was this tin left here and not on the summit? Or did Schulze leave more than one tin? Another mystery.
14 If Campbell is right this seems to make sense: a narrow couloir leading down from the Notch and a broader one below it.

Fig 9

Muratbi and Melitan at Betsho base camp. The priest's bearskin is also visible. Photo: JR Young

might have found Hodgkin's line above the Mazeri Notch: it certainly lay within their capabilities. (op. cit. p.361)

Raeburn condenses several days of exacting travel in his brief note in the SMCJ (1914): 'Reluctantly leaving Betsho and Ushba, the Dongusorun Pass was ridden up, and the glacier crossed with—*not on*—horses to Europe and the Bakshan Valley.' Even though the horses had been specially shod for glacier travel, understandably they still found it difficult and had to be belayed in several places. The day after their arrival, Raeburn, Ling and Martinson set off for Elbrus. 'Owing to the porters striking they had to carry all their baggage and wood themselves ...'

By 23 August, Raeburn and his friends were established for the night at 10,700 ft on Elbrus, the massive double-summited extinct volcano, then lying in southern Russia not far from the border with Georgia. They lit a fire, made supper, 'lay down till midnight and started at 12.10 am'. Their route initially lay 'amongst huge blocks of lava', but at 1.10 am they 'set foot on the vast snowfield ... The moon was bright and the snow hard, also the wind was very cold, so we made good progress unroped'. They sheltered by some rocks at 14,000 ft for bread and jam. (Despite the depredations of the brigands at Tsaya, they seem to have had an inexhaustible supply of jam.) Dawn came and 'The colouring in the sky was exquisite.'

The quality of the snow and thin air slowed their progress, but they laboured on till they came to some rocks below the ridge where they stopped for food until 10 am. Ling noticed that their aneroid had stopped registering at 15,000 ft. The rope was briefly necessary as they coped with some rocks, but then they 'plodded on very laboriously, stopping often for breath, up steep snow slopes and on to the ridge and finally to the highest snow summit', 18,510 ft,[15] at 12.25 pm. Ling says, 'The hollow of the former crater showed clearly and a crescent ran round to the rock summit probably 200 ft lower, which is generally visited and accounted the top.' The party had ascended some 8,000 ft to the east summit of the mountain at 5,621 m, which at that

---

15   Elbrus is actually the highest summit in Europe, if this part of the Caucasus on the Russo-Georgian border is counted as being in Europe; arguably it is geographically, the doubt is of a political nature. Elbrus is some 3,000 ft higher than Mont Blanc, the increased altitude accounting for their laboured breathing. Raeburn's party climbed the East Peak; the West is actually a few metres higher. Seven years later Raeburn admitted in his book that the intense cold almost caused them to fail.

time was believed to be the highest. Their descent was technically straightforward but exceedingly long. They coped with soft snow on the glacier and loose blocks of lava on the ridge, getting back to their bivouac spot at 3.40 am where they rested for just over an hour. 'Then along the ridge and down a scree gully to the meadows of the Baksan, and in gathering darkness through the wood back to the [Cossack] post at 7.30.' They had ascended over 8,000 ft and descended over 12,000 ft in one day. Ling remarks, as only he could, 'We were quite ready for food and a welcome sleep.'

The ascent of Elbrus brought the 1913 expedition to a close. Raeburn's experiences in the Caucasus had whetted his appetite, and he was determined to return. What this small party achieved in 1913 obviously impressed the mountaineering world well beyond Scotland. At the SMC Dinner held on 5 December 1913, Geoffrey Winthrop Young, representing the Alpine Club, delivered what Campbell calls 'the following impressive doggerel':

> *To think that they can eat, and drink, and talk as us*
> *These Alexanders of remote Caucasus!*
> *To think that rocks Circassian have rung*
> *Beneath the boot nails of a worthier Young!*
> *To think that other virgin peaks still ring*
> *With echoes from the hallowed heels of Ling!*
> *To think, as morn to eve, and night to day turns,*
> *The torch they kindled with a brighter Ra(y)e burns*
> *On seven vanquished peaks*
> *In scarce as many weeks!*
> *To think that they still climb, and rest, and talk as us—*
> *These fellows who have conquered half the Caucasus.*[16]

Although mock-heroic, these lines were no mean praise from one of the most respected Alpine mountaineers of his day.

---

16 Lines quoted by Campbell (SMCJ, 2014), some hundred years after they were declaimed at the annual Dinner.

Fig 10

One of the pack horses caught in the act of jumping a narrow crevasse on the Dongusoran glacier. Raeburn steadying the white horse to the right. Photo: JR Young

Fig 11

Panorama of the Caucasus from near the East Summit of Elbrus. Ushba prominent to the left. The expedition travelled from the far side of Ushba; the North or Russian side is seen here. Photo: Dave Broadhead

28. THE CAUCASUS EXPEDITION: 1914
KARAGOM, LABODA

Raeburn was climbing and exploring in the Caucasus again in 1914 (*SMCJ*, 1915). For reasons unknown, his old friend and staunch companion, Willie Ling, was not in the party, but Harold was accompanied by H Scott Tucker of the Alpine Club and RC Richards, allegedly of the Climbers' Club[1] and the Swiss Alpine Club. They were joined at Vladikavkaz by Rembert Martinson, who had been such a vital party member in 1913. They also engaged a Russian soldier, Alexander Mirandoff (Raeburn says Miranoff), as cook, and he proved 'a great improvement on the Imeritian native [Melitan] of last year'. Mirandoff, by contrast, was 'quite a dandy', and Raeburn had to persuade him to abandon many spare clothes and luxuries he had brought with him. His shaving mirror, however, proved useful because none of the others had one.

The Caucasus had been hit by violent rainstorms which had affected most of Europe that year. Floods made travel difficult, 'railways, roads and bridges being washed away in places'. They were told at Vladikavkaz that it would be impossible to approach the mountains for several weeks, but Raeburn was wise to this sort of pessimism: 'My reply ... was to order the lineikas for ... next morning, and we got through—with difficulty, naturally—in two days.' They camped as before in the idyllic pinewoods below the Tsaya glacier. At first the weather was 'rather broken', and there was soft, deep snow on the hill even in the early mornings.

---

1   'Raeburn describes Richards as being a member of the Climbers' Club but may have been mistaken. Their club archivist can find no record of him.' (Mitchell, SMCJ, 2000). Mitchell concedes that Richards may have been a member of the Swiss Alpine Club. According to Robin Campbell, 'Richards was a stalwart member of ABMSAC [Association of British Members of the Swiss Alpine Club], affectionately known as the Bumsacks'. Thus Mitchell was mainly correct.

Raeburn wanted to 'investigate the problems of a Tsaya–Karagom pass, first suggested by Mr Freshfield and still unsolved'. To do this they first decided to attempt the Adai–Songuta col and try to make the first ascent of Songuta. On 14 July, at the last grassy area at 9,000 ft, they pitched camp below the terminal ice cliffs of the hanging glacier of Uilpata.[2]

They left this camp at 3.05 am the next day and followed the right moraine under the south-east spur of Adai (Uilpata) to the glacier. Raeburn says that this glacier is 'formed in a very peculiar manner'. Inaccurate observation from a distance had led to 'very erroneous delineation on the 1-verst map'. On the north-east face of Adai:

> [C]an be seen from far off a great hanging mass of ice. Below this an almost three parts circular névé basin sweeps round below Adai, the Adai-Songuta col and the south ridges of Songuta ... the major part of the ice pours over a great cliff to another ... basin below the south-east spur of Adai and Songuta's south ridge, [but] a portion escapes through a deep gap cloven between Adai['s] main peak and its south-east spur to join the north Tsaya glacier. (Geographical Journal, 1915)

After passing through an easy icefall they gained the lower basin. From there they 'ascended the rocks of Songuta's south spur and, traversing left when these became overhanging, gained an ice couloir between these and the central ice cliffs. At the top of this we then entered the upper snow reservoir'. The direct col was guarded by an enormous cornice and appeared impossible, but they 'gained the watershed ridge by attacking a steep rock rib of Songuta'. In the event bad conditions on the final ridge led them to abandon the ascent, but Raeburn, by descending 200 ft, found that the descent on the north side of the pass was straightforward, whereas 'the difficulties on the south side will always be considerable'.

The expedition's next objective was 'Double Peak' (or Bubis). In reality this mountain consisted of not two but three 'sharp rock peaks separated by a huge vertical-looking couloir' lying between the shoulder of Adai and the broad snow peak at the western end of the north Tsaya glacier. Carrying

---

2 Where the terms 'Adai' or 'Adai Khokh' are used to refer to one mountain, the name 'Uilpata' is also used.

supplies up to the necessary camp, the porters wore 'crampons' of knotted rope fitted to their gloved feet 'for use on the steep snow slope by which the first icefall was passed'. Raeburn also notes that they carried their rifles and went after tur whenever relieved of their loads. Once the camp was established, Raeburn spent several hours in the afternoon 'hunting for a passage through the rocky walls barring access to the north Tsaya glacier' on the east side. The climbing was difficult, and in the end they decided to seek out the 'back-door route' around the glacier, indicated in Dr Ronchetti's photographs.

On Monday, 20 July they left high camp at 1.05 am:

Passing up the main Tsaya glacier, we climbed a steep snow-and-scree-filled gully which cuts off 'Woolley's peak' from the ridge behind. This gives easy access to the North Tsaya glacier above its formidable icefall. We then traversed this glacier in its whole length to the foot of the 'Double Peak' [Bubis]. The ascent was made to the dividing col of the chief peaks, mainly by the great couloir.

This precipitous couloir was upwards of 3,000 ft high, but because of the recent bad weather the ice was covered with 'good adhesive snow'. Later in the season, this route (like the great couloir on Ushba) could well be impossible. In fact, because of rotten rock and sheer steepness, they failed on the ridge of the south peak and had to retrace their steps to the couloir. Here they had 'an incident' when the two middle climbers on the rope slipped as the snow gave way. The men at the back were watching, however, and were able to check the slip.

From the col, which they reached at noon, 'a short climb up a corniced ridge led to the summit of the south peak' of Bubis; this, like that of Chanchakhi, consisted of a sharp point covered with 2 ft of fresh snow. Raeburn says that it looked just the same height as 'its twin summit to the north'. It was higher than all the other Tsaya peaks except Adai (Uilpata). Significantly for the expedition, 'Its only possible rival [was] the beautiful mountain Karagom, on the other side of the Karagom névé.' They returned the way they had come, and because of crusty snow on the glacier did not get back to their high camp till after dark.

A tremendous cloudburst which uprooted trees in the forest and destroyed the new bridge forced them to follow the path high above the gorge on the left bank of the swollen river on their way back down to the Tsaya villages. Descending by this path to St Nikolai on 23 July, Raeburn noticed that the villages were poor; some of the children went virtually naked. This, however, did not dampen their commercial instincts, for they were 'very persistent merchants' of the strawberries which they gathered from the forest. Further down, Sadon village looked 'as though recently bombarded'. Many houses were destroyed; in some with missing fronts, 'domestic work was calmly being proceeded with in public'. Down in St Nikolai they found a good shop selling 'excellent Russian bread'. They camped for the night and Raeburn and his friends were surprised and pleased when the horsemen produced a good fire from the sodden bushes.

Next day the expedition headed for Kamunta over the 8,000 ft Sadon pass. They passed the village of Sgid and Raeburn was amused by a man who kept a fox cub as a pet. To the north rose the Kion Khokh, a range of limestone mountains, but to the south the Tsaya pinnacles were enveloped in cloud. A long ridge of soft, dark shale led down to 'the stronghold village of Kamunta in the Urukh basin'. All wood and water had to be carried up to this village from below. The houses were built of enormous blocks of stone, 'cyclopean walls without mortar'. In the cemetery above the village the corpses of former inhabitants could be seen 'lying in rows through large holes in the stone mausoleum'. A true explorer, Raeburn was interested in all he saw. In the guesthouse where they stayed he was amazed and delighted to find 'a Russian treatise on aviation', a subject in which he was much interested; not long after, he applied to join the Royal Flying Corps in the Great War—unsuccessfully, as it transpired.

On 25 July they walked from Kamunta to Dsinago. The latter being a semi-Mohammedan village, several inhabitants were engaged in evening prayer. They were invited by a Dr Iokelson, in charge of the veterinary post, to camp in its enclosure, an offer they gladly accepted later, but now they hired four donkeys to carry the baggage to a camp as high up the Karagom glacier as possible. The donkeys were 'sturdy little beasts' but 'they seemed to fancy themselves as singers and cocks'—evening and dawn were rendered 'an aural inferno with their rasping brays'.[3]

---

3   An incident oddly reminiscent of one in Miguel de Cervantes' *Don Quixote* and described by Raeburn in a similar way.

Fig 1

Karagom icefall with the peaks of Karagom East and West to its left. The figures give some idea of the scale. Photo: Vittorio Sella

The Dsinago valley was wide and well cultivated. A few versts above it the track entered a pine forest and climbed steeply above the moraine-covered ice tongue of the Karagom glacier. They were intent on Karagom, and on 26 July Raeburn, exploring ahead as always, walked up the glacier for a couple of miles until the icefall became too difficult. He noted the remains of a hooded crow. The great Karagom icefall was 'a magnificent sight, pouring out of huge rock portals on either side in a tumbled mass of seracs'. Vittorio Sella's photo does it justice. The upper fall, Raeburn thought, was not less than 2,000 ft—the whole thing nearly 4,000 ft—'high rock peaks streaming with snow and hanging glaciers on all sides ... There are quite distinct traces of the path, which here descends the moraine for the crossing of the Fastag glen and the Gurdzivzek to Gebi.' [Fig 1]

On 27 July the expedition moved up to a high camp to explore the northern peaks of Karagom. In about two hours, by moraine and glacier, they reached 'the Blue Lake', which occupied a space dammed up by the moraine with steep rocks on its east side. Beyond this the hills at the side fell back and a 'wide grassy space of alternate ridges and flats of ancient moraine' came into view. They climbed the grass slopes in the direction of the north Karagom glacier to 9,000 ft and pitched the tents on 'a small flat just below a chaos of giant boulders'. Raeburn prospected 1,000 ft higher that afternoon but couldn't see over the ridge called Saudor, 'which runs up to join the great wall of Karagom'. Raeburn says, 'Adai-Khokh [Uilpata] looks very well from here and easily shows its dominance.' Almost in the same breath he says, rather confusingly, 'This peak [i.e. the third rocky summit of that which they have just climbed] I have ventured to name Vologata, though its connection with that glacier is not very direct. It is really in the Skaticom basin.'

As it was only 11.20 am, they decided to go on and climb the highest point on this massif, the east summit of Karagom, so they went back to the 'snow hump at the junction of Saudor ridge'. There a descent of about 300-400 ft placed them on the col below east Karagom. The 2,100 ft to the summit:

[G]ave some interesting climbing, mostly on a corniced ice arête where considerable care, judgment and labour was necessary in dealing with the frequently unstable snow surface. The first rocky top reached proved

not to be the highest. That was not gained till 4.45pm. The west summit was fully a verst[4] distant and is distinctly lower.

They enjoyed splendid views of all the Adai peaks, 'and of the giants Dykhtau, Koshtantau and the other central peaks'. The return journey was begun at 5.15pm, 'and hastened by a most threatening appearance in the western heavens' where a huge storm was brewing. The descent was slowed by soft snow. In the end only the fringes of the storm reached them, but Raeburn says:

[T]he sunset seen from the Saudor ridge at 12,000 ft surpassed anything any one of us had ever seen in his life, of sublimity and awful grandeur. The vast black clouds hanging over the huge cones of Dychtau and Koshtantau, rent in every direction by the zigzags of lightning, seemed to take fire as the sun dipped, and the whole spectacle was that of a world in flames.

They did not regain their camp until nearly midnight. Raeburn merely says, 'It was a hard day of 24 hours, but a very repaying one.'

Over the next couple of days they descended to Dsinago, where the bread was satisfactory and they got eggs for one rouble a hundred. Raeburn thought highly of this place, and because it had a good communication network believed that it was bound to develop as a tourist centre rather like Zermatt or Chamonix.

In the 'Excursions' piece in the SMCJ, Raeburn gives the ascent of Laboda one sentence: 'Time now running out, a short trip was made to the Laboda group lying south of the Shtuli Pass, and a successful ascent made of its virgin highest peak, Laboda[5] (14,170ft).' Happily he is more forthcoming in his article in the *AJ* (1915). Passing by haymakers' chalets where they were 'invited to the inevitable sour—very—goat's milk', they made their way to a camp on the dusty moraine of the Tana Glacier, which, Raeburn noticed, appeared to be in retreat.

They left camp at 3.45am, 'the morning windy and misty. Rain threatened

---

4   A verst is a, now obsolete, Russian measure of length equivalent to about 1.1km.
5   It is worth mentioning that Clinton Dent, the Alpine pioneer, made an ascent of one of the lower summits of Laboda in the 1890s (Campbell).

Fig 2

The settlement of Stir Digor; Laboda is seen at the far end of the valley. Once again, Martinson (in white) seems to be talking with the locals. It was here that Raeburn's party first caught an inkling of the coming war. Photo: SMC Image Archive

Fig 3

Women waiting at the well in Gebi. This image is taken from the 1913 Expedition, but it gives a good idea of the style of village life. Photo: William Ling

Fig 4

Local people at Bezingi, including the heavily armed headman of the village, centre. This picture is from the 1913 Expedition but is a good illustration of the sort of local society with which the two expeditions were, on the whole, pleased to have dealings. Photo: SMC Image Archive

but none fell'. Ascending a long ice hollow which led north-west, they crossed over to the south 'and got on the Tana-Laboda glacier above the very steep wide icefall'. The fall was awkward, but they found perhaps the only good line through it and 'gained the easy upper glacier'. The snow here was arduous and 'The rocky and icy [east] buttress of Laboda looked steep—there is no deception: it is—but it was the shortest way …' A 'most enjoyable climb' ensued:

> The ice slopes were steep and the snow thin, but it was sufficiently holding to serve and little cutting was required. We did not move fast but kept going … and at 12.45 quitted the last rocks and reached the top—14,169 ft. This was a corniced narrow ridge of ice 60 to 80 ft above the last rocks. There were driving mists and only partial … views, mostly confined to the neighbouring peaks of Bokhobashi on the other side of the Shtulu Pass.

They got back to camp by 5.30 pm and endured a 'heavily loaded march, mostly in the dark' down to the entrance to the Tana Gorge.

Next morning they 'intercepted a wood-cutter whose donkey had most convenient panniers, to convey the baggage to Stir-Digor'. It had been in Stir Digor on their way up that they had had an amusing incident while hiring porters. 'A man came forward, the … typical Ossete mountaineer, holding out his hand and grinning genially. His polite greeting from a Caucasian was unusual. He said, "Hullo, Johnny, what the hell you here for?" It appeared he had worked on the railway in Vancouver for two years …' It was while they were saying goodbye to this man that they got the first hint of war in Europe. 'He said, "You know—my brother, he soldier—he go 'way—I do' know."'

Raeburn liked the Caucasus and although he regarded the 1914 Expedition as only half accomplished, in the *Geographical Journal* he claims that their knowledge, at least of the Tsaya group, was tolerably complete. Nobody on the 1913 or 1914 Expeditions suffered 'any form of illness whatever'. No bad fish here then, and none of the gastric troubles which routinely afflict travellers in the Himalayas. He says: 'The weather in 1913 was heavenly and far superior to all my Alpine or Norse experience, while in 1914, though we had violent storms of rain, these never lasted long. As a rule, a wet day means that the next and perhaps the next again will be perfect.'

The political weather then, as now, was not so stable. Having been told that no horses were available for their journey to Elchatova station, they surmised that they were being 'collected for some purpose'. However,

Raeburn insisted that contracts must be honoured, and they eventually acquired horses and reached the station on 4 August to find it in the hands of the military authorities. Martinson reported, 'It is war ...'

29. THE JOURNEY HOME   1914

A speedy and easy journey home[1] was now out of the question: it took them practically the rest of the month. Harold's journey back to the UK is fascinating not just for its complications but for the light it throws on his character. His diary account reveals a thoughtful, perceptive man who took an interest in all he saw going on round about him. It also reveals his quiet but firm patriotism and his kindness to strangers.

On 3 August the expedition members—Raeburn, Richards, Tucker, Martinson and Mirandoff the cook—left Dsinago through a narrow gorge in which Raeburn noticed buzzards, wagtails, chats and quails. At Diechau they had tea for which they were not charged, but had to pay a high price for the horse-drawn vehicle to take them to the ferry at Tercyk. They couldn't attract the ferryman's attention and had to camp for the night, pestered by flies, mosquitos and people; one tent was kicked down by a horse. Raeburn was understandably very tired and characteristically unable to sleep.

They got across the river at daybreak, and at the station they received confirmation of the outbreak of war. Military mobilisation meant that many thousands of troops were on the move, making transport for the expedition and any other civilians caught up in these events difficult. The delay here lasted eight hours as troop trains passed constantly on the way to Vlad and Tiflis. The expedition ate in the first-class restaurant, but the third class was kept closed when troop trains were in the station, presumably to stop the private soldiers drinking. Raeburn, however, says he never saw officers drunk on the journey.

---

1   I am indebted to John Mitchell for allowing me to use his article, 'Harold Raeburn's Journey Home' (SMCJ, 2000), which forms the basis for this chapter.

Tea was the usual refreshment, but Raeburn the brewer noticed the quality of the inexpensive lager and 'the excellent cheap Crimean and Kaukasian [sic] wines'. They eventually boarded a train and squeezed into a corridor jammed with luggage. At Nalchik they found accommodation with 'defective sanitary arrangements' at the Hotel Ravkaz, but they had a good dinner in the orchard and were entertained by piano music. The 'fruit was unripe, as usual'. At least Raeburn had a good night's sleep.

The following day they had to collect visas from a local official. Young Martinson attracted some suspicion, but his passports were in order and he was too young for military service, so all was well. They treated themselves to a shave and a haircut at a 'very swell place' and then had to wait, the next day, for seven hours to catch the train to Kot. At this juncture Martinson and Mirandoff lost patience and jumped on a troop train going south. (Thereafter, Raeburn appears to have lost touch with Martinson, a gifted linguist whose recruitment had been crucial to the success of both Caucasus Expeditions.)

Eventually Raeburn, Tucker and Richards boarded an open wooden-seated day train, which lumbered to Min Vode. Raeburn describes 'an awful scene', with women and children struggling to get into already full carriages while porters dragged baggage over their heads. That evening they ate in the Gogoschurche restaurant, whose proprietor did not remember Harold. (This detail reveals that Raeburn probably chatted to casual acquaintances on his travels and rather expected to be remembered.) The restaurant was crowded, but 'few escaped without paying'. The train finally left Min Vode after midnight.

During the night they were disturbed by bottles being thrown through their carriage windows from a passing troop train. Nobody was seriously hurt, but a little girl got glass fragments in her back. Arriving at Rostov they booked into the Hotel Moscow, where Harold noticed that the boot boy was cheeky to a shabby, elderly German in a frock coat who had been the hotel manager. Then they visited the British Consul, a 'fattish young man' called Edwards, of whom Raeburn had a low opinion, finding him of 'very little use indeed, and to know very little of anything and care less'. They were advised to go home by way of Petrograd and the Gulf of Bothnia, but Raeburn rejected this suggestion at once because there was no guarantee that they would get to either. They decided instead to go to Odessa via the Sea of Azov and Kerch, and remained in Rostov for a further day, during which they managed to arrange to send the expedition's luggage to Britain.

In order to get to Odessa they boarded the *Eisk*, 'a small dirty steamer without boats'. The River Don was slow and wide. Passing villages and towns, they saw men and boys swimming far out. At one point the boat had to change course to avoid a dog swimming across a section of the river about three-quarters of a mile wide. As John Mitchell notes, 'It is this kind of detail that brings Raeburn's diaries to life.' Large flocks of geese were grazing on the banks, and they also saw gulls, pelicans and cormorants.

The *Eisk* entered the Sea of Azov by a shallow channel marked by posts. They called at Taganrog, a good port with lots of vessels in the roadstead, including nine Austrian and two German, seized by the Russians. The party was quite comfortable; they had open bunks without bedclothes but American cloth-covered cushions (perhaps early versions of the duvet). The food was reasonable and the beer 'excellent'—high praise from Raeburn.

The ship called at Yeysk, where a good harbour was being dredged and enlarged. As in south Russia generally, much building was going on, a sign of prosperity. There were excellent shops and a few guest houses. Pigs were rootling about on the shore and in the shallows. Raeburn observed that the girls wore bright dresses, hobble skirts and high heels, but that the young men were not so 'dandified'. He saw many children but few people of mature years. The people at Polsk were said to be Tartars, and were generally slim and shapely.

That evening the *Eisk* rolled in heavy seas and had to weather a thunderstorm; she was a small steamer with a low freeboard, and was making only five or six knots. Despite his sailing background, or perhaps because of his nautical knowledge, Raeburn did not fancy a day onboard her on the North Sea.

On 11 August they sailed slowly into the Straits of Kerch opposite the Yeysk peninsula. At Kerch, on the Glorious Twelfth, the trio transferred to the *Chernypore*, a 1,500-ton Caucasus steamer which departed immediately for Odessa. The ship was crowded, as many officers were making for Sevastopol. Tucker was fortunate to get a berth beside a porthole in the six-berth cabin, though even with this open the atmosphere was stuffy. But with the sea blue and sparkling, great black-backed gulls, herring gulls and terns overhead, and porpoises playing around the bow of the ship, Raeburn enjoyed a 'most charming day'. The three-course dinner was also excellent and included two cups (or glasses) of tea, sugar, bread and butter. There were Crimean, Caucasian and Bessarabian wines: a half bottle of *Krasny Sagen* cost merely 35 Kopeks (9d or 4p). Until his sad years in institutions at the end of his life, Raeburn always seems to have enjoyed fine food and drink.

There were also several characters aboard; one Raeburn named 'the Ancient Greek' was bitterly against the Germans. Another 15-stone Greco-Indian was dubbed the 'light horseman' because he claimed to be a member of the Behar Light Horse Regiment. Raeburn wondered 'what the horse thought'.

On 13 August they reached Feodas, a picturesque pleasure resort with first-rate hotels and stone villas with tennis courts. Richards had a bath in the muddy inshore waters and they found 'the best tea cakes we have struck in Russia'. They didn't have long to enjoy these, however, as the ship sailed for Sevastopol via the south point of the Crimea, passing picturesque sea stacks and a castle built on high crags.

As they neared Sevastopol they heard gunfire from warships. Suddenly a torpedo boat fired several shots into the air. The Captain of the *Chernypore* threw the engines into reverse and the ship shuddered to a stop. During a megaphone conversation between the vessels it transpired that they had sailed into a minefield and only narrowly avoided being blown up. The ship was escorted into Sevastopol's side harbour and officials arrived, suspecting that there was a spy on board. Everyone's passport was examined, and though no one was arrested, only those disembarking at Sevastopol were allowed on shore. In the evening the ship was cleared to sail on to Odessa.

After a fine breezy sail with dolphins again playing round the bow, they landed in the busy shipping harbour of Odessa and booked into the Hotel d'Europe. Raeburn thought Odessa a fine town—bustling, with good shops, hotels and an excellent electric train service. The cafés provided delicious tea and cakes. Paperboys were selling war news in the streets. The little party went to visit the British Consul, a JF Roberts. He too attracted Raeburn's scorn: 'young, fat and devoid of energy'. Roberts's Greek clerk planned a route home for them through Constanza and Greece to Italy, but they were already committed to sailing to Constantinople on the cargo steamer *Efrat*, which was due to leave in the morning.

Richards went to book cabins but was told there were no first or second-class ones left, and that he needed passports. When he returned with passports he secured three second-class cabins easily. Tickets, including meals with wine or vodka, cost two pounds and sixpence.

Of the war, they received news that there was a great battle in Northern France, in which two million men were said to be engaged. German ships had been captured in the North Sea. Turkey, which had not yet declared war but was considering it, was said to have bought two of these, but had been ordered by the Allies not to fit them. Amid a large French patriotic demonstration, the *Efrat* sailed late in the afternoon.

At dinner Raeburn met a Scotsman who had been an engineer on an Austrian vessel seized at Taganrog and was accompanying 15 Arab sailors to Alexandria. All his possessions had been lost or stolen. After yet another 'excellent meal', Raeburn attended a *Café chantant* between decks: some French ladies sang sentimental songs before falling victim to sea sickness, even though, according to Harold, the sea was calm.

At sunrise on 17 August the ship entered the heavily-mined Bosphorous, whose nearby cliffs were fortified, to find a British ship[2] had been sunk nearby with some loss of life. They reached Constantinople at about 9am. Raeburn admired the minarets and St Sophia.

An Italian steamer was due to sail to Venice, and with help from the British Consul (who, this time, attracts no adverse comment from Raeburn), Tucker was able to get first-class tickets on the *Sardegna* and they boarded her that evening. Raeburn noted kites scavenging garbage from the water where two warships, the *Goeben* and the *Breslau*, were at anchor, having escaped from the Black Sea and the Mediterranean.

The following day the ship sailed for Piraeus and they enjoyed fine views of the Asian and European sides of the narrow passage as they entered the Sea of Marmara: bare green hills, barley fields, scattered trees and villages, and several vessels, including a German yacht. The *Sardegna* had to stop at the east end of the Dardanelles because the Turks said it was too dark to go through the minefields. At sunset there was gunfire on the European side of the channel.

In the morning bumboats came out selling fruit, bread and sardines to the deck passengers. The ship was guided through the straits by a Turkish boat and a Franco-British fleet of warships was waiting off the Dardanelles.

---

2 *The Craigforth*, 2,900 tons, registered in Leith.

They reached Piraeus at night, and when dawn broke in the full harbour Athens could be seen through the smoky atmosphere. Locals came on board selling papers, cigarettes and fruit; a money changer tried to cheat Richards until one of the ship's stewards threatened him.

The Corinth Canal was said to be blocked, so they sailed across the Bay of Salamis and round Cape Matapan, stopping briefly at Patras. It was a warm and beautiful night with a phosphorescent sea and shooting stars. A German claiming to be half Dutch tried to ingratiate himself, but Raeburn's attention was drawn to a 'tall, good looking, very short-sighted elderly man, German, or more likely Austrian. Some high official in Turkey ... or on a diplomatic mission'.

On 21 August there was a partial eclipse of the sun in the middle of the afternoon. They sailed close to a French battle squadron and by sunset were off the island of Corfu. A friendly Greek passenger told Raeburn that Corfu gave excellent shooting—woodcock, hares, pig and small deer. He said that the Kaiser had a holiday estate there, and Raeburn suggested he might need it for a permanent residence after the war!

A day later they arrived at Brindisi, a dirty, unattractive town. Tucker and Richards went ashore to buy papers and post letters and got their first reliable news of the war. Sailing on from here, the ship was rather top-heavy in the rough sea and there were not enough lifeboats. Raeburn observed an anxious elderly man having a row with the ship's officers; he was 'nearly having a fit!' But any danger, real or imaginary, passed and Venice was sighted at midday.

The *Sardegna* went in past the Lido and anchored opposite the Grand Canal and St Mark's Square. Raeburn thought the Campanile 'a bit like a factory chimney but St Mark's very fine', particularly the interior. But war had affected Venice severely and there were few tourists. Here he received a letter from 'E', saying she would not come. Probably Harold had managed to contact one of his sisters during the journey and had suggested that they meet in Venice.[3]

After a day's halt they went on to Milan by train where Tucker and Richards left to make their own way home. Raeburn, seeming in no hurry,

---

3   Assuming always that 'E' stood for Edith or Ethel; his sister Ethel, as noted earlier, was a fine water-colourist who sometimes painted Venetian scenes.

went to visit Dr Ronchetti, who had sent him photos and information about the Caucasus. Ronchetti had lost part of his foot through frostbite on 'Adai', but was nevertheless still able to climb.

Before leaving for Switzerland, Raeburn looked round Milan and was impressed by the cathedral. Lake Maggiore, he thought, seemed just as beautiful as Loch Lomond but larger. Two motorcyclists raced the train towards the trans-alpine tunnel, and at Visp he had to deal with a supercilious booking clerk while attempting a transfer ticket to Zermatt.

When he reached Zermatt, Raeburn found most of the hotels shut. There were many English people and a few Americans in town. A train had been arranged on 28 August to evacuate the English, and one would have thought that Harold would be one of its passengers, but he seemed to have other ideas. He met Newmarch, who had climbed in the Caucasus in 1893 (with Solly of the SMC and Cockin), 1894 and 1895.

The 27th August was very cold with torrential rain, apparently the worst Raeburn had experienced in the mountains. (It must have been really bad.) He spent the day writing and reading newspapers. Hearing some English ladies being lectured by a German priest about German war successes, news of which was posted in all the hotels, Raeburn says that he attempted to 'put a spoke in the oily priest's wheel'. An Irish/British colonel was adamant that the Germans would be in Paris within days and that the British Army would be cut off and annihilated. Raeburn argued vigorously against this view, but the colonel remained unconvinced.

The following day most of the English departed on the special train, leaving only a few stray Americans. The torrential rain had turned to snow during the night, transforming the town into a winter picture. Raeburn climbed to 2,000m and then walked down the Trift Gorge. Later he visited a wine shop owned by a Matterhorn guide who told him that 44 men had been called up from Zermatt and so the women were doing most of the harvest work.

Still in no hurry to get home, and possibly hoping that the weather would improve, Raeburn went down the Mattertal and walked up to the Täschalp with a young American called Stephen, who had climbed in the Lake District and whose father raced a yacht on the Clyde. The weather improved slightly and the snow was melting. Although the mists had lifted a little, they had no view of the Weisshorn.

Probably because he was convinced that the climbing season was over, Raeburn left Zermatt on 30 August in a packed train. After a long wait at Lausanne he then caught a slow train to Geneva. He had a friendly argument with an American who claimed that the German army was invincible and that France was already as good as beaten. When Raeburn pointed out the economic difficulties Germany faced, the American replied that France was a fine orange to squeeze. Raeburn replied that the orange was 'not yet picked'.

At Geneva, he easily got a ticket valid for the journey to London via Paris, Calais or Boulogne, despite being told by an English clergyman and his wife that it was not possible. The Germans were already holding the Calais/Boulogne railway line and were close to Paris, so Raeburn was not overly optimistic about getting home. However, he boarded the train and found himself sharing a carriage with a 'very stout man' who knew no French and was in charge of five schoolgirls: an English girl called Johnson, an unnamed Scottish girl of 19 and three 'Kentish maids' called Reader, aged between 10 and 16. Their schoolmistress, who had come to see them off, recruited Raeburn to look after the girls, possibly because he did speak French. Both George Mallory and Ronald Burn speak of Raeburn's fatherly qualities, and he always seemed keen to help members of the opposite sex.

They had a pleasant but slow journey along the river Rhône. There were soldiers all along the line and stations had been prepared as hospitals, but there were no difficulties as they crossed from Switzerland to France.

On 1 September they waited for a connecting train from Marseilles. On being told that the train was full, a 5F bribe procured a very comfortable carriage. Trains of wounded soldiers passed incessantly: closed trucks converted to hold double tiers of hammocks.

Paris had not yet been attacked, but there were many refugees in the city. Raeburn managed to get two rooms for the girls and one for himself and 'Mr Light'. After breakfast Harold went to the Gare St Lazare to see if it was possible to leave Paris. The Germans were reportedly near Pontoise but, if the line was clear, a train would leave for Dieppe the next morning. Outside the British Consulate Raeburn saw several exhausted-looking British soldiers. There was much activity at the Ministry of the Interior, and he thought that this was caused by the French Government leaving for Bordeaux but he was told it was preparation for the Battle of the Marne, which stopped the German advance on Paris.[4]

While walking near the Opera House one of the girls remarked that it would be a pity if the Germans were to bomb such a beautiful building. Her words were prophetic, for shortly after there was a loud explosion and, looking up, they saw a German Taube aeroplane drop another bomb. Soldiers rushed out of cafés and started shooting at the plane, but it flew off unscathed. Raeburn took the girls to see the damage. The second bomb had fallen in the Rue Joubert, a narrow business street. Although there was much fallen plaster and broken glass no one was hurt, and people seemed neither afraid nor angry. Raeburn thought the bombing an act of 'mean blackguardism' and the dropping of bombs on civilians as futile as the dropping of ridiculous propaganda leaflets. Paris was blacked-out in the evening, but they nevertheless had a pleasant walk along the Champs Élysées.

In the morning Raeburn's party took taxis to the station where they found two enormous trains already nearly full. There was no room for a group of seven, so they commandeered an empty guard's van. The journey was halting, particularly near Pontoise where the Germans were nearby, and they saw large numbers of soldiers retreating to the south-west. Troops were resting and bathing in streams at the track side. The girls tried to give them presents, but officers were reluctant to allow men to approach the train.

At Dieppe they embarked on a crowded steamer and had a 'splendid passage' on a calm sea. At sunset they passed part of the British fleet steaming through the Channel, and arriving at Folkestone, passengers, all of whom had filled in landing cards, were allowed ashore without inspection. Spies could easily have passed through; Raeburn was not even asked for his passport.

'Mr Light' and the girls were to stay overnight at the port, so Raeburn travelled on to London on his own. He had, with considerable ingenuity, got his party out of what could have been a rather nasty situation. Characteristically, Raeburn's diary makes no mention of their thanks, which were probably effusive.

He found that recruiting was widespread across London. In the next couple of days he met Tucker and Richards, who had got home from Milan

---

4   In fact, the French Government left for Bordeaux on 2 September, so Raeburn's first surmise was probably correct.

in three days. When Raeburn finally arrived in Edinburgh on 4 September it was cold, wet and miserable. His journey home from the second Caucasus Expedition demonstrated his remarkable self-possession and reliance, his geographical knowledge, his gentle humour, his interest in whatever surroundings he happened to be in, and his care for the welfare of his fellow travellers, some complete strangers. These qualities would be tested to the full in the remaining years of his life.

LAST CLIMBS IN THE ALPS AND SCOTLAND

30. SOLO TRAVERSE OF THE MEIJE 1919

[Fig 1] In the year after the end of the War and five years after his 1914 expedition to the Caucasus, Harold made his way back to the Dauphiné to try to complete a cherished project: a first ascent of the West Arête of the Meije. He says: 'The route is no freak "variation". Since I first saw it in 1904 I have always considered it the correct, natural, and given suitable conditions, the quickest way of gaining the summit of the Meije' (*AJ*, 1920). However, when Raeburn arrived he found that the arête had just been climbed for the first time by two young climbers from Grenoble, Claudius Main and Albert Plossu. The latter, who was only 16, led the climb throughout. Harold had been admiring this route for some 15 years and had made several attempts, usually foiled by bad weather, but his article betrays not a hint of disgruntlement. Even though the young climbers had forgotten to leave their names in the 'summit receptacles'—leading to scepticism in the minds of some of the La Grave guides—Harold, who had some knowledge of the route, gave 'the fullest credence to every word of M. Claudius Main's modestly written and perfectly clear narrative'.[1]

For Harold it was 'rather surprising' that the West Arête (or Brèche Arête, as it is sometimes called) had been neglected for so long. He did not think it would be 'found of any extraordinary difficulty'. To some extent Main's account bore this out, but he stressed the difficulty of the 100 metres of smooth steep slabs that form the 'thin steep edge of the Petit Doigt de l'Épaule', which well-known guides had called the 'Barrière infranchissable'.[2]

1 Main's account was published in the local paper, *Le Dauphiné*.
2 'Impassable barrier.'

Fig 1

La Meije: the West Arête is on the left. Raeburn traversed from the opposite direction, hoping to descend that way.
Photo: Noel Williams

Main certainly found these the hardest part of the climb and 'admired the way in which his young friend, Plossu, overcame them'.

Raeburn says: 'I have myself had bad luck with the arête, and my acquaintance with it is, to the extent of the "100 metres" stretch, incomplete.' As recounted earlier, after first setting eyes on the arête in 1904, in 1907 he had spent four nights with Ling at the Promontoire Hut in poor weather. The Great Wall had been heavily iced, so they had 'resolved to have a look at the Brèche Arête'. They found the beginning of the arête 'steep though probably quite climbable', but they went round to 'an easy slope on the Étançons side' and followed this until 'a steep chimney' gave access to a gap in the ridge. Because of the fresh snow on the rock they 'cut the ridge again', this time on the La Grave side, but 'regaining the arête' was difficult. 'Very loose rocks covered with several inches of fresh snow made very delicate hand and footwork on the part of the leader necessary.' They reached the foot of the *Infranchissable* only to discover that it certainly was impassable. The '… mist, the cold wind, the falling snow and the snow-covered rocks put both of us in mind of climbs at Easter on the steeper ridges of the N Face of Ben Nevis. Prudence counselled a retreat', and they went back to the hut.

Two days later, the weather having slightly relented, they had been able to have a look at the top of the Brèche Arête. Raeburn even managed to take a photograph, which he later admitted makes no sense unless looked at through a magnifying glass. What he discovered by looking down on the climb was that the Petit Doigt de L'Épaule[3] 'is really only a step or steep shoulder on the arête'. In the conditions, however, no further exploration was undertaken, and Ling and Raeburn had abandoned the Dauphiné for 'Tarentaise and Italy'.

Twelve years later, in 1919, Raeburn returned to the Dauphiné and, having never completed the traverse of the Meije, decided to try it by climbing the Western Arête first. Learning that the two young Grenoblois had just made the first ascent, he resolved instead to traverse it by descending the arête. Characteristically he says: 'It would be perhaps more interesting and useful to reverse the route.' Many climbers might have said 'interesting', but few would have said 'useful'. He set off for the Refuge de l'Aigle on Friday, 12 September.

3   Literally, 'The little finger of the shoulder', i.e. a small tower or pinnacle.

At 3 pm on Saturday, I found myself on the ledge above the 'Pas du Chat'. This was a good deal later than I had hoped for. Friday night was bad at the Aigle. The wind howled and moaned through its steel rigging and the hail seldom ceased to rattle on the windows and roof. Not till after 7 am was it possible to make a tentative start in rather thick mist. It cleared somewhat on the Central [Peak], though the wind was still high and cold, and I went on over the arêtes.

After 3 pm the weather again got very thick, and it hailed rather heavily. Raeburn went down the Western Arête till he was just above the Petit Doigt de l'Épaule, but 'Prudence and the hour, the weather looking decidedly nasty, now counselled that, as I knew the Great Wall well, it would be wise to drop, not literally of course, down the Muraille to the Promontoire Hut before the early darkness of mid-September came on.' Raeburn even admits that a guides' superstition may have hastened his decision, because he heard the 'warning whistle' of an ancient Alpine chough which he had heard here on both previous visits.[4] He climbed down the familiar Wall without too much difficulty and at 5.50 pm he 'opened the door of the welcome Promontoire, just as a livid and evil-looking evening was closing in'. The traverse, which he had at last completed, though not the way he really wanted, had taken 'rather under 9¾ hours', not including stops. So far as we know, it was his last serious climb in the Alps.

---

4 The whistle of this solitary bird was supposed to mean that the climber should go back or perish. Given his dismissal of the appearance of ravens on the Black Shoot, the bad weather seems a more likely cause of Raeburn's caution, although he did pay attention to a raven on Napes Needle. Trying to descend steep hail or snow-covered slabs in gathering darkness would have been suicidal.

31. FIRST ASCENT OF OBSERVATORY RIDGE IN WINTER

1920

[Fig 1]

Before coming to the SMC Easter Meet of 1920 at Fort William, Raeburn, enjoying female company, spent a day with the LSCC at Tyndrum. On Monday, 5 April, before his historic first ascent of Observatory Ridge, he climbed the upper part of Tower Ridge with Ling and Goggs via the traverse from Observatory Gully to the base of the Great Tower, ascending the latter by the Recess Route.

The following day, Frank Goggs, Editor of the SMCJ, and Arthur Mounsey, with whom Raeburn had also climbed before, joined Harold at Achintee for, so far as we know, his last time on Ben Nevis. Goggs (SMCJ, 1920) begins his article on the first winter ascent of Observatory Ridge on an elegiac note, mentioning that in 1914 he had walked up the Ben with Harry Walker, who had subsequently died in the War. For Goggs, the Ben had been 'a mind picture, symbolising beauty and peace' during the War, and now that he can visit the mountain again, he feels 'sanctified by the memory of many who can no longer accompany us in the flesh'.

Of Walker, he says: 'Being alone, our conversation was more intimate and personal than usual, and under such conditions you get to know a man in a way that you rarely, if ever, do among bricks and mortar.' How true, and Ling and Goggs must have known Raeburn as well as anyone, for they—particularly Ling—had often been alone with him. It would have been fitting if Ling, too, had been in the party that day, but it didn't work out like that.

Remarking on Raeburn's fitness, Goggs says, 'If you can keep close to Raeburn as he skims along and down the slope, now on turf, now on scree, and now on boulders, with the perfect balance of the born hill man, you are in good training.'

Fig 1

'The only arrival to-day was Raeburn, from Tyndrum, where he had spent a day at the Ladies' Scottish Climbing Club Meet.' Frank Goggs in the Easter Meet Report of 1920. From left: Raeburn, Paton, Mabel Jeffrey (née Inglis Clark), Menzies, Murray, Finlayson and Ruth Raeburn. Paton and Menzies do not appear on the list of those at the SMC Easter Meet; perhaps they were attached to the LSCC Meet. Photo: LSCC Archive

They had a meal after the Douglas Boulder and then wondered what to do. Raeburn thought 'most routes would go'. Only he had climbed Observatory Ridge, in more or less summer conditions. The SMCJ Editor was in no doubt that this would be the first winter ascent. Decision made. They roped up, Raeburn leading, followed by Goggs then Mounsey. They gave Raeburn 'a generous share of the 100 ft rope'. One supposes that amounted to 50-60 feet; it can't have been much more and meant that most of the time the second pair probably climbed simultaneously.

The party made a good start on the first 200 ft, 'sound hitches, good standing room, the rocks reasonably broken up, and the demand on the muscles not excessive'. After this pleasant introduction they came to 'a big slabby face', which at first they thought impregnable. Round the corner to the right was no better, so 'Raeburn examined the slabs more carefully and suddenly exclaimed, "I have it."' Goggs comments on the reliability of Raeburn's memory, and he describes the pitch:

> [Y]ou clamber up a slight recess on the right, then when you can get no further and feel uncomfortable, you see a narrow ledge on your left, but out of reach; however, with the aid of a niche for the toe of your boot, and not much more than a balancing hand on the smooth rock face above, you manage to get your knees on the ledge.

It is indeed an awkward move. Goggs, with his usual self-deprecating humour, describes his eventual success: 'How I did it I frankly cannot say, and it really does not matter two straws ... Mounsey ... had watched my performance and had taken note how not to do it.' He came up 'in fine style'. But, Goggs adds, 'I had my revenge later'. On a more serious note, Goggs gives a good impression of the exposure: 'Looking down one never saw more than two slippery ledges at a time ... Looking up, steep frowning rocks were succeeded by steep snowslopes which lost themselves in cloudland.'

Raeburn agreed to pause for food, but such was the gradient that they could find nowhere to sit or stand in comfort and had to go on. Looking for a place to stop, they had deviated from the crest. Raeburn climbed a short gully back to the ridge, but Goggs had such difficulty following that he had to use Mounsey's shoulder, and then, of course, Mounsey, who was a heavy man, had to come up on a tight rope: '... there was rather a struggling and a kicking before the third man's head appeared on the ridge'. Goggs's revenge.

It had been snowing for some time, and 'Rocks ... which Raeburn said were easy in summer, now proved the reverse.' The direct way, over glazed rock, seemed impossible, so, as one does on a difficult and perplexing route, they manoeuvred about looking for an easier way. Making a short descent, they found a good hitch—'a curious spike of rock 15 inches long'—and Raeburn's rope was 'promptly drawn round it'. He tried to the left but soon came back and searched elsewhere. Looking up, Goggs and Mounsey wondered if the cornice would be surmountable, but retreat would have been desperate. Raeburn was unconcerned about the cornice, but he still couldn't find the way ahead. He tried a band of snow running down to a gully, but there was no ledge beneath it. Saying, 'It's got to go,' he disappeared left again and for the next 15 minutes they saw nothing of him, but heard and saw snow and ice hurtling down. They could only wait and hope. Eventually the rope went out more quickly 'and a halloo from our leader announced his conquest of the difficulty'. Goggs says that when he followed, he found the pitch comparatively easy as the second, but that 'the route, a clamber over ... rounded and holdless rock, was very difficult for the leader'.

They now took to the gully on the left (Zero Gully). It was high-angled and Raeburn ran out 'length after length of rope'. Moving one at a time they made slower progress, often without adequate belays of any kind because rock could not be reached, or because the snow was too thin or hard to embed an axe into. Spindrift frequently swept down, but gradually the weather improved. Goggs marked their progress by noting that they were slowly climbing above the height of Càrn Mòr Dearg and could see the Aonachs beyond it. He also comments on the strange, 'almost weird', absence of life: no birds, no insects. In good Romantic fashion, he quotes Lord Byron's lines[1] about the Alps seen as 'The palaces of Nature ...' Scottish palaces were all around.

On a more mundane level, Goggs feared the onset of cramp: '... the steps were ... small, the angle steep, the ice axe could rarely be depended on to give a satisfying sense of security'. While Raeburn ran out the notional 50 ft, Goggs and Mounsey presumably first had to move together and then remain on small stances Raeburn had cut from the steep ice or névé. They

---

1 From, appropriately, *Childe Harold's Pilgrimage*.

Fig 2

The North Face of Ben Nevis. Observatory Ridge, scene of Raeburn's last Scottish climb, is the middle of the three great ridges. Photo: Roger Robb

had to wait until Raeburn could protect them with some kind of hitch, but there were frequent calls to follow because Raeburn could find none. On these occasions, when all three moved together, a slip by any of them could have had fatal consequences.

At last Raeburn could assure them that 'victory was at hand'. A minor icefall between rocks had 'steps cut aslant the ice', and after another 20ft of névé Raeburn landed on 'snow-covered flat rocks'. Goggs says: 'At the icefall a few rocks jutted out on the right, and I remember the feeling of security and satisfaction there was in gripping a rough rock surface.' Even then they were not quite at the top but in a gently-angled snow bay fringed by a moderate cornice 'vulnerable at several points'. Half a dozen steps up the cornice 'landed us on the summit plateau'. Right on cue, 'the sun, which had been threatening to break through the scurrying clouds, bathed us in light …'.

Congratulating Raeburn on his magnificent leading, they celebrated with acid drops, brandy balls, a jam piece and chocolate. The climb had taken just five-and-three-quarter hours. Back at the Alexandra Hotel they delighted in telling Harry MacRobert that his newly-published guide to Ben Nevis was already out of date.

With the first winter ascent of Observatory Ridge on Tuesday, 6 April 1920, Raeburn's mountaineering career in Scotland comes to a glorious but abrupt end. He had been climbing new routes all over the Highlands for some 25 years, but now his name all but vanishes from the pages of the *SMCJ* until his old friend, Willie Ling, writes his obituary in 1926 and Sandy Mackay belatedly contributes his article on climbing the Barrel Buttress on Quinag in 1928. So far as Scotland is concerned, 'The rest is silence.' [Fig 2]

The ascent of Observatory Ridge in full winter condition was one of Harold's finest achievements; its accomplishment a reward for years of persistent effort. Raeburn had been the first ascensionist in summer; he had climbed the route several times since then and descended it at least once; he knew it well, but of course winter conditions change everything. We need constantly to remind ourselves that Harold and his companions had little protection except the dubious kind provided by hitching the rope behind some projection, or the use of an ice-axe belay in snow that was often too shallow or too hard. They had nailed boots, but no crampons. Most of the time they were moving together as a rope of three on 100ft of half-frozen hemp line of doubtful strength. They depended on their skill—particularly Raeburn's—experience and fitness to find the way, clear holds on the rock and cut steps in the ice. We should not forget that Goggs and Mounsey were also both very experienced mountaineers and that either of them could have taken over the lead in an emergency. But neither had climbed the route before, whereas Harold knew the lie of the land and was an acknowledged master. On virtually any route in the previous 25 years he had been expected to lead. The rule was 'the leader must not fall', and he never did.

Nowadays, Observatory Ridge is regarded by most experts as the hardest of the three great Nevis ridges in winter. It has been justly said that while modern long ropes and abundant belaying devices make the route safer, the advent of front-point climbing with crampons and the use of two axes has not made it any easier. The Ridge is now graded between IV,4 and V,4; a realistic grade in most conditions is probably IV,5 because of the technical difficulty of the harder pitches. How many parties of three, one wonders, better Raeburn's time of five-and-three-quarter hours? Most parties of two take longer.

Like the ascents of Green Gully, Crowberry Gully and many other fine, if less famous, routes, Raeburn's ascent of Observatory Ridge in winter has only come to be appreciated in modern times. As with his traverse of the Meije the previous year and his forthcoming expedition to Kangchenjunga in the same year, it provides sound evidence that his selection as Climbing Leader of the 1921 reconnaissance expedition to Everest was thoroughly justified.

32. MOUNTAINEERING ART: A BRIEF STUDY

Art cannot properly be acquired from the pages of a book.
— Harold Raeburn

It is tempting to think that few things date so quickly as mountaineering instruction manuals. Even in the last 50 years there have been radical changes in footwear, clothing and equipment, amongst many other things, and Raeburn's book was published over 100 years ago, in 1920. But one thing never goes out of date: mountaineering wisdom. Any worthwhile manual contains this, and Harold's book is no exception. What follows, then, focuses on Raeburn's wit and wisdom.

The prejudice against guideless climbing issuing chiefly from the Alpine Club is quickly disposed of: 'It was perhaps the successful ascent of … La Meije in 1879 by the Messrs. Pilkington and … Gardiner which most largely contributed to the breaking down of the British prejudice against guideless climbing' (Raeburn, 1920). He goes on to praise the exploits of Collie, Hastings and Slingsby abroad and Collier, Solly, Haskett Smith and Jones at home, who all achieved fine routes without guides in the 1890s. The idea that one should always employ guides is rightly seen as belonging to 'a century and conditions no longer existing'. Raeburn is right to spend no more than two pages on this. In one passage in particular, he summarises what the good mountaineering leader needs:

> *The ability to climb difficult rocks, to cut steps up and down steep ice, to have perfect balance and never slip, and to have great endurance, are the smaller, less important … requirements of a really good guide or leader.*

> *More important are the possession of an apparently intuitive eye for country, an 'instinct' for route finding ... a great power of judging time and space, and a wide knowledge of mountain structure. In short, a real mountaineering leader is the man who 'understands' mountains. (p.137)*

To this he would have been entitled to add 'and understands himself and those he climbs with'; this is implied here rather than stated, but in the chapter on Ethics and Rules, he says: 'There would be little need of mention of mountaineering ethics, if the golden rule of ethics were always kept in mind.' So far as mountaineering morality goes, one should consider oneself on an equal footing with others. But, as he says, 'We are all apt to be forgetful at times ... eager beginners, out of pure thoughtlessness or ignorance, may sometimes fail to exhibit a proper consideration for other mountaineers.' A striking example of the opposite was Raeburn's consideration for young Martinson on Ushba: he recognised that while he and Ling could have endured a bivouac on the summit, this could well have been too much for the 18-year-old. It is also worth remembering that in a long career as a leader, nobody ever suffered a fall or any serious injury climbing with Raeburn. In his own way he kept the Golden Rule.

So much then for mountaineering ethics, but what of more general rules? Raeburn is wise to insist that it is 'beyond the wisdom of anyone' to draw up a comprehensive list because of mountaineering's 'infinite variety', but he proposes a short general maxim: *Conserve energy, don't waste time, and always be careful.* He deplores racing on mountains. He thinks that record times are 'usually more or less fakes', depending more on the conditions than on the virtue of the climbers. He hopes that 'all record-breaking efforts will be avoided by real mountaineers'.

In both rock and snow and ice climbing Raeburn recommends the upright posture. He rightly insists that, summer or winter, the legs do most of the work. To press down on holds is safe; to get the feet at an angle on them is likely to cause a slip. This is especially so when on loose material. He links his discussion of climbing technique to the causes of mountaineering accidents, which are often the result of 'ignorance of climbing technique'. A proper knowledge of this, he says, 'is the very best accident insurance policy, and, unlike ordinary insurance policies, its benefits are preventive and anticipatory'. *(p.174-5)*

For Raeburn balance is key, and 'denotes an unusual quickness of brain telegraphy, and a corresponding rapidity in the execution of orders by the muscles and limbs'. Is this just a matter of practice? No. 'The highest rank as mountaineers can only be attained by those who have added persevering practice to innate ability.' As the man who could jump over three top hats and carve intricate figures on Duddingston Loch, Raeburn recommends skating to improve balance, since it gives 'the power of altering the balance quickly in any desired direction without losing control of it'. With this sort of training, 'a practised mountaineer hardly ever stumbles'.

Concerning rock climbing, Raeburn is consistent with the line he took against William Brown in their controversy over learning to climb on Skye. He says:

The granite slabs of the Cairngorms, and ... Arran give good practice in sound footwork; a climber trained upon these is much more likely to develop into a safe and competent mountaineer than if he were to confine himself to standard 'courses' in the English Lakes. (p.53-54)

Perhaps tactfully, he avoids mentioning Skye gabbro. His general line is that climbers should experience as many different rock types as possible and learn to deal with the peculiarities of each.

Travelling light is recommended both by Raeburn and his sister, Ruth. Harold's policy is to assemble all the food and clothing one might need, cut out anything not essential and then take only half of what is left.

It is sometimes a relief to get free from a whole host of time-wasting and useless knick-knacks such as a razor for instance, which civilisation has caused us to burden ourselves with ... It will be found that the weight of small extras, when added together, will mount rapidly. (p.45)

In these passages he is referring to fairly lengthy excursions, but the principle holds good. Ruth Raeburn quotes the French alpiniste, Mary Paillon: 'Abandon everything which is not absolutely essential, for comfort in climbing depends upon feeling oneself light and mobile.' Raeburn's advice is refreshingly full of common sense. It includes: 'The less washing at high elevation, the better'; remember matches and keep them dry; write a list of what you need and check the lists of other members of your party, thus avoiding the common error of supposing that your friend will have brought the vital item.

Chapter 9 is devoted to women in mountaineering. It is noticeable that Raeburn does not adopt a patronising tone or pretend to instruct. Rather, he offers 'some suggestions which may be of service to the girl or woman beginner ... these are derived from a long and extensive experience of the aims and abilities, the wants and ways of the feminine mountaineer from seven to umpty years of age'. This makes explicit what is partially revealed in Raeburn's writings: he has always been keen to foster the climbing careers of women and has helped some as children.

For beginners Raeburn recommends bouldering, moderate rock climbing and hillwalking. Of bouldering, he says: a woman will 'often be able to show a more experienced and much more powerful man, how a short piece of difficult rock can be climbed with ease and grace' (p.125).

Comparing two young novices of the same age, Raeburn holds that 'the girl is quicker at picking up right methods, and is safer at first than the boy'. The girl's advantages are: smaller feet, a lower centre of gravity and, rather paradoxically, *less* powerful hands and arms. The point being that she will 'pay all the more attention to footholds'. Raeburn links this advice to his general doctrine about rock climbing:

> *[I]t is a mistake to select the highest hold within reach and haul the body up by it. Rather the lowest possible should be used, and the press-down method employed. The weight should be pushed up, and the arms used as much like the legs as possible.* (p.122)

In the Alps, says Raeburn, the girl should avoid going too fast, and she also needs to avoid the wrong kind of Alpine day—the long, tedious snow grind. An interesting, moderate rock ridge is much more suitable. This might sound condescending to modern ears, but Raeburn, a man of his time, wanted everyone, regardless of gender, to enjoy and be involved in the intricacies of mountaineering.

Raeburn also gives good advice about nutrition, drinking, avoiding sunburn and snow-blindness. As for style, balance is always of the essence: 'If you are a good dancer, skater or ski-runner, balance will come easily to you.' Being good at all three, he knew what he was talking about.

Raeburn is against all dietary, medical and training fads. Climbing is the best training for climbing. As for food: eat what you like but in strict moderation; usually, on the hill, sugary things like jam and rusks, but back in the valley, plenty of bread and meat. He is against tinned food and carrying water—use what you find on the hill; carry a collapsible cup. A small portable stove is a good idea, as not only can you make tea but you can fry bacon and eggs as well. In all this Raeburn is reporting what has worked for him in a long career.

Raeburn's psychological approach to mountaineering is sound. The best climber should lead and come last on descent. The party should move at a pace which is comfortable for the weakest member. If the leader has to pause at some difficulty, he should not rush on after it, but remember that his second will also have to slow down. Of the psychological effect of the rope, he wisely says:

> [It] is the physical sign of the thread of will which connects the members of a roped party, and of them makes a single unit ... its moral assistance is very real. Its putting on puts everyone ... on their mettle. The leader's responsibility may be greatest, but the rope distributes part of this responsibility among every member, while at the same time giving just the confidence and courage required, to enable the less practised, or more diffident climbers to do themselves justice ... In a moral and physical sense, the rope represents l'esprit du corps. (p.173)

Throughout his career, Raeburn was a popular, sympathetic, safe and responsible leader; his partners climbed with him again and again. He understood the state of mind needed for mountaineering. He understood mountains and people. Until his ill-fated trip to Mount Everest you will search in vain in mountaineering literature for a single bad word spoken about him by anyone.

Concerning the mountain environment, and in particular mountain huts, he says that on leaving a hut one has a duty to leave it in a better state than before, adding, mordantly, 'As a rule this will not be found difficult.' He also deflates notions about the romantic charm of mountain huts. Quoting Clinton Dent: 'For those who are not afraid of solitude there is a great charm to be found in a stay at one of these huts,' Raeburn comments: 'Those who go in August will find … the "solitude" is of much the same nature as that enjoyed by the sardine in its tin'.

This, then, is an account of some of the timeless wisdom contained within *Mountaineering Art*. It is fascinating and entirely typical of Raeburn that he ends the book with an *Envoi* containing four questions:

> *Why do we mountaineers love the Alps? Is it their beauty and majesty of form which appeal to us? Is it because of the pure physical enjoyment of the struggle with the difficulties, maybe with the dangers of the ascent? Or the mental exhilaration of setting one's wits to discover the safe way to overcome the icy or rocky barriers that guard access to the heights?*

He does not answer the questions; that is up to us.

In his review of *Mountaineering Art*, William Naismith (SMCJ, 1920) spends time on technical matters such as the weight of boots, posture and technique on rock, the advantages of woven bootlaces, and the freedom given by braces as opposed to belts, but perhaps more interestingly, he says, 'In this book Mr Raeburn is downright and natural, and while we read it we can almost hear him speaking to us in his own quietly emphatic tones.' This is valuable, and rare, testimony as to how Raeburn talked and the firm way in which he held his opinions. One recalls Raeburn, quietly emphatic, telling William Clark not to waste his last exposure when they climbed the North-East Ridge of Aonach Beag.

In a generally favourable review, perhaps Naismith's most important criticism is of the commonly held view 'that on steep ground the climber must stand up straight'. Raeburn strongly endorses this doctrine, 'but', says Naismith, 'he will probably admit that there is always a more or less unconscious bias inwards. A man on a snow slope resembles in this respect a boy walking along the parapet of a bridge, who of course stands upright, or he would leave the parapet, but who also knows quite well on which side he is going to alight if he tumbles off'. A point nicely made, and which Raeburn might have grudgingly accepted. After all, as Sandy Mackay said, he was 'ultimately fair in debate'.

In 1920 Raeburn's book cost 16s. Today one can purchase a facsimile paperback edition for £16. It is significant that on the Everest reconnaissance expedition, Raeburn gifted a copy of *Mountaineering Art* to Guy Bullock.

33. THE HIMALAYA   1920

In his last article for the *AJ*, Raeburn (1921) chronicles his exploratory expedition to Kangchenjunga.[1] He says: 'In 1920 I was fortunate enough to be able to carry out a project, long thought of and planned, to make a reconnaissance of the southerly access to Kanchen.' It may have been one of the things that kept him going throughout the years of dreary, unceasing work in Glasgow during the War. Not only did Harold want to explore the access to Kangchenjunga, he also 'had another project, and that was to get as near as politically possible to ... Everest'.

[Fig 1]

At a Shangri-La in the foothills of the Himalaya, where high officials in the Raj sent their families during the 'hot weather', Raeburn found that a week or so of 'Darjeeling in the rains' was worse than 'the very worst weather Skye or the English Lakes can show'. However, it cleared at last and there 'rose into the northern heavens vast domes and peaks of purest white, the Kangchenjunga range'.

Raeburn set off from Darjeeling on 22 July 1920 with a party that included Col HW Tobin DSO, the Sherpa Sirdar Gyaljen, a Lama cook called Kusay and 21 porters, four of whom were women. Their objectives were to examine the south-east approach to the mountain, possible routes on its south-east face, and the complete traverse of the Talung Glacier.

They followed the 'raging glacier torrent' of the Rathong River through a thick jungle of 'great forest trees and tangled undergrowth', the unseen torrent 'roaring ... like a perpetual thunderstorm'. A missing bridge necessitated

---

1   Various spellings: this appears to be the widely accepted one. Abbreviated to 'Kanch' in modern mountaineering circles.

Fig 1

The South-West or Yalung Face of the Kangchenjunga massif. The triangular summit of the mountain just left of centre is flanked by Yalung Kang to the left and Kangchenjunga South to the right. Photo: John Cleare

Fig 2

Kabru just right of centre and Rathong Peak, previously named Little Kabru, to its right. Photo: John Cleare

a devious, ascending detour where 'the great oaks, magnolias and chestnuts changed to rhododendrons, pines and mountain bamboo'. They 'passed several bears within smelling distance—I mean of our noses, not Bruin's'. The bears would certainly have smelled them, but Raeburn characteristically dismisses the threat of an encounter with a witty aside, rather as he had dismissed the threat from feral dogs in the Caucasus.

They skirted the steep rocks of the summit of Longjong (15,500 ft) to camp in a little valley at 14,000 ft, and the next day reached another camp at Agluthang. Raeburn established that WW Graham's party of 1883 had ascended Jabonu and not the more significant Kabru, and thus was able to clarify some of the misunderstandings about the complicated geography of the area. (Raeburn was experienced in this sort of work: recall his disproof of de Déchy's ascent of Chanchakhi in the Caucasus [AJ, 1914].) [Fig 2]

From the camp at Agluthang some porters, including the four women, were sent back while the main party ascended 1,000 ft of steep, loose boulders to gain the Guicha La at 16,400 ft from where they descended to camp in 'a lovely flowery, grassy recess'. The weather remained settled and Raeburn could examine the south side of Kangchenjunga and other nearby mountains. His opinion of Kangchen's south-easterly aspect was that it was 'most repellent'. He identified a col which had been reached by Alexander Kellas in 1911: 'Dr Kellas, with his usual prudence and mountain wisdom, did not risk the descent on the south side,' and was able to make further corrections to the faulty maps he had been given.

The party then descended the length of the mighty Talung Glacier: '... such a vast mass of dirt and boulders fall on it from the frightfully steep walls that hem it in, that no ice is visible for miles'. On 4 August they began their descent of the Talung or Rinpiram River. In Raeburn's words:

> [T]he week following was spent in forcing the descent of the wonderful gorge ... no track exists and a way had to be hewn through dripping forests, through bamboo thickets, much enjoyed by the bears, and down clay and stone banks to the rugged boulders of the torrent bed. The walling precipices rise in some places from 3,000 to 4,000 ft above the river and from them leaped countless waterfalls, some completely vanishing in spray. At one place the furious Rinpiram plunges with a thunderous roar into a huge chasm some hundreds of feet deep. We had

> to construct improvised bridges over the various 'chhus' [side streams]. The coolies[2] behaved splendidly under most uncomfortable and depressing conditions, and carried their heavy loads without complaint ... Our only loss was a severe one to me. My ice-axe, a faithful friend of a dozen years, doubly valued as a gift of the late Harry Walker[3] ... was swept away by one of the flooded torrents.

Eventually, thanks to the woodsman skills of one of the porters, the party came upon a cultivated clearing in the forest, much to the joy and relief of the rest of the porters, whose supply of rice had finished that morning. In this clearing:

> A most picturesque aboriginal turned up. He was a Lepcha, dignified and taciturn, but guardedly friendly. His garment was a single sheet of cloth forming a kind of kilt, the upper part thrown over his right shoulder, leaving the left side of his body bare. At his side he wore the straight Lepcha 'ban' or knife, like a Roman sword. His colour was ... about that of old ivory, and features quite fine.

This local chieftain provided a guide so that Raeburn's party were eventually able to reach another settlement with ample food supplies. The real difficulties were now over, although they still had to cross the Talung River:

> [A] long bridge of rotten rattans, supported in V-shaped slings, a couple of bamboo stems as roadway. The crossing of this swinging, dancing, slack rope affair, over the leaping snowy cauldron of the great river was a first experience to Tobin and myself. Perhaps neither of us quite enjoyed it, but of course we acted ... as though we did.

After a couple more days of travel they reached Gangtok.[4] Tobin, whose leave was over, rode the final 60 miles while Raeburn followed:

---

2   A term once used to refer to unskilled labourers from some Asian countries, now widely considered offensive.
3   Killed in the War: see Chapter 31.
4   Where Raeburn was to recuperate after his illness on the Everest expedition in 1921.

> [M]ore leisurely on foot down the most beautiful and not too hot valley of the Teesta, riding the 22 miles up from Teesta Bridge. We were well satisfied with our coolies, nearly all Sherpas, like Gyaljen, our Sirdar ... I have said nothing about the leeches. These are unspeakable, and what I should like to say would be unprintable.

HW Tilman describes his own descent of the gorge in 1936 and makes it clear that the journey was a gruelling test for a strong party, which included Pasang Kikuli, a magnificent mountaineer who perished on a brave rescue attempt on K2 in 1939. On one occasion it took Tilman's party nine hours to travel barely a mile.[5]

Raeburn's second reconnaissance expedition left Darjeeling on 2 September. On this occasion he was accompanied by a member of the Indian Civil Service, the 'cheery CG Crawford', who was also a member of the Alpine Club. Crawford was particularly useful because, as well as being a good rock climber—having pioneered routes on Scafell Pinnacle and Pillar Rock in the Lakes with CF Holland and HM Kelly—he also had some knowledge of local dialects and customs. Gyaljen came again as Sirdar with 30 porters. The party had permission from the Indian and Nepalese authorities to explore the south-western approaches to Kangchenjunga from the Yalung Valley of Nepal.

The first four days were along the Singalila ridge, with comfortable bungalows at night and good views. Raeburn was in fact quite used to riding horses, having done so in the Caucasus, and the first few days were spent on pony back. (The porters, of course, would have walked.) At Sandakpu, a hill station at 12,000 ft, they had their best view yet of Everest, even if most of it was obscured by Makalu. The scene gave them a panorama 'of over 300 miles of the mightiest mountains on the globe'. Here the ponies were left behind and the party proceeded on foot.

They entered Nepal by the Chumbab La (15,900 ft), crossed the Semo La (the Cold Pass) at 15,300 ft, and 'ascended the Yalung Valley to the deserted village of Tseram', which seems to have consisted of 'one semi-ruined yak

---

5   'The only Europeans who had followed it down were Messrs Raeburn and Tobin in 1920. From the map it seemed about three days' journey—it had taken them eight.' Tilman (1946) says he was unaware of that or he might well not have undertaken that route.

hut', arriving there on 10 September. The weather was cold and misty and no use for reconnaissance. As Raeburn puts it:

> *After ten days' delay, Mr Crawford, unluckily having caught a chill, and the party having to seek a more genial climate lower down, the weather much improved. Camp was gradually shifted up the 13-mile Yalung glacier. The highest camp made was right under the highest peak of Kangchen at about 20,000 ft, and next day about 1,000 ft higher was reached ... However, food ... was running short and the only possible routes which could be discovered were judged to be too dangerous. The whole south-west face of Kangchenjunga is very steep and every possible looking way of access seems to be dominated at this season by overhanging ice masses, from which the avalanches fall almost ceaselessly.* (SMCJ, 1921)

In this 'Excursions' note in the *SMCJ*, Raeburn omits to mention that on 28 September, he and Crawford had crossed an inflowing glacier from the Talung Peak and climbed to 19,000 ft up a rock rib from which 'Splendid, but not encouraging, views of Kangchen's SW face and of the Talung saddle (22,000 ft) rewarded our exertions.' Raeburn found it interesting that quite hard rock climbing at 20,000 ft was easier than laborious snow plodding at the same height. Again, he was able to identify that the existing maps of the area were inaccurate in their depiction of the various Yalung glaciers and peaks.

Time and food running short, the expedition retreated to the highest yak pasture at Ramser (15,000 ft). From here Gyaljen led the main party of porters back to Pamionchi (now Pemayangtse). Raeburn's efforts were now concentrated on the search for a direct pass between the Yalung and Rathong valleys which he was sure must exist. 'After hours of heavy toil and being forced to apply the "whip" to our tired men in the shape of tots of cognac', Raeburn and Crawford with 'three picked and booted' porters managed to find what they were looking for—'a new pass (proposed name the Rathong La, 18,000 to 19,000 ft) just under Kabru ...' They did so by 'forcing a way through soft snow and heavy moraines of the Rathong cirque', reaching grass below the snowline as night fell: a remarkable achievement.

[Fig 3]

As Robin Campbell comments:

[I]t is disgraceful that this expedition is consistently ignored in published histories of Kangchenjunga. Raeburn's crossing of the Rathong La was the first recorded, but he thought that it might well have been an old route between Nepal and Sikkim. He suggested that Little Kabru [marked on the Garwood map] should be renamed Rathong Peak and this name is used today ... Raeburn's energy and drive in Sikkim in 1920 amply rebut the slanders levelled at him at the time of the 1921 Everest reconnaissance, and thereafter, that he was too old to have been the climbing leader of that expedition. (SMCJ, 2021).[6]

The party returned to Darjeeling on 9 October. Raeburn published a full account of the expedition, but he said nothing about his other declared purpose: '... to get as near as ... possible to Everest'. This may be partly because they did not get very near, but it might also be that he was not keen to put in the public domain any useful information he had gathered, for a rather obvious reason. Discretion was part of his makeup.

6   Concerning the silence of historians about Raeburn's Kangchenjunga Expeditions, Campbell makes an exception for Douglas Side's article, 'Towards Kangchenjunga', *AJ*, May 1955, 83–95.

Fig 3

The valley by which Raeburn and Crawford approached the Rathong La is probably the shadowed valley directly right of Rathong Peak with a distant snow peak visible. The other alternative, to the left of Rathong, looks too high and menaced by loaded slopes. Photo: John Cleare

34. EVEREST RECONNAISSANCE EXPEDITION—PART 1   1921

In January 1921 Harold Raeburn was officially invited to lead the mountaineering side of the Everest Reconnaissance Expedition. He accepted with great pride. His friends and his parent club the SMC were delighted by this honour bestowed on a hugely talented, experienced and popular member of the Scottish mountaineering community. Harold's friendly acquaintance, Geoffrey Winthrop Young, might also have been considered, but he had lost part of a leg in the Great War. The only real competition was from Lt-Colonel Edward Lisle Strutt, a distinguished soldier and diplomat who was also an experienced Alpinist and guidebook author. He, however, was held to be rather opinionated and prone to personality clashes. Raeburn, too, could be dogmatic, but there was no suggestion that he couldn't get on with his companions. He also had an outstanding record in the Alps, had led two successful small expeditions to the Caucasus and had only returned from Sikkim in the Himalaya in October, having led two reconnaissance expeditions to the Kanchenjunga area. Although at 56 there was a slight question mark against his age, he was the ideal choice.

Because of his recent Himalayan experience, it was agreed by the Mount Everest Committee, made up of representatives of the Alpine Club and the Royal Geographical Society and largely under the domination of Arthur Hinks, who was appointed Secretary,[1] that Harold should go out to India earlier than the main body of the Expedition so that he could arrange supplies and hire mountain porters. Harold's recent experience in India equipped

---

1   JEC Eaton of the Alpine Club was appointed Joint Secretary of the committee a little later, but he seems to have left most of the work to Hinks.

Fig 1

The Everest Expedition 1921, standing: Wollaston, Howard-Bury, Heron, Raeburn. Seated: Mallory, Wheeler, Bullock, Morshead. Photo: Wollaston Alpine Club

him to deal with these matters, as he had also done in the Caucasus.

On 9 February, in London, Raeburn met Francis Younghusband, instigator of the Everest plan and Chairman of the Committee, and George Mallory, rising star of the mountaineering world, who was to be a vital member of the team. Percy Farrar of the Alpine Club was also present. So far as is known the initial meeting went well. However, a few days later Raeburn was struck down with influenza (which had killed an estimated twenty million people worldwide in 1918/19). Because of this he was unable to attend a meeting of the full Mount Everest Committee some days later, and he wrote to Hinks saying his doctor had told him not to travel. Perhaps sensing some unease about his fitness, Raeburn also wrote to Younghusband:

> *I am deeply anxious to do everything possible for the success of the Expedition and regret exceedingly the trouble caused by my indisposition. I shall be all right on the sea and on the mountains and able to do good work for its safety and success.*[2]

Raeburn indicated that he would be able to attend the next meeting on 7 March, at which he was expected to give a short presentation on various relevant aspects of Himalayan mountaineering.

In fact all the participants were required to produce medical evidence stating that they were fit enough to cope with the rigours of the Expedition. Raeburn's doctor in Edinburgh examined him and sent him a report, which he forwarded to the Mount Everest Committee:

> *Dear Mr Raeburn, – Upon completing my examination of you, I find that there is no evidence of any organic disease. Your heart, lungs and kidneys are healthy. You are decidedly below par just now, probably the result of not laying up when you had mild influenza lately. You will require to give up this week entirely to recuperating and should avoid all work and worry as far as possible. By next week I think you will be fit to go to London and complete the necessary arrangements for your journey. I think that by taking care of yourself for the next week or so*

---

2   The letter from Raeburn to Younghusband is available at Box 2, Everest Archive, Royal Geographical Society.

you will be quite fit to go through with your expedition. Yours very sincerely, A.M. Ronaldson.[3]

The doctor's report, though not very detailed, is at least somewhat reassuring, although no mention is made of his mental health—probably rather a taboo subject at the time, but later evidence shows that Raeburn had been treated at home in 1911 for 'melancholia', now known as depression. One wonders also if Dr Ronaldson had any real grasp of the rigours of months of arduous living in the Himalaya, or the effects of altitude. To us the rather quaint advice about 'laying up' for a week, after which all would be well, seems rather inadequate. However, this report was probably no more or less adequate than those provided by the other members of the Expedition.

The choice of Raeburn as Climbing Leader was not welcomed by Mallory. He thought that Raeburn was 'too old' and that, in certain matters, he was 'incompetent'. In particular, the tents had not been 'thought through' and 'no proper provision for cold at great heights came within Raeburn's scheme of things'. The vexed question of Raeburn's age will be discussed later. The criticism of the tents and equipment seems unfair as the member of the committee who had overall responsibility for stores and equipment was not Raeburn but CF Meade.

As to 'incompetence', Mallory himself was prone to make hasty judgments, and as later events were to demonstrate, practical 'competence' was not high on his list of virtues. He disliked Oliver Wheeler from the outset simply because he was a Canadian. He was notoriously careless with his possessions: Hinks had to detail someone to see that he got all his luggage off the boat properly. He had trouble working both primus stoves and cameras. More seriously, by Raeburn's standards, Mallory's mountaineering judgment was not 'safe'. His complicity in the decision to attempt the North Col the following year in avalanche conditions led to the deaths of seven porters; and his personal decision to take Andrew Irvine instead of Noel Odell with him on his last summit attempt in 1924 was unwise. Mallory was an excellent and courageous climber, but his mountaineering judgment was questionable. In his magisterial work, *Everest: The Mountaineering*

---

3   The letter from Ronaldson to Raeburn, dated 28 February 1921, is available at Box 2, Everest Archive, Royal Geographical Society.

History (2000), Walt Unsworth has interesting things to say about Raeburn and Mallory: he accurately rehearses Raeburn's career, describing him as a 'great mountaineer' before, disappointingly, subscribing to the view that, at 56, he 'was already a crabbed and crusty old man'. However, of Mallory he says: 'His character was flawed by one serious weakness—he was a drifter, uncommitted and indecisive. He never seriously tried to shape events in his life; instead, it was the events themselves which did the shaping. He drifted into the Everest adventure as he drifted into everything else he did.' This makes a striking contrast with Raeburn, whose career builds in chosen stages, culminating in what should have been his greatest triumph.

Raeburn left Britain in the middle of March, travelling first-class on 'The City of Lahore' from Birkenhead to Calcutta (£129 return). When he got to Darjeeling he stayed at the 'Hotel Mount Everest', with which he was familiar from his trip the previous year. He must have been relieved to get to the cool mountain air of Darjeeling after the sweaty heat of Calcutta and the plains of India before the monsoon season. He was in India for some five to six weeks before the others began to arrive, and in that time he organised the Expedition's cohort of porters and saw to it that there was an adequate supply of food for them.

While waiting in Darjeeling, Raeburn wrote to Younghusband and Hinks expressing disappointment at the loss of George Finch from the climbing party, allegedly for failing a medical, but much more likely because his face did not fit. This was a matter in which Raeburn and Mallory were at one. The loss of Finch was a serious blow to the Expedition; he was one of the best Alpinists of his day and his eventual replacement, Mallory's old school friend, Guy Bullock, although willing and able, was not in the same class as a mountaineer.

The stores did not arrive in Calcutta until 14 May. It may seem like a trivial matter, but Raeburn and Charles Howard-Bury, the Expedition Leader, disagreed about the amount of sugar they should take. Raeburn wanted to take more, but Bury, who was notoriously stingy, vetoed it. But sugar is a vital commodity when people are engaged in strenuous exercise for prolonged periods; Raeburn knew this from experience and should have been listened to.

To cut to the chase: the expedition travelled in two parties, Sandy Wollaston (the Expedition Doctor), Wheeler, Mallory and Howard-Bury in the first and Raeburn, fellow Scot Alexander Kellas, Alexander Heron and Guy Bullock in the second. In order not to place too much strain on the limited accommodation in the Dhak bungalows on the first part of the journey, the second party gave the first a couple of days' head start. Raeburn's party finally left Darjeeling on 18 May, two months after his arrival in India. One suspects that all the irksome hanging about in Darjeeling did not improve Raeburn's state of mind or his health. At least until Kellas arrived, he may have felt rather the odd man out in that social setting with its grand receptions at Government House, polo matches and so on. However, as usual, he made no complaint. [Fig 1]

The Expedition gradually moved from 'forests blazing with rhododendrons, great trees and hanging mosses' to a 'more European-type country with oak and walnut trees, birch and juniper woods paved with anemones'. These impressed Wollaston, who said: 'it is impossible to exaggerate the beauty of the scenery and vegetation' (1933). They eventually crossed the Jelep La (14,000 ft) into Tibet 'with banks of old snow on either side of the track'. They descended to the Chumbi Valley with its 'prosperous villages', typically travelling some 15 miles a day. They passed by Yatung and came to Phari, which was a rude awakening: 'an extremely dirty village dominated by a stone fort and lying under the shadow of the great mountain Chomolhari (23,930 ft.)' (Arnold, 1922).

At Phari some of the team 'went over to have dinner with the Dzong Pen [village chief]. First we were given tea and sweetmeats, followed by strong ginger wine, which was most comforting to our stomachs in their delicate condition'. This note of warning in an otherwise laudatory comment on the Dzong Pen's dinner announces the arrival of the severe gastric trouble which was to cause the Expedition so much grief. Wollaston described the cooking as 'unspeakably bad' due to poor cleanliness, and most of the party, particularly Kellas and Raeburn, were affected by sickness and diarrhoea.

Apart from the 'bad fish' incident in the Alps, Raeburn, so far as we know, had never suffered from severe bacterial infection before while away climbing. He seems to have remained perfectly healthy in the Caucasus and, more relevantly, in the Himalaya the previous year. Kellas, too, had been mountaineering in the Himalaya in the months prior to joining the Expedition, and there are no reports of him being troubled by stomach problems. Raeburn, like his fellow Scot, had also been in India much longer than the others. It is possible that both men had picked up the micro-organism which causes amoebic dysentery and can remain in the gut for a long time before its effects become apparent. This, of course, is conjecture.

The consequences of sickness and diarrhoea in visitors to the Himalaya are very unpleasant but not usually serious or fatal, with symptoms typically subsiding in a matter of days. Most of the other members of the team had spells of the usual kind of trouble and recovered relatively quickly. In the case of Kellas, and later of Raeburn, things got much worse, as Howard-Bury confided in his diary:

> *Dr Kellas is … ill and won't take any food and is very depressed and is not at all encouraged by Raeburn. The next morning we were very late in starting. Dr Kellas said at first that he would go. Then, owing to Raeburn's dismal predictions, he changed his mind after all his kit had gone on and I had to persuade him to come on again, by being carried in an armchair on two poles.*[4]

Michael Jacob comments: 'Kellas needed medical supervision, good nursing and a suitable diet, and Phari was certainly not an appropriate place for such a convalescence. Equally, travelling just placed a further strain on his weakened constitution. In the event, the "least worse" option was for Kellas to continue and Raeburn's words of caution were over-ruled.'[5]

It is certainly possible to sympathise with Howard-Bury, who was faced with an acute dilemma. Whether it would have been any better to leave Kellas at Phari we cannot know. Dr Wollaston confirmed the generally poor health of the Expedition at this stage:

> *Dr Kellas is not at all well. I am afraid some of us already have our insides all wrong. Certainly I spent half today in bed having to starve myself. Our cooks are thoroughly bad and our food has been very bad all the way.* (1933)

---

4 *The Everest Diaries of Charles Howard-Bury* are available at the National Library of Scotland.
5 From an unpublished manuscript, by Michael CC Jacob, whose masterly account of the expedition and its aftermath plays an important part in what follows.

Illness was not the only problem affecting the equanimity of the Expedition's Leader; Howard-Bury complained in his diary:

Raeburn's mule threw him at Phari almost into the pond there, and when given the interpreter's pony, an excellent little beast, was thrown by this also and kicked. I am afraid our champion alpine climber is not an equally good equestrian.

Howard-Bury may very well have 'ridden to hounds' in Ireland and was, no doubt, good on horseback, but his rather unpleasant, sneering remark indicates irritation with Raeburn. In fact, Raeburn was likely quite adequate on horseback as he had ridden at times in the Caucasus and more recently on the Kanchenjunga venture. But it would be a mistake to make too much of this; most mountaineers know that petty animosities are the background to almost every expedition and usually mean very little. Bury was a man under pressure; things were going seriously wrong.

On 1 June, Howard-Bury wrote: 'Dr Kellas was carried on a bed, but is better though weak. He had had enough of being carried in a chair yesterday.' Mallory wrote: 'The old gentleman (such he seemed) was obliged to retire a number of times en route and could not bear to be seen in this distress.' Howard-Bury's diary of 3 June records:

Wheeler is not at all well, with bad indigestion. Dr Kellas is better but weak and has still to be carried in a litter. Raeburn is not feeling well with diarrhoea. Several people are still indisposed, which must be due to the height. Poor Raeburn got kicked by a mule today ...

Poor Raeburn indeed, for this seems to have been the start of his serious illness; but for the time being Kellas was the focus of medical attention. Wollaston again: 'Kellas very unwell, but no dysentery; pulse very poor, and he tells me that he has recently lost a stone in weight, which accounts for a good deal of his present weakness.' The weight loss was no doubt caused by the dehydrating effects of diarrhoea combined with Kellas not drinking or eating. In these circumstances, the cessation of the 'dysentery' (i.e. diarrhoea) would be a very dangerous sign: the body having nothing left to get rid of.

At all events, the Expedition 'left the Lhasa road and turned westwards, over high passes between 16,000 and 17,000 ft with views to the south ... of Pauhunri, Kangchenjau, and Chomiomo'.[6] Kellas had shown some signs of recovery and, according to Howard-Bury, on 4 June was carried on a yak, at his own request, 'propped up by his bedding, but he stopped at the top of the highest pass and refused to go on'.

Wollaston wrote: 'At about 5 miles beyond the pass I was told that Kellas had broken down just short of the pass.' The doctor went back and got Kellas into 'a Tibetan hut where a woman made hot water and we mixed Bovril and brandy from my saddle bags ... with six men we carried him very slowly about ten miles', and eventually got him into camp. One cannot help thinking that Kellas must have been exceedingly tough to survive these exhausting manoeuvres as long as he did.

The following day, seeming a bit better, Kellas returned to being carried in a litter. However, when Howard-Bury arrived in Khampa Dzong he had hardly time to turn round before 'an excited messenger arrived at the run to give them the shocking news that Kellas was dead'. Bury had passed Kellas on his way to Khampa Dzong and he had 'seemed to me to be still quite cheerful'.

Kellas's death was a disaster for the Expedition. Not only was he one of the few recognised climbers but 'the only man qualified to carry out the physiological tests with the oxygen apparatus' (Jacob, op. cit.). Raeburn must have been particularly affected: Kellas was a fellow Scot and in the somewhat rarefied social atmosphere of an expedition composed largely of the English upper classes, most of whom knew rather little about Scottish mountaineering, it must have been comforting for Raeburn to have a kindred spirit. Harold also seems to have felt a sense of guilt that he perhaps did not do more to persuade Howard-Bury that Kellas really was unfit to travel. We do not know, of course, what Raeburn actually said to Bury at Phari, but a lingering feeling that he ought to have done more is understandable.

On 6 June Kellas was buried at Khampa Dzong, and George Mallory described the brief funeral in a letter to his friend, Winthrop Young:

---

6   All mountains which Alexander Kellas had climbed.

It was an extraordinarily affecting little ceremony burying Kellas on a stony hillside—a place on the edge of a great plain and looking across it to the three great snow peaks of his conquest. I shan't easily forget the four boys, his own trained mountain men, children of nature seated in wonder on a great stone near the grave while Bury read out the passage from Corinthians.[7]

While the sympathy that Kellas received was fully deserved, it should be borne in mind that, as Wollaston revealed later, he did not help himself by stubbornly refusing to take 'drugs or stimulants'. Among the medicines carried by the Expedition there would almost certainly have been a small brown bottle with a white and red label containing Chlorodyne, invented at the end of the 19th century by Dr Collis-Browne of the Indian Army for the treatment of cholera, and without which no wise traveller ventured to Asia. It may not have been a 'stimulant', but it was certainly a 'drug' for it contained a potent mixture of laudanum (an alcoholic solution of opium), tincture of cannabis, and chloroform. A few drops dissolved in water produced an extremely soothing effect on the stomach of the traveller suffering from diarrhoea. A little of this remedy might have had a very beneficial effect.[8]

Severely crippled and saddened by Kellas's death and soon to be missing Raeburn as well, the Expedition continued on its way.

---

7   *Mallory's Letter Collection*, The Library of Magdalene College, Cambridge.
8   Needless to say, in its original composition, it has long since been banned as a narcotic.

35. EVEREST RECONNAISSANCE EXPEDITION—PART 2 1921

The Expedition's doctor, Sandy Wollaston, was growing increasingly concerned about Raeburn's health, writing:

> *Raeburn has been suffering for several days with much the same as Kellas; he does not get any better and is losing strength. He is really not suited to the strain of this altitude, and I have told Howard-Bury that he is not fit to continue ... but must go to some lower place where he can be properly fed and looked after.* (1933)

Altitude has many undesirable effects on mountaineers but, so far as is known, chronic diarrhoea is not one of them. However, Wollaston was certainly right that Raeburn needed proper care and attention.

Howard-Bury accepted Wollaston's advice. Writing to Arthur Hinks, he said: 'I must send Raeburn down to Lachen to recover,' adding morosely, 'It does not pay to send middle-aged men out to this country.'

Wollaston, a caring doctor, and remembering Kellas's lonely death, said he would accompany Raeburn. Raeburn, every bit as stubborn as Kellas, though perhaps not averse to swallowing medicine, wanted to stay with the Expedition 'at least as far as the valley of the Yaru, down which I might go to more genial conditions. Col. Bury decided, however, that not to embarrass the rest, I ought to go over the Serpo La to Lachen in Sikkim where there was known to be a Mission Station.' And Raeburn agreed to this, 'for the sake of not delaying the others'.[1]

1   From a report by Raeburn to the Mount Everest Committee.

Thus, according to Mike Jacob:

[O]n 8 June, whilst the others continued to Tinki, Raeburn and Wollaston, accompanied by some porters, departed in another direction. Their path lay over a bare, open plain to Gira, then a gentle rise to the Serpo La at 17,000 ft where there was a numbing headwind from which their clothing gave scant protection as they sat astride their plodding ponies. The pass was not a regular col but a stony saddle about two miles wide ... The wind howled and chilled them to the bone as they struggled on through rocky moraines until, late in the afternoon, they were very fortunate to find a Tibetan encampment.[2]

Wollaston wrote later: 'A fire of the usual yak dung occupied the middle and filled the place with acrid smoke, but the warmth was very comforting, especially to Raeburn, who had reached very nearly his limit and was quite done up.'

Raeburn was very unwell. He could not eat, even though the Tibetans willingly shared their Tsampa and ewe's milk cheese with the benighted travellers. Wollaston says, stoically: 'it filled a gap and we did not starve'. The porters, meanwhile, had been lagging some way behind, but one pack pony and its attendant managed to find the right tent in the dark and, fetching Wollaston's bedding, they wrapped Raeburn up in it, while Wollaston 'curled up in a space about four feet long, with one side of me against a large boulder ... but every night has its end, and Raeburn said in the morning that he had been quite warm thanks to my eiderdown sleeping bag'. Wollaston appears to be a sympathetic character who probably saved Raeburn's life by insisting that he go to Lachen for treatment. His attitude contrasts favourably with the irritation expressed by Howard-Bury, Mallory and Hinks as their plans were thwarted.

Jacob again:

The small party continued their slow journey across frozen swamp and river to Girzong, which at about 15,000 ft marked the boundary between Tibet and Sikkim [in India]. Raeburn was very weak but

---

2   *From Edinburgh to Everest*, an unpublished manuscript by Mike Jacob.

managed to stay aboard his pony by leaning on his arms. As they got lower down Wollaston welcomed the appearance of dwarf rhododendrons, pine trees and flowers.

On 10 June:

[T]hey crossed the river Zemu by a two-spanned bridge and eventually reached Lachen village where there was a mission station run by two Finnish women. They agreed to take Raeburn in and look after him until he could be carried to Gangtok some fifty miles further on where there was a doctor. Wollaston could do no more for his patient and returned to the Expedition whilst Raeburn languished at Lachen. All of this was reported to Arthur Hinks in London, who unfeelingly referred to … 'the breakdown of Mr Raeburn', adding 'and that is the last that anyone has heard of him'.

But it certainly wasn't.

Raeburn, in his report to the committee, wrote: 'I remained in bed … suffering severely and growing weaker. On the 19th [June] I left Lachen carried on a dandy[3] … and got to Gangtok on the 22nd.'

Jacob writes:

Raeburn was given every help and the best treatment that was available at Government House, the residence of the Political Officer for Sikkim, Major FM Bailey, and his wife. Bailey, a seasoned adventurer himself, was a close friend of Henry Morshead and had been with Younghusband in Lhasa. They nursed Raeburn back to health and he was regularly attended to by Dr Dyer, the Civil Surgeon, with whom he later stayed as he slowly regained his strength. So began a frustratingly slow recovery from a serious dysentery-like condition that had brought him near to death.

Raeburn said later in his report: 'I most keenly desired to rejoin the party at the earliest possible date, but it was not till nearly the end of July that Dr

---

3 The 'dandy' was provided by a local dignitary as were the men who carried it.

Dyer would consent to allow me to travel.' While staying with the doctor Raeburn had already been writing letters trying to engage an interpreter/servant in Darjeeling, Gangtok and Kalimpong, 'but without success', so he decided he must return to Darjeeling to organise and get stores. When he finally arrived there it took several days to hire one Gyanchen as his interpreter and cook.

Jacob again:

Raeburn left Darjeeling on 5 August and returned to Tibet via Gangtok and Lachen in the Teesta Valley. Ten days later he re-crossed the Serpo La and stayed for a day at Khampa Dzong, where he visited Kellas's grave. Now he was in unfamiliar territory but, fortunately, was assisted in route-finding by local guides provided by the village Headman. Raeburn had a copy of a sketchy map about which Howard-Bury wrote: 'The existing maps of the country were quite misleading and we could no longer depend on them. The rivers flowed in opposite directions to those shown on the map and mountains were shown where there were none.'

The exploration and survey of the northern approaches to Everest carried out by Wheeler, Mallory, Morsehead et al. have been fully described in other publications. However, a brief sketch of what Raeburn missed is in order here.

With Kellas dead and Raeburn out of the game, the mountaineering reconnaissance now fell to Mallory and Bullock, assisted by untrained porters. They explored the Rongbuk Valley and set up camp near the snout of the Rongbuk Glacier, from where they could investigate suitable approaches to the North Face of Everest. On 5 July they ascended a peak to the east of Kyachung-Kang (25,990ft), which they wished to name Mt Kellas.[4] The view from this mountain provided an overview of the area's complex geography. The following two weeks were spent gathering information about the glaciers and lower summits of the area and trying to form a mental picture of the geography of the ridges and faces of Everest. Mallory could see that the upper parts of the North Face were not impossibly steep and could be approached by the ridge leading from the North Col up to the north-east

---

4   It was subsequently given the Tibetan name, Ri-Ring.

shoulder. Access to the North Col was the key to the problem, but Mallory and Bullock failed to discover the significant East Rongbuk Glacier, which ultimately provided the solution.

Much of Mallory's effort had been aimed at getting into good positions to take photographs, and this involved long, arduous ascents of the surrounding ridges encumbered by the bulky photographic equipment of the day. Great was his chagrin, therefore, when he was informed by Howard-Bury that he had taken no photographs whatsoever because he had inserted the frames of the glass plates back-to-front, so that no light reached the plates when the shutter clicked. The error was due to his own technical incompetence, which manifested itself in many other ways, for example in his inability to deal with Primus stoves. However, in the two remaining days at that camp Mallory made heroic efforts to recover the situation by reascending ridges and retaking pictures.

Mallory and Bullock retreated to their base camp intending to investigate further, but monsoon storms and trouble with their Sirdar, whom Mallory, never short of a colourful phrase, dubbed 'a whey-faced treacherous knave', hampered their efforts. Apparently the Sirdar had been cheating the porters of their food.

Bullock and Mallory departed the north side of Everest at the end of July, around the time Raeburn was ending his long convalescence with Dr Dyer. Fortunately, Oliver Wheeler knew how to insert photographic plates and in the course of his photographic survey discovered the significance of the East Rongbuk Glacier, which proved to be the way to get to the North Col.[5]

Meanwhile, back at Kampa Dzong, Raeburn reckoned that the north-western reconnaissance of Everest would now be complete, and that the Expedition should be in the neighbourhood of Kharta, which was marked on his map. Of course, the maps were not accurate, and the Dzong Pen of Kampa Dzong had never heard of Kharta, but, in Raeburn's words: 'Some of his people had heard of Peruk (marked also on the old map). He stated, however, that he had word from his brother official at Shekar "that

---

5   In one way it might have been better if the discovery had not been made at that time as it led, indirectly, to the deaths of seven men in 1922, and indeed to the deaths of Mallory and Irvine in 1924. However, the discovery of the southern approach to Everest lay many years in the future, and depended on the co-operation of the Nepalese authorities, not granted in 1921.

the Expedition party had disappeared, he did not know where to".' To complicate matters further, 'The Tinki Dzong Pen had also stores and mails to forward [to the Expedition] but had no word as to where these were to go.' Raeburn says: 'I thought of taking on the mails, but thought better of it as any day runners from Col. Bury might arrive and the party might not, after all, be at Kharta or Peruk.'

The reason Raeburn gives for not taking on the mails seems perfectly adequate. He didn't know where the Expedition was, and they might be able to send runners to collect the letters much quicker than he could bring them. He also didn't know how long it would take him to find the Expedition. One wonders if he explained this properly to Howard-Bury and the others when he eventually caught up with them. The issue caused a lot of grumbling in various diaries and letters and has been used as a stick to beat Raeburn with. Of this more later.

Raeburn was advised by the Dzong Pen of Kampa Dzong to follow the trail to Shekar where he might cross the swollen Bhong Chu, but this meant going a long way round and he decided instead to try and save time by making for a bridge, said to be made of a few strands of twisted animal hide, near the junction of the Yaru and Arun Rivers. It was not one of his better decisions.

Thus, on 19 August, Raeburn and party crossed the Tinki La to Chussar where a large quantity of the Expedition's stores lay awaiting collection rather than being forwarded. Raeburn thought that this was due 'to the stupidity of the Shekar Dzong Pen'. Fortunately, he also met a couple of runners from the Expedition who had actually 'come from Kharta-Peruk by the bridge, which they described as bad and dangerous ... they had been right under water in crossing. If any more water came down the way would be impossible'. However, Raeburn, desperate to rejoin the Expedition, ignored the messengers' warning. 'It was so much nearer ... that I resolved ... to make an attempt to get over. From Chussar on 20 August my party crossed the plains here through which winds the Yaru ... but now was a sea of water and quicksands ... quite impossible.' In fact, the Expedition had traversed the same way in June, when the weather was dry, and even then the sluggish Bhong Chu was as much as 600 ft wide. Raeburn had to find another way of getting to the dangerous 'bridge'.

Resuming the trek in heavy storms, after many delays caused by understandable trouble hiring porters, Raeburn reached the town of Palè. More floods hindered his way and he made slow progress down a limestone gorge to examine the 'bridge' across the Yaru:

> On reaching the bridge nothing was visible except an old trunk of tree projecting out of the water about 10 yards from the shore ... From this hung a few strands of rope disappearing under water and no sign of connection with the other side. Crossing this raging leaping mass of chocolate-coloured waves was clearly impossible ... In deep disappointment I made the decision not to wait for the subsiding of the floods.[6]

Here, Raeburn had been only a day away from Kharta: so near and yet so far. He returned to Palè. Travelling north on 24 August, he finally managed to get his party across the Yaru at a place where it was 'only' three-and-a-half feet deep, and he was promptly benighted in sandhills east of Shillong. More high passes and river crossings were negotiated until, on 28 August, he reached Chumbab where he learned that the nearest way to Kharta was over yet another river, the Bhong, a crossing that was treacherous because of numerous channels and quicksands. Plainly there was some delay while Raeburn encouraged his followers:

> At last a party was persuaded. The men stripped naked and joined hands. I put the bulk of my clothes in a waterproof bag inside my rucksack, which I fastened on my shoulder. The crossing was most painful and hard from the cold water and wind and the heavy quicksands. It took me up to the shoulders and a small man up to the chin. Fortunately the water had not a swift current. On getting over I shivered for two hours.[7]

Raeburn too old and unfit to go on the Expedition? What nonsense. As Mike Jacob temperately remarks: 'This is another demonstration of Raeburn's remarkable determination, especially given his weakened state

---

[6] From a report produced by Raeburn for the Mount Everest Committee.
[7] Ibid.

after severe illness.' The following day was spent getting their baggage over the river, a task that took the efforts of 15 men, ropes and large copper vessels.

Raeburn's report continues:

On the 30th, Tsogo, a large village with many chortens and prayer wheels ... was left and the Gi La (about 17,000 ft) crossed to Te ... On the 31st one slants up hill to the south, [and] soon overlooks the Gadung Pa and the great bends of the Yaru. At the top one is on the Quiuk La (Cuckoo Pass) the barrier here flung across the river's path, forcing it to twist through the vast gorge behind Chomo Uri Peak [Cho Oyu]. The La is about 15,000 ft ... descending from the La it was necessary owing to the reported breaking of a bridge to descend into the valley of the Zacca, a tributary of the Yaru from the N ... we then spent the night at a farmstead and ... on 1 September I proceeded down the Yaru valley ... and then perceived a white tent ... this was the base camp ... at the mouth of the Kharta valley. I reached it in the afternoon and was able to greet again Col. Bury, Dr Wollaston, Major Morshead and Major Wheeler. The climbers [i.e. Mallory and Bullock] had started for the head of the valley the previous day and Dr Heron was away N on a geological expedition.

In his book, *Into the Silence*,[8] Wade Davis (2011) dramatises the re-entry of Raeburn into the Expedition. Apparently, Oliver Wheeler, on the afternoon of 1 September, had left his improvised darkroom and gone outside for a cigarette when, to quote Davis:

[S]uddenly he saw a short, ghostlike figure stumble toward their camp. To the utter surprise of all it was the irascible Scot, Harold Raeburn, whom they had not seen or heard from since Wollaston had left him in the care of Moravian nuns at Lachen in Sikkim on 12 June. At the age of fifty-six, he had walked across Tibet to rejoin the Expedition.

---

8   Davis does not give detailed references to all of the sources quoted in his book. One assumes that in the following passage he is paraphrasing Wheeler's Diary.

The passage is effective as storytelling, but it appears to be a mixture of source material and authorial opinion. Davis seems already to have swallowed Mallory's line on Raeburn as evidenced by the words 'irascible Scot', a term Wheeler was most unlikely to have used. Was Harold 'short'? Did he 'stumble'? Was he 'ghostlike'?

It seems the other members present were 'stunned' and 'gathered in the mess tent to hear the tale'. There follows what purports to be an account of Harold's illness, recovery and journey. Despite a lack of detail and some dubious passages, it is roughly what we already know. However, there is no mention of the missed opportunity to bring the mails or, crucially, of Harold's reason for not doing so.

Davis continues: 'In the official account, the return of Harold Raeburn, the titular leader of the climbing party, was cause for celebration. "We rejoiced," Mallory wrote, "to see [him] again." Private thoughts were less charitable. Howard-Bury, in a note to Francis Younghusband, said: "To our great surprise, Raeburn turned up yesterday after a three-month absence[9] ... He passed five bags of our mails near Tinki ... can you imagine anyone being such a fool!"' Bury evinced no sympathy for Raeburn's near-death experience, no delight at his survival and spoke no word of praise for his astounding journey back to the Expedition.

Worse than this, some days later, Mallory, in a letter to Geoffrey Young, wrote:

> *Raeburn turned up ... looking extraordinarily old and grizzled and being no less old than he looks. When he is not being a bore I feel moved to pity. But that's not often. He takes no part luckily ... Was he always such a very stupid man? It's impossible to understand how ever he can have got a party up a mountain.*

Readers of this book know a different story. One wonders if Mallory recalled his words when reflecting on his part in the decision which led to the deaths of seven men on the North Col the following year. Our own words often condemn us.

Davis (op. cit. p.340) also notes that 'Wollaston ... was appalled that

---

9   Two-and-a-half months.

[Raeburn] had returned. He felt that Raeburn was a serious liability to all, noting, "His internal trouble is at an end ... But he is definitely an old man, in mind as well as in body, and I very much wish he had not come, as there is nothing whatever for him to do ... He is become quite senile since his illness".' This comment from Dr Wollaston springs from a genuine concern for Raeburn and the Expedition members as a whole. However, two things should be noted: The first, far from taking no further part in the Expedition, Raeburn was with it to the end, reached a high camp, climbed a peak of some 21,000 ft and helped with the laborious business of evacuating the Expedition's stores and gear. He also made his own four-day reconnaissance of the Kama Valley and studied the southern aspect of Everest, writing a detailed report on what he observed. The other thing is the accusation of 'senility'. This surfaces again in a letter Mallory wrote to his wife in which he describes Raeburn as 'a senile, babbling, insignificant, almost broken and heart-breaking figure' (Davis, op. cit. p.346). It would certainly be no surprise if Raeburn looked exhausted and much older after all that had happened to him. But 'senility' implies impairment of mental function, and no evidence of this is offered.

Indeed, the detailed report Raeburn wrote for the Mount Everest Committee at the end of the Expedition shows no sign at all of mental incapacity, and on the very day after his reunion with the Expedition, Raeburn wrote to Arthur Hinks:

> *You would have news from other sources of the unfortunate death of Dr Kellas and of my serious illness, and being obliged to return to Gangtok and ... Darjeeling. Owing to the care and kindness received as a member of the Expedition from everyone ... I made a good if tardy recovery. Not being able to make arrangements for a travelling servant, provisions etc at Gangtok, I returned to Darjeeling. Here I equipped and left on the 5 August.*

Raeburn goes on to describe his journey until the day of his reunion with the Expedition. He had returned, he said:

> *[T]o find them practically isolated and without news for nearly two months. The rivers will fall at the end of September but the monsoon conditions, as I have always held, penetrate very thoroughly into this*

part of Tibet, up the Great Yaru-Arun Gap ... Mallory and Bullock, who have done splendid work in the hopelessly steep north-western region are up at a high camp where I hope to join them in a day or two, waiting and hoping for a break in the monsoon ... I learn with great interest and admiration that Mallory and Bullock have ascended a peak on the NW which they propose to call Mt Kellas [subsequently named Ri-Ring]. This is nearly 23,000 ft.[10]

Raeburn's perfectly coherent report concludes by praising the work of Kellas and noting that he visited Kellas's grave on his return journey.

As Mike Jacob comments:

Although written in a tent at 12,000 ft, and whilst recovering from his exertions, Raeburn's handwriting is perfectly legible, so Hinks had no reason for disregarding it. [Which, apparently, he did.] Raeburn manifestly acknowledged his obligations to his benefactors and paid tribute to the work of other team members. There is no hint of disparagement or criticism of anyone, despite his less-than-overwhelming welcome.

To extend to Mallory a fairness he denied to Raeburn, there is a passage in an earlier letter to Ruth in which a different picture of Raeburn emerges:

I had a friendly little walk with Raeburn before we left Darjeeling and rather played up to his desire to give advice, so we got on very nicely. He has some very nice qualities and he has a good deal of fatherliness and kindliness, but his total lack of calm and of sense of humour at the same time is most unfortunate.[11]

Raeburn's 'fatherliness and kindliness' are of course demonstrated by his helping new members of the SMC find their feet, and the way in which he took a benevolent interest in the emerging LSCC. It is also important to acknowledge his extreme modesty: he never sought to glorify himself or

---

10   Raeburn's letter to Arthur Hinks can be found in the Alpine Club Archive.
11   From Mallory's Letter Collection, Magdalene College, Cambridge.

his own achievements. Although the outstanding climber in the SMC, and apparently a good public speaker, he turned down the Presidency. In all his known writings there is not a nasty word about anybody. His courage and determination speak for themselves, and his love of nature and literature are admirable.

But the second part of Mallory's sentence is disputable. In all Raeburn's recorded climbing there is no evidence of lack of calm, indeed, quite the opposite. And Raeburn certainly had a sense of humour, albeit dry and understated. One wonders if Mallory ever read any of Raeburn's articles. They were both members of the Alpine Club and Raeburn contributed several articles to its *Journal*.

In a letter to Hinks, Howard-Bury says: 'Raeburn has become very old and is a great responsibility. We do not want a second heart failure and like all Scotch, he is very obstinate.' Bury, as leader of the Expedition, felt the loss of Alexander Kellas keenly and probably had a sense of guilt over it: if he had taken more notice of Kellas's condition and sent him down from Phari for treatment, he might have been saved. Naturally he felt responsibility for Raeburn, but if he had paused to reflect on the exceedingly arduous journey Raeburn had undertaken to rejoin the Expedition he would have seen that it was very unlikely that Raeburn's heart would give out. Yes, Raeburn was obstinate, no, not all 'Scotch' are obstinate, but Raeburn's obstinacy was one of his virtues—he didn't give up easily.

It must have been difficult for Raeburn, perhaps during the whole Expedition, but certainly on his return to it, to be a member of a group of which he was not the acknowledged leader. Throughout almost his whole career Harold had become accustomed to leading any party of which he was a member. Having to accept Howard-Bury's decisions—even about trivial things like the amount of sugar the Expedition should take—must have grated with him; it was something he wasn't used to. Although he was not egoistic, returning to the Expedition to find that his place as Climbing Leader had been taken by Mallory must have been a further blow to his self-esteem. Moreover, there was no clearly defined role for him to fulfil. He had expended a vast amount of energy to get back to an expedition which no longer really needed him: it was no doubt disorientating and, combined with the awkward atmosphere, clearly revealed in diaries and letters, he must have felt rather useless and the odd man out.

36. EVEREST RECONNAISSANCE EXPEDITION—PART 3   1921

The Mount Everest Committee Secretary, Arthur Hinks, wrote:

It will take some time to disband the party, sort out the stores and settle up the accounts, so that the members who are returning to England will hardly arrive before the middle of December ... They have, however, been warned that they are expected to give an account of themselves at a meeting of this Society and the Alpine Club.[1]

As Mike Jacob notes, it sounds as if Hinks was 'referring to a bunch of teenage merry-makers who had been out for a night on the tiles'.

Raeburn arrived in Plymouth on Saturday, 26 November and then accompanied the Expedition's collections of photographs and natural history specimens to London. His return to Britain was reported in *The Times*, which said: 'He declined to make any statement, the members of the party being bound down not to say anything. He stated that the first lecture will be given at Queen's Hall, London on 20 December.' In London, Raeburn was invited to meet both Hinks and Francis Younghusband.

The Mount Everest Committee had got what it wanted from the Expedition. A feasible way to the summit of Everest had been found and partially reconnoitred. As Jacob remarks, 'it was obvious that Mallory was the driving force behind the success of the mountaineering reconnaissance', although it was not he but Oliver Wheeler who discovered the all-important East Rongbuk approach to the North Col. Youth, it seemed, was more

---

[1] Hinks's letters are available at Box 12, File 1, EA, Royal Geographical Society.

important than experience or technical skill, though Mallory had plenty of the latter. As things transpired it was not quite so obvious that experience and sound judgment should be disregarded, but that was for the future. For Harold Raeburn the Expedition was a disaster, and the aftermath was fraught with sore vexations.

Raeburn returned to Edinburgh where he stayed with his sisters at Barnton Terrace in the west of the city. He was being harassed by Hinks on two counts: first, Hinks had written reminding him that he was not permitted to deliver any lecture about Everest until after Mallory's lecture tour on behalf of the Committee. It is not known why Hinks did this; perhaps he was just being characteristically officious, or perhaps Raeburn had been asked to give a talk in Edinburgh. All members of the Expedition had had to sign a strict undertaking barring them from publishing any material or communicating with the press, because Hinks was determined to retain control over publicity and, perhaps even more important, over finances, especially with the prospect of another expedition soon. If Raeburn had remained healthy on the Expedition, the lecture tour would primarily have been conducted by him as the Climbing Leader, but Mallory had superseded him in that role and thus as the lecturer also.

In the event, Mallory's two months of lectures went well and he was given a 25% share of the profits, earning him more in two months than a year's pay as a school-master at Charterhouse. The tour also cemented his reputation and allowed him to give his own version of events. Mallory was a person of integrity and probably did not seek to undermine Raeburn's position, but equally he held no brief for him and, for the most part, omitted him from the tale.

Perhaps Raeburn queried the generous terms given to Mallory—it does seem odd that one member of the Expedition should be financially rewarded for recounting an adventure in which all took part. However this may be, it seems that Hinks thought Raeburn was being 'awkward' about the lecture tour, and he allowed this slur to continue. Even in recent times, in a 1970 review in the *Geographical Journal*, Raeburn was described as 'a nuisance to those planning the lectures'. Jacob says, 'Where this notion comes from, if not Hinks, no-one seems to know.' The Committee had chosen Raeburn as Climbing Leader and then failed to show support for him, despite his undaunted efforts on its behalf. Norman Collie, President of the Alpine Club from 1920 to 1922, and JP Farrar, a former President, had both championed Raeburn initially, with good reason, but perhaps felt that they had made the wrong choice and chose to remain silent.

Not only was Raeburn removed from the lecturing position, but he was also passed over for any form of authorship of the inevitable Expedition book. As Climbing Leader he should by rights have had a say in that as well. Both would have brought financial rewards and, perhaps more importantly, prestige. But Hinks knew there was to be another expedition in 1922. Although he sneered at Mallory behind his back, calling him 'Master Mallory', he needed to keep him sweet for the future. Raeburn was yesterday's man and could be hung out to dry.

Hinks also niggled Raeburn with the petty accusation that he had not obtained a discount from the P&O Shipping Company for the cost of his boat ticket home on the *SS Delta*, and he hounded Raeburn for re-payment.

In the meantime, Raeburn was in London for the Alpine Club's noteworthy Winter Dinner, which was held in the King's Hall of the Holborn Restaurant on Tuesday, 13 December. The guest list included Howard-Bury, DSO, and Arthur Hinks, CBE, FRS. Raeburn cannot have been comfortable seeing these two being fêted by the members of his own club. If there was any conversation between him and Hinks it must have been strained, to say the least.

Raeburn seems to have remained in London until 20 December, when Howard-Bury, 'very much the toast of the town, was received at Buckingham Palace' before heading for the Queen's Hall, where the Alpine Club and the Royal Geographical Society united to welcome the team officially. Team members were supposed to speak on various aspects of the Expedition; Bury and Mallory went on at such length that Raeburn was given just half an hour, and Wollaston was excluded altogether. *The Scotsman* at least reported that 'appreciation was expressed at the work of Mr Raeburn'.

When Harold got back to Edinburgh he found a letter from Hinks, dated 16 December, continuing the demand for the payment of the shipping discounts. It seems that the collapse of Harold's health can be dated almost precisely to this period, for he had by now asked his friend, the lawyer George Sang, who was also Secretary of the SMC, to attend to the matter for him. This shows just how far Raeburn was alienated from the Committee's 'terrier-like' Secretary.

From his office in Forres Street, Edinburgh, Sang sent Hinks a peremptory letter dated 21 December: 'Mr Raeburn has handed to me your letter ... He is at present taking a rest cure under doctor's orders and is unable to attend to correspondence.' He continued by quoting from P&O: 'regret no rebate can be allowed [for] members [of] Everest Expedition. Rebate allowed was 25% off single tickets outward or 15% off return tickets [for] up to 6 members'. Hinks should have checked his facts. Sang delivered the *coup de grâce* with masterful underplay: 'Raeburn, you may be aware, went out by another line [the City Line]'. Raeburn obviously was not entitled to any discount; Hinks, desperately trying to recoup small sums of money, had blundered.

Harold's physician, the good Dr Ronaldson, no doubt considered that his patient required professional nursing care and Harold, run-down and in low spirits, agreed to move to a nursing home run by a Miss Cochrane at Highfield in leafy Colinton, not far from his old school. Despondent and dwelling on what might have been, he was starting to suffer from his old enemy, depression.

In early January 1922, Francis Younghusband visited him in Edinburgh, though sympathy was not the motive. Younghusband wanted Raeburn to write a detailed statement recording his recognition and appreciation of all the help he had received when recuperating in India. One suspects that this had to do with placating the Indian and Tibetan authorities to smooth the way for the 1922 Expedition, which was now being planned. In fact, Raeburn was extremely grateful for the help he had received and had acknowledged this in letters to both Hinks and Younghusband himself. It may well have seemed to Harold that the implication of this fresh, irritating request was that he was in some undefined way letting the side down. It seems that the members of the Committee did not think it was up to them to issue statements of gratitude, but rather up to a member of the Expedition to do so.

However, despite his poor state of health, Harold wrote out, yet again, all he had previously said, and shamefully none of this material was included in the official Expedition book, which was largely authored by Howard-Bury. Ironically, Mallory complained about the book in a letter to Ruth: 'There is not a word of appreciation of anyone's work or qualities—nothing that gives the feeling that the author liked any one of the party in the whole 180 pages whereas ... there are quite a number of remarks quite gratuitously pointing to their weaknesses.' Mallory acknowledges that Howard-Bury has been fair to him personally, but concludes, 'I don't like sharing a book with this sort of man.'

Significantly, the covering letter Raeburn sent with his 'appreciation' was addressed to both Hinks and John Eaton, joint Secretary of the Committee, hinting at his belated realisation of Hinks's devious and untrustworthy nature. Raeburn had done his utmost physically to play his part in the Expedition and had repeatedly shown his gratitude to those who had helped him. It was not his fault if Hinks and the Committee either failed to disseminate this information or spitefully suppressed it. The aftermath of the 1921 Everest Expedition, which should have been the high point of Raeburn's illustrious career, brought him only disappointment and alienation. Sadly, worse was to follow.

37. ILLNESS AND DECLINE   1922-26

Towards the end of January 1922 Raeburn's condition deteriorated. Dr Ronaldson reported that his patient: 'looks very depressed. He said that everything was hopeless. He told me that he heard voices which told him to do evil and wrong. He said there was a conspiracy against him.' Harold's depression became so severe that on Sunday, 5 February he 'threw himself on the road in front of a taxi-cab in a deliberate attempt to commit suicide'. He was taken to a nursing home at 93 Comiston Drive, and 'during his first night there he got out of bed, seized a poker and attempted to smash in the vault of his skull. Fortunately he only managed to raise a few weals'.

Raeburn was examined by two doctors: Dr Ronaldson, who wrote 'he said he was possessed by a demon', and Dr Duncan, who reported that:

> [H]e says that he has committed a great many secret sins during the past few years and that a visitation of God has come upon him. This takes the form of emanations of smells of wild beasts, lion's dens, dung etc. from his mind. He also states that voices told him to commit suicide in order that his funds might not be incriminated in his sins. He confesses therefore to have attempted suicide by throwing himself in front of a motor car.

Suicide was illegal then, so the doctors had no alternative but to transfer Harold to Craig House mental asylum, also located in the Colinton district of Edinburgh.

For its time, Craig House was a model of enlightenment, providing humane and sympathetic treatment for patients suffering from Nervous and Mental Disorders, and Raeburn could not have been in better surroundings. On 8 February 1922 he was given a full medical examination. Physically he was described as 'well-built, muscularly very well developed, with grey/blue eyes and grey hair, bald on top'. He was 5 ft 10 in and 9 st 10 lbs. This was some 10–11 lbs less than his usual weight, and it is surprising that in the 'fatness' category he was described as 'well covered'. Importantly there was no evidence of physical injury or disease, thus eliminating the idea that he might have been suffering from an illness such as tuberculosis.

In order to try to understand Harold's condition the doctors at Craig House interviewed his siblings at length and compiled a case history, using longhand to write their notes in a large, heavy book:

Mr Raeburn had an attack of melancholia [depression] about ten years ago and was treated at home.[1] *Last year he was a member of the Expedition which set out from this country to climb Mount Everest. Before setting out Mr Raeburn was described as being somewhat above himself, full of energy and enthusiasm and not nearly so reserved as was his wont. About the same time he published a book on climbing, which is said to be one of the recognised authorities on the subject. As an indication of the tireless energy which characterised him at this time it may be noted that the [manuscript] of the book was lost and the fruit of several years' labour seemed to have been lost with it. After communicating with his publishers, however, Mr Raeburn undertook to re-write the book, a task which he accomplished within three months. Eventually the book was published at the right time. What he regarded as the crowning point of his whole career was his selection as a leader of the climbing party in the Mount Everest Expedition. All seems to have gone well with him till the party reached the bays [base/base camp?] of Everest. There Mr Raeburn and another well-known climber both suffered ptomaine poisoning, and while the other succumbed Mr Raeburn eventually became well enough to be invalided home to this country. Naturally he was very crestfallen owing to the collapse of*

---

[1] This certainly fits with other evidence for there was a period in 1911–12 when Raeburn hardly climbed at all in Scotland and missed two Alpine seasons.

his ambition, and though he made a good physical recovery from the ptomaine poisoning his friends were conscious that he was somewhat depressed and that he needed a prolonged rest.[2]

The case history then describes Raeburn's attempted suicide and admission to Craig House before giving his State on Admission:

On admission, [the] patient was profoundly depressed and rather agitated. He regarded his condition as a just retribution for secret sins, of which he had been guilty. What these sins were he could not be induced to say. He explained that he had thrown himself in front of the taxi-cab in obedience to a voice which kept telling him that the wrongs he had done could only be expiated by his death. He again heard the voice in the nursing home prompting him to smash his skull. He believed that his brain was decaying and that foul smells resembling [that] of wild beasts were emanating therefrom. His whole outlook was utterly hopeless. He added that he had been sleeping badly for a considerable time and that interference with his sense of smell had destroyed his appetite, so that he took no pleasure in his food.

A few days later, on 17 February, progress notes state that:

Mr Raeburn remains very seriously depressed and still believes that nothing but his death can solve his difficulties. He is not now so harassed by the voices though occasionally they try to induce him to do away with himself. The hallucinations of smell [have] disappeared. Some days he is quite mute and he afterwards explains that by speaking he is only incriminating himself further. With the help

---

2   The account suffers from the usual ignorance of mountaineering by some involved: the Expedition was not going to climb Mt Everest, it was a reconnaissance. Also, Raeburn, as we know, was not 'invalided home': far from it. The account insists that he was suffering from ptomaine poisoning, i.e. food poisoning, but it could well have been amoebic dysentery. In the whole account one hears a well-meaning Scottish family not wishing to state Harold's case too dramatically: 'rather above himself', 'somewhat depressed', etc.

of 3drs [drachms] of paraldehyde³ he gets on the average about 6½ hours sleep. Since the hallucinations of smell disappeared his appetite has improved.

Within the limitations then existing, the doctors at Craig House relied on personal attention, patience, kindness, an investigative spirit, and the careful use of sedatives combined with psychotherapy to achieve recovery rates of 20-25% of the admissions. Ward rounds were made twice a day with an abbreviated late round about midnight to visit restless or sleepless patients. They could have hoped, therefore, to see a long-term improvement in Harold's health, although older, melancholic patients were always difficult to nurse back to full health.

On 28 February 1922:

Mr Raeburn is still very depressed and has strong suicidal inclinations ... he appears generally to be a case of Anxious Melancholia. He seldom speaks except to give monosyllabic replies to questions. He is frequently very restive, especially when in his 'panicky' moods. He has occasionally had fleeting delusions of a persecutory character, such as that his bed was a live electric plate, but these have never shown any tendency to be systematised and have never lasted long. His physical condition has improved under treatment in the open air.

One wonders what this open-air treatment consisted of. The Pentland Hills can be seen from Craig House, and this might momentarily have encouraged him.

On 14 March:

Mr Raeburn has become more composed and has had fewer outbursts of anxiety. At the same time he remains depressed and still has well-marked suicidal inclinations which necessitate constant supervision. He now sleeps better and with the help of 1dr. Paraldehyde will often

---

3   A potent anti-convulsive drug capable of controlling seizures. It has a sedative effect and was probably used to counter Raeburn's acute anxiety attacks. Unfortunately it imparts a foul pervasive smell to those using it. Production seems to have been discontinued in the USA.

sleep for eight hours. He has had one or two quite lucid days when he appeared to be perfectly well.

This looks a promising window of opportunity, but the notes continue:

These periods of enlightenment have come on quite suddenly and have disappeared as suddenly ... It would appear as if many of Mr Raeburn's difficulties are of a sexual character, as he has repeatedly requested that his condition be relieved by an incapacitating operation [i.e. castration].

We know nothing of Harold's sexual life. It was typical of conventional Victorian morality to have a disapproving attitude towards sex, especially outwith matrimony, and this attitude probably affected his relationships with women. There is ample evidence that he was interested in and enjoyed the company of women. Clearly he also enjoyed the company of men, but there is no evidence that he was homosexual, which was illegal at that time. One guesses that whatever Harold's 'sins' were, they were a great deal less sinful than his tormented imagination fancied. But this, of course, is conjecture.

Raeburn's weight increased to a more normal 10½ stone. But news of his misfortune had percolated to the wider world, and reached fellow Everest expeditioner, Henry Morshead, on the 1922 Everest attempt. During the walk-in, he wrote to his wife: 'Did you hear that old Raeburn has been off his head since his return to England last autumn? He is apparently under the delusion that he murdered Kellas!' The medical notes do reveal that Raeburn was tormented by feelings of guilt and quite possibly some of these did relate to the death of Kellas. As we know, at one stage he had persuaded Kellas, at Phari, that he was too weak to go any further. At that time Raeburn was the Climbing Leader. He had a right to be listened to. But Howard-Bury persuaded Kellas that it was better to continue. With the benefit of hindsight, Raeburn may have been right, but in his tortured mind he perhaps felt that he was responsible for his friend's death by his failure to protect him and, as Mike Jacob says, 'this may have translated itself into the notion of murder'. It is only in Howard-Bury's private diary that Raeburn's 'gloomy forebodings' become apparent, and as Jacob notes: 'Howard-Bury carefully omits any mention of the incident in the Expedition book.'

On 21 September 1922:

There is absolutely no change in Mr Raeburn's condition. He sits all day in a corner of the veranda in the hospital with his head slightly retracted, his eyes closed and remains absolutely silent. It is generally impossible to get him to reply to any question, and as for obtaining his signature to some documents recently forwarded to him the thing is out of the question ... It is with difficulty that he takes his food and has sometimes to be tube fed. On the whole his condition is very unsatisfactory.

Jacob says:

In the 21st century, this reference to force-feeding may seem barbaric ... but the medical staff had little choice. Refusal of food was typically symptomatic of severe melancholia and the doctors could only hope for recovery, as sometimes happened. This state of affairs continued into 1923. Harold's brother, John, died at the start of the year and Harold's state of health continued as a cause of anxiety for his remaining family. He often refused food, necessitating more tube feeding, and was quite silent apart from a curious noise resembling a cough, and he had to be supported whenever he got out of bed as he refused to straighten himself when he walked.[4]

In 1924, while another Everest Expedition was being prepared, Harold's remaining siblings, Florence, Edith, Ethel, Norman and Ruth, decided that it was time to petition the Lords of Council and Session that his sister, Ruth, be appointed as Curator Bonis, to act on his behalf on the grounds that he was 'a person of unsound mind and unfit to manage his affairs or to give directions for their management'. This was granted in January. At this time Raeburn's financial holdings were valued at about £1,300 (about £65,000 in 2023). He owned a property at 2 Advocates' Close, valued at £140, but most of his money, over £1,000, was invested in Exchequer Bonds.

On 17 March Harold's notes state that 'he lies in bed all day with his

4   *From Edinburgh to Everest*, an unpublished manuscript by Mike Jacob.

eyes shut and gets out of his own accord to go to the bathroom. As he does this he trots all the way bent almost double'. He was still being tube fed and his physical condition, surprisingly, was noted as 'remarkably good'. But he never spoke, except to shout Murder! Murder! Murder! at feeding times.

Ruth Raeburn had to be asked for permission for the doctors to give Harold a general anaesthetic to treat a severe inflammation of the right eye, as he violently resisted any attempt at treatment. Naturally, Ruth readily agreed. As Jacob comments: 'Mental patients generally co-operated in taking food and medicines prescribed for their well-being and showed gratitude for whatever was done for them, so Harold's steadfast refusals of help were not typical.' But, having a very strong will, he seldom changed course when once he had decided on a certain plan of action. Now he seemed bent on self-destruction.

Jacob again:

> On 8 June 1924 George Mallory and Andrew Irvine disappeared on Everest on their brave summit attempt, an event that became instant news around the world … Meanwhile another less dramatic tragedy was being played out in a leafy area of Edinburgh, where Raeburn's weight now fluctuated around the 8-stone mark.

Yet another year went by. His condition was unchanged; there was only one medical note recorded, in March, and it is apparent that the doctors had no further ideas about how to treat this most intractable of cases. Given his general demeanour and refusal of food, it is remarkable that Harold's overall physical condition was not much worse and that he remained alive for as long as he did.

It was over another year before the next note was recorded, in April 1926. Raeburn's physical condition was deteriorating and his weight had fallen to 7 stone. By this time, he had been moved to West House, a wing of the hospital with much more basic facilities. This may indicate that his funds were running low. Although West House was south-facing and attractive, patients were segregated in single-story wings. The wards were large units and all categories of patients were forced to live together, a source of great distress to many of them and to their visitors.

A final note was registered in the book on 21 December 1926:

For some time now Mr Raeburn has been in a very weak state. He has shown marked signs of endocrine disturbance and yesterday had a definite syncopal[5] attack. He recovered from this with treatment. He had another similar attack later on from which he also revived, but in the early hours of the morning a third attack proved fatal.

Died December 21st 1926. Age 60 years [in fact 61]. Causes of death: 1. Exhaustion from Melancholia. 2. Endocrine Insufficiency.

His death was certified by Dr McAlister and notified by his sister Ethel. The Death Certificate described him as a brewer (retired) and single. He had made a will in 1920, prior to his Kangchenjunga trip, in which he bequeathed all his heritable property in equal measure to any surviving brothers and sisters. His brother, Norman, had died in Mexico earlier in the year, so Florence, Edith, Ethel and Ruth inherited. In addition (intriguingly), he left £50 to Violet Binns, daughter of Alfred H Binns of Ingleby Close, Barwick Stockton-on-Tees, but it is not known how she had featured in Harold's life. His estate, which had fallen to a value of £450 (about £25,000 in 2023), was managed jointly by Ruth and George Sang. Obituaries written by Sang and Willie Ling appeared in various mountaineering club journals and in *The Scotsman*.

There seems to be no reason to dissent from Dr McAlister's opinion that one of the causes of Raeburn's death was exhaustion produced by a very prolonged period of 'melancholia' or depression. It is, of course, not the depression itself which is fatal but its physical effects, in this case, effectively self-starvation. The second cause of death avouched on the certificate, Endocrine Insufficiency, is too technical to be discussed here and the question is further complicated by uncertainty as to the medical knowledge at that time.

Harold was buried on 23 December 1926 in Warriston Cemetery in the Goldenacre district of north Edinburgh, two days after his death. The family monument is a mural, reasonably well preserved, and the inscriptions are legible. It is fitting to quote Mike Jacob's words:

It may seem a world away from the lonely moorland and rough, rocky mountains that he loved, but in its own way, it seems an appropriate

---

5   A loss of consciousness due to a cessation of blood reaching the brain.

destination ... Would Harold Raeburn, the young iconoclast who started his mountaineering life on remote and exposed cliffs in solitary pursuit of birds' eggs and nest photography ... not have smiled at this final irony ... that the forlorn nature of the cemetery today provides an ideal habitat for Tawny Owls, Sparrow-hawks and other urban wildlife?

In the mid-1990s, John Fowler, then Secretary of the SMC, went looking for Raeburn's grave. He said:

Many of Edinburgh's graveyards are in an appalling condition—a perfect example of the wrong sort of property being in private hands ... As graveyards became full and the popularity of cremation increased, profits dwindled and graveyards were abandoned to their fate. Inevitably, vandalism has since become rife.

As Fowler recounts, it was only after an expedition with a machete that he discovered Harold's grave 'in a hellishly desecrated corner' (*SMCJ*, 1997).

Raeburn's beloved club, the SMC, has done what it can to honour his name. In 1988 Ken Crocket, then *SMCJ* Editor, suggested that the new Club Hut between Dalwhinnie and Laggan should be named in Raeburn's honour, and in the living room of the hut are memorial photographs and information about his life. Raeburn's ice-axe is also ceremonially passed from President to President as part of the insignia of office.

EPILOGUE

Harold Raeburn's mountaineering record speaks for itself, and it is fitting at this stage to quote Robin Campbell's (*SMCJ*, 2021) considered assessment:

> Raeburn, so far as Scotland is concerned, was the greatest mountaineer of his age, perhaps of any age. But his determined efforts in Norway, the Alps, the Caucasus, and the Himalaya show him to have been a master of all forms of mountaineering.

Perhaps, among his contemporaries, Valentine Ryan and Geoffrey Young achieved more in the Alps:

> But they did it with guides ... and did not stray much beyond the Mont Blanc ranges and the great peaks of the Pennine Alps, whereas Raeburn employed no guide after 1902, climbed in every major Alpine range except the Mischabel and, of course, moved on to the Greater Ranges.

Campbell also mentions Raeburn's friend, Alexander Kellas, as a possible rival, and certainly, 'His record in the Himalaya ... especially in Sikkim, was extraordinary.' But Kellas 'did not seek out difficulty ... and his Alpine experience was limited'. Campbell concludes that Raeburn's record stands up well to comparison with any of these.

However, the man himself retains much of his mystery. His friend and climbing companion, Sandy (Lord) Mackay, writing in 1950 (*SMCJ*, 1950), described him as 'Physically and mentally hard as nails ... certain, unyielding and concise in every movement, both mental and physical.' Enough has been said about Raeburn's strength and climbing style, but Mackay also comments that 'In his mental get-up Raeburn was as sure of himself as he was in physical habit.' If one was arguing with him about routes or times required, 'he was a stern opponent'. Mackay also comments on his 'complete self-confidence', which 'made Raeburn assume or accept the lead on almost every occasion. Something, I sometimes thought, of Stalin[1] was in his make-up'. But, despite returning in argument again and again to his 'original assertions', Mackay thinks 'he was ultimately fair in debate'.

Mackay also relates a surprising anecdote in which Harold, returning from a climb on Arran, sat down and said that he wouldn't go another inch unless his friend, Harry Lawson, would go a bit slower. Lawson would not agree, so Harold said, 'Just go on, I'll wait.' Mackay and Lawson eventually got to the 'square of light before the door of Corrie Inn' and looked round 'casually', wondering where Raeburn had got to. There he was, 'on the edge of the same square of light from the inn door'. He was, in a quiet way, a proud man, unwilling to admit that he was anyone's inferior.

Determined, proud, self-reliant, intelligent, well-organised: all these adjectives apply to Raeburn. Particularly later in life, he seems to have had fatherly traits, something attested to by George Mallory, whose general opinion of Raeburn was unfavourable. This kindliness towards the younger generation is also spoken of by the Rev Ronald Burn, who, as a beginner, spent a couple of days climbing with Raeburn at New Year in 1918. Raeburn took him to a gully on Stùc a' Chroin and gave the young Burn a chance to cut steps and lead parts of the climb. At the end of this little holiday, Burn was moved to say: 'Raeburn, so kind and good—a man "who can walk and talk as us", despite his Caucasus fame ... I don't think I realise myself how good a time I've had.'[2] In fact, throughout his climbing career Raeburn took new members of the SMC out and climbed with them, and his kindly and positive attitude towards emergent women climbers has also been noted.

It seems that Raeburn had no difficulty in making friendly relationships with both sexes. As so many do, he developed particularly strong

---

1   In 1950 the reference to Stalin would imply only that Raeburn was very tough-minded and determined.
2   This comes from a piece put together by Iain Smart entitled 'Lest We Forget', *Forget'* (*SMCJ*, 1990). The line of doggerel quoted by Burn comes from the speech made by Geoffrey Young in honour of Raeburn at an SMC Dinner and noted earlier.

relationships with those he chose as his habitual companions, people like Willie Ling, Willie Douglas, Frank Goggs, Harry Lawson, William and Jane Clark and Sandy Mackay. There are few better ways of getting to know what someone is really like than going on the hill with them, and it was rare for someone to climb with Harold only once. He was safe and trustworthy, but he must also have been a considerate and agreeable companion in the mountains. In the minor key, he seems to have liked his food,[3] and the occasional bottle of sparkling Bouvier is mentioned as a little celebration at the end of at least two successful Alpine ascents.[4] He did not smoke, but seems to have had quite a sweet tooth. On the hill he liked jam sandwiches and the occasional acid drop.

It is not known why Raeburn never married or even whether he ever had an intimate relationship with a woman. In particular, we do not know whether he was in love with Natalia Yovitchitch or she with him.

There is little doubt that after the, for him, calamitous aftermath of the Everest Expedition, Harold plunged into a deep depression. The medical reports of the time record this in great detail.[5] As Robin Campbell has claimed, it is possible that some physical ailment was overlooked,[6] but the evidence suggests otherwise. Dr Dyer, the Civil Surgeon who treated Harold in India, Dr Wollaston on the Expedition, and the doctors at Craig House in Edinburgh all asserted that 'his digestive troubles are at an end' and that physically, he was in a surprisingly good condition. Thus we are left with the conclusion that Harold died of self-starvation caused by deep clinical depression.

It is worth asking whether this was the culmination of a pattern of events that had beset Raeburn since he was a young man. He had been treated at home for 'melancholia' in 1911 and missed two Alpine seasons in 1911–12. He seems to have done very little on Scottish or Lakeland hills in that period. There is mention, in *The Scotsman* obituary, of some injury he suffered, but there are no details. Mental illness was stigmatised at the time, and it is

---

3   It makes his long hunger-strike against a cruel world all the more poignant.
4   After the traverse of the Drus and the North Face of Monte Disgrazia.
5   Mike Jacob even went so far as to get a modern mental health expert to look at the reports and his professional opinion backed them up.
6   '… his psychiatric symptoms of suicidal depression may have distracted his doctors from dealing with his general physical condition', according to Robin Campbell (*SMCJ*, 2021).

possible that this 'injury' was a fiction put about by his friends.

It is perhaps of interest that Harold's life seemed also to consist of periods of tireless activity. One of these followed his appointment as Mountaineering Leader of the Everest Expedition; he appeared, in the words of his sisters, 'to be above himself' and to be much more talkative and forthcoming 'than was his wont'. Much earlier in his life, a similar state of mind can be sensed in the remarkable article he wrote after soloing Observatory Buttress on Ben Nevis (see Chapter 8). It is certainly true that some of Raeburn's other articles contain writing which is exuberant and artistic—his descriptive powers are excellent—but this article is crammed with expressions of joyous feelings and sensations. Raeburn can hardly concentrate on one subject for more than a few sentences together: he flits about like a butterfly from one topic to the next and at one point has to remind himself that he is supposed to be writing a serious description of a climb. He discusses anything but that: loosening his clothes, birdsong, the sunlight, his recent sailing adventures, the prospect of afternoon tea on the summit! It is a remarkable piece of writing, all the more so for its time, when mountaineering articles tended to be rather staid affairs.

The day before the climb, Raeburn had been enjoying his other passion, sailing, and had been very late getting back to the shore because he had been becalmed. With only a couple of hours rest he caught the early morning train to Fort William and stormed off up the Ben. One might expect him to have been exhausted by all this, but Raeburn was stimulated by it. In the end he virtually flies up Observatory Buttress and all he says in the entire article about the climb is 'I went up'!

Indeed, at times Harold seems possessed of abnormal amounts of energy. He climbed Tower Ridge, North-East Buttress[7] and Crowberry Gully in winter in just four days, cycling between Fort William and Glencoe in between. And this when he was well into middle age. We know he was extremely fit and determined, but some of his exploits display superabundant vitality.[8]

Given his distinguished record it is puzzling why Harold did not accept the Presidency of the SMC when it was offered to him. Perhaps, as Ling said

---

7   Up and down from Fort William on each occasion.
8   In view of Raeburn's periods of depression and euphoria, it may occur to readers to wonder if he suffered from bipolar disorder (manic depression). There is not, however, sufficient evidence to decide the matter.

in his obituary (SMCJ, 1927), modesty stopped him from doing so, though that did not stop him from accepting the job of Climbing Leader on the Everest Expedition. Harold was well organised, a good public speaker, and he valued the SMC highly. It might be that when he was offered the Presidency he was suffering depression or feared its onset, but this is conjecture.

Robin Campbell has already placed Raeburn on the European stage. In Scotland, mountaineering history has, to some extent, overlooked the fact that Harold Raeburn's achievements in the Edwardian era were no less impressive for their time than those of WH Murray, Robin Smith, Tom Patey, Dougal Haston, Jimmy Marshall or Hamish MacInnes in their respective periods, and Raeburn had far less sophisticated equipment. He deserves to be mentioned in the same breath as any of these great climbers, and it is appropriate to think of them as standing on his shoulders. Raeburn was not only an outstanding climber, he can also justly be called the Father of Scottish Mountaineering.

Epilogue

ACKNOWLEDGEMENTS

My most outstanding and obvious debts of gratitude are to Mike Jacob and Robin Campbell, whose research into the life of Harold Raeburn stimulated my interest. I had hoped that they would combine to complete a biography. When that did not happen, I took up the challenge. Mike supplied the Lakes chapter, and material about Raeburn's early life, ornithological interests, Everest adventure and untimely death. Robin gave me an electronic copy of Ling's Diary, an essential document, and took time out of other work to read chapters on the Caucasus and the Alps, saving me from many errors and adding his own valuable insights. He also provided many photographs.

Ken Crocket presented me with both volumes of *Mountaineering in Scotland*, which I reference copiously. David Stone, the SMC's Custodian of Images, visited me in Torridon and showed me the club's extensive archive of historic photos relevant to Raeburn, many of which he subsequently cleaned and supplied. Tom Prentice read early chapters on the Cobbler, Beinn an Lochain and Arran and provided invaluable information and diagrams. Noel Williams supplied many photographs of Scotland, some of which he made special trips to obtain, and maps and information about Norway and the Dauphiné. Geoff Cohen read chapters on the Alps and gave me the benefit of his vast experience and knowledge of French. Greg Strange read parts of my chapters on the Cairngorms and helped where my knowledge failed. Julian Lines made a special trip to photograph the Shelter Stone. Chris Bartle of Glacier Books selflessly looked out and photocopied articles by Raeburn and Ling in the Alpine Club Journal. Roger Robb twice accompanied me to Coire Ardair to get photos of Creag Meagaidh, supplied photos of other Scottish hills, making a special trip to Coire Lair, and provided photos and knowledge of the Alps. Peter Macdonald supplied valuable Alpine photos. Dave Broadhead and Thomas Priestley supplied modern photos of the Caucasus. Alison Higham, Archivist of the Ladies Scottish Climbing Club, supplied photos of Raeburn's involvement with that club and valuable information about Natalia Yovitchitch. Kenny Brookman supplied photos of La Meije. Barry Hard supplied a panorama from Skagastølstind's summit. Gordon 'Curly' Ross provided a photo of Neil J Barlow's painting of Lochnagar. Neil Adams supplied photos of Garbh Bheinn. Raymond Simpson supplied photos of the Matterhorn. Grahame Nicoll sent photos of the Aiguille Noire de Peuterey. Henning Wackerhage provided a photograph of the Post Face of Creag Meagaidh. I am indebted to John Cleare, who supplied excellent photos of the Alps and the Himalayas and information and clarification about Raeburn's routes and journeyings. My old friend Phil Gribbon was constantly encouraging. Mick Tighe supplied a photo by Alex Gillespie of Raeburn's altimeter. Thanks, too, to the Alpine Club, the Fell & Rock Climbing Club, the National Gallery of Scotland and the Scottish Mountaineering Club Image Archive for photographic material.

Warmest thanks to Simon Richardson for writing the foreword and supplying photos. Editor Deziree Wilson has a keen sense of how a story should 'flow'; she put up with my eccentricities with admirable patience and remained cheerful throughout. The Boss, Rob Lovell, was always there in the background to lend a hand and keep the show on the road. I am also very grateful to the Editor of the *Scottish Mountaineering Club Journal*, Graeme Morrison, for much help and encouragement and especially for his kind offer to compile the index. Ken Mackinlay provided technical help with matters photographic; both he and Mike Dixon provided enthusiastic encouragement.

I would also like to acknowledge the support I received from my son Richard, always an interested spectator, and the tolerance of a writer's absent-mindedness shown by my wife Angela during our long marriage; her pointed observations on my purple passages saved me from much self-indulgence.

To all the above, and anyone I have forgotten, a big 'Thank You!'

Peter J Biggar

Bibliography and References

Introduction

Raeburn, H., 1920. *Mountaineering Art*. London, T. Fisher Unwin Ltd, p.125.

Crocket, K., 1988. 'Raeburn's First Climb'. *Scottish Mountaineering Club Journal* (*SMCJ*), vol.34, no.179, pp.29–34.

Scottish Mountaineering Club (SMC)., 2004. *Guide to the Northern Highlands North*. Scottish Mountaineering Trust (SMT), ed. A Nisbet, p.442.

Raeburn, H., 1891. *The Zoologist*, pp.126–135.

Jacob, M., 2018. 'Figures on Ice'. SMCJ, vol.46, no.209, p.78.

Chapter 1

Raeburn, H. Application Form to SMC. SMC Archive.

Raeburn, H., 1895. Letter to William Douglas. Douglas Letters, vol.4, letter 15, SMC Archive in the National Library of Scotland.

Thomson, G., 1896. 'New Year Meet 1896—Tyndrum' from Proceedings of the Club. *SMCJ*, vol.4, no.20, pp.126–128.

Douglas, W., 1896. 'The Tower Ridge Pinnacle—Ben Nevis' from Excursions. *SMCJ*, vol.4, no.21, pp.172–173.

Tough, W., 1896. 'Corrie Arder'. *SMCJ*, vol.4, no.21, pp.141–148.

Raeburn, H., 1897. 'The Cobbler' from Excursions. *SMCJ*, vol.4, no.22, pp.248–249.

Prentice, T., 2022. Email correspondence.

Crocket, K., 2015. *Mountaineering in Scotland—The Early Years*. SMT.

Raeburn, H., 1897. 'Ben Nevis in November' from Excursions. *SMCJ*, vol.4, no.22, pp.244–246.

Chapter 2

Raeburn, H. Douglas Letters, vol.4, letter 65, SMC Archive in the National Library of Scotland.

'Proceedings of the Club'. *SMCJ*, 1897, vol.4, no.22, p.241.

Raeburn, H., 1897. 'Arthur's Seat and the Salisbury Crags'. *SMCJ*, vol.4, no.24, pp.335–341.

Munro, H., 1897. 'Loch Awe Meet, New Year 1897'. *SMCJ*, vol.4, no.23, pp.284–287.

Lodge, PR., 1897. 'Yachting Meet, Easter 1897'. *SMCJ*, vol.4, no.23, pp.288–293.

Raeburn, H., 1897. 'Askival and Allival, Island of Rum'. *SMCJ*, vol.4, no.23, pp.301–302.

Douglas, W., 1897. 'Mountaineering with Cycles'. *SMCJ*, vol.4, no.23, pp.279–283.

Bell, JH., 1897. 'Ladhar Bheinn, Saturday,

17th April 1897' from Excursions. *SMCJ*, vol.4, no.23, pp.299-300.

SMC., 2007. 'Raeburn's Gully 240m grade III*' from *Guide to the Northern Highlands South*. SMT, ed. by A Nisbet et al., p.38.

Brown, W., 1897. 'Ladhar Bheinn, 18th April'. *SMCJ*, vol.4, no.23, p.300.

Smith, W., 1897. 'Stuc a' Chroin (3,189 feet), "Hill of the Cloven Hoof"' from Excursions. *SMCJ*, vol.4, no.23, pp.296-298.

Thow, I., 2017. *Highland Scrambles South*. SMT, pp.361-362.

Raeburn, H., 1898. 'Ben Nevis' from Excursions. *SMCJ*, vol.5, no.25, p.41.

Crocket, K., 2015. *Mountaineering in Scotland—The Early Years*. SMT.

Chapter 3

Raeburn, H., 1898. 'A Wet Day in Glencoe' *SMCJ*, vol.5, no.25, pp.24-28.

Raeburn, H., 1898. 'Two Climbs on the Tarmachans'. *SMCJ*, vol.5, no.26, pp.70-76.

Crocket, K., 1997. *Arran, Arrochar and the Southern Highlands*. SMT, ed. G Little et al., p.236.

Munro, H., 1898. 'The Easter Meet—Ballachullish'. *SMCJ*, vol.5, no.26, p.80-81.

Bell, JH., 1898. 'Buachaille Etive Mor' from Excursions. *SMCJ*, vol.5, no.26, p.89-90.

Raeburn, H., 1898. 'The Cobbler—Central Buttress and South Peak'. *SMCJ*, vol.5, no.27, pp.141-143.

Bell, JH., 1898. 'The "Church Door" Buttress of Bidean nam Bian'. *SMCJ*, vol.5, no.27, pp.135-140.

Taylor, I., 2014. 'The History of Climbing on Church Door Buttress'. *SMCJ*, vol.43, no.205, pp.17-24.

Clark, WI., 1898. 'A Day on Cir Mhor'. *SMCJ*, vol.5, no.25, pp.29-36.

Brown, W., 1898. 'Climbing in Skye' from Correspondence. *SMCJ*, vol.5, no.26, pp.82-86.

Chapter 4

Bennet Gibbs, G., 1899. 'August at Sligachan' *SMCJ*, vol.5, no.28, pp.164-175.

Raeburn, H., 1899. 'The Storr Rock (2,3600 feet) and the Old Man of Storr' from Excursions. *SMCJ*, vol.5, no.28, pp.200-201.

Raeburn, H., 1899. 'The Castle—Ben Nevis' from Excursions. *SMCJ*, vol.5, no.28. pp.198-200.

Raeburn, H., 1899. 'A November Evening on Lochnagar'. *SMCJ*, vol.5, no.28, pp.176-181.

Crocket, K., 2015. *Mountaineering in Scotland—The Early Years*. SMT, p.184.

Raeburn, H., 1899. 'The Narnain Caves' from Excursions. *SMCJ*, vol.5, no.28, pp.200.

Borthwick, A., 1939. *Always a Little Further*. Faber.

Raeburn, H., 1902. 'The Maiden Rock, St Andrews' from Excursions. *SMCJ*, vol.7, no.37, pp.48-49.

Chapter 5

Mackay, AM., (1900). 'The Northern Pinnacles of Liathach'. *SMCJ*, vol.6, no.33, pp.87-90.

Gribbon, P., 2018. 'Craig Lug Lost in Translation'. *SMCJ*, vol.46, no.209, pp.104-108.

Raeburn, H., 1901. 'The Black Shoot—In White'. *SMCJ*, vol.6, no.35, pp.161-171.

Raeburn, H., 1901. 'Ben Nevis—The Observatory Gully' from Excursions. *SMCJ*, vol.6, no.35, pp.251-252.

Hinxman, L., 1901. 'The Easter Meet at Fort William 4th-9th April'. *SMCJ*, vol.6, no.35, p.210.

Ling, W., 1901. 'A Blizzard on Ben Nevis' from Excursions. *SMCJ*, vol.6, no.36, pp.249-250.

Crocket, K., 2015. *Mountaineering in Scotland*

—*The Early Years*. SMT, p.196.

Chapter 6

Raeburn, H., 1901. 'The Observatory Ridge, Ben Nevis'. *SMCJ*, vol.6, no.36, pp.213–217.

Clark, W., 1901. 'Stormy June Days in Skye and on Ben Nevis', *SMCJ*, vol.6, no.36, pp.218–230.

Newsroom, The., 2017. 'The hotel that once stood on the summit of Ben Nevis'. *The Scotsman*.

Duncan, G., 1901. 'An Eight Hours' Day in a Lochnagar Gully', *SMCJ*, vol.6, no.36, pp.231–234.

Chapter 7

Raeburn, H., 1902. 'Arran' from Excursions. *SMCJ*, vol.7, no.38, pp.113–115.

SMC., 1997. *Arran, Arrochar and the Southern Highlands*. SMT, ed. G Little et al., p.115.

King W, Mackay A, and Raeburn H., 1902. 'Sgoran Dubh'. *SMCJ*, vol.7, no.39, pp.117–123.

Lawson, HGS., 1902. 'Sgòran Dubh Pinnacle'. *SMCJ*, vol.7, no.38, pp.57–60.

Almond, HH., 1893. 'Ben-Y-Gloe on Christmas Day'. *SMCJ*, vol.2, no.5, pp.235–245.

Mackay, A., 1902. 'June 21: Again on Sgoran Dubh, Fourth Buttress' from Excursions. *SMCJ*, vol.7, no.39, pp.17–179.

Chapter 8

Raeburn, H., 1903. 'From Sea to Summit'. *SMCJ*, vol.7, no.40, pp.194–198.

Clark, Wl., 1903. 'New Climbs on Ben Nevis'. *SMCJ*, vol.7, no.40, pp.199–211.

Goggs, F., 1903. 'A Salvationist on Lochnagar'. *SMCJ*, vol.7, no.40, pp.185–193.

Strange, G. Email correspondence.

SMC., 1985. *Climber's Guide to the Cairngorms*. SMT, ed. A Fyffe et al., p.64.

Chapter 9

Penney, SM., 1902. 'Beinn Buidhe'. *SMCJ*, vol.7, no.39, pp.124–129.

Crocket, K., (1989). *Arran and Arrochar*. SMT.

Raeburn, H., 1903. 'Ben an Lochain (The Old Man): Climbs on North Face' from Excursions. *SMCJ*, vol.7, no.40, pp.242–243.

Walker, H., 1903. 'A Winter Climb on Creag na Caillich' from Excursions. *SMCJ*, vol.7, no.42, pp.365–366.

SMC., 2021. *Scottish Winter Climbs West*. SMT, p.90.

Smith, WC., 1903. 'Sligachan Meet—Easter, 1903'. *SMCJ*, vol.7, no.41, pp.282–283.

Ling, W., 1903. 'Sligachan to Glen Brittle by the Dubh Ridges'. *SMCJ*, vol.7, no.42, pp.301–303.

Clark, Wl., 1903. 'The Motor in Mountaineering—A Visit to Buachaille Etive Mor'. *SMCJ*, vol.7, no.42, pp.313–322.

Abraham, AP., 1902. 'Glencoe' from Excursions. *SMCJ*, vol.7, no.38, pp.110–111.

SMC., 2005. *Scottish Rock Climbs*. SMT, ed. A Nisbet et al., p.80.

Chapter 10

Raeburn, H., 1904. 'The Cliffs of Corrie Arder'. *SMCJ*, vol.8, no.43, pp.4–11.

Collie, N., 1894. 'Divine Mysteries of the Oromaniacal Quest'. *SMCJ*, vol.3, no.15, pp.151–157.

Crocket, K., 2015. *Mountaineering in Scotland—The Early Years*. SMT, p.218.

Raeburn, H., 1904. 'Ben Nevis' from Excursions'. *SMCJ*, vol.8, no.43, p.86.

Bell, JH., 1904. 'Thirty-second Meet of the Club, Fort-William, New Year 1904' from Proceedings of the Club. *SMCJ*, vol.8, no.44, p.100.

Douglas, W., 1904. 'Ben Lui Revisited'. *SMCJ*, vol.8, no.44, pp.95–99.

Chapter 11

Campbell, DS., 1904. From 'Proceedings of the Club'. *SMCJ*, vol.8, no.44, pp.115–116.

Clark, W., 1904. 'Thirty-third Meet of the Club, Aviemore, Easter, 1904'. *SMCJ*, vol.8, no.44, pp.110–115.

Raeburn, H., 1905. 'Sgurr Ruadh and Coire Lair' from Excursions. *SMCJ*, vol.8, no.46, pp. 221-223.

Hinxman, L., 1895. 'Strathcarron as a Climbing Centre'. *SMCJ*, vol.3, no.16, p.218.

SMC., 2007. *Guide to the Northern Highlands South*. SMT, ed. by A Nisbet et al., p.123.

MacPhee, G., 1954. *Climbers' Guide to Ben Nevis*. SMC, p.31.

Clark, Jl., 1904. 'Three on the Centre Grid of the Trident Buttress of Ben Nevis'. *SMCJ*, vol.8, no.45, p.149. [First female article in the SMCJ.]

SMC., 2007. *Scottish Winter Climbs*. SMT, ed. A Nisbet et al., p.154.

Clark, Wl., 1904. 'Garbh-Bheinn of Ardgour and the North-East Ridge of Aonach Beag'. *SMCJ*, vol.8, no.45, pp.142-148.

1905. 'Thirty-fifth Meet of the Club, Easter 1905'. *SMCJ*, vol.8, no.47, p.251.

Chapter 12

Naismith, W., 'Wastdale Head'. *SMCJ*, vol.4, no.21, pp.174-175.

Raeburn, H.,1898. 'Wastdale at Christmas' from Excursions. *SMCJ*, vol.5, no.26, p.87.

Raeburn, H., 1901. 'Two Days in Cumberland'. *SMCJ*, vol.6, no.34, pp.132-133.

Ling, W. Diary, Book 2, p.59.

Ling, W. Diary, Book 5, p.11-12.

Ling, W. Diary, Book 7, p.37.

Raeburn, H., 1910. From the Fell and Rock Climbing Club Journal, p.114.

Raeburn, H. Notebook. SMC Archive, acc. 11538/122, National Library of Scotland.

Perrin, J., 1993. Menlove. p.147.

Champernowne, D., 1959. 'Arthur Cecil Pigou (1877-1959)'. *Journal of the Royal Statistical Society*, Series A (General), vol.122, no.2, pp.263-265.

Ling, W. Diary, Book 12, pp.66-77.

Raeburn, H., 1920. Letter to Godfrey Solly, 9 February. Raeburn Archive, acc. 11538/122, National Library of Scotland.

Barker, MM., 1932-1934. *Pinnacle Club Journal*. No. 5.

Chapter 13

Raeburn, H., 1905. 'Scottish Snow'. *SMCJ*, vol.8, no.48, pp.285-298.

Naismith, W., 1893. 'Snowcraft in Scotland'. *SMCJ*, vol.2, no.4, pp.157-167.

Wilson, C., 1893. *Mountaineering*. G Bell.

Dent, C., 1892. *Mountaineering*. Longman's Green: London, Badminton volume.

Wilson, JDB., 1949. *District Guide to the Southern Highlands*. SMT, p.80.

Douglas, W., 1894. 'Ben More, Perthshire, in Bad Weather' from Notes and Queries. *SMCJ*, vol.3, no.14, pp.106-107.

Thomson, G., 1895. 'Beinn and Dothaidh and Beinn Dooireann'. *SMCJ*, vol.3, no.13, p.79.

Campbell, F., 1895. 'Inveroran Meet. Easter, 1894' from Proceedings of the Club. *SMCJ*, vol.3, no.13, pp.97-102.

Rickmers, WR., 1904. 'Aquatic Sport on Ben Nevis'. *SMCJ*, vol.8, no.45, pp.157-165.

Scully, TV., 'Snowdon at Christmas'. *SMCJ*, vol.3, no.14, pp.58-64.

Chapter 14

Clark, Wl., 1905. 'The Mystery of Crois'. *SMCJ*, vol.8, no.48, pp.309-312.

Raeburn, H., 1906. 'Cobbler, North Peak' from Excursions'. *SMCJ*, vol.9, no.49, p.54.

Crocket, K., 2015. *Mountaineering in Scotland—The Early Years*. SMT, p.228.

Raeburn, H., 'Ridge Walking on the Coolins at Easter, 1905'. *SMCJ*, vol.9, no.50, pp.59–70.

Williams, N., 2023. Email correspondence.

Raeburn, H., 1906. 'Skye—The Castles from Harta Corrie' from Excursions. *SMCJ*, vol.9, no.50, pp.101–102.

Chapter 15

Raeburn, H., 1906. 'The "Chasm", Buachaille Etive Mor' from Excursions. *SMCJ*, vol.9, no.51, pp.149–151.

Campbell, Robin N., 2006. '100 Years Ago'. *SMCJ*, vol.39, no.197, pp.402– 403.

Murray, WH., 1949. Rock *Climbing Guide to Glencoe and Ardgour*, SMC, p.150.

SMC., 2005. *Scottish Rock Climbs*. SMT, ed. A Nisbet et al, p.80.

Parker, JA., 1907. 'Buachaille Etive' from Excursions. *SMCJ*, vol.9, no.52, p.224.

SMC., 1979. *Climbers' Guide to Ben Nevis*. Ed. JR Marshall.

Raeburn, H., 1907. 'A Scottish Ice Climb'. *SMCJ*, vol.9, no.52, pp.153–158.

Campbell, RN., 1972. 'The First Scottish Ice Climbers'. *SMCJ*, vol.30, no.163, p.57.

Chapter 16

Goggs, F., 1906. 'A Climb on the Coire Arder Cliffs'. *SMCJ*, vol.9, no.51, pp.118–125.

Campbell, RN., 2006. '100 Years Ago'. *SMCJ*, vol.39, no.197, pp.401.

Chapter 17

M'Intyre, HA., 1907. 'Thirty-eighth Meet of the Club—New Year 1907, Corrie, Arran' from Proceedings of the Club. *SMCJ*, vol.9, no.53, pp252–254.

Herbert Boys., 1907. 'Thirty-ninth Meet of the Club. Easter 1907. Ichnadamph, Sutherland' from Proceedings of the Club. *SMCJ*, vol.9, no.53, pp.254–258.

Crocket, K., 2015. *Mountaineering in Scotland—The Early Years*. SMT, p.256.

Mackay, S., 1928. 'Sail Garbh: Its Barrel Buttress'. *SMCJ*, vol.18, no.106, pp.207–213.

SMC, 2004. *Guide to the Northern Highlands North*. SMT, ed. A Nisbet.

Clark, W., 1909. 'The Cliffs of Stob Coire an Lochan'. *SMCJ*, vol.10, no.59, pp.240–245.

SMC., 2008. *Scottish Winter Climbs*. SMT, ed. A Nisbet et al.

Pescod, M., 2010. *Winter Climbs Ben Nevis and Glencoe*. Cicerone.

Chapter 18

Raeburn, H., 1908. 'A Cairngorm Climb'. *SMCJ*, vol.10, no.55, pp.6–12.

Campbell, RN., 2007. '100 Years Ago: The Club in 1907'. *SMCJ*, pp.631–633.

Clark, Cl., 1908. 'Thirty Hours on Ben Nevis'. *SMCJ*, vol.10, no.56, pp.73–81.

Crocket, K., 2015. *Mountaineering in Scotland—The Early Years*. SMT, pp.281–286.

Raeburn, H., 1908. 'Garbhvein of Ardgour—Descent of North-East Buttress' from Excursions. *SMCJ*, vol.10, no.56, pp.123–124.

'Forty-first meeting of the Club—Easter, 1908. Braemar' from Proceedings of the Club. *SMCJ*, vol.10, no.57, pp.146–151.

Raeburn, H., 1909. 'The North Buttress, Carn Dearg of Nevis'. *SMCJ*, vol.10, no.58, pp.183–189.

Chapter 19

Smith, AD., 1909. 'Forty-second Meeting of the Club, New Year, 1909.

Killin.' from Proceedings of the Club. *SMCJ*, vol.10, no.59, pp.258–261.

Clark, MI., 1909. Entry from Excursions. *SMCJ*, vol.10, no.59, pp.270–271.

Campbell, RN., 2009. 'Some Old New Routes'. *SMCJ*, vol.40, no.200, pp.490–491.

Levack, J., 1909. 'Forty-third Meet of the Club, Easter 1909. Fort William' from Proceedings of the Club. *SMCJ*, vol.10, no.60, pp.335–342.

Raeburn, H., 1911. 'The Crowberry North Gully, Buachaille Etive'. *SMCJ*, vol.11, no.65, pp.255–262.

Ling, W. Diary, Book 8, p.87. Alpine Club Archives.

Raeburn, H., 1910. Letter to Geoffrey Winthrop Young, 13 April. Alpine Club Archives. Quoted by K Crocket in *Mountaineering in Scotland—The Early Years* (2015, SMT, p.307).

Chapter 20

Bell, JH., 1911. 'A Wintry Midsummer's Day on Nevis'. *SMCJ*, vol.11, no.64, pp.216–221.

Raeburn, H., 1912. 'Ben Nevis—Coire na Ciste—An Easy Way Out' from Excursions. *SMCJ*, vol.12, no.67, p.54.

Raeburn, H., 1913. 'Arran—Cir Mhor B1-B2 Rib' from Excursions. *SMCJ*, vol.12, no.70, p.236.

Raeburn, H., 1912. 'The Brack. The Elephant Gully'. *SMCJ*, vol.12, no.70, pp.209–214.

Wordie, J., 1913. 'The Brack: "Elephant Gully"' from Excursions and Notes. *SMCJ*, vol.12, no.71, p.294.

Raeburn, H., 1913. Review of Seton Gordon's The Charm of the Hills (1912). *SMJC*, vol.12, no.70, pp.246–248.

Raeburn, H., 1914. 'Skye' from Excursions. *SMCJ*, vol.13, no.73, pp.58–59.

'The Fifty-third Meet of the Club—Easter 1914. Fort William' from Proceedings of the Club. *SMCJ*, 1915, vol.13, no.74, pp.111–113.

Reid, WA., 1915. 'The S.M.C. in Clover Again'. *SMCJ*, vol.13, no.78, pp.337–340.

'Proceedings of the Club'. *SMCJ*, 1916, vol.14, no.79, pp.33–39.

Chapter 21

'New Expeditions in Norway in 1900.' *SMCJ*, 1901, vol.6, no.34, p.127.

'S.M.C Abroad in 1902' from Excursions. *SMCJ*, 1902, vol.7, no.37, p.40.

Raeburn, H., 1904-1905. 'Slogen. A day on the Seaward Face'. *The Yorkshire Ramblers' Club Journal* 2/6, pp.134–40.

Chapter 22

Douglas, W., 1905. 'S.M.C. Abroad in 1904' from Excursions. *SMCJ*, vol.8, no.46, pp.216–219.

Ling, W. Diary, Book 5, p.34–38.

Ling, W. Diary, Book 6, p.11–14.

Raeburn, H., 1920. *Mountaineering Art*. London, T. Fisher Unwin Ltd, p.32.

RN Campbell, 2021. *SMCJ*, vol.49, no.212, p.25.

Chapter 23

Ling, W. Diary, Book 6.

Ling, W., 1908. 'S.M.C. Abroad in 1908' from Excursions. *SMCJ*, vol.10, no.58, pp.219–220.

Ling, W. Diary, Book 7, pp.41–69.

Collomb, RG., 1975. *Guide to the Central Pennine Alps*. Alpine Club.

Campbell, RN., 2021. 'Harold Raeburn—His Pilgrimages Abroad'. *SMCJ*, vol.49, no.212, p.26.

Chapter 24

'S.M.C. Abroad in 1909' from Excursions and Notes. *SMCJ*, 1910, no.11, no.61, p.51.

Campbell, RN., 2021. 'A Master at Eton. See Croydon's Weekly Standard 14 August 1909, for Details'. *SMCJ*, vol.49, no.212, p.27.

Ling, W. Diary, Book 8, p.29.

Collomb, RG., 1987. *Pennine Alps Central*. Alpine Club.

Crocket, K., 2015. *Mountaineering in Scotland—The Early Years*. SMT, p.309.

Ling, W. Diary, Book 8, pp.21–50.

Chapter 25

Raeburn, R., 1937. Natalia Yovitchitch. *Ladies' Scottish Climbing Club Journal*.

Raeburn, H., 1911. 'The Disgrazia by the N. Face'. *Alpine Journal*, pp.691–699.

Ling, W. Diary, Book 8, p.84.

Ling, W. Diary, Book 9, pp.1–9.

Raeburn, H., 1911. 'S.M.C. Abroad in 1910'. *SMCJ*, vol.11, no.64, pp.238–239.

Raeburn, H., 1910. 'The Alps in 1910' from Notebook. SMC Archive, acc. 11538/122, National Library of Scotland.

Ling, W., 1927. 'In Memorium: Harold Raeburn'. *SMCJ*, vol.18, no.103, pp.26–31.

Sang, G., 1926. 'Harold Raeburn Obituary'. *Fell and Rock Climbers' Club Journal*, pp.300–302.

Ling, W., 1914. 'Some New Climbs in the Caucasus'. *Alpine Journal*, 204, p.132.

'S.M.C. Abroad: Caucasus' from Excursions and Notes. *SMCJ*, 1914, vol.13, no.73. pp.47–48.

Raeburn, H., 1915. 'The Adai Khokh Group, Central Caucasus'. *Geographical Journal*, 45, 3, pp.181–199.

Campbell, RN., 2013. 'The Caucasus Expedition of 1913'. *SMCJ*, vol.42, no.204, pp.353–361.

Raeburn, H. Diary.

Chapter 26

Campbell, RN., 2021. 'Harold Raeburn— His Pilgrimages Abroad'. *SMCJ*, vol.49, no.212, p.357.

Ling, W. Diary, Book 11.

Bell, JHB., 1955. 'Attempt on Ushba (From the unpublished diaries of Harold Raeburn)'. *SMCJ*, vol.25, no.146, pp.315–32.

Irving, RLG., 1940. *Ten Great Mountains*. J. M. Dent & Sons, London.

Campbell, RN., 2023. Email correspondence.

Raeburn, H., 1914. 'S.M.C. Abroad in 1913: Caucacus' from Excursions and Notes. *SMCJ*, vol.13, no.73, pp.48–49.

Campbell, RN, 2014. '100 Years Ago: The Club in 1914'. *SMCJ*, p.259.

Chapter 28

Raeburn, H., 1915. 'Caucasus' from Excursions and Notes. *SMCJ*, vol.13, no.76, pp.227–229.

Mitchell, J., 2000. 'Harold Raeburn's Journey Home'. *SMCJ*, p.308.

Raeburn, H., 1915. 'The Adai Khokh Group, Central Caucasus'. *Geographical Journal*, 45, 3, pp.181–199.

Raeburn, H., 1915. 'In the Caucasus—1914'. *Alpine Journal*, 29/208, pp.142–158.

Chapter 29

Mitchell, J., 'Harold Raeburn's Journey Home'. *SMCJ*, vol.38, no.191, pp.298–309.

Chapter 30

Raeburn, H., 1920. 'The Western Arête of the Meije'. *Alpine Journal*, pp.215–24.

Chapter 31

Goggs, F., 1920. 'Ben Nevis: Observatory Ridge'. *SMCJ*, vol.15, no.90, pp.310–318.

Chapter 32

Raeburn, H., 1920. *Mountaineering Art*. London, T. Fisher Unwin Ltd, p.125.

Naismith, W., 1920. 'Mountaineering Art by

Harold Raeburn' from Mountaineering Literature. *SMCJ*, vol.16, no.90, pp.346–348.

Chapter 33

Raeburn, H., 1921. *Alpine Journal*, vol.34, p.33–50.

Tilman, H., 1946. *When Men and Mountains Meet*. Reprinted in *The Seven Mountain Travel Books*, Diadem, 1983 p.312.

Raeburn, H., 1921. From Excursions and Notes. *SMCJ*, vol.16, no.92, p.96.

Campbell, RN., 2021. 'Harold Raeburn— His Pilgrimages Abroad', *SMCJ*, p.34.

Chapter 34

Raeburn, H., 1921. Letter to Francis Younghusband. Box 2, Everest Archive, Royal Geographical Society.

Ronaldson, DR AM., 1921. Letter to Harold Raeburn, 28 February. Box 2, Everest Archive, Royal Geographical Society.

Unsworth, W., 2000. *Everest: The Mountaineering History*. London: Baton Wicks, 3rd edition, pp.36–42.

Wollaston, A., 1933. *Letters and Diaries of A.F.R. Wollaston*. Cambridge University Press, ed. M Wollaston.

Howard-Bury, C., 1922. *Mount Everest Reconnaissance 1921*. London: Edward Arnold & Co.

Howard-Bury, C. *The Everest Diaries of Charles Howard-Bury*. National Library of Scotland.

Mallory, G., 1921. Letter to Winthrop Young. *Mallory's Letter Collection*, The Library of Magdalene College, Cambridge.

Chapter 35

Wollaston, A., 1933. *Letters and Diaries of A.F.R. Wollaston*. Cambridge University Press, ed. M Wollaston.

Davis, W., 2011. *Into the Silence: The Great War, Mallory and the Conquest of Everest*. London: The Bodley Head.

Raeburn, H., 1921. Letter to Arthur Hinks. Alpine Club Archive.

Mallory, G., 1921. Letter to Ruth 1921. *Mallory's Letter Collection*, The Library of Magdalene College, Cambridge.

Chapter 36

Hinks, A. Hinks's Letters. Box 12, File 1, Everest Archive, Royal Geographical Society.

Chapter 37

Jacob, M. Edinburgh to *Everest: The Life and Climbs of Harold Raeburn, 1865–1926* (unpublished manuscript).

Ling, W., 1927. 'In Memorium: Harold Raeburn'. *SMCJ*, vol.18, no.103, pp.26–31.

Fowler, J., 1997. 'Of Beer and Boats'. *SMCJ*, vol.36, no.188, pp.380–383.

Epilogue

Campbell, RN., 2021. 'Harold Raeburn—His Pilgrimages Abroad'. *SMCJ*, vol.49, no.212, pp.35–37.

Mackay, S., 1950. 'Vignettes of Earlier Climbers'. *SMCJ*, vol.24, no.141, pp.174–176.

Smart, I., 1990. 'Lest We Forget'. *SMCJ*, vol.34, no.181, pp.400–402.

Ling, W., 1927. 'In Memorium: Harold Raeburn'. *SMCJ*, vol.18, no.103, pp.26–31.

Index

Bold: image
fn: footnote

A' Chìr, 29
Adams, NGF, 451
Aiguille d'Argentière, 7, 263
Aiguille de l'M, 263, 286
Aiguille du Chardonnet, 280
Aiguille du Géant, 244
Aiguille du Grépon, 286, 287, **290**, 291
Aiguille du Midi, 286
Aiguille Noire de Peuterey, 257, **258**
Aiguille Verte, 286, **288**
Almond, George, 128
Alps, European, [see also entries by mountain name]
   Bernese Oberland, 264-265
   Bernina, 309-311
   Bregaglia, 301-309
   Dauphiné, 256, 259, 270, 378ff
   Dolomites, 244
   Graian Alps, 271ff
   Mont Blanc range, 257, 259-263, 275ff, 280ff, 286-289
   Pennine Alps, 264ff, 277ff, 289-296
   Tarantaise, 256
An Caisteal (Cuillin), Central Buttress, 176
Aonach Beag, North-East Ridge, 133, **134**
Arran, 29, 94, 200, 232
Arthur, David, 217
Azov, Sea of, 367

Barker, Mabel, 158
Barre des Écrins, **253**, 259
Bartle, C, 450
Basteir Tooth, 68
Beardmore, William, & Co, 238
Bec de l'Invergnan, 274
Beinn a' Bhùird, 217
Beinn a' Chliabhain (Arran), 94
Beinn an Dothaidh, 224
Beinn an Lochain (Arrochar), 110, **112**
Beinn Eunaich, Black Shoot, 47, 80-82
Beinn Narnain, **164**
Bell, James HB, 59, 186
Bell, John H, 50-53, 59, 61-64, 148, 214, 223, 226, 230
Ben Cruachan, 47
Ben Lomond, 29
Ben Lui (Laoigh), 30, 125
Ben Narnain, 74, **75**
Ben Nevis, **42**
   Castle Ridge, 38, 237
   Central Gully of Trident Buttress, 132
   Douglas Boulder, 30-33, 224, 384
   Gardyloo Gully, 40, 82-83
   Green Gully, 6, 187-194, **188**
   hotel at summit, **88**, 89, 230
   No 2 Gully, 232
   No 3 Gully, 39

   North Trident Buttress, 124
   North-East Buttress, 54, 70, 90, 224, 231, 237
   observatory at summit, 40, 70, 124
   Observatory Buttress, 83-84, 102-103
   Observatory Ridge, 86-89, 217, 311, **386**
      first winter ascent, 7, 384-388
   Raeburn's 18-Minute Route, 123
   Raeburn's Arête, 103, **107**
   Raeburn's Buttress, 217-220, **219**
   Raeburn's Easy Route, 232
   The Castle, 68-70, **69**, 214
   The Comb, 187, 194
   Tower Ridge, 54, 125, 224, 230, 382
   Zero Gully, 385
Ben Vorlich (Perthshire), 28
Berg, Ole, 247
Bernina, Piz, **308**, 311
Berthau, Thérèse, 247fn, 252, 254, 286
Bidean nam Bian, Church Door Buttress, 56, 61-64, 63
Biggar, PJ, 7
Black Shoot (Beinn Eunaich), 47, 80-82

boots & clothing, 55, 271fn
Bouquetins, Les, 298
Boyd, Herbert, 50-53, 62-64, 98, 200, 222-223
Brack, The, Elephant Gully, 233-235
Braeriach, 217
brewing & Raeburn Brewery, 16, 17, 144, 197, 367, 441
Brigg, JJ, 180
Brigg, WA, 180, 224, 277
Broadhead, DJ, 451
Brookman, K, 451
Brown, William, 30, 38, 50-53
  disputes Raeburn's opinion of Skye, 64-65
  Buachaille Etive Mòr
    Crowberry Gully, 7, 59-60, 224
    Crowberry Ridge, 114-115
    North Buttress, 186
    The Chasm, 117, 184-185
Bullock, Guy, 395, **407**, 411
Burn, AR, praises Raeburn, 445
Burns, James, 125

Caisteal Abhail (Arran), 29
Camasunary, 176
Campbell, Miss CM, 286
Campbell, RN, 8, 10, 194, 212, 224fn, 319fn, 350, 403, 444, 450
  The First Scottish Ice Climbers, 8, 187fn
Caucasus, 314ff, 330ff, 354ff
  Adai (Uilpata), 355
  Chanchakhi, 318, **322**, 324, **325**, **326**
  Elbrus, 350, 353
  Karagom, 358, 359
  Laboda, 360, 361
  Mamison Khokh, 318fn, 320, 322
  Nuamkuam, 330-334, 332, 335
  Tsaya Aiguilles, 317
  Tur Khokh, 317
  Ullargh Khokh, 317

Ushba, 338-348, **339**, **346**
Charmoz, Grand, 263, **291**
Charmoz, Petit, 262, 286
Cìr Mhòr, 29, 95-96, 232
Clark, Charles Inglis, 55, 90, 125, 132, 176, 179, 181, **182**, 213, 234
Clark, Jane Inglis, **88**, 89, 103, 114-117, **115**, 125, 234, 244, 446
Clark, Mabel Inglis, 90, 110, 132fn, 132, 207, 222, **225**, 234, **383**
Clark, William Inglis, 55, 61, 64, **88**, 89, 103, 110, 114-117, 125, 182, 244, 446
Cleare, J, 451
Cobbler, The, 29, 35-37, **37**, 55, 60-61, 174
  Cave Route, 61
  Ramshead Gully, 38
  Recess Route, 38, 175
  Right-Angled Gully, 6, 38
  The Fold, 38, 175
Cohen, G, 450
Coire an t-Sneachda, Pygmy Ridge, 128
Col du Géant, 257
Collie, Norman, 138, 390, 429
Collins, George Lissant, **225**
Corrie Boulders (Arran), 95
Craig House mental asylum, 434-435
Crast' Agüzza (Bernina), 309
Crawford, Colin, 401-403
Creag Meagaidh, **32**, 33, 118-121, 197-199
  avalanche in 1896, 34
  Centre Post, 34, 120-121
  Eastern Corner, 8
  Raeburn's Gully, 8, **32**
Creag na Caillich (Tarmachans), 57, 111-113, 223
Creag nan Adhaircean (Dalwhinnie), 35
Crocket, KV, 9, 18, 38, 54, 84, 110, 200, 442, 450

Cuinneag, [see Quinag]
Darjeeling, 411
Daudet's *Tartarin sur les Alpes*, 29
Davis, Wade (Into the Silence), 423
Dent Blanche, 278-280
Disgrazia, [see Monte Disgrazia]
Dolomites, 244
Dôme de la Sache, 271
Douglas, William, 29ff, 44, 47, 53-54, 83, 125, 180, **181**, 187, 196, **225**, 244, 446
Dru, Grand, 281
Dru, Petit, 260, **261**, 281-283
Duncan, George, 38, 90-92

eagle, golden, 23, **24**
Écrins, Barre des, **253**, 259
Edinburgh, 16, 429
  Abercromby Place, 18
  Craig House mental asylum, 434-435
  Craigmillar, Raeburn Brewery, 144
  Duddingston Loch, 25
  Grange Loan, 16
  Granton, Wm Raeburn drowned at, 17
  Heriot-Watt College, 17
  Manor Place, 16
  Merchiston Castle School, 16-17
  Raeburn's fondness for, 46
  Royal Forth Yacht Club, 25
  Salisbury Crags, 6, 29, 30, **31**, 44-46, **45**
  St George's School, 18
  Usher's Brewery, 16
  Warriston Cemetery, 16, 441-442
Everest Expedition of 1921, [see Himalaya]

Farrar, Percy, 408, 430
Fell & Rock Climbing Club, 148
Finch, George Ingle, 410
Finsteraarhorn, 264

Fowler, JRR, 442
Froebel method, 18
Froswick, 28
Gaelic spellings, 14
Galbraith, William A, 237
Gall Inglis, J, **45**, 78, 79
Garbh Bheinn, 124, 215, **216**
Garden, William, 90–92, 128, 186, 215, **225**, 244
Gibbs, George Bennett, 224
Gibson, Thomas, 68fn
Gillies, Daisy, **225**
Gillon, Stair Agnew, 98
Glasgow, 238
Glen Sannox, 95
Glover, George Tertius, 73, 103, 141, **142**
Glyders, The, 29
Goatfell, 29
Goggs, Frank, 105–109, 148, 182, 196ff, 210, 224, 382, 446
Goodeve, Thomas Edward, 145, 213, 215, 231
Gordon, Seton, 235
Gran Paradiso, 271–274, **272**
Grande Casse, 257
Gray, Edith, 226, 295
Great Gable, 141, 144
Greenwood, Eric, 180, 263, 277
Greig, Francis, 226
Grépon, [see Aiguille du Grépon]
Gribbon, PWF, 451
gullies in climbing history, 57

Hard, BG, 451
Haystacks, Stack Ghyll (VS), 159
Hechle, Hilda, 262
Heriot-Watt College, 17
Heron, Alexander, **407**, 411
Higham, Alison, 451
Himalaya, 396ff
 Everest in 1921, 7, 406ff, 416ff, 428ff
  approach through Tibet, 411ff
  death of Kellas, **414**
  E Rongbuk Glacier identified, 420
  evacuation of Raeburn, 417
  lecture tours, 429–430
  mail left at Kampa Dzong, 421
  Mt Everest Committee, 406
  official book, 431
  party rejoined by Raeburn, 423
  Raeburn appointed climbing leader, 406, 409
  Raeburn organises stores & porters, 410
 Kabru, 398, **399**
 Kangchenjunga, 7, 10, **397**, 397–403
  Talung Peak, 402
 Hinks, Arthur, 406, 408, 410, 428, 432
  criticises & pursues Raeburn, 430
 Hinxman, Lionel, 30, 128
 homosexuality, 438
 Hope, Robert, 226
 Howard-Bury, Charles, **407**, 410
  diaries of, 412fn
  opinion of Raeburn, 427
 Hurrungane (Hörunger), 176fn, **246**, 247ff

Inglesi, Spigolo degli (Disgrazia), 302–306
Inglis Clark, [see entries under Clark]
Inglis, Gall, [see entries under Gall Inglis]

Jacob, MCC, 8, 9, 16fn, 138ff, 412, 441, 450
Johns, WG, 314ff, **315**, **316**, **321**, **325**
Johnston, Miss M, 283

Kellas, Alexander, 399, 411, 411, 412
 joins SMC, 73
 compared with Raeburn, 444,
 death, 414
Kerch, 368
Kern Knotts Crack, 145
kletterschuhe or scarpetti, 115, 116, 144, 153, 176, 249, 260
Kurz, Marcel, 263
Kynaston, H, 98
Ladhar Bheinn, 51–53, **52**
Ladies Scottish Climbing Club, 18, 222, 382
Laggan, 196
Lake District, 9, 28, 138ff
 Great End, 29
 Great Gable, 29
 Napes Needle, 141–144
 Haystacks, Stack Ghyll (VS), 159
 High Street, 28
 Pillar Rock, 29, 145–152
 Scafell
 Pinnacle, 29
 Slingsby's Chimney, 29
La Meije, [see Meije, La]
Lawson, Harry, 57, 71, 82, 94, 96, 98fn, 141, **142**, 446
Lester, William, 80
Liathach, Northern Pinnacles, 78–80, **79**
Lindertis, 237
Lines, JT, 450
Ling, William Norman, 238, 247, 268fn, 446
 diaries, 7, 247, 450
 in Caucasus, 314ff
 in Lake District, 141ff, 144
 in Scotland, 78, 83, 113, 184, 200, 214, 215, 222, 224, 226, 230, 382
 in the Alps, 259ff, 380
 joins SMC, 73
 obituary of Raeburn, 387
 photographs of, **79**, **142**, **155**, **225**, **252**, **299**, **315**, **316**, **325**, **332**, **335**
Lochnagar
 Black Spout Buttress, 215
 Black Spout Pinnacle, 106–109
 Douglas-Gibson Gully, 90–92, 105–106, 215
 Raeburn's Groove, 106fn
 Raeburn's Gully, 8, 71–73
 West Gully, 105

Macdonald, PF, 451
McIntyre, John, 213
Mackay, Alexander, 73, 78, **79**, 80, 94, 97fn, 98, 105-109, 111, 200, **225**, 387, 446
   appraisal of Raeburn, 444
Maclay, James, 47, 123
MacRobert, Harry, 217, 223, 232, 387
Maggiore, Lake, 372
Maiden Rock (St Andrews), 76
Mallory, George, 11, 327, **407**, 408ff, 431
   disappearance in 1924, 440
   lectures after Everest expedition, 429
   opinion of Raeburn, 409, 424, 426-427
   personality contrasted with Raeburn's, 410
   technical incompetence, 420
Martinson, Rembert, 314ff, **315**, **316**, **321**, **325**, **332**, 354ff, **361**
Matterhorn, 244
   Zmutt Ridge, 7, 193, 265, **266**
Mayar, 237
Meall nan Tarmachan, Arrow Chimney, 6, 58-59
Meije, La, 7, 256, 270, 311, 378-381, **379**, 390
Merchiston Castle School, 16-17
Mitchell, John, 366fn
Mont Blanc, 276
Mont Pourri, 271
Monte Disgrazia, 7, **300**, 301-306
Monte Rosa, 244, 289-295
Morshead, Henry, 438
Mounsey, Arthur, 98, 224, 382
Munro, Hugh, 47, **48**, 78, **79**, 179, 237, 264, 286
Murray, WH, 39, 101, 121, 172, 185, 318, 448

Naismith, WW, 30, 55, 78, **79**, 98, 139, 395
Napes Needle, 141
   Arrowhead Ridge, 144
   Eagle's Nest Ridge, 144
Napier, John Stewart, 56
Napier, Robert Graham, 62-64, 124
Newbigging, William, 125
Nicoll, GS, 451
Norway, 247ff
   Brekketind, 248
   Dyrhaugstinder, 247
   Gjeithorn, 248
   Grøtdalstinder, 248
   Hurrungane (Hörunger), 176fn, **246**, 247ff
   Jakta, 248
   Kjerringa, **253**, 254
   Maradalstind, 247
   Sætretinder, 247
   Skagastølstinder, 247
   Slogen, 249-250, **251**
   Store Ringstind, 250
   Sündmore, 248

Obergabelhorn, 296, **297**
Odessa, 369
Ossian's Cave (Glen Coe), 56

paraldehyde, 437fn
Paris, in August 1914, 373
Parker, James, 30, 176, 244
Phildius, Eberhard, 6, 190ff, 263
Pigou, Arthur Cecil, 150
Pillar Rock, 145, **152**
   Central Jordan Climb, 147
   North-East Climb, 151
   North-West Climb, 147
Piz Bernina, **308**, 311
Piz Scerscen, **308**, 309
Pontoise in August 1914, 374
porridge, ways of eating, 88
Prentice, RT, 36, 450
Priestley, T, 451
Priestman, Howard, 247

Quinag (Cuinneag), Barrel Buttress, 200-203, **204**

Raeburn Brewery & brewing, 16, 17, 144, 197, 367, 441
Raeburn Hut (SMC), 442
Raeburn Cup (yacht racing), 25
Raeburn, Edith, 18, 439, 441
Raeburn, Elizabeth Mary (née Meakin), 16
Raeburn, Ethel Maud, 18, 19, 439, 371fn, 441
Raeburn, Florence, 439, 441
Raeburn, Harold Andrew
   addresses FRCC dinner, 148
   advice on winter climbing, 162ff, 391
   ancestry, 16
   assessments of, 6-7, 444-448
   attempts suicide, 434
   bequests, 441
   childhood, 16-17
   chosen for Everest reconnaissance, 406
   climbs, [see mountain or district, or Raeburn's ...]
   concern for others, 366, 375, 426, 445
   compared with contemporaries, 444
   cycling, 56, 60, 68, 71, 73, 74, 114, 118, 120, 149, 196, 210, 214, 224, 447
   death, 441
   diaries & letters, 13, 19, 149fn, 150, 158, 228, 239, 314fn, 327, 337fn
   disparages Skye climbing, 64
   elected SMC Vice-President, 220
   elected to Royal Physical Soc., 19

elected to SMC
  Committee, 73
enters Craig House
  asylum, 434
enters nursing home,
  431
feelings of guilt, 438
grave of, 442
guided climbing, 244-247
injuries & illness, 200,
  227ff, 231, 259, 311,
  314, 408, 411-413,
  416-418, 430, 434ff
medical reports, 408,
  413, 416, 435-437,
  439-440, 441
joins SMC, 44
leadership, 55, 92, 99,
  114, 159, 196, 327,
  394, 406, 427
life summarised, 11ff
Mountaineering Art, 238,
  390ff
motorcycling, 151, 238
ornithology, 18ff, 35, 177,
  240, 249
personality & intellect,
  13-14, 17, 39-41, 46,
  80, 93, 100-101, 109,
  125, 136, 182, 197,
  203, 223, 229, 277,
  366, 375, 395, 426,
  445
photographs of, **15**, **31**,
  45, **48**, **49**, **75**, **79**,
  142, **143**, **155**, **163**,
  192, **225**, **252**, **299**,
  315, **316**, **321**, **332**,
  383, **407**
physique & fitness, 63,
  82, 125, 408, 425,
  434, 438, 440
prose style, 17, 39, 71,
  95, 100, 102, 118-119,
  176, 191
relations with women,
  223, 264, 283fn, 373,
  393, 445, 446
response to mountains
  & nature, 47, 95,
  100-102, 120, 121, 177,
  180, 233, 235, 395

safety, 93, 109, 173, 229,
  232, 287
sexual orientation, 438
siblings, 16-18, 439, 441
skating, 25
skiing & glissading, 25,
  128, 169, 170, **192**,
  199, 237, 254
sporting prowess, 17, 25,
  413
war work, 237-238
wealth, 439, 441
yachting, 25, 47, **49**, 101,
  114, 372
Raeburn, John, 25, 439
Raeburn, Margaret (née
  Ramsay), 16
Raeburn, Norman, 439,
  441
Raeburn, Ruth, 148, **225**,
  226, 232, 234, 295, 298,
  299, **383**, 439, 441
schooling, 18
Raeburn, Sir Henry, 25
Raeburn, William (brother),
  17, 41
Raeburn, William (father),
  16
Raeburn, William
  (grandfather), 16
Raeburn's 18-Minute Route,
  123
Raeburn's Arête (Ben
  Nevis), 103, **107**
Raeburn's Buttress (Càrn
  Dearg), 217-220, **219**
Raeburn's Buttress (Sgùrr
  Ruadh), 129-130, **131**
Raeburn's Buttress
  (Shelter Stone Crag),
  210, **213**
Raeburn's Easy Route (Ben
  Nevis), 232
Raeburn's Groove
  (Lochnagar), 106fn
Raeburn's Gully (Creag
  Meagaidh), 8, **32**
Raeburn's Gully
  (Lochnagar), 8, 71-73
Raeburn's ice-axe, 442
Raeburn's Route (An
  Caisteal, Skye), 176

Raeburn's Route (Sgùrr
  Coire an Lochain), 236
Raeburn's Route (Stob
  Coire nan Lochan), 7,
  205, **206**
Ranken, Anna, **225**
Ranken, Pauline, **225**
ravens, 57, 58fn, 80, 80fn,
  102, 148, 381fn
Reid, SJH, 153
Reid, Walter, 237
Rennie, John, 47, 60, 71, 83,
  124, 180
Richards, RC, 354ff
Richardson, SM, 6, 451
Rimpfischhorn, 295
Robb, RJC, 450
Robertson, AE, 190, 197fn
Robertson, Euan Barclay,
  128-130
Rogerson, JJ, 16
Ronaldson, Dr AM, 409,
  431, 434
Ronchetti, Vittorio, 318,
  320, 356, 372
Ross, RG, 451
Roth, A, 128
Royal Forth Yacht Club, 25
Rum, 50
Russell, Arthur, 74, 232
Ryan, VJ, compared with
  Raeburn, 444

Salisbury Crags, 6, 29, 30,
  31, 44-46, 45
Sang, George, 73, 80, 149
  acts on Raeburn's behalf,
  430-431, 441
Satarma Needle (Arolla),
  298
scarpetti or kletterschuhe,
  115, 116, 144, 153, 176,
  249, 260
Scerscen, Piz, **308**, 309
Schreckhorn, 264
Scott-Tucker, H, [see
  Tucker, H Scott]
Scottish Mountaineering
  Club, 28, 29, 44
  Raeburn Hut, 442
  Raeburn's ice-axe, 442
  SMC Journal, 7, 8, 29, 46,
  73, 187, 233

Yacht Meet in 1897, 47–53, **49**
Sgòran Dubh, 96–99
Sgùrr Coire an Lochain (Cuillin), 236
Sgùrr MhicChoinnich, 235
Sgùrr Ruadh, Raeburn's Buttress, 129–130, **131**
Shakespeare, 47, 78, 120
Shelter Stone Crag, **213**
Raeburn's Buttress, 210ff
Shetland, 19–23
Simpson, GR, 451
Skye, 113ff, 137, 175–182, 235
   An Caisteal, Central Buttress, 176
   Basteir Tooth, 68
   Sgùrr Coire an Lochain, 236
   Sgùrr MhicChoinnich, 235
   Theàrlaich-Dubh Gap, 178, 235
Slingsby, William Cecil, 141, **143**, 176, 390
Smith, Joan, **225**
Smith, Lucy, 225, 226
Smith, Walter, 53
Smith, William Charles, 114
Snowdon, 28, 29
Solly, Godfrey, 143, 144, 157, 176, 337
Spigolo degli Inglesi (Disgrazia), 302–306
Squance, Conradi, 61, 98
Stone, David, 450
Stob Coire nan Lochan, Central Buttress, 7, 205, **206**
Storr, Old Man of, 76
Strange, GS, 450
Strutt, Edward Lisle, 406
Stùc a' Chroin, 28, 29, 53–54, 238
   accident on, 149, 227
Sündmore, 247

Taganrog, 368
Theàrlaich-Dubh Gap, 178, 235
Thomson, Austen, 223
Thomson, Gilbert, 30, 224

Tilman, HW, 401
Tobin, Harry Walter, 396, 400
Tough, William, 33, 35
Tryfan, 29
Tucker, H Scott, 224, 354ff

Ullén, Erik, 176ff, **252**, 254, 283
Unna, Percy, 224
Usher's Brewery, 16

Vanoise, 257
Venice in August 1914, 371

Wackerhage, H, 451
Wales
   Glyders, The, 29
   Snowdon, 29
   Tryfan, 29
Walker, Charles, 111, 113, 118, 123, 182, 231, 256
Walker, Harry, 111, 113, 118, 123, 214, 223, 237, 382
   ice-axe lost by Raeburn, 400
Wallwork brothers, 235
War, First World, 237–240, 366ff, 382
Warriston Cemetery, 16, 441–442
Watson, Henry, 217
Weisshorn, 244, **245**
Wellenkuppe, 296, **297**
Wheeler, Oliver, **407**, 409, 410
Wigner, John, 125
Williams, DN, 176, 450
Wollaston, AFR, 407, 410, 416

Yeysk, 368
Yorkshire summits, 28
Young, Geoffrey Winthrop, 111, 228, 257, 351, 406, 415, 424
   compared with Raeburn, 444
Young, James R, 231, 314ff
Younghusband, Francis, 408, 410, 428, 431
Yovitchitch, Maria, 283
Yovitchitch, Natalia, 147, 284, 295, **299**, 446
   winter sports prowess, 298
Yovitchitch, Persida, 283

Zermatt, 264, 281, 295
   in August 1914, 372
Zinalrothorn, 277

All profits from Scottish Mountaineering Press books go to help fund the Scottish Mountaineering Trust, a Scottish charity that provides grants to projects and organisations that promote recreation, knowledge and safety in the mountains, especially the mountains of Scotland.

www.thesmt.org.uk